The Global Competitiveness of Regions

The aim of this book is to consider theoretically the notion of the *global competitiveness of regions*, as well as to give attention as to how such competitiveness may be empirically measured. With this in mind, the book has three specific objectives: first, to place the concept of regional competitiveness within the context of regional economic development theory; second, to present a rationale and method for quantifying the global competitiveness of regions; and, third, to undertake the most geographically widespread analysis of regional competitiveness differences across the globe. With regard to the third goal, the analysis incorporates more than 500 regions across Europe, North and South America, Asia-Pacific, the Middle East, and the so-called BRIC economies of Brazil, Russia, India, and China.

The importance of the concept of competitiveness has increased rapidly in recent years, with the issues surrounding it becoming, simultaneously, more empirically refined and theoretically complex. The focus on regions reflects the growing consensus that they are the primary spatial units that compete to attract investment, and it is at the regional level that knowledge is circulated and transferred, resulting in agglomerations, or clusters, of industrial and service sector enterprises. This growing acknowledgement of the region's role as a key spatial unit of organisation has led to attention turning to competitiveness at a more regional level.

The book explores the results of the World Competitiveness Index of Regions (WCIR), covering the rankings and results of the 2014 edition. The WCIR provides a tool for analysing the development of a range of regional economies across the globe. It enables an illustration of the changing patterns of regional competitiveness on the international stage to be generated. In fundamental terms, the WCIR aims to produce an integrated and overall benchmark of the knowledge capacity, capability, and sustainability of each region, and the extent to which this knowledge is translated into economic value and transferred into the wealth of the citizens of each region.

Robert Huggins is Professor of Economic Geography at the School of Planning and Geography, Cardiff University, and Director of its Centre for Economic Geography.

Hiro Izushi is a Senior Lecturer in the Innovation, Economics and Strategy Group, Aston Business School, Birmingham, UK.

Daniel Prokop is currently studying for a PhD at the School of Planning and Geography, Cardiff University. He previously worked as a research associate in the Centre for International Competitiveness, Cardiff Metropolitan University, Wales.

Piers Thompson is a Lecturer in Economics within Nottingham Trent University, UK.

Regional Studies Association
THE GLOBAL FORUM FOR CITY AND REGIONAL RESEARCH, DEVELOPMENT AND POLICY

Routledge
Taylor & Francis Group

Regions and Cities

In today's globalised, knowledge-driven and networked world, regions and cities have assumed heightened significance as the interconnected nodes of economic, social and cultural production, and as sites of new modes of economic and territorial governance and policy experimentation. This book series brings together incisive and critically engaged international and interdisciplinary research on this resurgence of regions and cities, and should be of interest to geographers, economists, sociologists, political scientists and cultural scholars, as well as to policy-makers involved in regional and urban development.

For more information on the Regional Studies Association visit www.regionalstudies.org

75. The Global Competitiveness of Regions
Robert Huggins, Hiro Izushi, Daniel Prokop and Piers Thompson

74. The Social Dynamics of Innovation Networks
Edited by Roel Rutten, Paul Benneworth, Dessy Irawati and Frans Boekema

73. The European Territory
From historical roots to global challenges
Jacques Robert

72. Urban Innovation Systems
What makes them tick?
Willem van Winden, Erik Braun, Alexander Otgaar and Jan-Jelle Witte

71. **Shrinking Cities**
A global perspective
Edited by Harry W. Richardson and Chang Woon Nam

70. **Cities, State and Globalization**
City-regional governance in Europe and North America
Tassilo Herrschel

69. **The Creative Class Goes Global**
Edited by Charlotta Mellander, Richard Florida, Bjørn Asheim and Meric Gertler

68. **Entrepreneurial Knowledge, Technology and the Transformation of Regions**
Edited by Charlie Karlsson, Börje Johansson and Roger Stough

67. **The Economic Geography of the IT Industry in the Asia Pacific Region**
Edited by Philip Cooke, Glen Searle and Kevin O'Connor

66. **Working Regions**
Reconnecting innovation and production in the knowledge economy
Jennifer Clark

65. **Europe's Changing Geography**
The impact of inter-regional networks
Edited by Nicola Bellini and Ulrich Hilpert

64. **The Value of Arts and Culture for Regional Development**
A Scandinavian perspective
Edited by Lisbeth Lindeborg and Lars Lindkvist

63. **The University and the City**
John Goddard and Paul Vallance

62. **Re-framing Regional Development**
Evolution, innovation and transition
Edited by Philip Cooke

61. **Networking Regionalised Innovative Labour Markets**
Edited by Ulrich Hilpert and Helen Lawton Smith

60. **Leadership and Change in Sustainable Regional Development**
Edited by Markku Sotarauta, Ina Horlings and Joyce Liddle

59. **Regional Development Agencies: The Next Generation?**
Networking, knowledge and regional policies
Edited by Nicola Bellini, Mike Danson and Henrik Halkier

58. **Community-based Entrepreneurship and Rural Development**
Creating favourable conditions for small businesses in Central Europe
Matthias Fink, Stephan Loidl and Richard Lang

57. **Creative Industries and Innovation in Europe**
Concepts, measures and comparative case studies
Edited by Luciana Lazzeretti

56. **Innovation Governance in an Open Economy**
Shaping regional nodes in a globalized world
Edited by Annika Rickne, Staffan Laestadius and Henry Etzkowitz

55. **Complex Adaptive Innovation Systems**
Relatedness and transversality in the evolving region
Philip Cooke

54. **Creating Knowledge Locations in Cities**
Innovation and integration challenges
Willem van Winden, Luis de Carvalho, Erwin van Tujil, Jeroen van Haaren and Leo van den Berg

53. **Regional Development in Northern Europe**
Peripherality, marginality and border issues
Edited by Mike Danson and Peter De Souza

52. **Promoting Silicon Valleys in Latin America**
Luciano Ciravegna

51. **Industrial Policy Beyond the Crisis**
Regional, national and international perspectives
Edited by David Bailey, Helena Lenihan and Josep-Maria Arauzo-Carod

50. **Just Growth**
Inclusion and prosperity in America's metropolitan regions
Chris Benner and Manuel Pastor

49. **Cultural Political Economy of Small Cities**
Edited by Anne Lorentzen and Bas van Heur

48. **The Recession and Beyond**
Local and regional responses to the downturn
Edited by David Bailey and Caroline Chapain

47. **Beyond Territory**
Edited by Harald Bathelt, Maryann Feldman and Dieter F. Kogler

46. **Leadership and Place**
Edited by Chris Collinge, John Gibney and Chris Mabey

45. **Migration in the 21st Century**
Rights, outcomes, and policy
Kim Korinek and Thomas Maloney

44. **The Futures of the City Region**
Edited by Michael Neuman and Angela Hull

43. **The Impacts of Automotive Plant Closures**
A tale of two cities
Edited by Andrew Beer and Holli Evans

42. **Manufacturing in the New Urban Economy**
Willem van Winden, Leo van den Berg, Luis de Carvalho and Erwin van Tuijl

41. **Globalizing Regional Development in East Asia**
Production networks, clusters, and entrepreneurship
Edited by Henry Wai-chung Yeung

40. China and Europe
The implications of the rise of China as a global economic power for Europe
Edited by Klaus Kunzmann, Willy A Schmid and Martina Koll-Schretzenmayr

39. Business Networks in Clusters and Industrial Districts
The governance of the global value chain
Edited by Fiorenza Belussi and Alessia Sammarra

38. Whither Regional Studies?
Edited by Andy Pike

37. Intelligent Cities and Globalisation of Innovation Networks
Nicos Komninos

36. Devolution, Regionalism and Regional Development
The UK experience
Edited by Jonathan Bradbury

35. Creative Regions
Technology, culture and knowledge entrepreneurship
Edited by Philip Cooke and Dafna Schwartz

34. European Cohesion Policy
Willem Molle

33. Geographies of the New Economy
Critical reflections
Edited by Peter W. Daniels, Andrew Leyshon, Michael J. Bradshaw and Jonathan Beaverstock

32. The Rise of the English Regions?
Edited by Irene Hardill, Paul Benneworth, Mark Baker and Leslie Budd

31. Regional Development in the Knowledge Economy
Edited by Philip Cooke and Andrea Piccaluga

30. Regional Competitiveness
Edited by Ron Martin, Michael Kitson and Peter Tyler

29. Clusters and Regional Development
Critical reflections and explorations
Edited by Bjørn Asheim, Philip Cooke and Ron Martin

28. Regions, Spatial Strategies and Sustainable Development
David Counsell and Graham Haughton

27. Sustainable Cities
Graham Haughton and Colin Hunter

26. Geographies of Labour Market Inequality
Edited by Ron Martin and Philip S. Morrison

25. Regional Innovation Strategies
The challenge for less-favoured regions
Edited by Kevin Morgan and Claire Nauwelaers

24. **Out of the Ashes?**
The social impact of industrial contraction and regeneration on Britain's mining communities
Chas Critcher, Bella Dicks, David Parry and David Waddington

23. **Restructuring Industry and Territory**
The experience of Europe's regions
Edited by Anna Giunta, Arnoud Lagendijk and Andy Pike

22. **Foreign Direct Investment and the Global Economy**
Corporate and institutional dynamics of global-localisation
Edited by Jeremy Alden and Nicholas F. Phelps

21. **Community Economic Development**
Edited by Graham Haughton

20. **Regional Development Agencies in Europe**
Edited by Charlotte Damborg, Mike Danson and Henrik Halkier

19. **Social Exclusion in European Cities**
Processes, experiences and responses
Edited by Judith Allen, Goran Cars and Ali Madanipour

18. **Metropolitan Planning in Britain**
A comparative study
Edited by Peter Roberts, Kevin Thomas and Gwyndaf Williams

17. **Unemployment and Social Exclusion**
Landscapes of labour inequality and social exclusion
Edited by Sally Hardy, Paul Lawless and Ron Martin

16. **Multinationals and European Integration**
Trade, investment and regional development
Edited by Nicholas A. Phelps

15. **The Coherence of EU Regional Policy**
Contrasting perspectives on the structural funds
Edited by John Bachtler and Ivan Turok

14. **New Institutional Spaces**
TECs and the remaking of economic governance
Edited by Martin Jones and Jamie Peck

13. **Regional Policy in Europe**
S. S. Artobolevskiy

12. **Innovation Networks and Learning Regions?**
James Simmie

11. **British Regionalism and Devolution**
The challenges of state reform and European integration
Edited by Jonathan Bradbury and John Mawson

10. **Regional Development Strategies**
A European perspective
Edited by Jeremy Alden and Philip Boland

9. **Union Retreat and the Regions**
The shrinking landscape of organised labour
Ron Martin, Peter Sunley and Jane Wills

8. **The Regional Dimension of Transformation in Central Europe**
Grzegorz Gorzelak

7. **The Determinants of Small Firm Growth**
An inter-regional study in the United Kingdom 1986–90
Richard Barkham, Graham Gudgin, Mark Hart and Eric Hanvey

6. **The Regional Imperative**
Regional planning and governance in Britain, Europe and the United States
Urlan A. Wannop

5. **An Enlarged Europe**
Regions in competition?
Edited by Louis Albrechts, Sally Hardy, Mark Hart and Anastasios Katos

4. **Spatial Policy in a Divided Nation**
Edited by Richard T. Harrison and Mark Hart

3. **Regional Development in the 1990s**
The British Isles in transition
Edited by Ron Martin and Peter Townroe

2. **Retreat from the Regions**
Corporate change and the closure of factories
Stephen Fothergill and Nigel Guy

1. **Beyond Green Belts**
Managing urban growth in the 21st century
Edited by John Herington

The Global Competitiveness of Regions

Robert Huggins, Hiro Izushi,
Daniel Prokop and Piers Thompson

Routledge
Taylor & Francis Group
LONDON AND NEW YORK

First published 2014
by Routledge
2 Park Square, Milton Park, Abingdon, Oxon OX14 4RN

and by Routledge
711 Third Avenue, New York, NY 10017

Routledge is an imprint of the Taylor & Francis Group, an informa business

British Library Cataloguing in Publication Data
A catalogue record for this book is available from the British Library

Library of Congress Cataloging in Publication Data
The global competitiveness of regions / Robert Huggins, Hiro Izushi, Daniel Prokop and Piers Thompson.
pages cm. — (Regions and cities)
1. Competition, International. 2. Regional planning. 3. Sustainable development. I. Huggins, Robert.
HF1414.G55896 2014
338.9'048—dc23
2013049406

ISBN: 978-0-415-85943-1 (hbk)
ISBN: 978-0-203-79913-0 (ebk)

Typeset in Times New Roman
by FiSH Books Ltd, Enfield

Contents

List of illustrations

Figures

Tables

1 Introduction

From the 1980s onwards, patterns of economic development across the globe have changed significantly. The opening-up of former communist and socialist national economies has produced a new economic tapestry that is continuing to evolve with mind-boggling speed. The accompanying growth and prevalence of information and communications technologies has increased the speed of change, resulting in economies appearing to suffer disturbances and shocks with increasing frequency. As a result, the spatial nature of economic development is now firmly viewed as a phenomenon subject to evolutionary and dynamic forces.

In his seminal study on *The Competitive Advantage of Nations*, Michael Porter (1990) laid down the foundations for a better understanding of how economic development, as manifested by *competitiveness*, was evolving across nations due to changes in a number of key forces driving productivity and economic growth. Porter (1998, 2000) soon came to realise that many of these forces were not generic or distributed evenly across nations, but 'clustered' within particular regions *within* national economies. Nevertheless, much of the work on locational competitiveness has continued to focus on examining global competitiveness differences from the national perspective, with little attention given to analysing the competitiveness of regions within a global context (World Economic Forum, 2012; IMD, 2013).

In light of this apparent gap, the aim of this book is to consider theoretically the notion of the *global competitiveness of regions*, as well as giving attention as to how such competitiveness may be empirically measured. On a number of fronts, this is no easy task, with 'the theory of regional competitiveness' emerging in a fragmented fashion, along with a range of measurement techniques that do not always appear to be aligned to any particular theory or discourse. Despite this, there is a broad school of academic and policy research that has sought to progress our understanding of the nature of regional economic development in a global evolutionary context.

With this in mind, the book has three specific objectives: first, to place the concept of regional competitiveness within the context of regional economic development theory; second, to present a rationale and method for quantifying the global competitiveness of regions; and, third, to undertake the most geographically widespread analysis of regional competitiveness differences across the globe. With regard to the third goal, the analysis incorporates more than 500 regions across Europe, North and South America, Asia-Pacific, the Middle East, and the so-called BRIC economies of Brazil, Russia, India, and China.

Regional competitiveness in a globalizing world

The importance of the concept of competitiveness has increased rapidly in recent years, with the issues surrounding it becoming, at the same time, more empirically refined and theoretically complex (Porter, 1990, 2000; Huggins and Izushi, 2011). Porter (1990) first defined national competitiveness as an outcome of a nation's ability to innovate in order to achieve, or maintain, an advantageous position over other nations in a number of key industrial sectors. Porter's (1990) early studies linked national competitiveness to productivity and, principally, a nation's ability to innovate. However, regions are increasingly considered to be an important source of economic development and organization in a globalized economy (Scott, 1995; Cooke, 1997; Amin, 1999; Werker and Athreye, 2004; Malecki, 2007). The focus on regions reflects the growing consensus that they are the primary spatial units that compete to attract investment, and it is at the regional level that knowledge is circulated and transferred, resulting in agglomerations, or clusters, of industrial and service sector enterprises. This growing acknowledgement of the region's role as a key spatial unit of organization has led to attention turning to competitiveness at a more regional level. From this spatial perspective, Porter's (2000) major contribution was to take a micro-level understanding of the conditions determining firm competitiveness, such as the capacity to innovate, and apply it to the territorial unit – be it a city, region, or nation. It is Porter's (2000) notion of the microeconomic determinants of prosperity and wealth generation, as opposed to determinants related to monetary exchange rates and the like, that is at the heart of the concept of regional competitiveness.

Regional competitiveness models are usually implicitly constructed in the lineage of endogenous growth frameworks, whereby deliberate investments in factors such as human capital and knowledge are considered to be key drivers of growth differentials. In the context of this book, therefore, regional competitiveness is defined as the difference in the rate of economic development across regions and the capacity and capability of regions to achieve future economic growth relative to other regions at a similar stage of economic development.

Such competitiveness is far from a zero-sum game, with the more integrated nature of the global economy making cooperation and coordination between regions increasingly important (de Bruijn and van Oort, 2007). The need to access global knowledge flows to retain competitiveness has been highlighted by a number of studies (Bathelt *et al.*, 2004), implying that as well as understanding competitiveness within a particular region it is also important to understand how competitiveness is determined through the global network of regions (Huggins and Thompson, 2014). At the same time, the resources, institutions and infrastructure present in regions are vital for utilizing externally sourced knowledge to generate outputs, including new knowledge.

Regional organizations may benefit from local knowledge spillovers as an undirected and spontaneous 'buzz' (Storper and Venables, 2004), but they may also need to consciously build non-local 'pipelines' to tap into knowledge from outside their region (Bathelt *et al.*, 2004). For instance, knowledge spillovers are found to be greater in the presence of knowledge investments, and vice versa, with those regions possessing higher rates of knowledge investment experiencing a higher level of knowledge spillover – with interregional spillovers contributing significantly to regional knowledge production (Bathelt *et al.*, 2004). In particular, globalization and technological progress are considered to spur openness in the innovation process across the globe by expanding the extent of the market, allowing for increased divisions of labour and providing new ways to collaborate and coordinate across geographical distances (Gassmann, 2006; Drejer and Lund Vinding, 2007; Moodysson, 2008; Crevoisier and Jeannerat, 2009; Trippl *et al.*, 2009; Dahlander and Gann, 2010).

According to Malmberg and Power (2006: 61),

> knowledge in clusters is seldom created through local inter-organizational collaborative interaction . . . in a localized cluster the majority of firms tend to have most of their important suppliers and customers somewhere else and innovation and knowledge creation tend to follow value chains that are most often global.

Somewhat contrary to Porter (1990), therefore, if the local market does not have the most sophisticated customers, firms are required to look for them elsewhere. Von Hippel (2005) highlights how markets and user-led innovation in a number of industries, such as design, are becoming increasingly international in scope.

The complementary effects of 'local buzz' and 'global pipelines', enabled by information and communications technology advances, are leading to new patterns of knowledge sourcing and an economic geography that is as spiky as it is flat (Florida, 2005; Friedman, 2005; Huggins, 2008). This spikiness is typified by the existence of key and leading concentrations of knowledge-based economic activity within a relatively limited number of regional locations (Hoekman *et al.*, 2009). These regions, however, are increasingly connected through the networks resulting from the internationalization of markets and the broadened scope of knowledge networking activities. As Rodríguez-Pose and Crescenzi (2008) indicate, knowledge will spill over beyond regional borders as a consequence of the existence of different forms of inter-regional contacts, with flows of inter-regional knowledge acting as important agents of innovation. They further find that accessibility to extra-regional innovation is positively associated with regional growth performance, with the 'amount of knowledge' available in a region reinforcing the effect of local innovative activities (Rodríguez-Pose and Crescenzi, 2008). Similar results are produced by Badinger and Tondl (2002), who find that an inflow of knowledge has a positive impact on the growth of a region, with this effect having a larger magnitude if neighbouring regions also exhibit high growth rates.

Regional economies in a global context

Changing patterns of economic activity and their consequential impacts on rates of development have brought competitiveness to the top of many political and policymaking agendas. Ensuring that regional competitiveness is retained and enhanced is a common concern across the globe, although the nature of these concerns may differ according to their past histories and future expectations.

In the case of Europe, the changing patterns of global trade and development has made the resilience of competitiveness in European regions a core concern of the European Union and the governments of constituent nation states, as well as aspiring members (Koschatzky and Stahlecker, 2010; Reiner, 2010). The Lisbon Strategy, for instance, emphasized the importance of confronting the structural problems faced by European regions in their bid to increase productivity growth (Denis *et al.*, 2005; European Commission, 2010a). Interestingly, a study of regional growth across European regions finds that only within certain northern nations of Europe is there a significant relationship between regional growth and the intensity of R&D and higher education, suggesting a fragmented pattern of knowledge-based growth across regions (Sterlacchini, 2008). Such fragmentation and growth disparities across European regions have also been found by other empirical studies (Rodríguez-Pose and Crescenzi, 2008; Rodríguez-Pose and Tselios, 2010; Huggins and Izushi, 2013).

Concerns about the loss of regional competitiveness have moved further up the agenda of European governments with the onset of the financial crisis in 2007 and the recession that followed (European Commission, 2010b). Structural problems and the direct exposure of banking systems to the US sub-prime mortgage market have resulted in European economies not only suffering deeper and longer recessions than other national economies, but also weaker recoveries (Claessens *et al.*, 2010; Yurtsever, 2011). Competitiveness disparities within European nations mean that the capability to withstand and overcome shocks is likely to vary across European regions. These concerns, however, are not only associated with more recent downturns, but also the changing patterns of economic activity experienced in the latter half of the twentieth century and onward into the twenty-first century.

In North America, the US faces an ongoing erosion of its competitiveness on the international stage, with it continuing to slip down national competitiveness rankings, a fall that has undoubtedly been accentuated by the 2007 financial crisis (World Economic Forum, 2012; IMD, 2013). Other research concerning growth across US regions suggests that growth rates in per capita income are associated with knowledge-based inputs whereas labour market growth rates are mainly associated with industry structure characteristics, which can be further related to economic history and industrial legacy (Barkley and Dudensing, 2011). In the case of regions in Canada, the evidence suggests that productivity gains emerge from knowledge spillovers, coupled with strong employment growth (Baldwin *et al.*, 2008). Although these studies highlight the role played by the knowledge economy in generating regional growth in North America, policy intervention appears to have been less successful in achieving standard of living improvements via an expanded knowledge economy. For the period 2000–6 there was found to be only a limited role for knowledge-based economic development policies with respect to enhancing job growth across many US regions (Barkley and Dudensing, 2011).

While research on European and North American regions has raised concerns about competitiveness erosion, the images and messages presented for the BRIC economics are usually of a more converse nature. Much of the research on the BRIC economies has concentrated on the expected and actual capability of these economies to dominate the manufacturing of basic products by taking advantage of the low labour costs associated with their massive labour forces (Stone and Ranchhod, 2006; Ranjan and Agrawal, 2011). Other work has concentrated on the potential offered by these nations as huge markets for resources (Bhar and Nikolova, 2009; Samake and Yang, 2011; Cairns and Meilke, 2012) and more advanced goods and services as these economies develop (Hussain and Faes-Cannito, 2008). However, it has become more apparent in recent years that advanced goods and services may also be supplied by these nations (Gouvea *et al.*, 2013). In part, this has reflected purposeful developments encouraged by policymakers who are aware that the footloose nature of low-cost labour intensive manufacturing means that this source of wealth cannot be relied upon in the long-term (Perkmann, 2006).

However, as with more developed economies, emerging economies include regions that vary in terms of their rates of growth and development. In particular, China has not only a cadre of regions that have become key players in the global knowledge economy, but also a large set of regions that have not enjoyed the same level of economic success (Krugman, 2009; Ke, 2010). China's leading regions also provide evidence of a number of potential different modes of growth being available, due to varying development processes in terms of key pre-existing regional resources and institutions (Fleisher *et al.*, 2010; Huggins *et al.*, 2013). In Shanghai, for instance, growth has evolved through a model incorporating both indigenous and external knowledge sources in the form of foreign investment (Wu, 2007). In Beijing, both state and local governments have allocated large human and financial resources to education and technology, as well as the setting-up of spin-off enterprises to commercialize technology and the establishment of high-technology development zones within the region (Zhao and Tong, 2001). By contrast, in Guangdong growth has been particularly associated with foreign direct investment (FDI)-driven characteristics, especially overseas Chinese-owned FDI (Huang *et al.*, 2012; Huggins *et al.*, 2013).

Elsewhere in Asia-Pacific, regional growth in Australia is found to be a complex interaction between population growth, human capital and economic structure (Stimson *et al.*, 2009), whilst in Japan regional competitiveness and growth has been related to a pattern of rising overseas investment coupled with the increased import penetration of less technology-intensive products to Japan (Essletzbichler and Kadokawa, 2010).

With regard to Middle Eastern regions, their economies have long been aware that whilst their reserves of oil and gas have been plentiful, they are also finite. This means that governments and regional policymakers need to ensure that the rents from natural resources are invested in the creation of alternative capital, whether it is produced physical capital and infrastructure or human capital, in order to ensure that the overall assets of a region are not depleted (Auty, 2007). Interestingly, the World Bank (2005) have developed an Adjusted Net Savings indicator, which adjusts national savings for the depletion of mineral resources, with the results suggesting that not all countries have taken a sustainable approach to the use of their wealth (Auty, 2007).

One approach adopted by Middle Eastern national governments has been to invest their oil wealth in businesses and infrastructure within other economies (Winder, 2010). An alternative approach adopted by some regions, particularly those with lower oil and gas reserves, has been to try to diversify their economies and utilize their wealth to fund a rapid increase in knowledge resources (Herb, 2009). However, access to technology must also be accompanied by the capability to effectively adapt and adopt such technology (Basu and Weil, 1998; Acemoglu and Zilibotti, 2001; Los and Timmer, 2005).

In order to gain insights into the specifics of regional competitiveness and growth trajectories within these continental blocs and nations, it is necessary to unpack the distribution of endogenous and knowledge-based resources underpinning global rates of regional economic development. The tool used here to achieve this is the *World Competitiveness Index of Regions* (WCIR).

World Competitiveness Index of Regions (WCIR)

The concept of regional competitiveness has evolved beyond those studies and measures that previously regarded it as simply consisting of the ability to compete with other regions for export markets, often relying on labour productivity alone as a measure of competitiveness differentials. It is now recognized that whilst regions compete, the main competition between regions is not only in terms of attracting and nurturing highly productive firms (Tewdwr-Jones and Phelps, 2000), but also the productive knowledge stemming from the attraction and nurturing of the creative knowledge-based workers and entrepreneurs who underpin the innovative capacity of regional firms (Rohr-Zänker, 2001; Florida, 2002a; Mellander *et al.*, 2011). This competition occurs through the provision of sufficiently high returns on capital, attractive wages and employment prospects (Krugman, 2003).

In order to capture these mechanisms, this book explores the results of the World Competitiveness Index of Regions (WCIR), covering the rankings and results of the 2014 edition. The WCIR provides a tool for analysing the development of a range of regional economies across the globe. It enables an illustration of the changing patterns of regional competitiveness on the international stage to be generated. The methodology employed by the WCIR attempts to integrate the key influences on changes in contemporary rates of economic development identified by the relevant literature, which is critiqued in Chapter 2.

In fundamental terms, the WCIR aims to produce an integrated and overall benchmark of the knowledge capacity, capability, and sustainability of each region, and the extent to which this knowledge is translated into economic value and transferred into the wealth of the citizens of each region. In other words, the WCIR is explicitly tied to the theoretical discourse stemming from endogenous growth theory, with knowledge and human capital at the centre of its analysis. The WCIR analysis presented in this book covers 546 regions (see Appendix 1 for a full list) across 51 nations.

This benchmarking approach is based on an adaptation of the methodology previously used by the authors in their World Knowledge Competitiveness Index (WKCI) series of reports (Huggins and Izushi, 2002; Huggins *et al.*, 2003, 2004, 2005, 2008a), which largely concentrates on analysing and benchmarking regions in North America and Western Europe. The WCIR, however, is far more ambitious in both scope and scale, and provides a far more complete picture of the global competitiveness of regions.

The book

The book is organized in such a way that it first reviews the theoretical and measurement aspects of regional competitiveness, followed by a global comparison of regional competitiveness differences based on the WCIR results. A comparative regional analysis is then presented across Europe, North America, the BRIC economies, and Middle Eastern regions. A summary of each chapter is provided below.

The aim of Chapter 2 is to place the regional competitiveness discourse within the context of theories concerning regional economic growth. In particular, it situates the concept of regional competitiveness within the prevailing paradigms of endogenous and knowledge-based economic development. The final part of the chapter introduces the rationale and method underlying the WCIR.

Chapter 3 presents the overall rankings of the WCIR. The rankings enable an identification of the general patterns of regional competitiveness across the globe. Given the large number of regions included in the WCIR it can be considered to represent one of the most comprehensive measures of global regional competitiveness. Chapter 4 assesses in more detail the components of regional competitiveness and the links with broader notions of regional economic development.

Regions may reach different stages of economic development depending on their geospatial location, and Chapter 5 analyses the sources of competitiveness across the continental blocs, including an assessment based on the particular stage of economic development that a region has reached. This allows a more in-depth analysis of the different drivers of regional competitiveness. Importantly, it is found that regional competitiveness differences are not necessarily related to national or geospatial characteristics, with regions undertaking economic change and evolution that is more related to their position within a global network of regions.

Clearly, the evolution of a regional economy and its competitiveness capacity may involve multiple independent trajectories, through which different sets of resources and capabilities evolve together. Little is known, however, on the nature of these trends across the globe. Chapter 6 presents evidence on the recent development of some of the globe's most productive regions from the viewpoint of their growth trajectories, in particular the form of growth that they are experiencing. The analysis identifies three key trends by which the economic evolution and growth patterns of these regions are differentiated based on growth wave theory. Overall, the knowledge-based growth of leading Chinese regions is evident, which highlights a continued shift of knowledge-based resources to Asia.

Chapter 7 focuses upon the competitiveness of the European regions surveyed by the WCIR. In order to understand the extent to which regions have been able to withstand, or otherwise, the economic buffeting from the financial crisis of 2007, those regions displaying the greatest changes in competitiveness since 2008 are explored. The chapter further examines the differing nature of the regions within Europe based on the underlying components of the WCIR. It is found that, although there have been concerns about a loss of competitiveness within Europe relative to both the US and other emerging competitors, European regions have, on average, retained their competitiveness, although this competitiveness is not evenly spread.

In Chapter 8, the focus switches to the North American regions. In general, it is found that North America continues to be home to some of the globe's most competitive regions. Silicon Valley remains at the summit followed by a range of other economically advanced and leading regions, especially on the western and eastern seaboards. Nevertheless, there remains significant differentiation in competitiveness across regions, manifested by economic divides within the continent. In aggregate terms, North American regions are seeing their global competitiveness coming under continued pressure as regions in Europe, Asia-Pacific, and the BRIC nations challenge for investment, resources and subsequent economic activity.

The competitiveness of regions within the BRIC economies forms the focus of Chapter 9. It seeks to disaggregate the global rise of the BRIC economies to a regional level in order to understand the patterns and nature of changing competitiveness trajectories in these emerging economies. It is found that leading Chinese regions are, to some extent, a breed apart in terms of the rapid rates of development occurring in these locations, which are far beyond that seen in India and most of Brazil. The analysis of the Russian regions finds that some locations possess massive competitive strengths in terms of natural resources, whereas others are continuing to convert to more knowledge-based regional economies.

Chapter 10 provides one of the first available analyses of the competitiveness of Middle Eastern regions. The analysis finds that whilst there are a small number of globally competitive regions, most still have some way to go before they move into the higher competitiveness echelons. Although there has been much investment in regional economies within nations such as Saudi Arabia and the United Arab Emirates, these still perform below the global average.

In Chapter 11, the global competitiveness of regions is discussed in terms of the broader context of regional benchmarking and policymaking. It is argued that performance measurement – such as that undertaken in the preceding chapters – should form part of a suite of regional benchmarking exercises that also covers the benchmarking of the processes and institutions underlying the functioning of regional economic systems, along with the public policies that impact on regional competitiveness. It is suggested that regional competitiveness benchmarking exercises should employ a '3P' methodology encompassing the performance, process, and policy contexts in order to provide a rounded assessment and evaluation of the economic development trajectories of regions.

Chapter 12 concludes by suggesting that, alongside the need for further technical development to improve regional competitiveness measures, there is also scope for theoretical development, especially with regard to integrating and connecting regional competitiveness with concepts concerning institutions, resilience and well-being, each of which has gained prominence in bids to better explain uneven development. The book concludes with some thoughts on the scope for future public policy intervention in less competitive regions, especially in emerging economies.

2 Regional competitiveness

The notion of the competitiveness of regions remains an area of contested theoretical debate, with some arguing that firms, and not places, compete for resources and markets. Nevertheless, a significant forum of scholarly and practitioner-based research has developed in recent years with the aim of theorizing upon and empirically measuring the competitiveness of regions. However, the somewhat disparate and fragmented nature of this work has led to the lack of a substantive theoretical foundation underpinning the various analyses and measurement methodologies employed.

This chapter seeks to place the regional competitiveness discourse within the context of theories concerning regional economic growth. It positions the concept of regional competitiveness, and models related to its measurement, within those theories that attempt to understand and determine the means through which economic development occurs across regions. To achieve this, it contains a critique of a range of literature from both a theoretical and methodological perspective, allowing a more concrete conceptualization of regional competitiveness to be framed.

The above aims are addressed in the following manner: the chapter first presents an understanding of the concept of regional competitiveness based on the extant literature; it then theorises a link between regional competitiveness and knowledge-based regional economic growth; and following this there is a discussion of the methods for measuring regional competitiveness. This leads to the suggestion that certain measurement models have implicitly sought to connect regional competitiveness with the factors underlying future regional growth. The final part of the chapter introduces the rationale and method underlying the *World Competitiveness Index of Regions* (WCIR).

The concept

The competitiveness of regions generally refers to the presence of conditions that both enable firms to compete in their chosen markets and for the value these firms generate to be captured within a particular region (Begg, 1999; Huggins, 2003). Regional competitiveness, therefore, is considered to consist of the capability of a particular region to attract and maintain firms with stable or rising market shares in an activity, while maintaining stable or increasing standards of living for those who participate in it (Storper, 1997). Given this, competitiveness may vary across geographic space, as regions develop at different rates depending on the drivers of growth (Audretsch and Keilbach, 2004).

While the competitiveness of regions is intrinsically bound to their economic performance, there exists a growing consensus that competitiveness is best measured in terms of the assets of the regional business environment (Malecki, 2004, 2007). These include the level of human capital, the degree of innovative capacity, and the quality of the local infrastructure – all of which affect the propensity to achieve competitive advantage in leading-edge and growing sectors of activity. The influence these assets and other externalities can have on firm competitiveness, such as the ability of regions to attract creative and innovative people or provide high-quality cultural facilities, are all important features of regional competitive advantage (Kitson *et al.*, 2004). In other words, competitiveness is increasingly concerned with creativity, knowledge, and environmental conditions, rather than being purely based on accumulated wealth (Huggins, 2003).

As Martin (2005) outlines, concern with competitiveness has filtered down to the regional, urban, and local levels, particularly the role of regionally based policy interventions in helping to improve the competitiveness of regions and city-regions. In many advanced nations, these interventions form part of a strategic framework to improve productive and innovative performance. From this policy perspective, the key drivers of regional competitiveness are usually considered to consist of the enhancement of knowledge and creativity through clusters (Porter, 1998) or networks (Huggins and Izushi, 2007) of firms and complementary organizations. This perspective resembles the views of the endogenous school of regional development, which argues that regions themselves act as an organizational form of coordination facilitating sustainable competitive advantage (Courlet and Soulage, 1995; Maillat, 1998a; Lawson and Lorenz, 1999; Garofoli, 2002).

Despite these developments, both the concept and the measurement of competitiveness at a regional level remain contested areas of analysis, with some suggesting that 'competitiveness league tables are inevitably seductive for regional development agencies and the media keen to absorb "quick and dirty" comparative measures of regional economic performance' (Bristow, 2005: 294). When conceptualizing regional competitiveness, it is crucial to distinguish it from the concept of competition. Certainly, by writing in terms of competitiveness, one inevitably invites the reader to think of head-to-head conflict. Yet, the concept of competitiveness at the national or regional level is only competitive in the sense that it refers to the presence of conditions that will enable firms to compete in local, national, and international markets. Regions 'compete' in trying to provide the best platform for operating at high levels of productivity, but this is very different from the kind of direct competition undertaken by firms. It is the zero-sum conceptualization of regional competitiveness that often leads to the premise that there must inevitably be both winners and losers (Bristow, 2005).

Malecki (2004) usefully distinguishes between low-road and high-road competition. As he points out, regions may compete on the basis of low wages, docile labour, and low taxes, but such low-road competition will simply perpetuate an inability to upgrade to an economic base with higher skills and wages. Conversely, competition on the high road involving, for example, knowledge policies aimed at promoting entrepreneurship and knowledge-based economic development can lead to positive-sum outcomes that bring benefits to all regional economic and social activities (Leborgne and Lipietz, 1988; Malecki, 2004). For regions, therefore, it is important that competitiveness not only leads to increasing market shares in a particular industry but also raises, or at least maintains, the standard of living, as this should be the end goal of competitive activity (Storper, 1997; Aiginger, 2006). In general, regional development concerns the upgrading of the economic, institutional, and social base, with entrepreneurship that is able to unlock wealth being a prime source of development (Amin, 1999). Consequently, entrepreneurship is central to regional economic growth and competitiveness (Audretsch and Keilbach, 2004; Malecki, 2007).

Spatial economics that does not incorporate entrepreneurship factors may fail to understand and identify key sources of regional development (Andersson, 2005), with regions that are open and creative often able to attract human capital and enjoy more dynamic entrepreneurship (Benneworth, 2004; Lee *et al.*, 2004). In a competitive environment, entrepreneurs will be alert to opportunities and contribute to regional economic growth (Audretsch and Keilbach, 2004). However, changes in levels of entrepreneurship and contributions to regional economic development will take time to emerge, and as such, any effects are only likely to be seen in the long term (Huggins and Johnston, 2009; Huggins and Williams, 2009). Alternatively, regions can be uncompetitive and lack entrepreneurial dynamism because they lack the key strengths that make leading regions prosper and develop (Huggins, 1997; North and Smallbone, 2000; Benneworth and Charles, 2005; Lagendijk and Lorentzen, 2007; Virkkala, 2007; Chaston, 2009; Huggins and Johnston, 2009; Huggins and Williams, 2011).

As already indicated, regional competitiveness remains a contested concept. However, Paul Krugman, a renowned sceptic of the national competitiveness concept (e.g., Krugman, 1994a), suggests that the competitiveness of a region is based on its ability to provide sufficiently attractive wages and/or employment prospects and a return on capital (Krugman, 2003). This proposition, along with others, has led to competitiveness becoming a more generally accepted concept when discussing uneven development across regions. Camagni (2002) further argues that the concept of regional competitiveness is theoretically sound, due to the role territories play in providing competitive environmental tools to firms and in processes of knowledge accumulation.

Regional competitiveness and growth

Some commentators have suggested that although policymakers everywhere are appropriating the term regional competitiveness, it remains 'complex and contentious' and 'we are far from a consensus on what is meant by the term'

(Kitson *et al.*, 2004: 992). Nevertheless, the regional entrepreneurial, knowledge, and innovation capacity of regions are generally considered to be key factors underpinning the future economic development and growth trajectory of regions. It is this link, therefore, between the knowledge, entrepreneurial, and innovation bases of regions and their growth capacity and capability that is at the heart of the concept of competitiveness. In this respect, regional competitiveness concepts are strongly tied to the lineage of Schumpeterian theory (Schumpeter, 1934) – or 'Schumpeter's competitiveness', as it has been termed (Beugelsdijk and Maseland, 2011) – as well as more contemporary theories relating to the endogenous nature of economic growth.

Both competitiveness and endogenous growth theory are rooted in the notion that the sources of high rates of economic performance and subsequent growth stem from the role that the production, distribution, and use of knowledge play within and across economies (Grossman and Helpman, 1994; Harris, 2001; Ibert, 2007; Zucker *et al.*, 2007; Vaz and Nijkamp, 2009; Antonelli *et al.*, 2011). The knowledge-based economy is generally considered to consist of the sphere and nexus of activities and resources centred on, and geared toward, innovation (Romer, 2007). The innovation systems literature, in particular, pinpoints the flow of knowledge across organizations as a crucial factor for effective innovation (Freeman, 1987, 1994; Cooke, 2004; Andersson and Karlsson, 2007; Lundvall, 2010; Cooke *et al.*, 2011; Harris, 2011).

Early models of economic growth are rooted in the work of Solow (1956, 1957) and Swan (1956), which focused on physical capital and the supply of labour as the key sources of growth (Andersson and Karlsson, 2007). In contrast with these earlier models and echoing the key tenets of regional competitiveness, endogenous growth theory stresses that knowledge is a key driver of productivity and economic growth, which departs from the traditional emphasis on the accumulation of physical capital (Lucas, 1988; Romer, 1986, 1990; Aghion and Howitt, 1998). Theorists of economic development have increasingly drawn upon models of endogenous growth to better understand the factors underpinning such development. Endogenous growth theory generally assumes that economic growth is at least partly a function of stocks of knowledge in the form of human capital or the outcomes of research and development (R&D) activities. The use of the term endogenous is recognition that economic growth is influenced by the use of investment resources generated by economies themselves, rather than the exogenous factors associated with traditional growth models.

At the regional level, it is generally recognized that there is a need to better understand the mechanisms underlying regional growth patterns (Andersson and Karlsson, 2007; Capello and Nijkamp, 2009; Stimson *et al.*, 2011). As indicated above, economic growth rates are increasingly considered to be dependent on endogenous factors with most treatments commonly assuming that economic growth is partly a function of either stocks of human capital, as proposed by Lucas (1988), or R&D, as proposed in Romer's (1986) model. Romer (1986), for instance, specified a model of long-run growth in which knowledge is assumed to be an input into production that has increasing marginal productivity. Adapting

Romer's (1986) model to the regional context, it can be proposed that the output of a region (r) is a function not only of physical capital and labour, but also the stock of results from expenditure on R&D:

$$Y_r = A(R)F(K_r, R_r, L_r)$$

Where: Y = economic output
A= current global state of knowledge
K= physical capital
R= stock of results from expenditure on R&D
L = supply of labor

In the Lucas (1988) model, it is investment in human capital (H) that largely determines the output of a region (r):

$$Y_r = A(H)F(K_r, H_r)$$

These models make clear that endogenous growth is considered to be driven by technological change arising from intentional investment decisions made by profit-maximizing agents, with the stock of human and research capital – and investments in such capital – determining the rate of growth (Romer, 1990; Ha and Howitt, 2007). In this respect, regional competitiveness models possess many similarities, with the key difference being that output measures are transferred to the right-hand side of the equation – see, for example, the equations developed by Aiginger (2006) outlined in the measurement and methodologies section below – with the left-hand side being a measure of overall competitiveness. This makes logical sense as endogenous growth models are seeking to explain the factors underlying past output growth. Competitiveness models, on the other hand, are seeking to measure the capacity and capability for future output growth, with the factors used to explain this encompassing the explanatory factors adopted by growth theorists as well as current rates of output and productivity.

In relation to competitiveness and endogenous growth theories, knowledge refers to the cumulative stock of information and skills concerned with connecting new ideas with commercial values, developing new products and processes, and, therefore, doing business in a new way. This may be called knowledge for innovation or innovative knowledge. Whereas innovation is a process, knowledge consists of the recipes and the ingredients to be processed. Therefore, as illustrated by Figure 2.1, the relationship between the concepts of knowledge, innovation, and competitiveness are closely associated and interlinked.

For Porter (1998), the localized productivity advantages of agglomeration, such as access to specialized inputs, employees, information, and institutions, will encourage firms to cluster, and reinforce clusters over time, as new firms become attracted by the same advantages of concentration. Many of the factors that increase current productivity will also encourage innovation within the cluster and, therefore, increase the productivity growth of firms. For example, access to

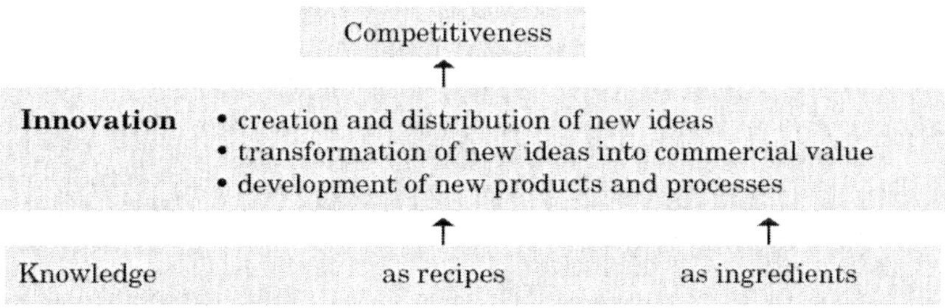

Figure 2.1 Relationship between competitiveness, innovation and knowledge

specialized information via personal relationships will, over time, provide localized advantages for firms in perceiving new technological opportunities and new buyer needs. Therefore, as traditional forms of advantage become nullified, competitive advantages lying outside of firms – i.e. in the business environment in which they are located – increase in importance.

With advances in telecommunications and information technologies allowing the instantaneous transfer of information, regardless of location, it might appear logical to consider that geography would become increasingly less important in economic analysis. In fact, in a number of ways, the reverse is true (Porter, 1990). Although it has become possible for firms and individuals to source work far more widely, the geographic concentration of related resources and industries, in particular knowledge-intensive activities, remains one of the most striking features of any nation or region, especially in the most advanced economies. Furthermore, although the historic factors influencing location, such as proximity to inputs and markets, are being undercut, the ability to source from anywhere is, paradoxically, increasing the importance of local competitive advantage; in many respects, globalization is reinforcing localization.

Despite contemporary theoretical developments in the field of economic growth, Aghion and Howitt (1998) suggest that there is a need to further widen our conception of the investment resources underpinning economic growth. At the regional level, it is similarly recognized that there is a need to better understand the mechanisms underlying regional growth patterns (Andersson and Karlsson, 2007; Capello and Nijkamp, 2009; Stimson *et al.*, 2011). Indeed, it is suggested that perhaps the most interesting implications of endogenous growth theory relate to the impact of the spatial organization of regions on flows of knowledge. In particular, it is considered that differences in regional growth can potentially be explained by differences in the conditions for creating, accumulating and – crucially – transmitting knowledge (Roberts and Setterfield, 2010). For instance, it is argued that increasing returns are realized through both the geographic and organizational processes resulting from localization, and in time the spatial and economic diffusion of knowledge (Pred and Hagerstrand, 1967; Storper, 2009).

Fundamentally, a key driver of regional growth consists of the capability of organizations in a region to access and subsequently utilize appropriate economically beneficial knowledge. According to Storper (1997: 44), 'the status of the region is now not merely as a locus of true externalities, but – for the lucky regions – as a site of important stocks of relational assets'. These relational assets in the form of the network capital of firms and other organizations (Huggins, 2010a; Huggins and Johnston, 2010; Huggins *et al.*, 2012) and the social capital of individuals (Tura and Harmaakorpi, 2005; Hauser *et al.*, 2007; Lorenzen, 2007; Walter *et al.*, 2007; Tappeiner *et al.*, 2008; Cantner *et al.*, 2009) distinguish Storper's (1997) 'lucky' from 'unlucky' regions, as well as forming part of the territorial capital of regions, which includes not only relational assets but the wider set of natural, human, and organizational assets underpinning regional competitiveness (Camagni and Capello, 2010, 2013; Capello *et al.*, 2011).

Knowledge and endogenous regional development

In general, it is widely observed that the location where innovation occurs is evolving, with the stock of knowledge and other knowledge-based resources constantly shifting, reflecting ever-changing contexts for new and more advanced knowledge requirements (Dicken, 2007). Furthermore, the sources of regional productivity and growth are increasingly based on the role that knowledge plays within and across regional economies (Capello and Nijkamp, 2009). As a result, the concept of the knowledge-based economy has emerged to aid a better understanding of how the effective production, distribution and use of knowledge underpin innovative and competitive modern economies (Huggins and Izushi, 2007). The concept of 'regional innovation systems', for instance, is recognition of the role of knowledge for growth through innovation (Cooke, 2004). Innovation systems theory views an economy as an interlinked systemic network of components facilitating innovation (Freeman, 1987; Lundvall, 1992).

In an evolutionary context, the knowledge-based development of a regional economy involves multiple threads of relationships among its actors and resources at both a firm and spatial level, which interact in a complex manner (Maskell and Malmberg, 2007). For instance, under growing competitiveness pressures in virtually all sectors, firms are increasingly focusing on their core activities and searching external knowledge sources as part of their innovation management strategies. These firm-level strategies may facilitate knowledge-based investment and stimulate the growth of related resources and capabilities within their region, resulting in productivity improvement at both firm and regional level. Yet, there are growing concerns that such knowledge-based development may not necessarily contribute to employment growth at the regional level and may in fact lead to 'jobless growth' (Vivarelli and Pianta, 2000; Döpke, 2001).

As indicated above, endogenous growth theory has placed knowledge at the centre of economic development (Romer, 1986, 1990), but whilst endogenous growth can be considered the desired outcome of knowledge-based development and innovation, it is the process of endogenous development which underpins the growth trajectories of economies (Vázquez-Barquero, 2007). In particular, regions are increasingly considered to be key territorial units within which endogenous forms of development flourish through their innovative milieu – or what some have referred to as 'technopoles' (Castells and Hall, 1994), 'industrial districts' (Capello, 1999), or 'clusters' (Porter, 1998) – facilitating knowledge flow and new knowledge creation. Implicit is the contention that regional development and growth is best promoted through bottom-up activity focused on the enhancement of local production systems, rather than top-down processes of exogenous development focused on seeking to redistribute resources from elsewhere (Maillat, 1998a, 1998b; Garofoli, 2002).

Cooke (2004), for instance, suggests that regional innovation systems are a vital component for regional economic development, while others have focused on the notion of clusters as the key focus of regional economic theory and policy, with the underlying argument being that competitiveness is determined by the strength of key concentrations of specific industries (Porter, 1998; Huggins and Izushi, 2011). The innovative milieu of urban settings, in particular metropolitan regions, means that they are often singled out by scholars such as Maillat (1998b), Fischer *et al.* (2001), Revilla Diez (2002) and Vázquez-Barquero (2007) as being key territorial units within which endogenous forms of development flourish.

The principles of the endogenous development school of regions are rooted in the role that factors such as collective learning and cooperative behaviour play in the establishment of an innovative milieu. As Garofoli (2002) argues, endogenous development primarily concerns the capacity to innovate and produce 'collective intelligence' in a localized environment, which explicitly recognizes the relevance of the spillover, diffusing, accumulating, creating and internalizing of knowledge. The centrality of knowledge spillovers within processes of endogenous development is evident in the way through which, for example, cluster boundaries are defined (Porter, 1998). As Porter (1998: 202) argues,

> Drawing cluster boundaries is often a matter of degree, and involves a creative process informed by understanding the most important linkages and complementarities across industries and institutions to competition. The strength of these 'spillovers' and their importance to productivity and innovation determine the ultimate boundaries.

Although it could be argued that agglomeration forces beyond technological development will also play a significant role in delineating cluster boundaries, it is clear that the extent of knowledge spillovers is also of significance in shaping these boundaries, as well as forming the basis of a region's overall innovativeness (Huggins and Izushi, 2011).

Measurement and methodologies

This section considers the establishment of methodologies to measure competitiveness across regions. In general, the development of regional competitiveness indices stems from the initial establishment of composite indices of the national sources and outputs of competitiveness, such as the *Global Competitiveness Report* (World Economic Forum, 2012) and *World Competitiveness Yearbook* (Institute for Management Development [IMD], 2013), which combine a number of variables to produce a single composite competitiveness measure.

There are a number of approaches to creating indices, including those that look into a single aspect of an economy and produce a single index. When economists analyse the economic performance of nations and regions, the most typical approach is to take a certain economic variable as a proxy for the degree to which economies are knowledge-based. One example is the work of Porter and colleagues in establishing an innovation index, whereby the number of patents granted acts as a proxy for the nation's innovativeness (Porter and Stern, 1999; Furman *et al.*, 2002). Although this approach has advantages in the operational ease of benchmarking, the choice of the variable leaves much room for subjectivity concerning the relationship between the variable and the extent of the knowledge base of an economy.

A second approach is one that analyses more than one aspect of an economy and produces an index for each of these aspects. By examining more than one aspect of an economy in understanding and defining the extent of the knowledge base, this approach avoids the assumption that a single variable represents a fully encapsulated measure (Castellacci and Archibugi, 2008). An example is the Organization for Economic Co-operation and Development (OECD)'s *Science, Technology, and Industry Scoreboard* (OECD, 1999). This approach provides a range of perspectives by which to evaluate economies but does not provide a single benchmark index.

A third approach is one that investigates more than one aspect of an economy and produces a single composite benchmark index. Studies taking this approach vary in the way in which they aggregate sub-indices, derived from different aspects of an economy, into a single composite index. For example, the Milken Institute's *New Economy Index* (DeVol, 1999) measures US states across a dozen aspects and produces a single composite index by taking a mean of the scores for those original indices. Similarly, the *Metropolitan New Economy Index* (Atkinson and Gottlieb, 2001) uses a set of weights that vary but are arbitrarily set.

The World Competitiveness Yearbook, published annually by the IMD (2013), analyses the competitiveness of nations based on both quantitative and qualitative data (consisting of an annual survey of executives within each nation), which are classified into sub-factors. Each sub-factor, independent of the number of criteria it contains, has the same weight in the composite index produced. The quantitative criteria represent a weight of two thirds in the overall composite, whereas the qualitative data represent a weight of one third. These examples indicate some subjectivity or arbitrariness in arriving at weightings used in the aggregation.

Some studies attempt to avoid this by employing more complex methods for the calculation of weights. An example is the World Economic Forum's (2012) *Global Competitiveness Report*. The report employs both quantitative (one third of variables) and qualitative data (two thirds of variables) and classifies them into nine factors (institutions, infrastructure, macro-economy, health and primary education, higher education and training, market efficiency, technological readiness, business sophistication, and innovation). The weight given to each factor varies across countries as a function of their overall level of economic development.

Building on measurement work at the national level, Aiginger (2006) offers two different perspectives on the definition of competitiveness in order to try to reduce some of the confusion in conceptualizing and measuring competitiveness. The first type of competitiveness he describes consists of outcome competitiveness, where competitiveness is measured as a form of welfare function.

$$Competitiveness \equiv W(Y,S,E)$$

Where: Y = income per capita
S = social and distributional indicators
E = ecological indicators.

The second type of competitiveness Aiginger (2006) describes is process competitiveness, which is related to the production function linking inputs to output (generally in terms of income per capita), with inputs including a wider range of factors than just physical capital and labour.

$$Competitiveness = F(K,L,TFP,C,I,T)$$

Where: K = physical capital
L = labour
TFP = total factor productivity representing technical progress
C = capabilities
I = institutional effects
T = trust.

Although Aiginger's (2006) work and national level competitiveness indices provide a useful analytical tool, they fail to tell the full story regarding subnational trends, with different industries tending to cluster in particular regions, leading to performance gaps across regions. In response, a number of alternative measures of regional competitiveness have been developed, with a rapid increase in the use of regional competitiveness benchmarking exercises to monitor differentials in competitive performance and economic development trajectories across regions (Huggins, 2010b). Regional competitiveness benchmarking exercises have become increasingly popular within the sphere of regional policymaking, with such popularity linked to notions concerning the means by which regions are able to learn (Morgan, 1997), particularly through methods based on comparison (Rose, 1993) or monitoring (Sabel, 1996). Regional economic development, competitiveness, and innovation policies, and the manner in which such policies are implemented, form part of the institutional architecture through which regions learn (Asheim, 1996; Morgan, 1997). Indeed, establishing such policies is itself a process undertaken by regional stakeholders to facilitate regional learning (Rutten and Boekema, 2007).

Regional competitiveness benchmarking has become a feature of this policy-making and facilitated-learning process, which seeks to understand regional contexts and promote improved regional competitiveness outcomes (Huggins, 2010b). The main purpose of regional benchmarking is to ascertain how certain regions, or a particular region, are performing based on an identified set of metrics representing a particular set of regional characteristics. To date, most regional benchmarking exercises undertaken in Europe and North America have been restricted to comparing regions within a particular continental bloc or nation (e.g., DeVol, 1999; Atkinson and Gottlieb, 2001; Wong, 2002; Florida, 2002b; Parkinson *et al.*, 2004; DeVol *et al.*, 2004, 2007; Fox and Treuhaft, 2006; Hollanders, 2007; Atkinson and Correa, 2007; Dijkstra *et al.*, 2011). These regional benchmarking exercises have usually either explicitly or implicitly sought to incorporate: (a) the input factors associated with process competitiveness; (b) the output factors measuring output competitiveness; and (c) the outcome factors associated with the welfare of the population (Huggins, 2003).

Figure 2.2 highlights the fundamental model underlying regional competitiveness models. The purpose of this model is to understand the relationship between the main determinants of regional competitiveness and to integrate them to understand competitiveness differences across regions. Regional competitiveness inputs are principally the factors of production that produce goods and services and drive economic activity and outputs, consisting of the human capital factors at the heart of endogenous growth theories, as well as factors such as the availability of physical and financial capital. Inputs are not an end in themselves; they provide the means to achieve outputs and long-term outcomes. Regional competitiveness outputs are the direct results that yield from inputs, while competitiveness outcomes are the long-term result of outputs in the form of rising living standards.

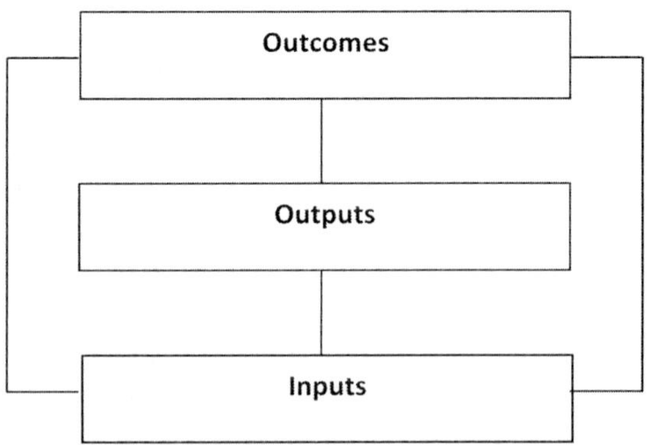

Figure 2.2 Three-factor regional competitiveness framework

One example of the use of this approach is the *UK Competitiveness Index* (UKCI) which draws on the model presented in Figure 2.2 to construct a single index that reflects, as fully as possible, the measurable criteria constituting regional and local competitiveness across the United Kingdom (Huggins, 2003; Huggins and Thompson, 2014). In this model, the input factors are measures of the resources available within the economy of a particular region, including research and development expenditure, economic activity rates, business start-up rates, number of businesses, human capital as measured by educational qualifications, and the proportion of knowledge-based businesses. These measures are mostly associated with the potential of a region to continue to compete, and therefore they primarily concern process competitiveness (Aiginger, 2006).

The second group consists of factors relating to outputs. These include gross value added per capita, exports per head of population, imports per head of population, proportion of exporting companies, productivity (output per hour worked), and employment rates. To capture favourable outcomes for the population of a region, a third group of factors is also included, that is, those relating to outcomes: gross weekly pay (median) and unemployment rates. Both these latter two factors are more strongly associated with outcome competitiveness (Aiginger, 2006). Given the uncertainty relating to the exact relationship between the three sets of factors, the overall index weights the three-factor indices equally.

Whilst recognizing the potential limitation of drawing upon single composite index measures, in particular its implicit universalism (Lall, 2001a; Bristow, 2005), such an approach does go some way towards reflecting the link between regional economic performance and innovative firm-level behaviour.

World Competitiveness Index of Regions (WCIR)

In this section the rationale and method underlying the *World Competitiveness Index of Regions* (WCIR) is discussed and presented. The aim of the WCIR is to provide a tool for analysing the development of a wide variety of regional economies based within differing national economies. The WCIR enables an illustration of the changing patterns of competitiveness across the globe to be generated, as well as exemplifying the outcomes suggested by the latest theories on regional development. As already indicated, the concept of regional competitiveness, along with its measurement is not an undisputed field (Bristow, 2005), and no index can fully capture all the resources, both tangible and intangible, provided to firms operating within a region, or the impact these have on the welfare and well-being of the population of a region (Thompson and Ward, 2005). The WCIR, therefore, seeks to accommodate the key influences identified by previous literature within the broad conceptual and analytical framework presented above.

The WCIR represents an integrated and overall benchmark of the knowledge capacity, capability, and sustainability of each region, and the extent to which this knowledge is translated into economic value and transferred into the wealth of the citizens of each region. Therefore, the WCIR is explicitly tied to the theoretical discourse stemming from endogenous growth theory, with knowledge and human capital at the centre of its analysis.

The WCIR is designed to address the growing attention that regions have attracted as an economic unit of analysis, with firms increasingly locating their functions in select regions within the global space. It is widely recognized that economic divides across regions are usually related to the different industries located, and functions performed, in these regions, as well as differences in their supporting environments (Huggins and Izushi, 2007). Such supporting environments consist of, for example, universities and research establishments, business and producer service providers, and information and communication technologies (ICT) infrastructure.

The approach adopted by the WCIR acknowledges that although the competitive advantage of firms can arise from size and position within their industry, alongside their physical assets (Porter, 1980), the pattern of competition in advanced economies has increasingly come to favour those firms that can mobilize knowledge and technological skills to create novelty in their products (Prahalad and Hamel, 1990). Along with this, the mode by which knowledge is produced has shifted from traditional linear processes of innovation to more complex incremental and iterative chain-link models based on the interactions between knowledge actors (Kline and Rosenberg, 1986; Rothwell, 1994).

The evolving characteristics associated with the new models of knowledge production include the following: (a) the number of sites where innovation occurs is rising rapidly alongside an increasing variation in the types of sites where innovation is occurring; (b) the stock of knowledge is in part an outcome of the intensity of interaction between knowledge actors; (c) the pattern and dynamics of these interactions are constantly shifting, reflecting ever-changing contexts; and (d) the density of interactions is increasing rapidly, as is the number of knowledge actors (Florida, 2002b; Chesbrough, 2003). The links between knowledge creation and diffusion processes, through individuals, organizations, and systems of institutions and organizations, are clearly required to be understood as fully as possible, as knowledge becomes the key value creator in modern economies.

Given the apparent linkage, therefore, between competitiveness and knowledge, it appears logical to test whether the distribution of knowledge and the capacity of the knowledge economy are unequal across regions at the global level, which is the task the WCIR sets itself. Through the construction of a composite competitiveness index based on a series of knowledge-based input factors and relevant output and outcome factors, the WCIR is able to identify the relative capacity and capability to achieve long-term regional growth. In this sense, the regional competitiveness measured by the WCIR can be defined as the difference in the rate of economic development across regions and the capacity and capability of regions to achieve future economic growth relative to other regions at a similar stage of economic development.

As suggested earlier, there exists a growing consensus that competitiveness is best measured in terms of the 'assets' of the regional business environment (Malecki, 2004, 2007). As such, the competitiveness of a region will depend on its ability to anticipate and successfully adapt to internal and external economic and social challenges by providing new economic opportunities, including higher quality jobs. In order to empirically analyse competitiveness at a regional level, the framework presented by Figure 2.3 is adopted, which builds on the three-factor model presented by Figure 2.2, introducing a means for measuring feedbacks via the long-term sustainability of knowledge, and thus competitiveness. Within this model, regional competitiveness inputs are distinguished according to whether or not they can be best considered as 5th-wave or 4th-wave knowledge capital. Fifth-wave knowledge capital inputs concern the acknowledged role played by the digital revolution and the Internet as the enabling innovation underpinning twenty-first century economic growth (Hall and Preston, 1988; Wymbs, 2004; Devezas *et al.*, 2005; Linstone and Devezas, 2012). Fourth-wave knowledge capital is related to the prior dominance played by innovation and technological developments stemming from investment in R&D, principally in manufacturing activities (Hall and Preston, 1988). (A fuller discussion of these waves of growth is presented in the section entitled 'Waves of growth: Factor analysis' in Chapter 6.)

Overall, the framework employs a set of 19 indicators. In the input domain of new knowledge production, we choose the number of employees in five high-tech sectors as proxies for the human capital devoted to innovation. A number of studies attempt to classify sectors based on criteria related to research and technology intensity (Lee and Has, 1996). The WCIR uses the Eurostat (the European Commission's statistical office) scheme of industry classification, which was developed in collaboration with the OECD (Hatzichronoglou, 1997; Laafia, 1999). It classifies into five groups those sectors considered by Eurostat as 'higher-tech manufacturing sectors', 'medium–high-tech manufacturing sectors' and 'high-tech service sectors'. The five groups are: IT and computer manufacturing; high-tech services; biotechnology and chemicals; instrumentation and electrical machinery; and automotive and mechanical engineering.

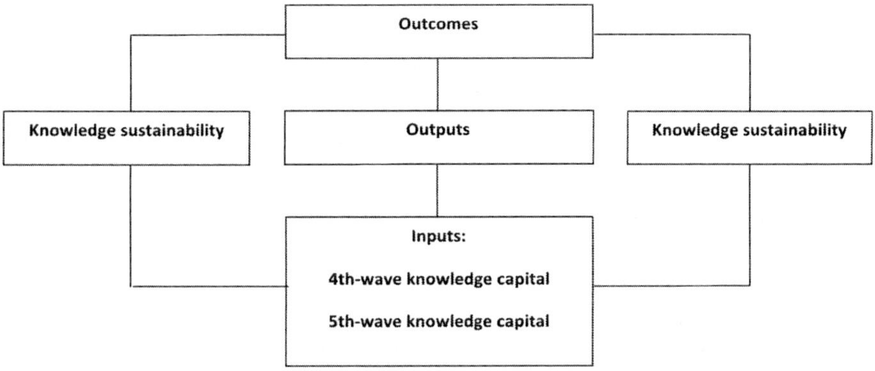

Figure 2.3 Framework underpinning the World Competitiveness Index of Regions (WCIR)

Other technology-input measures include R&D expenditures performed by the business and government sectors. Compared with corporate R&D, the impact of public sector R&D is less direct in its route in terms of both diffusion and timing. Nonetheless, there is evidence that spillovers from public sector R&D raise an economy's productivity (Jaffe, 1989a; Adams, 1990).

Another technology measure used is the number of patents granted. The propensity to patent is known to vary widely across industries, with many patents turning out to be worthless, while a few are extremely valuable (Pavitt, 1982; Griliches, 1990). However, there is some evidence that suggests a close association between patents and other productivity-based measures at the national and regional level (Fagerberg, 1996; Acs *et al.*, 2002).

Private equity investment capital is used as a proxy of the availability of funds for knowledge-based, start-up firms. Private equity funding is often concentrated in small or medium-sized firms, including venture capital and start-up investments, which tend to be in knowledge-based activities.

For indicators of the long-term competitiveness sustainability, public expenditures on primary and secondary education and higher education are included. There is a sequential interaction between a region's education and training system and its stock of high-skilled workers. The rate of enrolment in education is influenced by a region's employment and career prospects, as well as the socioeconomic background of pupils and the quality of schooling. Enrolment, in turn, determines the region's workforce skills, productivity and economic performance (Bradley and Taylor, 1996). Public investment in education plays an important role in this sequential cycle, particularly improving the quality of local schooling over time. In addition, three indicators of internet-based infrastructure are employed: numbers of internet hosts, secure servers, and broadband access – as measures of knowledge competitiveness sustainability.

Other measures included are the regional unemployment rate and economic activity rate (defined by the ratio of the labour force to the working-age population). Also included is the proportion of workers employed in a managerial capacity, which is used as a proxy of human capital. Although this is hardly a perfect indicator of human capital, a similar indicator is used in international studies of the labour market (OECD, 1994). The wages of managers are generally higher than those of other occupations, reflecting the greater amount of investment made in education and training. Lastly, we adopt labour productivity and mean gross monthly earnings as indicators of competitiveness outputs and outcomes, respectively.

To remove effects of the size of each region analysed, per capita figures are taken for the following variables: R&D expenditures performed by the business sector and government sector; patents granted; private equity investment capital; internet hosts; secure servers; broadband access; and public expenditures on primary and secondary education, and higher education. Employment in the five high- or medium-high-tech industries and the number of managers are based on a per total regional employment basis. To avoid individual indicators having an excessive influence on the four components of the WCIR or the composite

WCIR index, the individual indicators are standardized after appropriate scaling. Below the rationale underlying the grouping for each of the indicators is presented.

Fifth-wave knowledge capital inputs

As already argued, knowledge economies compete on value and innovation, rather than costs alone. As regions make the transition to knowledge economies, we would expect increases in the number and proportion of knowledge-based businesses and employment. In particular, 5th-wave knowledge-capital-based sectors have a higher potential for innovation and competitive advantage. Due to their intense requirements for innovation, these sectors have a higher propensity for developing a knowledge-driven economy, with the outputs from these sectors being more likely to generate knowledge spillovers for the rest of the regional economy. High venture capital/private equity activity is also essential to the translation of new ideas into innovation, as without the necessary availability of finance, a region's investments in R&D and human capital would yield little return. As such, the 5th-wave knowledge capital indicators are:

- employment in IT and computer manufacturing per 1,000 employees
- employment in biotechnology and chemicals per 1,000 employees
- employment in high-technology services per 1,000 employees
- per capita private equity investment.

Fourth-wave knowledge capital inputs

Investment and employment in research and development activities signal the strength of efforts to develop and exploit new technology in order to enlarge the knowledge base. Similarly, the number of patents indicates how successful a region is in converting knowledge into potentially commercially valuable products and processes. Also, more traditional manufacturing knowledge-based sectors are a good measure of knowledge employment concentration. High activity rates and managerial density are also considered to be strong indicators of the potency of the human capital stock in a region. As such, the 4th-wave knowledge capital indicators are:

- employment in automotive and mechanical engineering per 1,000 employees
- employment in instrumentation and electrical machinery per 1,000 employees
- economic activity rate
- number of managers per 1,000 employees
- per capita expenditures on R&D performed by government
- per capita expenditures on R&D performed by business
- number of patents registered per one million inhabitants.

Outputs/outcomes

Economic 'performance' indicators are clearly vital components of competitiveness, and are usually the most established and well-known measures used. Those indicators considered here portray a specific image of a region: how productive its economy is, and the living standards enjoyed by its citizens. To this end, the WCIR analyses the following indicators:

- labour productivity
- mean gross monthly earnings
- unemployment rates.

Knowledge sustainability

Future knowledge capital is embodied within those individuals currently undertaking education. Although strong regions will be able to attract talent from elsewhere, in the long-term, reinvestment of returns into local human capital through education will help ensure that a region's knowledge economy maintains a sufficient flow of human capital. Likewise, local investment in ICT infrastructure is also fast becoming a necessity in order to transfer knowledge effectively and efficiently. Based on these factors, the following indicators of knowledge sustainability are included:

- per capita public expenditures on primary and secondary education
- per capita public expenditures on higher education
- secure servers per one million inhabitants
- internet hosts per 1,000 inhabitants
- broadband access per 1,000 inhabitants.

Regional coverage

The WCIR covers 546 regions globally, which are listed by continental bloc in Appendix 1. In the European Union (EU) member states, a total of 137 regions are benchmarked. This not only gives a wide perspective across EU regions, but provides insights into the regional disparities that are so important to the EU's economic convergence goals (Keating and Loughlin, 1997). The regions of the EU states are based on the NUTS (Nomenclature of Territorial Units for Statistics) classification, with a majority of them belonging to NUTS-1 group (Austria, Belgium, Bulgaria, Estonia, France, Germany, Greece, Hungary, Latvia, Lithuania, Luxembourg, Malta, Netherlands, Poland, Portugal, Romania, Spain, and the UK), and the remaining ones to NUTS-2. The inclusion of the three European Economic Area (EEA) states – Iceland, Norway, and Switzerland – means that there is coverage of 140 regions within the wider European free trade area.

Due to the rapid development in the performance of the BRIC nations (Brazil, Russia, India, China), the WCIR gives the regions of these nations prominent coverage. Under the European continental bloc, 56 Russian regions are included, bringing the total of European regions to 196. Russia, being a transcontinental country, posed a separate challenge, with a number of the more eastern regions classified within the Asian continental bloc. The splitting of the Russian regions was considerably eased by the Russian administrative regional divisions, allowing the use of the conventional continental border of the Ural Mountains and the Ural River to distinguish between the European and Asian Russian regions. Only one region was divided between the two continents – Orenburg Oblast. It is classified here as European, due to the majority of its territory clearly being on the European side.

In North America, 90 US regions are benchmarked along with 12 Canadian regions (based on their defined provincial units). The US regions are based on the Metropolitan Statistical Areas (MSAs) as defined by the US Census Bureau. MSAs consist of an area with a substantial population centre and adjacent counties having a high degree of economic homogeneity, which is – compared with counties, cities and states – more robust for economic analysis, as they reflect the boundaries of clusters of firms in related industries.

In the case of Asia and Pacific regions, 164 regions are included from Australia, Japan, South Korea, China, India, Kazakhstan, Taiwan, Singapore, New Zealand, and 'Asian Russia'. The Asian and Pacific regions are defined by city or provincial/prefecture boundaries for most nations (for example, provinces for China).

In the Middle East, 35 regions covering Israel, Qatar, and Kuwait (each as region-states), as well as 13 Saudi Arabian, 7 United Arab Emirates, and 12 Turkish regions are benchmarked. Finally, the WCIR covers regions from two South America nations: Brazil (27 regions) and Colombia (22 regions).

As data are available on a time series basis for a selection of 145 regions – due to the datasets associated with the previous WKCI initiatives, it is possible to undertake a degree of longitudinal comparison – based on the WCIR methodology – that forms the basis of some of the analysis presented in following chapters and helps identify regional convergence or divergence trends more clearly (Romer, 1986; Krugman, 1999).

WCIR composite indicator

In order to establish the composite WCIR measure each of the four components are first calculated as an average of its sub-listed indicators (with the exception of the Knowledge Sustainability, where first an average of the three ICT infrastructure variables is taken, and then with the remaining two indicators another average is calculated). A mean average of the value of the components is taken to give a raw WCIR score. In order to calculate the final index, the raw scores are first transformed so that their average becomes 100. Then a geometric mean of the variances of the converted variables is taken, which is termed (variance)original. Finally, the scores for all regions are standardized, multiplied by the square root of (variance)original.

In the following analysis and data presentation, all scores are converted into scores whose average is 100. Within the bottom 10% of the regions there are a number with a negative index score. This has no particular meaning and should not affect the interpretation of the scores by the reader, as it is simply an expression of the wide range of differences between regions.

Data collection

As the WCIR covers 546 regions from 51 nations across the globe, this clearly poses a range of data collection challenges. Appendix 2 shows the data sources used for collecting the data, and although much regional data are available from respective national statistical offices, this is not always the case, and other reliable sources are used for accessing statistics for particular regions. The main challenges arising include the fact that: different national statistical offices often collect information on different indicators; collect information at different geographical levels (i.e. national, regional, or sub-regional); or use slightly different definitions in the statistical data they provide (e.g. working-age population according to the OECD is customarily defined as 15–64 years old; however, among the WCIR regions some statistical offices report only data for the population aged 15+ or 16+). In order to overcome these challenges, some of the indicators had to be sourced from a number of international organizations. In some hard-to-access cases, regional indicators are estimated using the closest possible statistical data that could act as a proxy variable for a particular WCIR indicator; for example, in a small number of cases broadband access is proxied from internet usage.

It is important to stress that the WCIR is not free of data gaps, and it is necessary to acknowledge that not all possible data are available. For the main composite WCIR indicator, the gaps are estimated using the national arithmetic average for the specific indicator and a geometric mean of all existing indicators for the considered region. The reason for this estimating process is to avoid disproportionate effects of the indicators on the WCIR regions.

Concluding remarks

This chapter has sought to identify regional competitiveness as a dual concept that explains relative differences in rates of economic development across regions, as well as an understanding of the future economic growth trajectories of regions at a similar stage of economic development. As with endogenous growth and development theory, the notion of regional competitiveness presented here has placed knowledge and innovation at the forefront of our understanding of regional economic differentiation. It has further been suggested that such differentiation needs to be increasingly understood from an international perspective, with the WCIR presenting a means for undertaking such an analysis, and, as will be shown in the following chapters, it represents a rich and unique insight into the global competitiveness of regions.

3 World Competitiveness Index of Regions

This chapter presents the overall rankings of the *World Competitiveness Index of Regions* (WCIR). The rankings enable an identification of the general patterns of regional competitiveness across the globe. Given the large number of regions included in the WCIR, it represents the most comprehensive available measure of global regional competitiveness. As described in the previous chapter, the WCIR has been designed so that the average competitiveness of the 546 regions included in the index is represented by a WCIR score of 100. The index has a variance related to the geometric mean of the individual sub-indices that make up the overall index. This means that it is possible to have a negative WCIR, as is the case for some of the less competitive regions included in the index. However, obtaining a positive or negative index score has no special meaning.

WCIR rankings

As shown by Table 3.1, the leading region holds no great surprise, consisting of San Jose-Sunnyvale-Santa Clara region of the United States, which is commonly referred to as *Silicon Valley*. As has been very well documented, this region has a long history of innovation and engagement in the knowledge economy. Its origins stem from the 1940s with Stanford University's world leading research and government investment in defence research playing a key role (Sölvell, 2008). In many ways, Silicon Valley has been viewed as the ideal or model region for policymakers to draw best practice from (Hospers, 2006). Studies as far back as Saxenian (1994) have noted the role that the proximity of a group of highly innovative IT corporations have played in the success of Silicon Valley. Along with this, work on clusters, such as that of Porter (1998), has led many regions to attempt to emulate the success of San Jose (Boschma, 2004; Hospers, 2005). The next most competitive region is the Région de Bruxelles-Capitale, the Belgian capital, with there being a clear gap between these two leading regions and those that follow.

Table 3.2 outlines some of the characteristics of the WCIR. The index scores range from the 359.98 obtained by San Jose-Sunnyvale-Santa Clara to –50.28 for Nariño in Colombia. This means that there is a range of 410.26 for the index, with a standard deviation of 79.31. The regions that form the median score of 99.37

Table 3.1 World Competitiveness Index of Regions (2014) (mean average = 100)

Rank	*Region*	*Index*
1	San Jose-Sunnyvale-Santa Clara, CA, US	359.98
2	Région de Bruxelles-Capitale, Belgium	328.50
3	Tokyo, Japan	307.02
4	Washington-Arlington-Alexandria, DC-VA-MD-WV, US	301.65
5	Ulsan, Korea	297.72
6	Stockholm, Sweden	292.80
7	Norway	291.32
8	Bridgeport-Stamford-Norwalk, CT, US	290.86
9	Luxembourg	289.46
10	Singapore	287.91
11	Boston-Cambridge-Quincy, MA-NH, US	278.00
12	Oxnard-Thousand Oaks-Ventura, CA, US	269.07
13	San Francisco-Oakland-Fremont, CA, US	266.72
14	Australian Capital Territory, Australia	262.82
15	Hovedstaden, Denmark	260.27
16	Île de France, France	259.08
17	Baltimore-Towson, MD, US	258.75
18	Chungnam, Korea	258.24
19	Durham-Chapel Hill, NC, US	255.39
20	Nenets Autonomous Okrug, Russia	250.93
21	Etelä-Suomi, Finland	246.75
22	Taiwan	245.62
23	San Diego-Carlsbad-San Marcos, CA, US	242.18
24	Switzerland	240.14
25	Gyeongnam, Korea	237.91
26	Gyeongbuk, Korea	237.52
27	Hartford-West Hartford-East Hartford, CT, US	234.72
28	New South Wales, Australia	233.63
29	Yukon, Canada	233.61
30	Western Australia, Australia	231.05
31	Baden-Württemberg, Germany	228.12
32	Los Angeles-Long Beach-Santa Ana, CA, US	225.12
33	Seattle-Tacoma-Bellevue, WA, US	223.49
34	Zuid-Nederland, Netherlands	219.57
35	Västsverige, Sweden	219.57
36	Bremen, Germany	219.02
37	Chungbuk, Korea	218.60
38	Hamburg, Germany	218.17
39	Jeonnam, Korea	217.43
40	Praha, Czech Republic	216.70
41	Shanghai, China	216.50
42	Beijing, China	214.21
43	New York-Northern New Jersey-Long Island, NY-NJ-PA, US	213.92
44	Ontario, Canada	213.72
45	London, UK	212.85
46	Hessen, Germany	212.80
47	Worcester, MA, US	211.92
48	West-Nederland, Netherlands	211.02
49	Des Moines-West Des Moines, IA, US	209.00
50	Victoria, Australia	208.11
51	Salt Lake City, UT, US	207.48
52	Northwest Territories and Nunavut, Canada	207.16
53	Bayern, Germany	205.56
54	Minneapolis-St. Paul-Bloomington, MN-WI, US	204.89
55	Östra Mellansverige, Sweden	204.72
56	Philadelphia-Camden-Wilmington, PA-NJ-DE-MD, US	204.72
57	Sydsverige, Sweden	204.29
58	Midtjylland, Denmark	203.69
59	Houston-Sugar Land-Baytown, TX, US	203.62
60	Incheon, Korea	200.72
61	Southern and Eastern, Ireland	200.67
62	Northern Territory, Australia	199.31
63	Gyeonggi, Korea	198.82
64	New Haven-Milford, CT, US	197.64
65	Pohjois-Suomi, Finland	197.35
66	South East, UK	195.70
67	Madison, WI, US	194.48
68	Sacramento–Arden-Arcade–Roseville, CA, US	194.27
69	Indianapolis-Carmel, IN, US	193.37
70	Länsi-Suomi, Finland	191.44
71	Honolulu, HI, US	191.16
72	Denver-Aurora-Broomfield, CO, US	190.46
73	Nordjylland, Denmark	189.97

Table 3.1 continued

Rank	*Region*	*Index*	*Rank*	*Region*	*Index*
74	Dallas-Fort Worth-Arlington, TX, US	188.36	111	Israel	168.75
75	Rochester, NY, US	187.82	112	Charlotte-Gastonia-Rock Hill, NC-SC, US	168.16
76	Alberta, Canada	186.57	113	South Australia, Australia	168.11
77	Noord-Nederland, Netherlands	185.24	114	Lombardia, Italy	167.81
78	Portland-Vancouver-Hillsboro, OR-WA, US	185.10	115	Harrisburg-Carlisle, PA, US	167.74
79	Syddanmark, Denmark	184.38	116	Shizuoka, Japan	167.35
80	Grand Rapids-Wyoming, MI, US	183.56	117	Colorado Springs, CO, US	166.71
81	Richmond, VA, US	182.32	118	Greensboro-High Point, NC, US	166.39
82	Vlaams Gewest, Belgium	181.80	119	Südösterreich, Austria	166.39
83	Nordrhein-Westfalen, Germany	180.59	120	Jeonbuk, Korea	165.98
84	Osaka, Japan	179.88	121	Iceland	165.19
85	Åland, Finland	179.56	122	Pittsburgh, PA, US	164.59
86	Oost-Nederland, Netherlands	179.51	123	Albany-Schenectady-Troy, NY, US	164.36
87	Cleveland-Elyria-Mentor, OH, US	179.51	124	Raleigh-Cary, NC, US	164.19
88	Queensland, Australia	178.88	125	Syracuse, NY, US	163.98
89	Aichi, Japan	178.87	126	Mie, Japan	163.52
90	Milwaukee-Waukesha-West Allis, WI, US	178.85	127	Cincinnati-Middletown, OH-KY-IN, US	162.56
91	Bakersfield-Delano, CA, US	178.05	128	South West, UK	162.03
92	Småland med öarna, Sweden	177.77	129	Birmingham-Hoover, AL, US	161.21
93	Austin-Round Rock-San Marcos, TX, US	177.46	130	Kansas City, MO-KS, US	161.18
94	Wichita, KS, US	177.25	131	Mellersta Norrland, Sweden	160.42
95	Ostösterreich, Austria	176.71	132	Kyoto, Japan	160.00
96	Omaha-Council Bluffs, NE-IA, US	176.41	133	Centre-Est, France	159.87
97	Övre Norrland, Sweden	176.14	134	Buffalo-Niagara Falls, NY, US	159.61
98	Albuquerque, NM, US	175.99	135	Chukotka Autonomous Okrug, Russia	159.49
99	Toyama, Japan	174.60	136	North West, UK	158.26
100	Baton Rouge, LA, US	174.50	137	Providence-New Bedford-Fall River, RI-MA, US	155.64
101	Virginia Beach-Norfolk-Newport News, VA-NC, US	174.32	138	Bratislavský kraj, Slovakia	155.40
102	East of England, UK	173.88	139	Scotland, UK	155.24
103	Westösterreich, Austria	173.43	140	Norra Mellansverige, Sweden	155.16
104	Rheinland-Pfalz, Germany	172.67	141	Memphis, TN-MS-AR, US	153.49
105	Chicago-Joliet-Naperville, IL-IN-WI, US	172.25	142	Yamaguchi, Japan	153.31
106	New Orleans-Metairie-Kenner, LA, US	171.98	143	Yamanashi, Japan	153.30
107	Columbus, OH, US	171.23	144	East Midlands, UK	152.83
108	Shiga, Japan	170.53	145	Daegu, Korea	152.58
109	Sjælland, Denmark	170.46	146	Quebec, Canada	151.92
110	Detroit-Warren-Livonia, MI, US	169.68	147	Fukui, Japan	151.59
			148	Tulsa, OK, US	151.56
			149	Nagano, Japan	151.49
			150	Tochigi, Japan	149.93

Table 3.1 continued

Rank	*Region*	*Index*
151	Lazio, Italy	149.17
152	Greenville-Mauldin-Easley, SC, US	148.78
153	Akron, OH, US	148.43
154	Niedersachsen, Germany	147.71
155	Emilia-Romagna, Italy	147.61
156	Gwangju, Korea	147.48
157	Zahodna Slovenija, Slovenia	147.47
158	Tokushima, Japan	147.28
159	Allentown-Bethlehem-Easton, PA-NJ, US	147.06
160	Ibaraki, Japan	146.90
161	West Midlands, UK	146.69
162	Busan, Korea	146.49
163	Louisville/Jefferson County, KY-IN, US	146.00
164	Little Rock-North Little Rock-Conway, AR, US	145.97
165	Saarland, Germany	145.90
166	Oklahoma City, OK, US	145.70
167	British Columbia, Canada	145.58
168	Boise City-Nampa, ID, US	145.58
169	Gunma, Japan	144.81
170	Seoul, Korea	144.77
171	Atlanta-Sandy Springs-Marietta, GA, US	144.74
172	Berlin, Germany	144.64
173	Toledo, OH, US	144.56
174	St. Louis, MO-IL, US	143.70
175	Kanagawa, Japan	143.20
176	San Antonio-New Braunfels, TX, US	143.00
177	Portland-South Portland-Biddeford, ME, US	142.84
178	Dayton, OH, US	142.51
179	Lancaster, PA, US	142.41
180	Ishikawa, Japan	142.33
181	Qatar	142.33
182	Phoenix-Mesa-Glendale, AZ, US	141.40
183	Columbia, SC, US	140.66
184	Jackson, MS, US	140.55
185	Saskatchewan, Canada	140.49
186	Moscow, Russia	140.06
187	Wales, UK	139.71
188	Fukushima, Japan	139.69
189	Gangwon, Korea	139.65
190	New Zealand	139.42
191	Tasmania, Australia	139.18
192	Tianjin, China	138.68
193	Northern Ireland, UK	138.56
194	Daejeon, Korea	138.55
195	Yamagata, Japan	138.12
196	North East, UK	137.48
197	Oita, Japan	137.43
198	Veneto, Italy	137.40
199	Border, Midland and Western, Ireland	137.09
200	El Paso, TX, US	136.58
201	Région Wallonne, Belgium	135.18
202	Provincia Autonoma Trento, Italy	134.93
203	Okayama, Japan	133.69
204	Itä-Suomi, Finland	133.67
205	Yorkshire and The Humber, UK	133.64
206	Hiroshima, Japan	133.35
207	Schleswig-Holstein, Germany	132.89
208	Piemonte, Italy	131.41
209	Friuli-Venezia Giulia, Italy	131.39
210	Tottori, Japan	130.49
211	Közép-Magyarország, Hungary	129.98
212	Charleston-North Charleston-Summerville, SC, US	128.86
213	Shimane, Japan	128.06
214	Palm Bay-Melbourne-Titusville, FL, US	127.46
215	Severovýchod, Czech Republic	127.24
216	Hyogo, Japan	126.67
217	Sud-Ouest, France	125.76
218	Comunidad de Madrid, Spain	125.57
219	Est, France	122.96
220	Nashville-Davidson–Murfreesboro–Franklin, TN, US	122.51
221	Akita, Japan	122.37
222	Yamalo-Nenets Autonomous Okrug, Russia	121.72
223	Bassin Parisien, France	121.19
224	Gifu, Japan	120.90
225	Scranton–Wilkes-Barre, PA, US	120.86
226	Niigata, Japan	120.73
227	Augusta-Richmond County, GA-SC, US	120.61

Table 3.1 continued

Rank	*Region*	*Index*
228	Sachsen, Germany	120.57
229	Orlando-Kissimmee-Sanford, FL, US	120.12
230	Strední Cechy, Czech Republic	119.34
231	Jihovýchod, Czech Republic	119.21
232	Provincia Autonoma Bolzano, Italy	119.18
233	Méditerranée, France	119.08
234	Ouest, France	119.06
235	Manitoba, Canada	118.77
236	Chattanooga, TN-GA, US	118.36
237	Jihozápad, Czech Republic	117.24
238	Hong Kong	117.13
239	Jacksonville, FL, US	115.99
240	Toscana, Italy	115.64
241	Thüringen, Germany	115.61
242	Knoxville, TN, US	115.32
243	Saga, Japan	114.95
244	Kuwait	114.95
245	Kagawa, Japan	114.72
246	Jeju, Korea	113.14
247	Liguria, Italy	112.15
248	Iwate, Japan	111.97
249	Wakayama, Japan	111.46
250	Distrito Federal, Brazil	111.13
251	Marche, Italy	110.94
252	Zhejiang China	110.20
253	Jiangsu, China	109.78
254	Khanty-Mansi Autonomous Okrug-Yugra, Russia	108.99
255	Ehime, Japan	108.72
256	Miyagi, Japan	108.66
257	Guangdong, China	108.21
258	Miami-Fort Lauderdale-Pompano Beach, FL, US	107.59
259	Nord-Pas-de-Calais, France	106.50
260	Prince Edward Island, Canada	106.39
261	Noreste, Spain	105.58
262	Tampa-St. Petersburg-Clearwater, FL, US	105.52
263	Kumamoto, Japan	105.21
264	Abruzzo, Italy	104.83
265	Fukuoka, Japan	104.08
266	Strední Morava, Czech Republic	101.99
267	Sachsen-Anhalt, Germany	101.58
268	Valle d'Aosta, Italy	101.38
269	Saitama, Japan	101.15
270	Malta	101.13
271	Saint Petersburg, Russia	101.03
272	Cyprus	100.53
273	Vzhodna Slovenija, Slovenia	99.42
274	Chiba, Japan	99.33
275	Miyazaki, Japan	99.15
276	Las Vegas-Paradise, NV, US	99.03
277	Nova Scotia, Canada	97.01
278	Newfoundland and Labrador, Canada	96.06
279	Kagoshima, Japan	96.03
280	Umbria, Italy	94.89
281	Nara, Japan	93.00
282	Sakhalin Oblast, Russia	91.16
283	Moravskoslezsko, Czech Republic	89.68
284	Santa Catarina, Brazil	89.61
285	Hokkaido, Japan	89.29
286	Kochi, Japan	89.19
287	Nagasaki, Japan	88.79
288	Brandenburg, Germany	87.76
289	Severozápad, Czech Republic	87.44
290	Dunántúl, Hungary	86.99
291	São Paulo, Brazil	86.28
292	Almaty city, Kazakhstan	85.07
293	North Port-Bradenton-Sarasota, FL, US	83.62
294	Mecklenburg-Vorpommern, Germany	83.03
295	Magadan Oblast, Russia	81.76
296	New Brunswick, Canada	80.30
297	Nizhny Novgorod Oblast, Russia	79.98
298	Novgorod Oblast, Russia	79.84
299	Aomori, Japan	79.55
300	Estonia	78.61
301	Region Centralny, Poland	78.41
302	Yaroslavl Oblast, Russia	78.19
303	Cape Coral-Fort Myers, FL, US	77.66
304	Sakha (Yakutia) Republic, Russia	77.42
305	Kamchatka Krai, Russia	77.17
306	Moscow Oblast, Russia	76.90
307	Kaluga Oblast, Russia	76.51
308	Tomsk Oblast, Russia	74.51
309	Západné Slovensko, Slovakia	74.32
310	Samara Oblast, Russia	74.27
311	Tyumen Oblast, Russia	74.16
312	Molise, Italy	73.81

Table 3.1 continued

Rank	*Region*	*Index*	*Rank*	*Region*	*Index*
313	Novosibirsk Oblast, Russia	73.01	361	Macroregiunea trei, Romania	50.57
314	Paraná, Brazil	72.35	362	Irkutsk Oblast, Russia	50.44
315	Okinawa, Japan	72.01	363	Dubai, UAE	50.40
316	Perm Krai, Russia	68.47	364	Sardegna, Italy	49.76
317	Rio Grande do Sul, Brazil	67.26	365	Minas Gerais, Brazil	49.63
318	Krasnoyarsk Krai, Russia	67.21	366	Sicilia, Italy	49.51
319	Basilicata, Italy	67.02	367	Fujian, China	48.89
320	Abu Dhabi, UAE	66.44	368	Oryol Oblast, Russia	48.85
321	Republic of Tatarstan, Russia	66.21	369	Mato Grosso, Brazil	48.61
322	Atyrau, Kazakhstan	66.18	370	Region Pólnocny, Poland	48.60
323	Sverdlovsk Oblast, Russia	66.11	371	Kursk Oblast, Russia	47.84
324	Vologda Oblast, Russia	65.92	372	Republic of Mordovia, Russia	47.17
325	Lipetsk Oblast, Russia	65.78			
326	Este, Spain	65.58	373	Makkah Al-Mokarramah, Saudi Arabia	46.91
327	Al-Riyadh, Saudi Arabia	65.43			
328	Vladimir Oblast, Russia	65.19	374	Republic of Bashkortostan, Russia	46.78
329	Attiki, Greece	64.77			
330	Tula Oblast, Russia	62.17	375	Pskov Oblast, Russia	45.55
331	Chelyabinsk Oblast, Russia	61.83	376	Noroeste, Spain	45.18
332	Arkhangelsk Oblast, Russia	59.96	377	Kirov Oblast, Russia	44.65
333	Campania, Italy	59.31	378	Liaoning, China	44.44
334	Udmurt Republic, Russia	59.09	379	Goa, India	44.36
335	Eastern Region, Saudi Arabia	58.95	380	Yugozapadna i yuzhna tsentralna Bulgaria, Bulgaria	44.35
336	Region Poludniowo-Zachodni, Poland	57.55	381	Penza Oblast, Russia	44.20
337	Republic of Karelia, Russia	57.52	382	Omsk Oblast, Russia	43.98
338	Astana city, Kazakhstan	57.29	383	Kostroma Oblast, Russia	43.95
339	Smolensk Oblast, Russia	57.17	384	Départements d'outre-mer, France	43.73
340	Ryazan Oblast, Russia	57.01			
341	Khabarovsk Krai, Russia	56.90	385	Calabria, Italy	43.66
342	Murmansk Oblast, Russia	56.81	386	West Anatolia, Turkey	42.85
343	Voronezh Oblast, Russia	56.63	387	Chuvash Republic, Russia	42.71
344	Tver Oblast, Russia	56.61	388	Tambov Oblast, Russia	42.37
345	Belgorod Oblast, Russia	55.75	389	Volgograd Oblast, Russia	42.30
346	Ivanovo Oblast, Russia	55.62	390	Amur Oblast, Russia	42.06
347	Istanbul, Turkey	55.48	391	Kemerovo Oblast, Russia	41.83
348	Leningrad Oblast, Russia	55.42	392	Mato Grosso do Sul, Brazil	41.83
349	Al-Qaseem, Saudi Arabia	55.40	393	Mari El Republic, Russia	41.79
350	Shandong, China	54.96	394	Alföld és Észak, Hungary	41.35
351	Mangistau, Kazakhstan	54.51	395	Amazon, Brazil	41.15
352	Ulyanovsk Oblast, Russia	54.39	396	Primorsky Krai, Russia	40.42
353	Rio de Janeiro, Brazil	53.97	397	Goiás, Brazil	40.35
354	Continente, Portugal	53.89	398	Bryansk Oblast, Russia	40.23
355	Holy Spirit, Brazil	53.61	399	Rostov Oblast, Russia	39.50
356	Region Poludniowy, Poland	53.55	400	West Marmara, Turkey	39.19
357	Region Pólnocno-Zachodni, Poland	52.85	401	Macroregiunea patru, Romania	38.52
358	East Marmara, Turkey	52.22	402	Sharjah, UAE	37.95
359	Puglia, Italy	51.24	403	Saratov Oblast, Russia	37.82
360	Komi Republic, Russia	50.72	404	Orenburg Oblast, Russia	37.34

Table 3.1 continued

Rank	*Region*	*Index*	*Rank*	*Region*	*Index*
405	Kaliningrad Oblast, Russia	36.42	449	Tuva Republic, Russia	20.98
406	Jewish Autonomous Oblast, Russia	34.94	450	Sergipe, Brazil	20.77
407	Altai Republic, Russia	34.56	451	Central Anatolia, Turkey	20.67
408	Ajman, UAE	34.50	452	Al-Baha, Saudi Arabia	20.51
409	Região Autónoma da Madeira, Portugal	34.43	453	Daman and Diu, India	20.48
410	Republic of Buryatia, Russia	34.02	454	Stredné Slovensko, Slovakia	20.42
411	Aseer, Saudi Arabia	32.92	455	Para, Brazil	20.41
412	Kurgan Oblast, Russia	32.83	456	Republic of North Ossetia-Alania, Russia	19.98
413	Aegean, Turkey	32.28	457	Najran, Saudi Arabia	19.98
414	Roraima, Brazil	32.24	458	Region Wschodni, Poland	19.64
415	West Black Sae, Turkey	31.66	459	Republic of Adygea, Russia	19.42
416	Aktobe, Kazakhstan	29.98	460	Republic of Kalmykia, Russia	19.41
417	Rondônia, Brazil	29.92	461	Kentriki Ellada, Greece	19.16
418	Umm Al - Quwain, UAE	29.84	462	Voreia Ellada, Greece	18.42
419	Centro, Spain	29.65	463	Ras Al–Khaimah, UAE	18.21
420	Hail, Saudi Arabia	29.44	464	Tabouk, Saudi Arabia	18.16
421	Acre, Brazil	29.40	465	Kostanai, Kazakhstan	17.81
422	Região Autónoma dos Açores, Portugal	29.19	466	Fujairah, UAE	17.60
423	Krasnodar Krai, Russia	29.10	467	Pernambuco, Brazil	16.89
424	Nisia Aigaiou, Kriti, Greece	28.72	468	Nord, Kazakhstan	16.34
425	Astrakhan Oblast, Russia	28.18	469	Paraíba, Brazil	16.16
426	Bogotá, D.C., Colombia	28.15	470	Kabardino-Balkar Republic, Russia	15.38
427	Lithuania	28.03	471	East, Kazakhstan	15.30
428	Altai Krai, Russia	27.81	472	Bahia, Brazil	14.83
429	Tocantins, Brazil	27.68	473	Latvia	12.85
430	Republic of Khakassia, Russia	26.83	474	Santander, Colombia	12.75
431	Zabaykalsky Krai, Russia	26.21	475	Maranhão, Brazil	12.66
432	Piauí, Brazil	25.74	476	Cundinamarca, Colombia	11.70
433	East Black Sea, Turkey	25.61	477	Zhambyl, Kazakhstan	11.51
434	West, Kazakhstan	24.54	478	Middle East Anatolia, Turkey	10.88
435	Macroregiunea unu, Romania	24.51	479	South, Kazakhstan	10.80
436	Al-Madinah Al-Monawarah, Saudi Arabia	24.26	480	Southeast Anatolia, Turkey	10.34
437	Kyzylorda, Kazakhstan	23.91	481	Meta, Colombia	9.02
438	Chongqing, China	23.73	482	Východné Slovensko, Slovakia	8.93
439	Pavlodar, Kazakhstan	23.42	483	Almaty, Kazakhstan	8.75
440	Ceará, Brazil	23.02	484	Bolívar, Colombia	6.47
441	Hubei, China	22.79	485	Northeast Anatolia, Turkey	6.39
442	Alagoas, Brazil	22.72	486	Al-Jouf, Saudi Arabia	6.25
443	Rio Grande do Norte, Brazil	22.69	487	Dadra and Nagar Haveli, India	5.70
444	Karachay-Cherkess Republic, Russia	22.46	488	Atlántico, Colombia	5.22
445	Akmola, Kazakhstan	22.03	489	Macroregiunea doi, Romania	5.20
446	Karaganda, Kazakhstan	21.84	490	Severna i iztochna Bulgaria, Bulgaria	4.67
447	Meditterranean, Turkey	21.75	491	Valle del Cauca, Colombia	3.40
448	Stavropol Krai, Russia	21.19	492	Chandigarh, India	2.15
			493	Republic of Dagestan, Russia	1.42
			494	Antioquia, Colombia	1.26
			495	Sur, Spain	1.10

Table 3.1 continued

Rank	*Region*	*Index*	*Rank*	*Region*	*Index*
496	Tamil Nadu, India	1.00	521	Tolima, Colombia	–19.10
497	Córdoba, Colombia	0.23	522	Karnataka, India	–20.97
498	Amapá, Brazil	–1.54	523	Northern Borders, Saudi Arabia	–21.84
499	Magdalena, Colombia	–1.85	524	Gujarat, India	–22.22
500	Delhi, India	–2.02	525	Mizoram, India	–22.49
501	Cesar, Colombia	–2.87	526	Arunachal Pradesh, India	–22.50
502	Boyacá, Colombia	–3.32	527	Lakshadweep, India	–24.52
503	Huila, Colombia	–6.60	528	Sikkim, India	–24.62
504	Kerala, India	–7.76	529	West Bengal, India	–25.75
505	Norte de Santander, Colombia	–7.92	530	Manipur, India	–27.40
506	Sucre, Colombia	–8.43	531	Nagaland, India	–28.13
507	Republic of Ingushetia, Russia	–8.60	532	Uttarakhand, India	–28.80
508	Canarias, Spain	–8.72	533	Tripura, India	–28.87
509	Maharashtra, India	–8.83	534	Jharkhand, India	–29.67
510	Chechen Republic, Russia	–9.79	535	Quindio, Colombia	–29.90
511	Cauca, Colombia	–10.91	536	Meghalaya, India	–30.43
512	Andhra Pradesh, India	–13.38	537	Risaralda, Colombia	–31.40
513	Puducherry, India	–13.39	538	Orissa, India	–33.10
514	Haryana, India	–13.57	539	Chattisgarh, India	–33.39
515	Himachal Pradesh, India	–14.63	540	Rajasthan, India	–34.18
516	A. and N. Islands, India	–15.51	541	Madhya Pradesh, India	–35.61
517	Caquetá, Colombia	–16.64	542	Assam, India	–36.82
518	Jazan, Saudi Arabia	–17.86	543	Jammu and Kashmir, India	–37.85
519	Punjab, India	–18.64	544	Uttar Pradesh, India	–42.40
520	Caldas, Colombia	–18.99	545	Bihar, India	–46.90
			546	Nariño, Colombia	–50.28

Table 3.2 Distributive statistics of the WCIR

	WCIR	*Region*	*Nation*
Maximum	359.98	San Jose-Sunnyvale-Santa Clara, CA	US
Minimum	–50.28	Nariño	Colombia
Median	99.37	Vzhodna Slovenija Chiba	Slovenia Japan
Mean	100.00		
Range	410.26		
SD	79.31		
Skewness	0.35		
Kurtosis	–0.50		

Note: SD = Standard deviation.

are located in Slovenia (Vzhodna Slovenija) and Japan (Chiba). The most competitive region possesses a WCIR score that is slightly more than three standard deviations above the mean, with the least competitive region having a WCIR score of less than two standard deviations below the mean. The negative Kurtosis (platykurtic) value of –0.50 is consistent with a flatter distribution of WCIR scores than would be the case if the scores were normally distributed. Overall, this means that the WCIR scores are not concentrated around the mean.

Figure 3.1 presents the overall pattern of WCIR scores for the regions by ranking. There are some distinct groups of regions, and as well as the top two regions appearing to be outliers, there are also other smaller, but still distinct drops in competitiveness scores. For example, between Singapore ranked 10th (WCIR score 287.91) and the Californian region of Oxnard-Thousand Oaks-Ventura ranked 12th (WCIR score 269.07) there is a drop of nearly 19 points, similar to the difference between Tokyo ranked 3rd (WCIR score 307.02) and Singapore. It is also notable that whilst the scores appear to flatten out in the early part of the top 300, beyond the 244th region, which is Kuwait (WCIR score 114.95), the fall in WCIR scores once more accelerates. Although it may at first be suspected that this reflects the change from regions in nations that are the most developed to emerging economies, no simple grouping such as this is present.

The regions ranked between 200 and 300 include a mix of less competitive regions from developed economies such as Shimane in Japan (ranked 213th WCIR score 128.06), Sachsen-Anhalt in Germany (ranked 267th WCIR score 101.58) and North Port-Bradenton-Sarasota in the US state of Florida (ranked

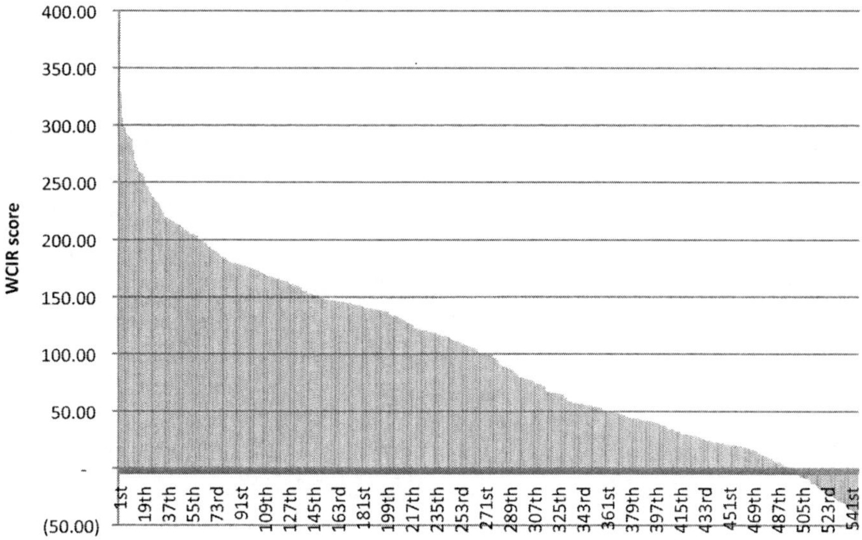

Figure 3.1 Distribution of WCIR scores

293rd WCIR score 83.62). Within this range of regions, however, there is not only a Middle Eastern region, in the form of Kuwait, but also East European regions such as Severovýchod in the Czech Republic (ranked 215th WCIR score 127.24), plus regions from the BRIC nations – for example Distrito Federal in Brazil (ranked 250th WCIR score 111.13), Saint Petersburg in Russia (ranked 271st WCIR score 101.03) and Guangdong in China (ranked 257th WCIR score 108.21).

It would be inappropriate to compare the rankings of the WCIR in 2014 with the rankings for the previous WKCI published in 2008 (Huggins *et al.*, 2008a) given the large number of additional regions included in the WCIR. However, it is possible to consider the 145 regions that were included in both the 2008 and 2014 indices by applying the same WCIR methodology. If these regions are ranked against one another in each period it is possible to establish the degree to which relative competitiveness remains stable within this subset of regions. Figure 3.2 plots the 2008 rankings, as calculated using the 2014 WCIR methodology, for the 145 regions against the change in these relative rankings by 2014.

It is understandable that there is a negative correlation between rank and change in rank, as the very highly ranked regions generally only have one direction that their ranking can go, and conversely those ranked 100th to 145th have much more potential to improve their rankings, and to some extent this relationship suggests that certain regions are catching up; for instance, the lowest ranked 25 regions in 2008 all improved their ranking, with the exception of Noreste in Spain (ranked 129th, moved down by 1 rank) and Hong Kong (ranked 124th in both 2008 and 2014). Five regions improved their ranking by more than 50

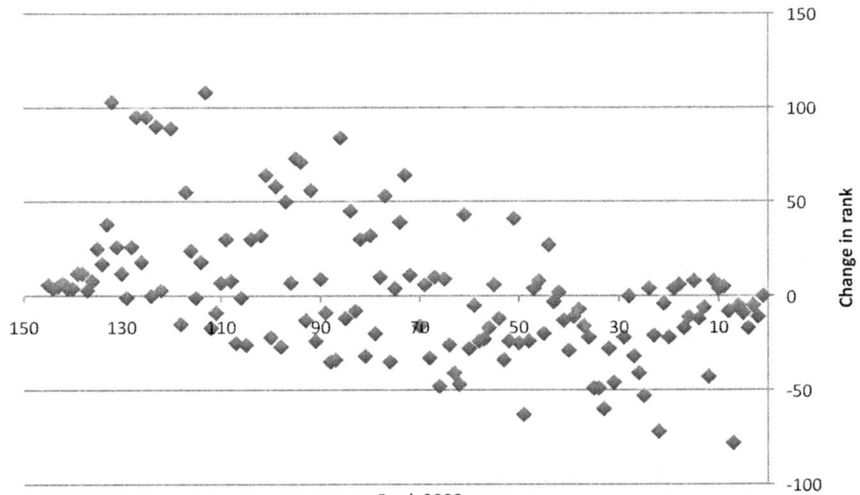

Figure 3.2 2008 WCIR rankings and change in rankings 2008–2014 for a subsample of regions

positions, and the degree to which the relative competitiveness of regions has changed in recent years may reflect the unusual economic conditions. In particular, it is likely that many of these patterns would have manifested themselves in years to come, but in this case the global financial crisis has speeded up events through a process of creative destruction not experienced within recent history (Pieterse, 2011).

Considering those regions that displayed the greatest improvement in their ranks across this subsample, it is reasonable to assume that many would be regions in emerging economies. However, as Table 3.3 indicates, this is not necessarily the case. Although Ulsan in Korea, along with Shanghai and Beijing in China fulfil the expected pattern of rapidly rising emerging market hotspots, it is clear that the vast majority of those regions making the largest relative improvements in competitiveness are in Europe. In particular, of the 16 regions recording ranking improvements of 50 or more places, six of these are German regions. This is consistent with the relative robustness of the German economy throughout the Euro zone crisis, despite the difficulties faced by many of its major trading partners and neighbours.

Both the Republic of Ireland and the UK were hit hard by the financial crisis. In the Republic of Ireland the construction and property bubble spectacularly imploded (Regling and Watson, 2010). However, the effect on the banking sector, whilst severe, was partly mitigated against by limits on risky lending in the lead-up to the crisis (Honohan, 2010). It appears, therefore, that the key components that originally underpinned the emergence of the Celtic Tiger economy have

Table 3.3 Regions displaying greatest improvement in ranking across the 2008–2014 sub-sample

2014 rank	*Region*	*Nation*	*Consistent ranks*		*Change in rank 2008 to 2014*
			2014	*2008*	
5	Ulsan	Korea	5	113	108
36	Bremen	Germany	29	132	103
38	Hamburg	Germany	30	125	95
41	Shanghai	China	32	127	95
42	Beijing	China	33	123	90
40	Praha	Czech Republic	31	120	89
2	Région de Bruxelles-Capitale	Belgium	2	86	84
28	New South Wales	Australia	22	95	73
30	Western	Australia	23	94	71
9	Luxembourg	Luxembourg	9	73	64
46	Hessen	Germany	37	101	64
53	Bayern	Germany	41	99	58
45	London	UK	36	92	56
83	Nordrhein-Westfalen	Germany	62	117	55
31	Baden-Württemberg	Germany	24	77	53
61	Southern and Eastern	Ireland	47	97	50

enabled Southern and Eastern Ireland to improve its relative ranking by 50 places, and move into the top 70 global regional economies. Similarly, London was hit severely by the financial crisis, but the unique combination of knowledge inputs present in the economy have allowed it to retain its competitiveness.

A combination of being more exposed to the financial crisis and not possessing the unique and valuable knowledge resources that other regions enjoy is likely to lead to the greatest declines in regional competitiveness. As shown by Table 3.4, the twenty regions displaying the largest falls in their relative regional competitiveness across the 2008–2014 sub-sample are predominately locations in the US. In total, sixteen of the regions are from the US. Other nations with regions experiencing large falls in their competitiveness are Japan, Canada and Iceland. In the case of Iceland much of its competitiveness and associated economic success had been linked to a massive banking sector as measured relative to the size of the domestic economy. At its peak, the banking sector's loans were more than 10 times the nation's GDP. Unlike other financial centres such as London and New York, the rapid development of the banking sector without the accumulation of knowledge and infrastructure resources, made it exceptionally vulnerable to the changes in the global economy (OECD, 2009). This was

Table 3.4 Regions displaying greatest declines in ranking across the 2008–2014 sub-sample

2014 rank	*Region*	*Nation*	*Consistent ranks*		*Change in rank 2008 to 2014*
			2014	*2008*	
80	Grand Rapids-Wyoming, MI	US	59	27	–32
176	San Antonio-New Braunfels, TX	US	113	81	–32
153	Akron, OH	US	101	68	–33
124	Raleigh-Cary, NC	US	87	53	–34
220	Nashville-Davidson–Murfreesboro–Franklin, TN	US	121	87	–34
174	St. Louis, MO-IL	US	111	76	–35
235	Manitoba	Canada	123	88	–35
90	Milwaukee-Waukesha-West Allis, WI	US	67	26	–41
163	Louisville/Jefferson County, KY-IN	US	104	63	–41
75	Rochester, NY	US	55	12	–43
108	Shiga	Japan	77	31	–46
171	Atlanta-Sandy Springs-Marietta, GA	US	109	62	–47
182	Phoenix-Mesa-Glendale, AZ	US	114	66	–48
117	Colorado Springs, CO	US	83	34	–49
118	Greensboro-High Point, NC	US	84	35	–49
110	Detroit-Warren-Livonia, MI	US	78	25	–53
134	Buffalo-Niagara Falls, NY	US	93	33	–60
175	Kanagawa	Japan	112	49	–63
137	Providence-New Bedford-Fall River, RI-MA	US	94	22	–72
121	Iceland	Iceland	85	7	–78

compounded by the reliance of the Icelandic banking system on international finance sources (Ólafsson and Pétursson, 2010), and the possession of its own currency, which although aiding recovery makes it more difficult to resolve long-term economic issues (Thorhallsson and Kirby, 2012).

Reflecting the shifting patterns of global regional competitiveness, the third and fifth ranked regions on the WCIR are both located in Asia, with Tokyo in Japan ranked third (WCIR score 307.02) and Ulsan in Korea fifth (WCIR score 297.72). Although two other US regions alongside San Jose are found in the top 10 regions (Washington-Arlington-Alexandria ranked 4th score 301.65, and Bridgeport-Stamford-Norwalk ranked 8th score 290.86), the most competitive regions are not as tightly clustered geographically in the US as they were in the past. In 2008, US regions dominated the top of the rankings. Seven of the top ten regions were located in the US with San Jose-Sunnyvale-Santa Clara and San Francisco-Oakland-Fremont in California leading the way. The remaining three positions in the top ten were occupied by European regions led by Île de France, ranking fifth on the overall WCIR for 2008. In fact, Tokyo in Japan (ranked 11th) was the only non-US or European region in the top 30 regions, which compares with three Asian regions in the top ten alone in 2014, with Singapore ranked 10th (WCIR score 287.91) joining Tokyo and Ulsan in 2014.

Figure 3.3 provides an indication of the geographical distribution of the leading 30 regions in 2008 and 2014. While it must be remembered that some of the changes will represent the inclusion of new regions in the 2014 analysis, the inclusion of these regions reflects their increasing competitiveness since 2008, when they would have been unlikely to be ranked in the top 30 regions.

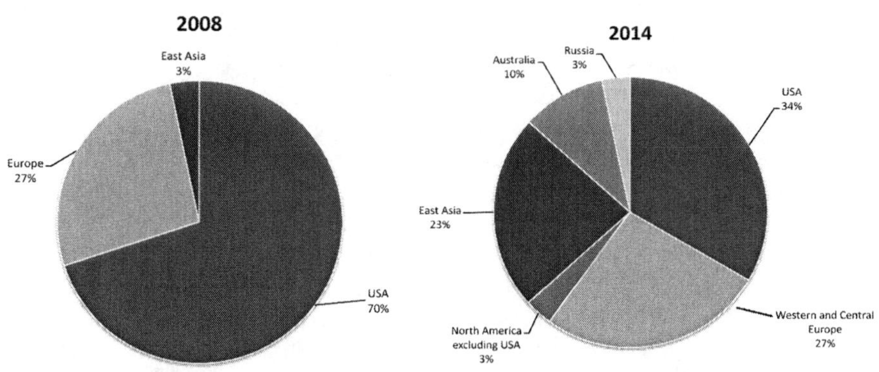

Figure 3.3 Geographical location of the 30 most competitive regions in 2008 and 2014

The 2014 rankings show that the US clearly continues to account for a large proportion of the most competitive regions, but many of the US regions that were in the top 30 in 2008 have been surpassed by rising regions located largely around the Pacific. In particular, Korea now has four entries in the top 30 most competitive regions. The ability of regions to catch up and improve their competitiveness has been linked with the opportunity to start with a clean slate, which provides regions with the advantage of being less bound to earlier investments, enabling them to leverage advantages from leading regions (Gerschenkron, 1962; Mathews, 2001). For instance, Mathews (2001) suggests that there are three model routes that latecomer regions can take to catch up with previously more competitive regions:

1 Large established firms in the industrially upgrading country.
2 Public sector laboratories and institutions, linked to consortia of small firms.
3 External leverage via multinational corporations.

Evidence of the success of all three models of economic development and knowledge diffusion are present in the results of WCIR. In the case of South Korea, Mathews (2001) suggests that the government has pursued a policy of promoting large state-sponsored enterprises, which have acquired knowledge from existing producers and developed strong absorptive capacity. This is not to suggest that this is the most effective manner through which latecomer nations can increase their competitiveness, as other routes have been utilized by different countries, but South Korea's greater population means that multiple regions have achieved high levels of competitiveness, whilst other nations are often smaller and effectively form a single region.

Other East Asian regions – or 'region-states' within the top 30 are Singapore and Taiwan. In the case of the former, Mathews (2001) suggests that the external leverage of multinational corporations has been used to enable the economy to catch up. The fact that Singapore now stands 9th in WCIR shows the success of such an approach. Taiwan, on the other hand, has used public sector institutions, rather than the private sector, to absorb knowledge, and it is now ranked 20th confirming the multiple routes to global competitiveness.

The choice of approach facing other regions that wish to emulate this success, in terms of breaking into the upper echelons of regional knowledge economies globally, is likely to be determined by the existing resources within the economy, such as the strength of domestic private sector enterprises or the extent to which a commercially orientated public sector research network exists. It is also likely that particular approaches may be appropriate at the national level, depending on the size of the economy and the geographical spread of the population. However, where a region enjoys sufficient autonomy it would seem probable that an individual region within a nation could pursue any of the three routes outlined above.

As indicated by Figure 3.3, along with the rise of the East Asian regional economies within the Pacific region, Australia now boasts three entries in the top 30, with the Russian region of Nenets Autonomous Okrug and the Yukon in

Canada also making an appearance. Given the changes in the geographical location of the top 30 regions in the last five years it would be no surprise if the reduced dominance of the US economy was a pattern that continued into the future. Although there is only one representative from the BRIC nations currently in the top 30, this is likely to reflect the relatively recent liberalization and opening of these economies, but the experience of Korea is likely to see regions from these emerging economies become fixtures as some of the most competitive regions in future years.

The leading Chinese region is Shanghai ranked 41st (WCIR score 242.03), whilst Distrito Federal is the foremost Brazilian region ranked 264th (WCIR score 103.92). Although the Indian economy has enjoyed considerable growth over the last decade (Dasgupta and Singh, 2005), and was thought by some to have even greater growth potential than China given its high level of institutional development (Rodrik and Subramanian, 2004), it has not so far seen the emergence of a dominant regional economy that could be considered as globally leading, with Goa the highest ranked at 373rd (WCIR score 36.02).

Regional specialization

The overall rankings of the WCIR provide a picture and understanding of the development of regional competitiveness in geospatial terms, and in this section the individual indicators contained within the WCIR are examined to further identify those regions that perform most strongly in different ways, especially in terms of regional specialization (Cooke, 1992; Storper, 1992, 1995; Krugman, 2011), which should be particularly observable among regions with developing economies (Scott and Storper, 2003). Through this analysis, it is possible to understand the extent to which different theories of regional economic development are presenting themselves in the global economy, however challenging such a task might be (Dicken *et al.*, 2001).

It is first worth acknowledging that there is likely to be considerable correlation between the individual variables that go into the making of the WCIR and its four key components. This is to be expected as the underlying culture and institutions that help to promote and sustain the knowledge economy will be similar across the different aspects of the WCIR. This means that where a region performs strongly in terms of 4th-wave knowledge capital, it is also likely to perform strongly in terms of 5th-wave knowledge capital, with the sustainability of the knowledge economy increasing the probability of these capital stocks remaining high. However, whilst they may be positively correlated, these measures are unlikely to be perfectly correlated, as the underlying context, history and institutions are likely to differ across regions, so that two highly competitive regions may enjoy subtly different strengths and weaknesses.

In order to understand the extent to which the components of WCIR move together Table 3.5 reports the Pearson and Spearman rank correlation coefficients. The Pearson correlation coefficients give a clear indication of the expected change in one component when another increases, but this may be partly influenced by outliers such as those regions with extreme values for both components. The Spearman rank nonparamentric measure of correlation is not influenced by these outliers to the same extent, as it is just concerned with whether those regions that rank highly in terms of one component also rank highly in terms of another component.

As shown by Table 3.5, there is a significant positive relationship between each of the components of the WCIR. However, in some cases they are far from perfectly correlated, confirming the importance of including all elements of the WCIR to enable the differing methods and patterns of achieving competitiveness across regions to be encapsulated. The strongest relationship reported, with a high value in both correlations, is found between competitiveness outputs and outcomes and knowledge sustainability. This is consistent with those studies that have noted that the most successful regional economies are those that have been able to adapt and reinvent themselves on an ongoing basis, adjusting to changing external forces and avoiding the dangers associated with internal lock-in (Simmie *et al.*, 2006; Martin and Sunley, 2011a; Ter Wal and Boschma, 2011). However, it would be inappropriate to regard this relationship as being uni-directional – that is, from the inside-out – with a variety of studies acknowledging the importance of outside-in approaches whereby regions attract and retain both talented individuals and firms from elsewhere (Florida, 2002b). These actors may contribute to the funding of education and digital infrastructure either directly through collaboration with public bodies or indirectly through their contribution to the local tax base.

Table 3.5 Pearson and Spearman rank correlation coefficients for the four WCIR components

	4th-wave knowledge	*Outputs/ outcomes capital*	*Knowl. sustain.*
Pearson correlation coefficients			
5th-wave knowledge capital	0.638 (0.000)	0.506 (0.000)	0.451 (0.000)
4th-wave knowledge capital		0.493 (0.000)	0.432 (0.000)
Outputs/outcomes			0.750 (0.000)
Spearman rank correlation coefficients			
5th-wave knowledge capital	0.779 (0.000)	0.600 (0.000)	0.575 (0.000)
4th-wave knowledge capital		0.534 (0.000)	0.490 (0.000)
Outputs/outcomes			0.772 (0.000)

Notes: *p*-values in parenthesis.
Knowl. sustain. = Knowledge sustainability.

The weakest associations are found between 4th-wave knowledge capital, which as discussed above incorporates labour inputs in general, as well as those positions associated with managerial functions (Huggins and Izushi, 2007). It also incorporates the R&D spending by both the public and private sectors, along with the outputs of this process, patents. These are the variables that are often more strongly associated with knowledge-based manufacturing rather than knowledge service sectors (de Bruijn and van Oort, 2007).

In this regard, the rise of Chinese regions is spectacular, given that the process of opening the economy to the rest of the world only began in earnest in 1978. Three regions are now found in the top 200 regions: Shanghai (ranked 41st WCIR score 216.50); the capital Beijing (ranked 42nd WCIR score 214.21); and Tianjin (ranked 192nd WCIR score 138.68). Much of the success of Chinese regions in catching up has been through links with multinational corporations and suppliers from other East Asian economies (Gereffi, 2009).

The differing modes of achieving regional economic competitiveness are best seen by looking at the indicators separately and under broader geographies, exposing the best performing regions within the set criteria. There are five continental blocs that such an overview incorporates here: Asia and Pacific; Europe; Middle East; North America; and South America. Within the five continental blocs used in the following analysis, regions in Russia are split between the two respective continents of Asia and Europe (details of which are described in Chapter 2).

The indicators analysed in the following sections are organized under their respective WCIR component group, which allows for a greater understanding of how each of the indicators contribute to a particular region's final index score. In order to compare the regions in a meaningful way, an index is created for each of the indicators. However, all follow the same design framework. Each region's score for a particular indicator is divided by this indicator's mean and the result is then multiplied by 100. The resultant average mean for all 19 indices takes a value of 100.

Fifth-wave knowledge capital

This component of the WCIR is built from four indicators, which in broad descriptive terms cover perhaps the most important high-knowledge-intensive manufacturing sectors – IT and computers, and biotechnology and chemicals – as well as high-technology services and private equity investments. It is well-established that the technological and knowledge-production intensity of a region is essential to its competitiveness (Archibugi, 1992; Florida, 1995; Storper, 1995), and as such it can be observed that the regions in Tables 3.6 to 3.9 with the highest index scores are also the regions that belong to the top 10% of the overall WCIR.

Within the 5th-wave knowledge capital indicators perhaps the most clear continental disparities can be observed among the employment in IT and computer manufacturing measures, clearly depicting regional sector specialization (Storper, 1995; Krugman, 2011) and regional economic development more generally as result of their export orientation (Storper, 1992). As shown by Table

Table 3.6 Top three regions by continental bloc: Employment in IT and computer manufacturing per 1,000 employees

Rank	*Region*	*Index*
	Asia and Pacific	
1	Ulsan, Korea	1,190.59
2	Gyeongnam, Korea	1,156.95
3	Gyeongbuk, Korea	1,132.31
	Europe	
1	Pohjois-Suomi, Finland	380.77
2	Dunántúl, Hungary	339.19
3	Severovýchod, Czech Republic	263.09
	Middle East	
1	Israel	164.21
2	Istanbul, Turkey	29.95
3	East Marmara, Turkey	29.40
	North America	
1	San Jose-Sunnyvale-Santa Clara, CA, US	1,239.05
2	Palm Bay-Melbourne-Titusville, FL, US	574.06
3	Boise City-Nampa, ID, US	349.63
	South America	
1	Santa Catarina, Brazil	47.11
2	São Paulo, Brazil	33.49
3	Rio Grande do Sul, Brazil	31.15

3.6, which presents the top three performers in each continental bloc, the uncontested leader in this measure of competitiveness is San Jose-Sunnyvale-Santa Clara in California, scoring 1,239.05. However, there remains a large gap between this region and its continental second best region: Palm Bay-Melbourne-Titusville in Florida, with a score of 574.06. Alongside these regions, the increasing dominance of Asian regions comes into play, with three of its regions subsequently following the top performing San Jose-Sunnyvale-Santa Clara. These regions are all located in South Korea: Ulsan (score 1,190.59), Gyeongnam (score 1,156.95) and Gyeongbuk (score 1,132.31).

Although leading European regions still perform above the WCIR average for the employment in IT and computer manufacturing, with Finland's Pohjois-Suomi taking a clear lead (score 380.77) in the continent, they are some distance below the top performing North American and Asian and Pacific regions, albeit performing better than the third North American region of Boise City-Nampa of Idaho, US (score 349.63). Among the Middle Eastern regions, the top performer, Israel, comes as no surprise (score 164.21), followed by two Turkish regions: Istanbul (score 29.95) and East Marmara (score 29.40). Within South America, all 3 top performing regions are Brazilian: Santa Catarina (score 47.11), São Paulo (score 33.49), and Rio Grande do Sul (score 31.15). However, there is still some way before they catch up with the rest of the world.

There are clearly different dynamics observable among the continental groups of regions when it comes to biotechnology and chemical manufacturing (see Table 3.7), with biotechnology being a sector characterized by firms clustered close to key knowledge bases (Cooke, 2002a, 2002b). All of the top trios of regions score above average, suggesting a strong global breadth in this particular sector of the economy. Overall, there appears to be a particular concentration of the top Asian regions in biotechnology and chemicals manufacturing in South Korea, with the same three regions as is the case for IT and computer manufacturing taking the top continental spots: Ulsan (score 494.76), Gyeongnam (score 480.78), and Gyeongbuk (score 470.54).

Behind the South Korean regions are the leading Europe regions – with two German regions: Rheinland-Pfalz (score 457.18), Hessen (score 333.81), and the Italian Lombardia (score 293.38) – and the leading North American regions which are clustered in the US: Oxnard-Thousand Oaks-Ventura in California, Durham-Chapel Hill in North Carolina (score 473.18), and Baton Rouge in Louisiana (398.17), all three of which are renowned for their economies being strongly based on the biotechnology and chemical manufacturing sectors (Enright and Roberts, 2001).

In the Middle East, Israel again takes primacy (score 178.85), followed by two closely performing Turkish regions: Istanbul (score 139.02) and East Marmara

Table 3.7 Top three regions by continental bloc: Employment in biotechnology and chemicals manufacturing per 1,000 employees

Rank	*Region*	*Index*
	Asia and Pacific	
1	Ulsan, Korea	494.76
2	Gyeongnam, Korea	480.78
3	Gyeongbuk, Korea	470.54
	Europe	
1	Rheinland-Pfalz, Germany	457.18
2	Hessen, Germany	333.81
3	Lombardia, Italy	293.38
	Middle East	
1	Israel	178.85
2	Istanbul, Turkey	139.02
3	East Marmara, Turkey	136.49
	North America	
1	Oxnard-Thousand Oaks-Ventura, CA, US	645.11
2	Durham-Chapel Hill, NC, US	473.18
3	Baton Rouge, LA, US	398.17
	South America	
1	Santa Catarina, Brazil	241.00
2	São Paulo, Brazil	171.29
3	Rio Grande do Sul, Brazil	159.33

(score 136.49). Within South America, Brazilian regions lead the way again: Santa Catarina (score 241.00), São Paulo (score 171.29), and Rio Grande do Sul (score 159.33). This remarkable proximity of the top scores among the continental blocs is suggestive of how biotechnology and chemical manufacturing activity is distributed globally compared to other knowledge-based sectors.

Employment in high-technology services is a particularly important measure of regional competitiveness, as it goes beyond the traditional focus on manufacturing, and accounts for the knowledge-based services that support regional economic activities (inclusive of manufacturing firms) (Muller and Zenker, 2001; Wood, 2006). Firms operating in this sector often act as knowledge diffusers, and hence are particularly important for regional economic development (Keeble *et al.*, 1991; Muller and Zenker, 2001).

Table 3.8 reveals interesting patterns of global concentrations of high-technology service sector economic activity. The leading Canadian region of the Yukon (score 1,264.26) is considerably distant from the second best overall, Région de Bruxelles-Capitale in Belgium (score 785.98). Second best in its continental bloc is Northwest Territories & Nunavut (score 488.63), also in Canada, which highlights a particular feature of resource-oriented economies.

In all continental blocs, with the exception of the Middle East, the top trios score well above average. It appears that the high concentration of high-technology

Table 3.8 Top three regions by continental bloc: Employment in high-technology services per 1,000 employees

Rank	*Region*	*Index*
	Asia and Pacific	
1	Tokyo, Japan	472.31
2	Australian Capital Territory, Australia	424.64
3	New South Wales, Australia	404.56
	Europe	
1	Région de Bruxelles-Capitale, Belgium	785.98
2	Île de France, France	411.54
3	Praha, Czech Republic	340.37
	Middle East	
1	Israel	229.67
2	Kuwait	63.54
3	West Anatolia, Turkey	56.95
	North America	
1	Yukon, Canada	1,264.26
2	Northwest Territories and Nunavut, Canada	488.63
3	Washington-Arlington-Alexandria, DC-VA-MD-WV, US	334.18
	South America	
1	Distrito Federal, Brazil	311.95
2	São Paulo, Brazil	280.03
3	Rio de Janeiro, Brazil	263.06

services is not just a North American or European phenomenon, with such concentrations also being observed in regions in Asia and Pacific, with Tokyo in Japan (score 472.31) taking the continental lead, and in South America, where Brazilian Distrito Federal (score 311.95) dominates. Nevertheless, it would be wrong to dismiss the Middle East, with Israel (score 229.67) not ranked far behind the top performers from other continental blocs – followed by Kuwait (score 63.54) and Turkish West Anatolia (56.95).

Per capita private equity investment is an important indicator of the finance available for firms, with regional financial systems stimulating the start-up rate and growth of firms (Florida, 1995; Klagge and Martin, 2005). Furthermore, the development of financial markets has been found to be linked to economic growth (Bekaert *et al.*, 2001), with the specific presence of venture capitalists often found to be closely clustered around better performing regions (Florida and Kenney, 1988; Martin, 1989; Martin *et al.*, 2005).

As shown by Table 3.9, all but one of the top regions across the continental blocs score above the average of 100 (with the exception being Brazilian Paraná, score 92.11), with all the continental bloc 'leaders' having at least 5 times the regional average private equity investment. There is a clear lead among the Asia and Pacific trio over the other continental blocs, with Taiwan scoring approximately 200 points less than Singapore, with New South Wales in Australia a further 84 points behind.

Table 3.9 Top three regions by continental bloc: Per capita private equity investment

Rank	*Region*	*Index*
	Asia and Pacific	
1	Singapore	1,131.24
2	Taiwan	932.87
3	New South Wales, Australia	848.17
	Europe	
1	Stockholm, Sweden	895.55
2	Norway	839.13
3	London, UK	749.67
	Middle East	
1	Israel	598.04
2	Istanbul, Turkey	114.76
3	East Marmara, Turkey	103.96
	North America	
1	Worcester, MA, US	642.34
2	Boston-Cambridge-Quincy, MA-NH, US	590.84
3	Los Angeles-Long Beach-Santa Ana, CA, US	537.54
	South America	
1	Distrito Federal, Brazil	535.66
2	São Paulo, Brazil	229.80
3	Paraná, Brazil	92.11

In Europe, Stockholm in Sweden leads the way (score 895.55), followed by Norway (score 839.13) and London, UK (score 749.67). North America is represented by the US regions with Worcester, Massachusetts (score 642.34) topping the table, followed by Boston-Cambridge-Quincy in Massachusetts and New Hampshire (score 590.84), and Los Angeles-Long Beach-Santa Ana in California (score 537.54). In the Middle East, the dominating Israel scores 598.04, which is nearly five times that of the second best, Istanbul in Turkey (score 114.76), closely followed by Turkish East Marmara (score 103.96). In South America, the second-placed Brazilian region of São Paulo scores less than half of the index value of Distrito Federal (score 535.66) also in Brazil. From this summarized comparison, it is noticeable how much unexplored entrepreneurial potential appears to lie in the Middle Eastern and South American regions, which would more than likely be mobilized if further venture capital were made available.

Fourth-wave knowledge capital

The 4th-wave knowledge capital component consists of the greatest number of indicators (i.e. seven), resulting in each having a lower contribution in terms of their weight to the overall WCIR score. This does not decrease the importance of these inputs, but rather makes them core parameters. In particular, 4th-wave knowledge capital includes three indicators that relate to medium-knowledge-intensive manufacturing, which depict the global shifts in production from the traditional western regional economies to the lower-cost eastern regions (Maskell and Malmberg, 1999; Storper *et al.*, 2002), such as those in Asia, Eastern Europe or South America. Tables 3.10 to 3.16 present the top performing regions for each of the indicators.

First, the automotive and mechanical engineering manufacturing sector is a good measure of not only large firm turnover and employment, but also substantial export orientation. This, in the current internationalization period of manufacturing, has an additional characteristic – i.e. it is closely associated with foreign direct investment (FDI) and respective knowledge flows (Gentile-Lüdecke and Giroud, 2012; Giroud *et al.*, 2012). Within the selection of regions presented in Table 3.10, the difference between the top region Bremen in Germany (score 661.82) and lowest performing Rio Grande do Sul in Brazil (score 58.96) is more than ten-fold, clearly pointing to very diverse geographical performances just within the top trios.

The European trio can be described as representing the highest concentration of automotive and mechanical engineering manufacturing, in particular Bremen, Strední Cechy in Czech Republic (score 624.34), and Baden-Württemberg (score 532.82). The 'mid'-level is located in Asia and Pacific, as represented by Aichi in Japan (score 387.85), Daman & Diu in India (score 308.55), and Ulsan in South Korea (score 296.31). The moderate level is observed among the Middle Eastern Turkish trio: Istanbul (score 168.47), East Marmara (score 165.41) and West Marmara (score 122.04).

North America's top three are slightly less easy to categorize, as Wichita in Kansas scores very high (score 514.36), whilst the subsequent two US regions –

Table 3.10 Top three regions by continental bloc: Employment in automotive and mechanical engineering manufacturing per 1,000 employees

Rank	*Region*	*Index*
	Asia and Pacific	
1	Aichi, Japan	387.85
2	Daman and Diu, India	308.55
3	Ulsan, Korea	296.31
	Europe	
1	Bremen, Germany	661.82
2	Strední Cechy, Czech Republic	624.34
3	Baden-Württemberg, Germany	532.82
	Middle East	
1	Istanbul, Turkey	168.47
2	East Marmara, Turkey	165.41
3	West Marmara, Turkey	122.04
	North America	
1	Wichita, KS, US	514.36
2	Seattle-Tacoma-Bellevue, WA, US	200.06
3	Hartford-West Hartford-East Hartford, CT, US	160.94
	South America	
1	Santa Catarina, Brazil	90.70
2	São Paulo, Brazil	64.47
3	Rio Grande do Sul, Brazil	59.96

Seattle-Tacoma-Bellevue in Washington (score 200.06) and Hartford-West Hartford-East Hartford in Connecticut (score 160.94) – are closer to the moderate-level Middle Eastern group. The top trio from South America could be classed as below-average performers, even though within South America alone these three Brazilian regions – Santa Catarina (score 90.70), São Paulo (score 64.47), and Rio Grande do Sul (score 59.96) – are undoubtedly well above average.

When the instrumentation and electrical machinery manufacturing sector is considered, there appears to be a wide gap between the top performing Severovýchod in Czech Republic (score 759.92) and the lowest performing Rio Grande do Sul in Brazil (score 20.28) (Table 3.11). Overall, this indicator has been found to be strongly correlated with employment in automotive and mechanical engineering sector (Huggins and Izushi, 2009), indicating similarities in regional economic development effects, especially FDI flows.

Here, the European trio show a clear lead, and is composed of the Central and East European regions of Severovýchod in the Czech Republic, Západné Slovensko (score 743.39) in Slovakia, and Jihozápad (score 738.09), which is also in the Czech Republic. The next in line with a good concentration of well-performing regions is Asia and Pacific represented by Japanese Shiga (score 292.59) and Gunma (score 246.92), and Chinese Guangdong (score 235.24). A

Table 3.11 Top three regions by continental bloc: Employment in instrumentation and electrical machinery manufacturing per 1,000 employees

Rank	*Region*	*Index*
	Asia and Pacific	
1	Shiga, Japan	292.59
2	Gunma, Japan	246.92
3	Guangdong, China	235.24
	Europe	
1	Severovýchod, Czech Republic	759.92
2	Západné Slovensko, Slovakia	743.39
3	Jihozápad, Czech Republic	738.09
	Middle East	
1	Israel	114.35
2	Istanbul, Turkey	84.63
3	East Marmara, Turkey	83.09
	North America	
1	San Jose-Sunnyvale-Santa Clara, CA, US	163.11
2	Milwaukee-Waukesha-West Allis, WI, US	158.30
3	Palm Bay-Melbourne-Titusville, FL, US	112.67
	South America	
1	Santa Catarina, Brazil	30.68
2	São Paulo, Brazil	21.80
3	Rio Grande do Sul, Brazil	20.28

clear global focus, albeit with a more moderate intensity, is observed among the North American US regions: San Jose-Sunnyvale-Santa Clara in California (score 163.11), Milwaukee-Waukesha-West Allis in Wisconsin (score 158.30), and Palm Bay-Melbourne-Titusville in Florida (score 112.67). The regions of the remaining two continental blocs show less dense levels of employment in this sector, although Israel (score 114.35) is performing above the average of 100.

As shown by Table 3.12, economic activity rates suggest that the percentage of the population mobilized into the labour market is highest in the Asia and Pacific regions, specifically in three Chinese regions: Zhejiang (score 158.98), Chongqing (score 157.87), and Beijing (score 151.59), which could indicate a greater pooling of labour resources into low-skilled low-paid jobs (Huggins and Izushi, 2009), such as basic manufacturing – a dominant feature of the Chinese economy. The remaining continental bloc trios appear to differ very little, apart from the outstanding Middle Eastern economy of Qatar (score 139.48). In Europe, the lead is taken by Moscow (score 118.02), and in North America by Washington, DC (score 120.07), and in South America by Brazil's Mato Grosso (score 122.81).

The rate of management employment within a regional economy can be treated as an efficiency indicator of local economic actors, as well as being correlated with entrepreneurial activity (Acs *et al.*, 2008). Furthermore, as employees

Table 3.12 Top three regions by continental bloc: Economic activity rate

Rank	*Region*	*Index*
	Asia and Pacific	
1	Zhejiang, China	158.98
2	Chongqing, China	157.87
3	Beijing, China	151.59
	Europe	
1	Moscow, Russia	118.02
2	Saint Petersburg, Russia	118.02
3	Murmansk Oblast, Russia	117.05
	Middle East	
1	Qatar	139.48
2	Dubai, UAE	120.06
3	Abu Dhabi, UAE	118.59
	North America	
1	Washington-Arlington-Alexandria, DC-VA-MD-WV, US	120.07
2	Alberta, Canada	118.56
3	Austin-Round Rock-San Marcos, TX, US	116.84
	South America	
1	Mato Grosso, Brazil	122.81
2	Piauí, Brazil	122.74
3	Acre, Brazil	122.64

in any organization act as knowledge and innovation sources (Nonaka, 1991, 1994; Florida, 1995; Grant, 1996), the effective management of human capital is understandably crucial, and as regional economies grow their local management skills improve (Acs *et al.*, 2008).

Among the top trios from the five continental blocs there appears to be quite similar performances across the Asia and Pacific and European regions for this indicator, led by Singapore (score 276.83) and Northern Ireland in the UK (score 272.58), respectively (Table 3.13). It is interesting to note that both these continental trios have very little variation within their respective groups. Across the Middle Eastern regions, Sharjah in the United Arab Emirates leads the way (score 210.86). In North America, San Jose-Sunnyvale-Santa Clara (score 132.85) tops the ranking, whilst in South America the Brazilian region of Amapá (score 108.74) has the highest concentration of managers.

Tables 3.14 and 3.15 highlight two key innovation inputs: public expenditure on research and development performed by either government or business. R&D activity is clearly crucial to economic development (Wang, 2007) even though not all regions may have the necessary social foundations to either stimulate R&D activity or benefit from it (Rodríguez-Pose, 1999). R&D activity is generally considered to be led by the business sector (Mowery, 1998), although public R&D laboratories may also play a key role, especially with regard to engagement

Table 3.13 Top three regions by continental bloc: Number of managers per 1,000 employees

Rank	*Region*	*Index*
	Asia and Pacific	
1	Singapore	276.83
2	New Zealand	267.96
3	Kerala, India	267.87
	Europe	
1	Northern Ireland, UK	272.58
2	North East, UK	268.64
3	Wales, UK	266.15
	Middle East	
1	Sharjah, UAE	210.86
2	Istanbul, Turkey	181.22
3	West Anatolia, Turkey	174.48
	North America	
1	San Jose-Sunnyvale-Santa Clara, CA, US	132.85
2	Bridgeport-Stamford-Norwalk, CT, US	128.50
3	Durham-Chapel Hill, NC, US	120.32
	South America	
1	Amapá, Brazil	108.74
2	Paraíba, Brazil	94.53
3	Alagoas, Brazil	94.44

Table 3.14 Top three regions by continental bloc: Per capita expenditure on R&D performed by government

Rank	*Region*	*Index*
	Asia and Pacific	
1	Australian Capital Territory, Australia	1,357.15
2	Beijing, China	891.73
3	Tottori, Japan	570.84
	Europe	
1	Praha, Czech Republic	792.14
2	Bremen, Germany	658.12
3	Berlin, Germany	630.07
	Middle East	
1	Qatar	363.90
2	Israel	87.28
3	Kuwait	68.01
	North America	
1	Baltimore-Towson, MD, US	2,011.33
2	Washington-Arlington-Alexandria, DC-VA-MD-WV, US	1,975.41
3	Richmond, VA, US	621.63
	South America	
1	Distrito Federal, Brazil	107.57
2	São Paulo, Brazil	53.14
3	Rio de Janeiro, Brazil	47.90

Table 3.15 Top three regions by continental bloc: Per capita expenditure on R&D performed by business

Rank	*Region*	*Index*
	Asia and Pacific	
1	Ulsan, Korea	452.48
2	Mie, Japan	410.80
3	Tottori, Japan	407.00
	Europe	
1	Hovedstaden, Denmark	455.05
2	Pohjois-Suomi, Finland	407.64
3	Stockholm, Sweden	397.73
	Middle East	
1	Israel	267.33
2	Istanbul, Turkey	19.76
3	East Marmara, Turkey	17.63
	North America	
1	Worcester, MA, US	779.72
2	Boston-Cambridge-Quincy, MA-NH, US	747.89
3	Bridgeport-Stamford-Norwalk, CT, US	710.95
	South America	
1	Distrito Federal, Brazil	34.31
2	Antioquia, Colombia	25.38
3	Atlántico, Colombia	25.38

in more basic research. The downturn of the late 2000s affected regional innovation convergence, as noted by Archibugi and Filippetti (2011), and therefore an analysis of R&D expenditure trends may provide insights into new emergent trends.

As shown by Tables 3.14 and 3.15, both R&D measures are characterized by a large disparity between the top continental trios, equating in both cases to over 40 times difference between the two. The top index score for the R&D performed by government – Baltimore-Towson in Maryland, US (score 2,011.33) – is nearly three times the top index score for the R&D performed by business achieved by Worcester in Massachusetts. Baltimore-Towson is closely followed by Washington, DC (score 1,975.41) and Richmond in Virginia (score 621.63). The close geographic proximity of these three regions clearly highlights the clustering of government labs engaged in publicly-funded research in this part of the US.

Asia and Pacific and European regions also score very high, led by Australian Capital Territory (score 1,357.15) and Praha in Czech Republic (score 792.14), respectively. There is a distinct gap between Tottori in Japan (score 570.84) and the top performing Middle Eastern Qatar (score 363.90). There are further gaps between the top regions in both the Middle East and South America (Distrito Federal in Brazil with a score of 107.57), suggesting that publicly-performed R&D is also highly geographically concentrated in these continental blocs.

In terms of private sector R&D investment (Table 3.15), the North American trio noticeably score over seven times the average – led by Worcester in Massachusetts (score 779.72) – although Europe and Asia and Pacific have similar rates of performance amongst the top regions. In Europe the way is led by Hovedstaden in Denmark (score 455.05) and in Asia and Pacific by Ulsan in South Korea (score 452.48). Israel scores disproportionately high among the Middle Eastern regions, with the two Turkish regions separated by a gap of nearly 250 points, both well below the overall average. The South American regions also score below the average, but are led by Brazilian Distrito Federal (score 34.31), followed by the Colombian regions of Antioquia and Atlántic.

One of the most established, yet controversial, measures of innovation are patent registrations (Archibugi, 1992), which depict how R&D activity is transformed or translated into knowledge of potential commercial value. At the same time, one of the major downsides of patents is the limits they impose on the knowledge exploitation by different users. Nonetheless, as Storper (2009) points out, newly created knowledge needs to be eventually diffused, otherwise it will constrain long-term growth. On a similar note, Romer (1986: 1003) points to knowledge spillover being a natural process, 'because knowledge cannot be perfectly patented or kept secret'.

As shown by Table 3.16, the most patent active region is Boise City-Nampa in Idaho (score 465.47) achieving a score 507 times that of the South American

Table 3.16 Top three regions by continental bloc: Number of patents registered per 1 million inhabitants

Rank	*Region*	*Index*
	Asia and Pacific	
1	Tokyo, Japan	451.71
2	Osaka, Japan	235.56
3	Shanghai, China	217.79
	Europe	
1	Switzerland	445.82
2	Baden-Württemberg, Germany	375.22
3	Zuid-Nederland, Netherlands	370.55
	Middle East	
1	Israel	121.36
2	Istanbul, Turkey	4.16
3	East Marmara, Turkey	3.71
	North America	
1	Boise City-Nampa, ID, US	465.47
2	Worcester, MA, US	330.19
3	Seattle-Tacoma-Bellevue, WA, US	326.79
	South America	
1	Santa Catarina, Brazil	1.19
2	São Paulo, Brazil	1.07
3	Paraná, Brazil	0.92

Paraná in Brazil (score 0.92). Tokyo in Japan (score 451.71) is ranked second overall, and first within Asia and Pacific. The remaining two regions in Asia and Pacific achieve approximately half that of Tokyo's performance: Osaka in Japan (score 235.56) and Shanghai in China (score 217.79). Overall, the performance of the North American and European leading trios of regions is fairly similar, whilst in the emerging continental blocs the Middle Eastern trio performs better than the South American.

Table 3.17 shows the relationship between R&D expenditure and patent activity across regions, with both government and business expenditure significantly correlated with patent activity. The Spearman correlation between the R&D performed by government and patents is slightly lower than that for R&D performed by the business, although both point to a strong and positive relationship between the measures.

Outputs and outcomes

Within the output and outcomes component of the WCIR there are three economic indicators: labour productivity; mean gross monthly earnings; and unemployment rates. At a micro level, labour productivity may vary depending on the flexibility of internal labour markets (Lucidi and Kleinknecht, 2010), or the shifting of business production operations to low-cost countries, which over time can stimulate the rate of skilled employment in incumbent regions (Navaretti *et al.*, 2010). As shown by Table 3.18, six traditionally oil-rich regions across three continental blocs lead the way in terms of labour productivity, headed by Russian Nenets Autonomous Okrug (score 764.00) located in the European side of the country. A further two Russian regions on the Eastern side of the Ural Mountains top the Asia and Pacific table in the form of Khanty-Mansi Autonomous Okrug-Yugra (score 271.84) and Yamalo-Nenets Autonomous Okrug (score 270.72). The third region in the trio, Jeonnam in South Korea, is separated by a gap of over 60 points from the Russian oil regions' primacy. In the Middle East the way is led by Qatar (score 215.05), Kuwait (169.72), and Abu Dhabi in United Arab Emirates (score 164.28).

Among the leading European regions are Luxembourg (score 334.27) and Région de Bruxelles-Capitale in Belgium (score 290.54), both far below the Russian leader in the trio. The North American regions are led by Bridgeport-Stamford-Norwalk in Connecticut, US (score 291.65), followed by San Jose and San Francisco. The South American trio, with the exception of Distrito Federal in

Table 3.17 Spearman rank correlations (rho) for innovation measures

Indicators correlated with number of patents per 1 million inhabitants	*Correlations*
Per capita R&D expenditure performed by government	0.5007***
Per capita R&D expenditure performed by business	0.7979***

Notes: *** denotes significance level <0.001.

Table 3.18 Top three regions by continental bloc: Labour productivity

Rank	*Region*	*Index*
	Asia and Pacific	
1	Khanty-Mansi Autonomous Okrug-Yugra, Russia	271.84
2	Yamalo-Nenets Autonomous Okrug, Russia	270.72
3	Jeonnam, Korea	206.46
	Europe	
1	Nenets Autonomous Okrug, Russia	764.00
2	Luxembourg	334.27
3	Région de Bruxelles-Capitale, Belgium	290.54
	Middle East	
1	Qatar	215.05
2	Kuwait	169.72
3	Abu Dhabi, UAE	164.28
	North America	
1	Bridgeport-Stamford-Norwalk, CT, US	291.65
2	San Jose-Sunnyvale-Santa Clara, CA, US	277.45
3	San Francisco-Oakland-Fremont, CA, US	261.61
	South America	
1	Distrito Federal, Brazil	105.15
2	Meta, Colombia	80.15
3	São Paulo, Brazil	55.15

Brazil (score 105.15), achieve below-average labour productivity, consisting of Meta in Colombia (score 80.15) and São Paulo in Brazil (score 55.15).

Table 3.19 shows the leading regions in terms of mean gross monthly earnings, which do not just determine the quality of life of a region, but also point to the relative global competitiveness of regional firms. In particular, firms located in regions with greater earnings are more likely to be focused on knowledge creation as their main competitive capability (Maskell and Malmberg, 1999). For this indicator there is a much smaller variation among the top trios, with the top region, Région de Bruxelles-Capitale in Belgium (score 354.39), scoring over four times higher than the lowest of the trios, which is Abu Dhabi in the United Arab Emirates (score 80.61).

The top performing trios are in Europe and North America, with the latter led by San Jose-Sunnyvale-Santa Clara (score 352.21). More moderate earnings can be found among the Asia and Pacific trio, with Tokyo (score 216.65) at the top. The Middle Eastern and South American trios have a relatively similar performance, with both having one outstanding region scoring above the average: Kuwait and Córdoba in Colombia, respectively.

From the correlations presented in Table 3.20, it is clear that there is a strong and significant relationship between earnings rates and the measures of innovation presented above, which confirms Cooke's (2001) argument that high economically performing regions tend to have more market-led innovation

Table 3.19 Top three regions by continental bloc: Mean gross monthly earnings

Rank	*Region*	*Index*
	Asia and Pacific	
1	Tokyo, Japan	216.65
2	Osaka, Japan	179.53
3	Kanagawa, Japan	175.84
	Europe	
1	Région de Bruxelles-Capitale, Belgium	354.39
2	Luxembourg	321.95
3	Île de France, France	237.24
	Middle East	
1	Kuwait	165.21
2	Israel	89.72
3	Abu Dhabi, UAE	80.61
	North America	
1	San Jose-Sunnyvale-Santa Clara, CA, US	352.21
2	Bridgeport-Stamford-Norwalk, CT, US	343.93
3	Washington-Arlington-Alexandria, DC-VA-MD-WV, US	300.95
	South America	
1	Córdoba, Colombia	145.98
2	Sucre, Colombia	93.26
3	Bolívar, Colombia	87.14

systems, which is manifested in terms of the very significant correlation between earnings and rates of private sector R&D expenditure. Furthermore, such systems are built on human capital in the form of the skills regional firms require (Cohen and Levinthal, 1990; Cooke, 1992; Maskell and Malmberg, 1999), which is highlighted by the strong correlations between the education indicators and earnings rates.

It is surprising, perhaps, to find no Brazilian region among the South American trio for earnings, suggesting that despite significant economic growth, Brazilian regions do not necessarily present the best living conditions for the local labour force. Table 3.21 presents the bottom trios for earnings across the continental

Table 3.20 Spearman rank correlations (rho) of mean gross monthly earnings with knowledge indicators

Indicators correlated with mean gross monthly earnings	*Correlations*
Per capita R&D expenditure performed by government	0.4620***
Per capita R&D expenditure performed by business	0.8126***
Number of patents registered per one million inhabitants	0.6683***
Per capita public expenditures on primary and secondary education	0.7571***
Per capita public expenditures on higher education	0.6544***

Notes: *** denotes significance level <0.001.

Table 3.21 Bottom three regions by continental bloc: Mean gross monthly earnings

Rank	*Region*	*Index*
	Asia and Pacific	
1	Bihar, India	7.27
2	Uttar Pradesh, India	10.23
3	Madhya Pradesh, India	12.45
	Europe	
1	Severna i Iztochna Bulgaria, Bulgaria	13.22
2	Macroregiunea doi, Romania	15.02
3	Macroregiunea patru, Romania	19.16
	Middle East	
1	Tabouk, Saudi Arabia	15.92
2	Jazan, Saudi Arabia	16.35
3	Al-Madinah Al-Monawarah, Saudi Arabia	23.46
	North America	
1	Prince Edward Island, Canada	98.68
2	Nova Scotia, Canada	105.70
3	New Brunswick, Canada	105.92
	South America	
1	Piauí, Brazil	20.32
2	Ceará, Brazil	21.16
3	Maranhão, Brazil	21.81

blocs, highlighting that some of these regions are major manufacturing locations (i.e. India, Eastern European states, and Brazil). It can be expected that over time these currently low-cost regions will tend to converge with the high-cost ones (Kaldor, 1957; Romer, 1986), especially as they tend to attract FDI, which facilitates knowledge diffusion (Florida, 1995).

In terms of unemployment rates, the top performing region is Qatar (score 108.04), with the lowest performing across the trios being Honolulu in Hawaii, US (score 102.77). The Middle Eastern regions have some of the lowest levels of unemployment, followed by Asia and Pacific, Europe, South America and North America (Table 3.22).

Knowledge sustainability

The final WCIR component consists of five indicators: two measuring public expenditure on education; and the remaining three measuring information and communication technology (ICT) infrastructure in the form of secure servers, internet hosts, and broadband access. All are clearly essential foundations of regional knowledge economies, and through combined nation-level policies further improve regional human capital (Selwyn and Brown, 2000).

Although knowledge sustainability and economic development are clearly associated, the relationship is complex, whereby an ageing population and lower

Table 3.22 Top three regions by continental bloc: Unemployment rate (reverse order)

Rank	*Region*	*Index*
	Asia and Pacific	
1	Beijing, China	106.97
2	Guangdong, China	105.71
3	Singapore	105.60
	Europe	
1	Åland, Finland	105.67
2	Westösterreich, Austria	105.30
3	Norway	105.04
	Middle East	
1	Qatar	108.04
2	Kuwait	107.15
3	Dubai, UAE	106.60
	North America	
1	Saskatchewan, Canada	103.24
2	Omaha-Council Bluffs, NE-IA, US	103.19
3	Honolulu, HI, US	102.77
	South America	
1	Piauí, Brazil	104.19
2	Santa Catarina, Brazil	103.65
3	Paraná, Brazil	103.54

birth rates may take a toll on education expenditure (Green, 1999). The effects of this require further insight, especially given the OECD's PISA (Programme for International Student Assessment) results (OECD, 2010), which provide a very inconclusive picture as to the relationship between education and output, or the education performance of students and related expenditures. The results of previous PISA surveys were analysed in detail by Hanushek and Woessmann (2008), who seek to measure cognitive skills, rather than expenditures alone, and find a strong link between these factors and individual income and economic growth.

Public expenditure on education, regardless of the level, is difficult to compare across regions given different national education systems, as in some nations there might be a considerable proportion of the private sector involved (e.g. higher education sector in the US). Furthermore, differences in levels of expenditure across regions may not necessarily directly translate into education outcomes (OECD, 2010). Nevertheless, it is well recognized that education or human capital accumulation is a crucial element of economic development (Lucas, 1988), and plays a particularly important role at the micro level of firms and organizations – contributing to their innovative capacity (Cohen and Levinthal, 1990). Caution, however, needs to be applied, as highlighted by Lewis (1962: 686):

> Human capacity is improved by education, public health, research, invention, institutional change, and better organization of human affairs, whether in business or in private or public life. To attribute all improvements in productivity to education would therefore be more than a little naïve.

This is partially confirmed among the European regions, where culture overall, inclusive of education, is found to influence economic development (Tabellini, 2010). This is why the WCIR takes education as only one of the indicators that provide a meaningful picture of the regional competitiveness. In addition, the picture is even more blurred given the inverse relationship between a nation's natural resource contribution to GNP (Gross National Product) and public expenditure on education, as found by Gylfason (2001). As evidence for this relationship is not based on the last two decades, but a period prior to that, it could be suggested that since Gylfason's study natural resource-rich regions have moved on, especially bearing in mind the Middle Eastern nations' and Kazakhstan's endeavours to diversify their economies.

As shown by Table 3.23, there is a moderate variation among the top trios in terms of the levels of per capita expenditure on primary and secondary education. The Russian regions of Chukotka Autonomous Okrug (score 444.79) in Asia and Pacific and Nenets Autonomous Okrug (score 394.56) in Europe lead the way,

Table 3.23 Top three regions by continental bloc: Per capita public expenditure on primary and secondary education

Rank	*Region*	*Index*
	Asia and Pacific	
1	Chukotka Autonomous Okrug, Russia	444.79
2	Sakha (Yakutia) Republic, Russia	201.94
3	Yamalo-Nenets Autonomous Okrug, Russia	191.60
	Europe	
1	Nenets Autonomous Okrug, Russia	394.56
2	Luxembourg	274.36
3	Norway	252.77
	Middle East	
1	Qatar	187.49
2	Kuwait	166.45
3	Tabouk, Saudi Arabia	152.28
	North America	
1	Bridgeport-Stamford-Norwalk, CT, US	296.58
2	New York-Northern New Jersey-Long Island, NY-NJ-PA, US	290.70
3	Honolulu, HI, US	288.59
	South America	
1	Acre, Brazil	56.52
2	Amapá, Brazil	53.56
3	Sucre, Colombia	52.94

with one possible explanation for such comparatively high expenditures being the climate conditions and remoteness of the two regions; another could be more directly related to the natural-resources wealth in these regions and perhaps some form of response to the trends identified by Gylfason (2001). In the Middle East, Qatar (score 187.49) heads the table, whilst in the North America Bridgeport-Stamford-Norwalk in Connecticut achieves the highest score (296.58). All trios, except those in South America, score above the average.

The importance of higher education to economic development is significant (Kimenyi, 2011), especially given the role of the universities in providing regional labour markets with the human capital and the research and knowledge commercialization they require (Cooke, 1992), or what can also be termed the absorptive capacity (Cohen and Levinthal, 1990) or locational capability for firms (Maskell and Malmberg, 1999). Although the causality of the positive relationship between higher education and economic development remains an area open for further research, there is growing evidence pointing to higher education exerting an effect on economic development (de Meulemeester and Rochat, 1995; Huggins and Izushi, 2007).

As indicated by Table 3.24, high per capita tertiary education expenditures are particularly concentrated in the North American and European regions, led by Albuquerque in New Mexico (score 379.65) and Hovedstaden in Denmark (score

Table 3.24 Top three regions by continental bloc: Per capita public expenditure on tertiary education

Rank	*Region*	*Index*
	Asia and Pacific	
1	Western Australia, Australia	291.34
2	Australian Capital Territory, Australia	278.70
3	Northern Territory, Australia	254.68
	Europe	
1	Hovedstaden, Denmark	374.38
2	Norway	336.70
3	Région de Bruxelles-Capitale, Belgium	307.09
	Middle East	
1	Qatar	168.30
2	Kuwait	110.95
3	Al-Riyadh, Saudi Arabia	93.56
	North America	
1	Albuquerque, NM, US	379.65
2	Des Moines-West Des Moines, IA, US	359.69
3	Salt Lake City, UT, US	353.83
	South America	
1	Distrito Federal, Brazil	165.04
2	Roraima, Brazil	113.72
3	São Paulo, Brazil	88.98

374.38), respectively. These are followed by the Asia and Pacific trio, with all three being Australian regions topped by Western Australia (score 291.34). In the Middle East, the most notable performer is again Qatar with a score of 168.30, whilst in South America the Brazilian Distrito Federal region (score 165.04) again takes the continental lead.

ICT infrastructure is also generally considered to be positively related to economic development (Kozma, 2005; Czernich *et al.*, 2011), particularly at a regional level (Gibbs and Tanner, 1997), albeit not always in the revolutionary way that is often thought (Heeks, 2010). ICT infrastructure plays an important role in knowledge diffusion, with specific positive effects on education (access to, and the development of, the relevant skills for ICT-based employment), and knowledge creation and innovation (Kozma, 2005). Fagerberg and Srholec (2008) identify the role of ICT based on a national-level study that finds a strong and positive correlation with economic output.

In the context of emerging economies, based on a study of Taiwan's ICT infrastructure development, Wang (1999) points out that these positive national or regional economic effects require a competent centralized strategy of infrastructure development in order to reach fruition. Frieden (2005) further argues that ICT infrastructure development needs not only governmental vision and coordination, but also a partnership with the private industry to deliver the necessary investments. Nevertheless, these governmental approaches would not necessarily reflect the ICT infrastructure development issues of developing regions, as other institutional factors appear to play an important role, for example domestic legal regulations or distribution of income (Chinn and Fairlie, 2010).

Secure servers allow for safe online transactions and can be considered a useful proxy measure of ICT infrastructure. As shown by Table 3.25, amongst the leading continental bloc trios there is a large gap between the top performing region of Ontario in Canada and the lowest, Santa Catarina in Brazil. In general, there appears to be three distinct levels of performance, with the greatest numbers of secure servers concentrated in the North America, Asia and Pacific, and Europe.

Internet hosting is essential for the development of worldwide web services, and a clear concentration can be observed in Europe, with Åland in Finland (score 711.92) leading the table (Table 3.26). The North American trio, which are all Canadian, is again led by Ontario (score 471.84), whilst in Asia and Pacific Australian Capital Territory (score 434.01) is the leading region. In the Middle East, there is relative disparity in internet hosting, with Israel (score 133.67) being well above the average, with the remaining two leading regions achieving less than half the average scores – Abu Dhabi in UAE and Istanbul in Turkey. South American regions perform quite strongly with two of the trio above the average, led by Bogotá in Colombia (score 125.72), Distrito Federal in Brazil, and São Paulo.

Regional broadband access is a measure of a region's knowledge transmission capability, with the highest levels found in North America and Asia and Pacific, led by Ontario in Canada (score 580.43) and Ulsan in South Korea (score 425.79),

Table 3.25 Top three regions by continental bloc: Secure servers per 1 million inhabitants

Rank	*Region*	*Index*
	Asia and Pacific	
1	Ulsan, Korea	442.00
2	Australian Capital Territory, Australia	365.45
3	Queensland, Australia	324.06
	Europe	
1	Iceland	436.46
2	West-Nederland, Netherlands	430.05
3	London, UK	424.44
	Middle East	
1	Israel	68.48
2	Abu Dhabi, UAE	45.94
3	Istanbul, Turkey	26.62
	North America	
1	Ontario, Canada	742.50
2	Bridgeport-Stamford-Norwalk, CT, US	469.80
3	San Jose-Sunnyvale-Santa Clara, CA, US	438.50
	South America	
1	Distrito Federal, Brazil	14.23
2	São Paulo, Brazil	10.61
3	Santa Catarina, Brazil	9.80

Table 3.26 Top three regions by continental bloc: Internet hosts per 1,000 inhabitants

Rank	*Region*	*Index*
	Asia and Pacific	
1	Australian Capital Territory, Australia	434.01
2	Tokyo, Japan	424.13
3	Queensland, Australia	384.86
	Europe	
1	Åland, Finland	711.92
2	Etelä-Suomi, Finland	565.27
3	Hovedstaden, Denmark	545.46
	Middle East	
1	Israel	133.67
2	Abu Dhabi, UAE	47.36
3	Istanbul, Turkey	40.10
	North America	
1	Ontario, Canada	471.84
2	Quebec, Canada	247.88
3	Alberta, Canada	201.72
	South America	
1	Bogotá, D.C., Colombia	125.72
2	Distrito Federal, Brazil	121.00
3	São Paulo, Brazil	90.18

Table 3.27 Top three regions by continental bloc: Broadband access per 1,000 inhabitants

Rank	*Region*	*Index*
	Asia and Pacific	
1	Ulsan, Korea	425.79
2	Beijing, China	321.00
3	Shanghai, China	316.67
	Europe	
1	Etelä-Suomi, Finland	250.92
2	West-Nederland, Netherlands	214.99
3	Norway	212.02
	Middle East	
1	Israel	138.87
2	Abu Dhabi, UAE	92.88
3	Istanbul, Turkey	78.84
	North America	
1	Ontario, Canada	580.43
2	Quebec, Canada	304.93
3	Bridgeport-Stamford-Norwalk, CT, US	299.43
	South America	
1	Distrito Federal, Brazil	85.58
2	São Paulo, Brazil	63.78
3	Bogotá, D.C., Colombia	59.04

respectively. Slightly more moderate broadband access is observed within the European trio with Etelä-Suomi in Finland (score 250.92) at the top. In the Middle East, only Israel performs above average (score 138.87), whilst in South America the whole trio achieves scores lower than the average, topped by Distrito Federal in Brazil (score 85.58).

Concluding remarks

It is evident that the top performing regions in each of the continental blocs are not necessarily a representative selection of the performance of all respectively grouped regions. However, what seems to be quite observable is that there are regions that follow different strategies in terms of their endeavour to achieve economic competitiveness. Some, like Ulsan in South Korea, Norway, Israel, San Jose-Sunnyvale-Santa Clara, and Brazilian Distrito Federal, have developed a range of strengths, which make them very competitive regions not just within their respective broader geospatial blocs, but also at a global level. Other regions develop more specialist approaches to their locational capabilities (Maskell and Malmberg, 1999), e.g. Tokyo, Praha, Kuwait, Yukon, or Bogotá, D.C. In the following chapters the WCIR indicators are analysed in more detail across a range of parameters in order to further understand the global competitiveness of regions.

4 Regional competitiveness and economic development

The aim of this chapter is to look in more detail at the components of regional competitiveness and the links with other notions of regional economic development. Regional economic development can be conceptualized and measured in a range of ways (Pike *et al*., 2007), some of which necessarily overlap and interlink with the notion of regional competitiveness, but this chapter focuses on the connection between regional competitiveness as a measure of economic development and one of the most widely used measures – Gross Domestic Product (GDP) per capita (measured throughout the chapter in US dollars), which generally equates to the rate of regional economic output per person resident in a particular region. It is far from an ideal measure of economic development – hence, one of the rationales for the establishment of regional competitiveness measures – with its weaknesses relating to its imperfect correlation with measures of financial welfare such as purchasing power adjusted incomes, particularly when its distribution is taken into account (Ravallion, 2001), and even more so when considering broader measures of social well-being such as happiness (Diener and Biswas-Diener, 2002; Stevenson and Wolfers, 2008). Nevertheless, it is associated with increases in these measures, which are less widely measured. This makes the link between a region's competitiveness and GDP per capita an important issue to examine.

In order to establish the link between regional competitiveness and GDP per capita both the overall measure of regional competitiveness and the individual indicators are examined. In doing so, this chapter, and those that follow, also consider some of the results of other competitiveness indices that may have importance for a particular set of regions (ITIF, 2012), or a focus on competitiveness from one particular perspective, for example, the Xinhua-Dow Jones International Financial Centers Development Index (CFC Holding Company and CME Group, 2011).

Gross domestic product per capita and the key competitiveness components

Before considering the individual competitiveness indicators and the precise relationship they have with GDP per capita, Table 4.1 presents the Pearson

Table 4.1 Correlations for GDP per capita and the components of the WCIR

	Pearson correlation coefficients	*Spearman rank correlation coefficients*
5th-wave knowledge capital	0.397 (0.000)	0.539 (0.000)
4th-wave knowledge capital	0.402 (0.000)	0.490 (0.000)
Outputs and outcomes	0.824 (0.000)	0.843 (0.000)
Knowledge sustainability	0.757 (0.000)	0.839 (0.000)
WCIR score	0.765 (0.000)	0.826 (0.000)

Notes: *p*-values in parenthesis

correlation coefficients for the four components of the WCIR along with the nonparametric Spearman rank measure. This gives an indication of the overall association between the components of the WCIR and economic development, as measured in its traditional sense. Overall, the key components of the competitiveness of regions and their GDP per capita are all significantly correlated. The overall WCIR score is also significantly related to the GDP per capita.

Reflecting the fact that each competitiveness component will contribute to economic development in different ways, the overall WCIR is more strongly related to GDP per capita than its individual components, with the exception of the outputs and outcomes measure. It should be acknowledged that this relationship is likely to be bidirectional with those regions with higher levels of GDP per capita in a better position to invest in key knowledge inputs, which explains the strong correlation with the knowledge sustainability component. Considering the individual components, the outputs and outcomes component is understandably strongly linked to GDP per capita, although this need not be the case given that more capital intensive production in higher income economies may reduce the likelihood of full employment. Although significantly related to GDP per capita the 4th- and 5th-wave knowledge capital components do not display relationships that are as strong.

Considering the relationship between the overall WCIR score and GDP per capita in more detail, Figure 4.1 illustrates the relationship between the two.[1] It shows that more competitive regions are also those with higher levels of GDP per capita. However, for more competitive regions the dispersion of GDP per capita appears to increase. This means that there is considerable variation in the GDP per capita values obtained for those regions with WCIR scores of approximately 100. For example, Khanty-Mansi Autonomous Okrug-Yugra in Russia has a WCIR score of 109.0, slightly less than Marche in Italy (WCIR = 110.9), but whilst the Russian region – which is highly reliant on its wealth in natural resources, particularly oil – has a GDP per capita of over $80,000, this compares to only $32,735 in Marche.

As well as bringing wealth to a region, studies have also suggested that there is a danger associated with an abundance of natural resources in that it can have a demotivating effect on the workforce, as a mindset of entitlement takes over,

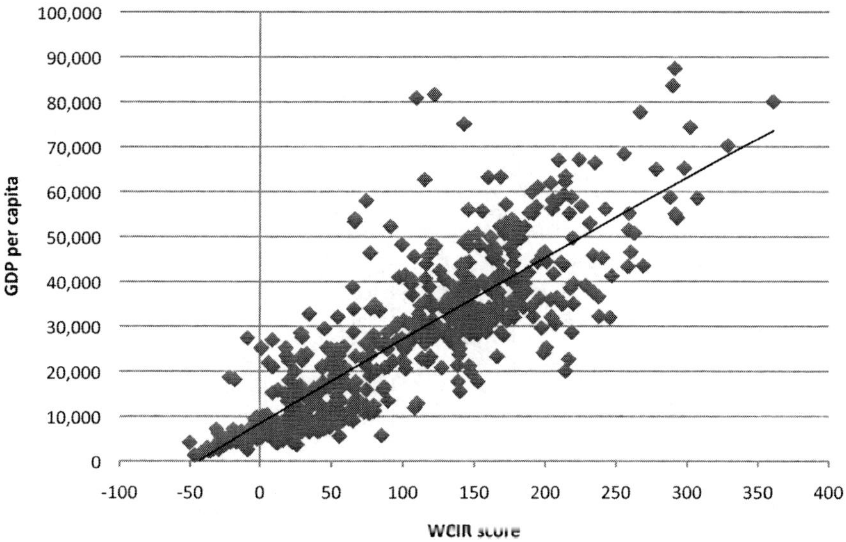

Figure 4.1 Relationships between GDP per capita (US$) and WCIR score

commonly termed the 'resource curse' (Leamer, 1999; Marcel, 2006). Other studies have attributed the weaker growth of resource-rich economies to weaker institutions and markets (Sachs and Warner, 2001). However, this finding has been disputed, with it argued that although growth in these regions may be slower, income levels tend to remain higher both in the short and medium term through the appropriate exploitation of resources in order to maximize welfare (Boyce and Emery, 2011).

A polynominal line of best fit is estimated for the relationship between the WCIR and GDP per capita. A positive relationship between the WCIR and GDP per capita is evident and the quadratic term has a very small negative coefficient suggesting that increasing competitiveness appears to be consistently linked to higher GDP per capita. The fitted equation explains just under 70 per cent of the variation in GDP per capita ($R^2 = 0.693$). Overall, there is evidence to suggest that competitiveness and GDP per capita are strongly linked, although other factors such as natural resource wealth creates a degree of variation. However, these supplies of natural resources are limited, and at some point regions will have to reduce their reliance on these in order to maintain the standard of living enjoyed by their populations.

In order to partly account for differences between the groups of regions, a simple linear regression is run with GDP per capita as the dependent variable and the WCIR score centred on the average of 100, along with the square of this centred WCIR score (divided by 100 to ensure that the standard deviation of the two variables are not too dissimilar). The controls for different groups of nations are provided by dummies representing whether the region is located in Europe, North America, BRIC nation, the Middle East, or outside these groups (Other). The excluded group is Europe. The results of this regression are presented in Table 4.2. Overall, the regression explains just under two thirds of the variation in the GDP per capita of regions ($R^2 = 0.655$). The null of collective insignificance of the variables is rejected by the F-test at the 0.1 per cent level. As with the simple line of best fit, the positive relationship between competitiveness and GDP per capita remains. The squared term is only weakly significant indicating that the relationship does not change greatly in nature as competitiveness increases or decreases. The region group dummies are all significant at the 5 per cent level or better, with the exception of the Middle East.

Compared with Europe, the predominance of US regions in the North America group means these regions experience a higher level of GDP per capita than those in Europe. This comes as no surprise given the dominance of US cities in other rankings of the most affluent urban areas; for instance, of the 100 cities with the highest GDP per capita, two thirds are in the US (Cox, 2013). However, by concentrating on city level analysis such as the Global Metro Monitor (Istrate and Nadeau, 2012), these studies ignore those regions that are sparsely populated but rich in natural resources.

After controlling for whether or not a region is located in the BRIC group, a negative effect is found. This is likely to reflect the heterogeneous nature of the BRIC regions, with many of the Russian regions enjoying high GDP per capita from their natural resource wealth, whilst Chinese and Indian regions have not had these advantages to the same degree.

Overall, the Middle East group is not found to be wealthier than their current level of competitiveness. However, this is likely to reflect the inclusion of Turkey within this group. When Turkey is excluded a weakly significant positive result is found, indicating greater wealth than is consistent with their current level of competitiveness, with their output being boosted by their oil and gas industries,

Table 4.2 Regression for GDP per capita on WCIR and region group

	Coefficient	*p-value*
WCIR	146.3	(0.000)
$WCIR^2/100$	12.418	(0.064)
Region group[a]		
North America	10029.2	(0.000)
BRIC	–6454.4	(0.000)
Middle East	1149.1	(0.605)
Other	–4071.3	(0.005)
Constant	27190.9	(0.000)
R^2	0.655	
F-test	170.6	(0.000)

Note: [a] Reference group Europe.

which has led to Abu Dhabi and Kuwait City being ranked in the top 50 most affluent cities (Cox, 2013).

Analysing the individual indicators included within the index allows further investigation of those factors associated with competitiveness that have the strongest relationship with GDP per capita. As with the overall index, any relationships found here should not be regarded as causal, as bi-directional effects are extremely likely. The Pearson and Spearman rank correlation coefficients are reported in Table 4.3. As found above, the nonparametric Spearman rank correlation coefficients are sensible to include given the outliers found when considering GDP per capita for isolated resource-rich regions. An examination of the correlation statistics shows that the majority of the indicators are positively and significantly associated with GDP per capita at the 0.1 per cent level. A larger number of the nonparametric correlation coefficients are significant, which can be attributed to the outliers. However, once the effect of these sparsely populated resource-rich regions with extremely high GDP per capita have been reduced, significant results continue to be found, and more so in the case of some variables. A number of the 4th-wave knowledge capital variables are affected in this manner. Employment in Automotive and Mechanical Engineering and Employment in Instrumentation and Electrical Machinery change from not being significantly associated, or only significantly related at the 5 per cent level, with GDP per capita, to being associated at the 1 per cent level.

There are quite sizeable differences in the correlation coefficients between GDP per capita and employment within the different industries associated with knowledge capital. For example, when considering the 5th-wave knowledge capital component, there is a moderate correlation between employment within the High Technology Services per 1,000 employees, but the correlation coefficients are about half the size for Employment in IT and Computer Manufacturing, and Biotechnology and Chemicals.

Industrial specialization

Figure 4.2 shows the relationship between employment representation in the High Technology Services industry and GDP per capita. This is after the removal of the outlier region of Nenets Autonomous Okrug, along with the region of the Yukon in Canada, which is excluded from the analysis due to its exceptionally high rates of employment in the High Technology Services sector, accounting for more than a third of total regional employment (341 employees per 1,000).

Despite the significant relationship found, it is clear that a high level of employment within the High Technology Services sector is not a prerequisite for high levels of GDP per capita. For example, the natural resource-rich regions such as Qatar and Khanty-Mansi Autonomous Okrug-Yugra in Russia both have a GDP per capita of over $75,000, but less than 15 employees per 1,000 employed in High Technology Services. Equally, Northwest Territories and Nunavut in Canada has the third highest representation in this area of activity with more than one in eight employees working in this sector (132 per 1,000 employees), but a

Table 4.3 Correlations for GDP per capita and the individual indicators

	Pearson correlation coefficients	*Spearman rank correlation coefficients*
5th-wave knowledge capital		
Employment in IT and computer manufacturing per 1,000 employees	0.134 (0.002)	0.312 (0.000)
Employment in biotechnology and chemicals per 1,000 employees	0.159 (0.000)	0.217 (0.000)
Employment in high-tech services per 1,000 employees	0.370 (0.000)	0.547 (0.000)
Per capita private equity investment	0.345 (0.000)	0.515 (0.000)
4th-wave knowledge capital		
Economic activity rate	0.137 (0.001)	0.142 (0.001)
Employment in automotive and mechanical engineering per 1,000 employees	0.072 (0.093)	0.181 (0.000)
Employment in instrumentation and electrical machinery per 1,000 employees	0.102 (0.017)	0.248 (0.000)
Number of managers per 1,000 employees	–0.020 (0.638)	–0.099 (0.021)
Per capita expenditures on R&D performed by government	0.267 (0.000)	0.441 (0.000)
Per capita expenditures on R&D performed by business	0.496 (0.000)	0.696 (0.000)
Number of patents registered per one million inhabitants	0.256 (0.000)	0.633 (0.000)
Output/outcomes		
Labour productivity	0.947 (0.000)	0.935 (0.000)
Mean gross monthly earnings	0.749 (0.000)	0.826 (0.000)
Unemployment rates (inverse)	0.066 (0.125)	0.082 (0.056)
Knowledge sustainability		
Per capita public expenditures on primary and secondary education	0.733 (0.000)	0.771 (0.000)
Per capita public expenditures on higher education	0.602 (0.000)	0.684 (0.000)
Secure servers per one million inhabitants	0.654 (0.000)	0.802 (0.000)
Internet hosts per 1,000 inhabitants	0.294 (0.000)	0.394 (0.000)
Broadband access per 1,000 inhabitants	0.646 (0.000)	0.757 (0.000)

Notes: *p*-values in parenthesis

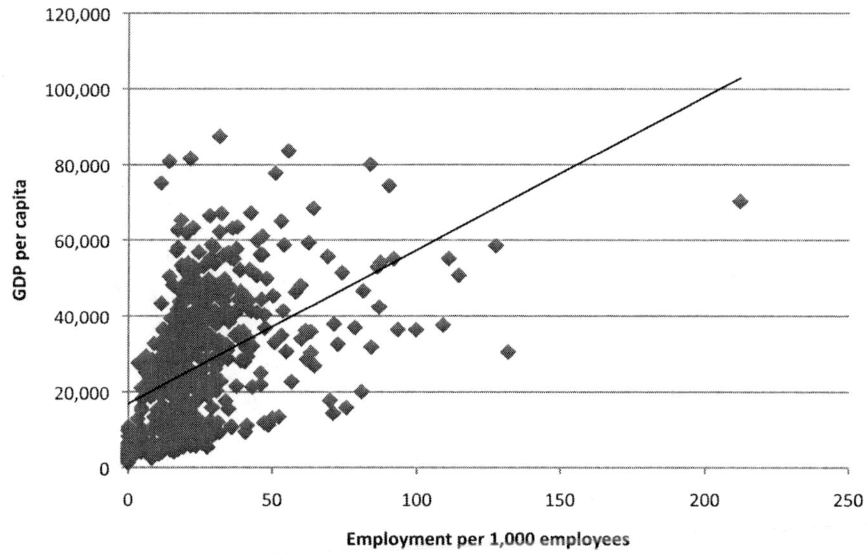

Figure 4.2 Relationship between employment in high-technology services per 1,000 employees and GDP per capita (US$)

GDP per capita of just over $30,500, which is a little over the median GDP per capita of $26,150 for the regions covered by the WCIR.

Considering another of the other industries associated with the 5th-wave knowledge capital component, the Biotechnology and Chemical sector, although significantly correlated with GDP per capita, these relationships are relatively weak (Figure 4.3). Whereas the line of best fit in Figure 4.2 for the High Technology Services sector explains just under 24 per cent of the variation in GDP per capita, the equivalent for Biotechnology and Chemicals explains less than 4 per cent of the variation. A similar result is found when considering the industries associated with the 4th-wave knowledge capital component. For example, Figure 4.4 illustrates the relationship between employment in the Instrumentation and Electrical Machinery sectors and GDP per capita.

In the cases of both the Biotechnology and Chemicals and the Instrumentation and Electrical Machinery sectors, for most regional economies – even those that are the most competitive – they only account for a small proportion of employment. The vast majority of regions have less than one per cent of total employment related to these sectors. Previous studies have shown that sectors such as biotechnology are highly important for the knowledge economy, innovation, exports and the creation of high-value jobs (Arundel, 2003). However, their limited size and applicability to other sectors of the economy mean that for most regions they only have a relatively small direct impact on total output (Hopkins *et al.*, 2007). It is the indirect effects of the industries that often have the biggest impact; in particular, future regional growth potential is likely to be significantly

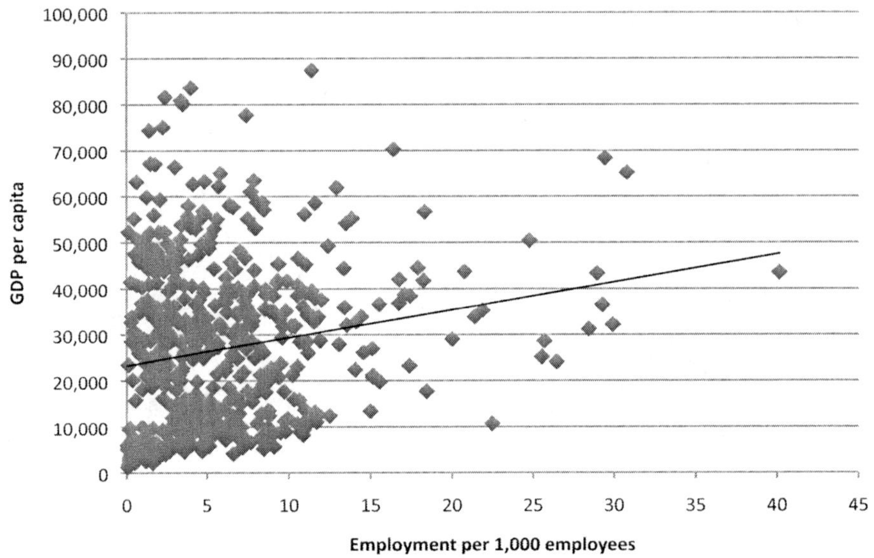

Figure 4.3 Relationship between employment in biotechnology and chemicals per 1,000 employees and GDP per capita (US$)

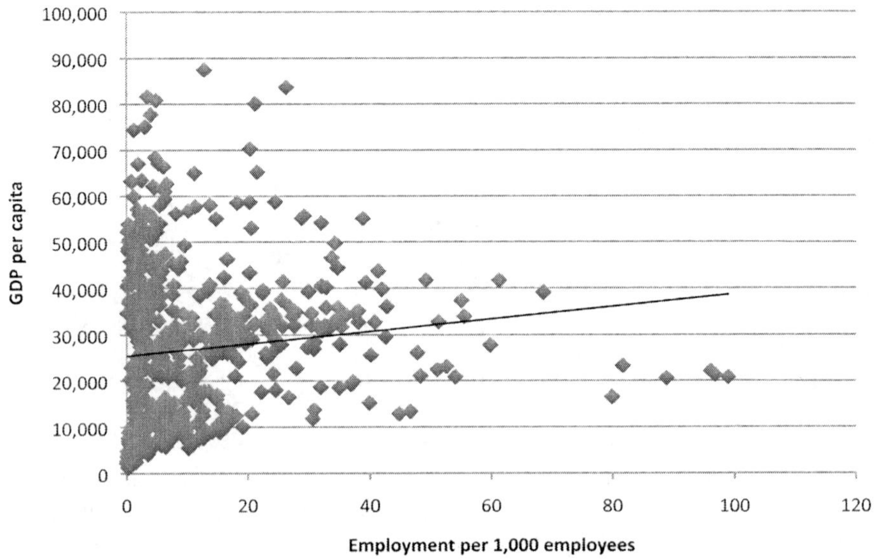

Figure 4.4 Relationship between employment in instrumentation and electrical machinery per 1,000 employees and GDP per capita

related to the downstream industries applying the outputs of these enterprises (Clark, 2007; Wydra and Nusser, 2011).

The positive relationship between the presence of industries constituting sources of 4th-wave knowledge capital and GDP per capita has led to numerous cities and regions around the world expressing a desire and objective to develop clusters of firms in these industries (Hospers, 2005, 2006). However, as theories of cluster development, such as those of Carlsson (2006) and Feldman *et al.* (2005) imply, the development of a successful region will rely on far more than the attraction and formation of a core of relevant firms. These theories envisage some kind of exogenous shock as being critical in moving a region with the appropriate infrastructure and industrial base towards the development of a self-sustaining cluster. Such a shock could come from downsizing or disbandment of a major employer (Stoerring and Dalum, 2007). In the case of Feldman *et al.*'s (2005) model, this leads to a second phase of entrepreneurial activity creating networks to develop infrastructure and attract resources. Carlsson (2006) also suggests that a triggering event must exist to move a cluster to a more rapid development stage, but it is the development of a second generation of firms which are a key feature in his model, as they enable greater knowledge transfer and spillovers. Given the impossibility of unleashing a constructive shock or triggering event, efforts by policymakers to copy the success of other regions are unlikely to be successful in the short term, and whilst efforts can concentrate on providing the basis of a cluster, its successful emergence may be less controllable.

Innovation and R&D

Other contributions to 4th-wave knowledge capital come from the direct inputs into the knowledge production process such as R&D activities. Previous studies have found evidence of both complementary and substitute style relationships between R&D expenditure by the public and private sectors (David *et al.*, 2000), where the additionality of public spending might actually be smallest for those projects with the greatest spillover effects (Takalo *et al.*, 2013). However, for some types of R&D, particularly at the pure research rather than the commercializable innovation end of the spectrum, work suggests that the two are more likely to be complementary rather than substitutes (Nelson, 1959), although the form and extent of the benefits may vary across scientific fields, industries and technologies (Salter and Martin, 2001). Fundamentally, government-sponsored R&D expenditure is associated with market failure relating to pure research that has no immediate commercial application, but is vital as a foundation for the private sector R&D activity that builds upon it (Guellec and van Pottelsberghe de la Potterie, 2004).

The public good nature of pure research means it is naturally both non-excludable, in that anyone can use it without payment, and non-rival in that one party's use does not reduce its availability to others. This means that it will not be created efficiently by the private sector without government intervention. Firms would choose instead to free ride on the work of others, so that no firm would be prepared to undertake the earlier stage research, given that others will exploit its efforts and enjoy a cost advantage in the commercial innovations developed. One solution to this is provided by the patent system, but given the potential for pure research to be used in multiple products and innovations, this approach would mean that society as a whole would lose out (Kremer, 1998). Instead public sector knowledge production is more appropriate (Nelson, 1959).

Although regions could choose to free-ride on the knowledge created by other regions, the ability to absorb information may deteriorate with distance (Jaffe, 1986, 1989b; Huang *et al.*, 2012), and there can be no guarantee that the knowledge relevant for a region's businesses will be created by others (Huggins and Thompson, 2014). The Pearson and Spearman rank correlation coefficients reported above initially suggest that the relationship between public sector R&D spending and GDP per capita should be relatively strong. However, as Figure 4.5 illustrates, the relationship is not as strong as may be supposed. This may reflect the access that regions have to global pipelines enabling acquisition of this form of knowledge (Bathelt *et al.*, 2004). In particular, research-oriented institutions such as universities may not only create and disseminate their own research outputs to the surrounding region, but may also act as aerials to draw in knowledge from networks with other international institutions of a similar type (Fritsch and Schwirten, 1999; Benneworth and Hospers, 2007). Regions such as Singapore and Makkah Al-Mokarramah in Saudi Arabia have created research-oriented institutions to form partnerships of just this type (Wong *et al.*, 2007; Fischer, 2008).

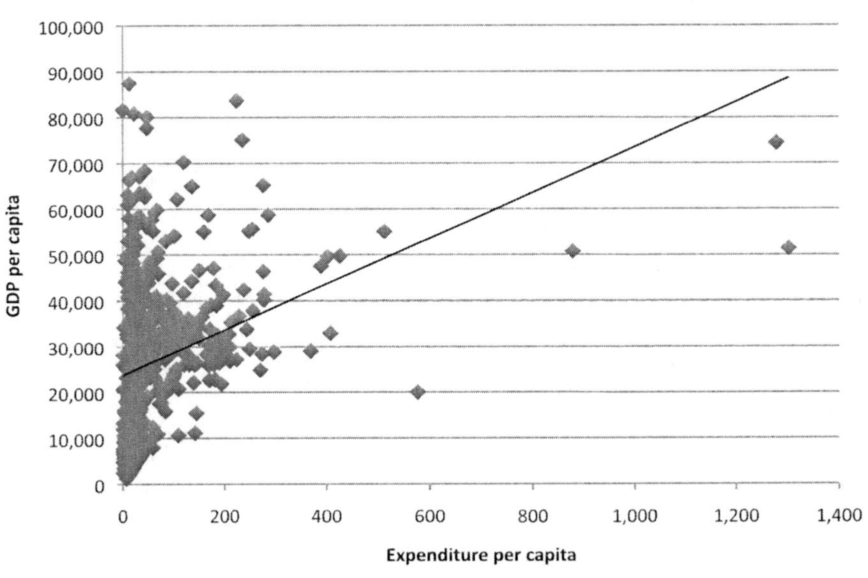

Figure 4.5 Relationship between R&D expenditure by government per capita and GDP per capita (US$)

Overall, government-sponsored R&D is dwarfed by the equivalent spending coming from private sources, although government may act as a possible source or ingredient for the stimulation of private R&D (Agrawal and Henderson, 2002). Across the WCIR regions the correlation between public and private sector R&D expenditures added together and GDP per capita is significant (Pearson correlation 0.289, *p*-value 0.000; Spearman rank correlation 0.627, *p*-value 0.000), although the key driver of this association is the rate of private sector investment.

The link between private sector R&D expenditure alone and GDP per capita is shown in Figure 4.6. The line of best fit suggests that each pound of private sector R&D has an effect on GDP per capita of only two fifths that of public sector spending. However, with median regional public expenditure being \$28 per capita, compared to \$134 in the private sector (there is a similar pattern for mean expenditure – public expenditure of \$64 per capita compared to private expenditure of \$369 per capita), the greater link with GDP per capita is understandable. However, it should be remembered that this relationship is likely to be bidirectional with richer regions better positioned to fund R&D activities.

Outputs and outcomes

Of the WCIR's output and outcome component indicators, the strongest link with GDP per capita is with labour productivity, which is why labour productivity has consistently been included within competitiveness measures (Porter, 1990) or in some cases is considered to effectively drive these measures of competitiveness

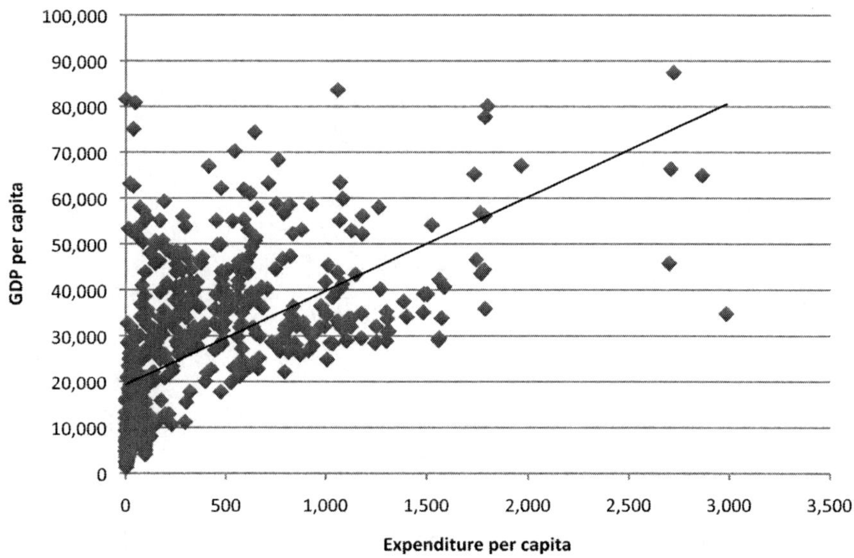

Figure 4.6 Relationship between R&D expenditure by business per capita and GDP per capita (US\$)

(Krugman, 1994a). Although the line of best fit in Figure 4.7 indicates a relationship that explains just under 94 per cent of the variation in GDP per capita, there are still some outliers. For example, Northwest Territories and Nunavut in Canada has the ninth highest labour productivity ($135,122 per employee), but a GDP per capita of just over $30,000. This is likely to be partly associated with its strong presence in the High Technology Services sector combined with a relatively low economic activity rate. This shows the importance of competitiveness measures such as the WCIR, which account for the extent that productivity is converted into increased living standards for the population as a whole (Storper, 1997). At the other end of the scale, another Canadian region, Ontario, enjoys a GDP per capita that is considerably higher ($62,183) than its labour productivity rate would suggest. This highlights the quite different development paths that may be pursued by regions even within the same nation. Likewise, it highlights the inappropriateness of simply copying policies utilized in successful regions, when the underlying economic and social structures across regions will require differing approaches (Asheim, 2002).

Although it is clear and understandable that labour productivity is closely associated with GDP per capita, current labour productivity is no guarantee of future competitiveness. With greater access to knowledge and greater international competition, it is important that a regional economy is able to constantly update and absorb new information and knowledge efficiently, and to adapt it appropriately (Martin and Sunley, 2011b). The education system is seen as being a key component in this process (Hershberg *et al.*, 2007). Not only will institutions such

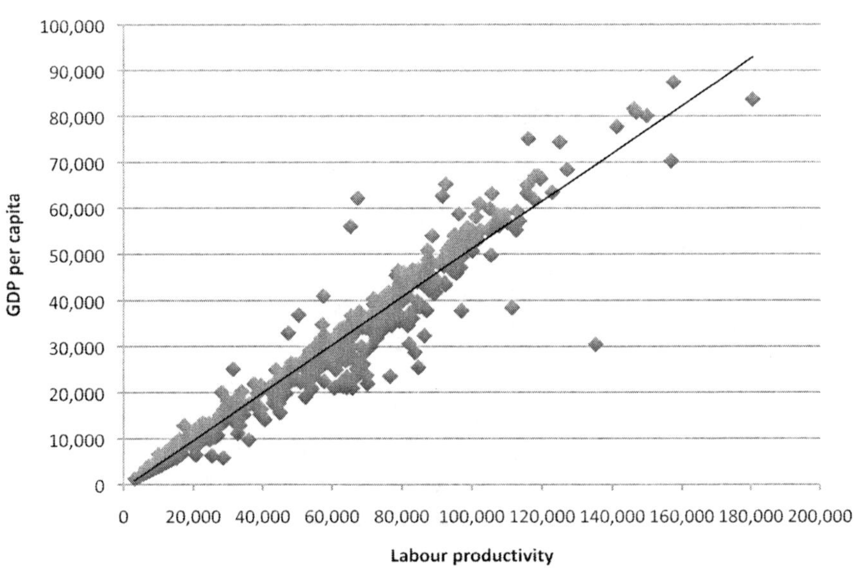

Figure 4.7 Relationship between labour productivity and GDP per capita (US$)

as universities have a direct influence in accessing new knowledge and disseminating it within the regional economy, but in training the future workforce they also directly influence the absorptive capacity of regional enterprises, which is important in allowing regions to absorb knowledge from outside sources such as foreign affiliates (Romer, 1993). As noted above, expenditure on regional primary, secondary and higher education may not directly convert into greater regional output. First, because higher expenditure may not be a perfect proxy of human capital development; second, because the success of a region's education system is reliant not just on it producing talent, but also attracting and retaining it (Glaeser *et al.*, 2001; Carlino and Saiz, 2008; Mellander *et al.*, 2011); and third, causation may also run from GDP per capita to expenditure on education.

As studies such as Gottlieb (1994) and Mellander *et al.* (2011) suggest, the school system also forms an important component in helping to retain talented individuals who wish their children to enjoy the best prospects for their future development. Bearing all these factors in mind, it is understandable that the relationship between expenditure on higher education per capita and GDP per capita, as shown in Figure 4.8, is far from perfect. Nevertheless, there is clear evidence of a positive relationship between the two.

As with many of these indicators, there are a number of outliers; for example, the Chinese capital Beijing spends \$784 per capita on higher education, but currently only has a GDP per capita of just over \$20,000. Such patterns are to be expected for those regions based in emerging economies that are rapidly moving from economies based on large-scale low-cost labour-intensive manufacturing to more knowledge-

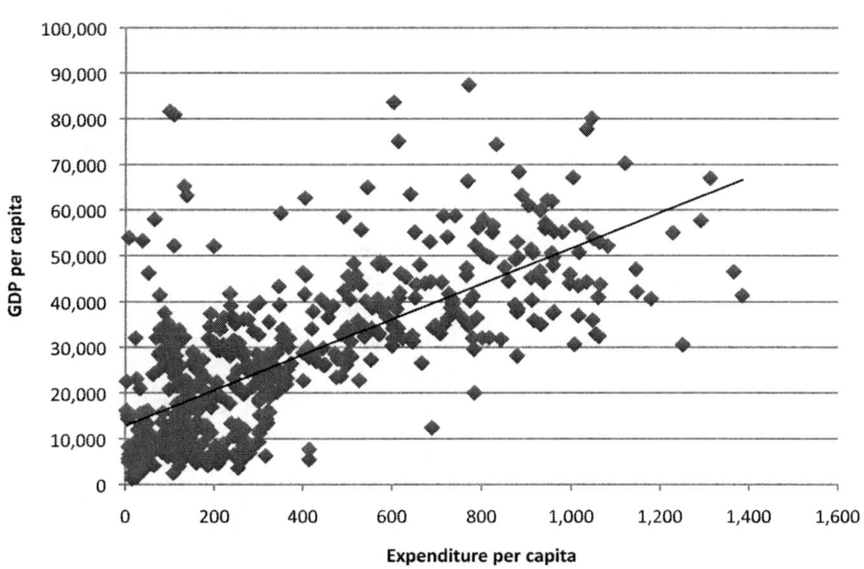

Figure 4.8 Relationship between expenditure on higher education per capita and GDP per capita (US\$)

intensive industries (Hershberg *et al.*, 2007). Given the lack of sustainability of low-cost mass production, as global manufacturers move from one location to the next as costs rise, it is understandable that regional policymakers look to make investments in increasing the absorptive capacity of the regional economy as a means of providing additional value beyond low costs and to access alternative industries (UNDP, 2003). However, it should be noted that some prior studies have suggested that whilst education may have a key role in attracting foreign direct investment (FDI), it has not always been possible to identify a direct causal link with economic growth in nations such as China (Narayan and Smyth, 2006).

A number of other outlier regions with higher levels of GDP per capita fall into the category of being resource-rich regions in emerging economies. For example, Khanty-Mansi Autonomous Okrug-Yugra in Russia has a relatively low rate of expenditure on higher education per capita at only $109 (compared to a median expenditure of $250 per capita and a mean expenditure of $361 per capita in the WCIR regions), but it enjoys a GDP per capita of just under $81,000. However, the success of other regions relative to their spending on higher education can be attributed to other industrial clusters that draw in talent from elsewhere, such as Luxembourg, which spends less than half the rate per capita of the US region of Alburquerque ($1384) and the Danish region Hovedstaden ($1365), but still enjoys the third highest GDP per capita of $83,646, largely reflecting its strong presence in the financial sector.

Human capital and entrepreneurship

One WCIR indicator that does not possess a positive relationship with GDP per capita is the proportion of the workforce employed within managerial positions (Figure 4.9). In fact, there is actually a negative relationship between the proportion of the workforce employed as managers and GDP per capita. In the modern knowledge-based economy, the role of managers in organizing and directing the knowledge creation process has been noted by a number of authors (Bradley and Taylor, 1996; Lall, 2001b; Huggins and Izushi, 2007). Importantly, whilst being imperfect as a measure of managerial talent, the proportion of the workforce employed in management is a better measure of this human capital than flow measures such as the number of high-quality public schools or first-class business schools (Lall, 2001a). However, where economies are based on larger-scale Taylorist manufacturing or the primary sectors, the ratio of managers to other workers may be much lower (Wennekers *et al.*, 2005).

As discussed in Chapter 2, and noted above, the competitiveness measures here are not designed purely to capture the current ability of a region to compete, but also its ability to continue to compete into the future. Where economies are relying heavily on large-scale low-skill production and primary and extractive sectors, economic output may be currently high, but, as regions in nations such as China have found, it is only with the development of management skills and training gained from working within foreign affiliates that entrepreneurial cultures and indigenous innovative ventures have started to emerge (Zhou *et al.*, 2011).

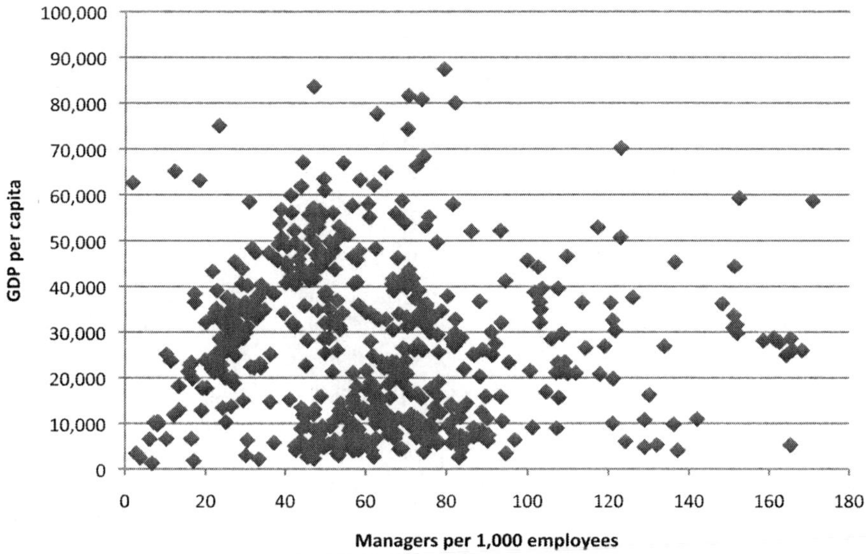

Figure 4.9 Relationship between employment in managerial positions per 1,000 employees and GDP per capita (US$)

The fact that no clear pattern exists between the number of managers as a proportion of regional employment and GDP per capita may reflect some of the patterns observed in entrepreneurial activity as economies develop. Using data from the Global Entrepreneurship Monitor (GEM), Wennekers *et al.* (2005) find a U-shaped relationship between the porportion of the population starting businesses (nascent entrepreneurship) and the GDP per capita of countries. This means that whilst the highest rates of nascent entrepreneurship are in the least developed countries, this rate initially falls before rising again for the richest nations, such as the US, Norway and Sweden. Given that owners of businesses are usually classed in labour statistics as managers, this means that no clear pattern is observed with GDP per capita.

As economies develop large-scale manufacturing, wages rise, making marginal entrepreneurs choose employment over self-employment (Lucas, 1978). However, Acs *et al.* (1994) observe that in the case of 12 OECD countries over the second half of the twentieth century, self-employment rates increase as services and the knowledge economy take over from manufacturing. This phenomenon has been described as an "Industrial Divide" (Piore and Sabel, 1984), a "Third Industrial Revolution" (Jensen, 1993), or a change from a "managed to an entrepreneurial economy" (Audretsch and Thurik, 2001). In other words, whilst managerial talent and abilities are likely to be important at all stages of development (Wennekers *et al.*, 2005), new firm creation has a much stronger relation with economic growth in more developed countries (van Stel *et al.*, 2005).

Further explanations for this rise in entrepreneurship in the most advanced economies include: increasing consumer demands for variety (Jackson, 1984); satiation of basic material needs, resulting in a higher need for self-realization and autonomy (Maslow, 1970); along with the rise of new industries such as biotechnology and software, where flexibility is of importance, aided by new technologies (Carree *et al.*, 2002).

Overall, effective management and entrepreneurial activities appear to be key elements of the economic and innovation systems of regions, with the primary role being to bring together and reorganize regional resources (Schumpeter, 1934). However, the nature of the predominant industries and institutions within a region will subtly alter the role they play and the appropriate combination of management, self-employment and labour at any particular point within a region's development. In part, this is reflected by the relationship between employment in management positions and the other indicators.

Table 4.4 presents the Pearson and Spearman rank correlation coefficients for management employment and the other indicators ordered so that positive relationships are at the top of the table and negative relationships towards the bottom. There are positive relationships found for the number of internet Hosts per 1,000 inhabitants, and per capita private equity investments. It has been suggested that the Internet and other developments in ICT favour smaller more flexible businesses that are able to adapt more quickly to the changing demands of the market (Howcroft, 2001; Carree *et al.*, 2002; Bayo-Moriones and Lera-López, 2007; Beynon-Davies, 2010; Thompson *et al.*, 2013). In the case of the latter, there is clear complementarity between these indicators, with the availability of private equity allowing the funding of entrepreneurial ventures (Berger and Udell, 1998; Mason and Harrison, 2003; Jones-Evans and Thompson, 2009). However, these ventures will also need entrepreneurial talent to be present if they are to be successful (Ewers and Malecki, 2010).

Equally, it is also notable that managerial employment is negatively correlated with a number of indicators, in particular those 4th-wave knowledge capital measures associated with formalized R&D activities, including private sector R&D expenditure per capita and the output measure of patents registered per million population. These activities are likely to be associated with those regional economies that place a greater reliance on larger scale production (de Bruijn and van Oort, 2007), where the role of the manager is still important, but favours a lower proportion of managers as a share of the workforce. In a similar fashion, the outcome measures of gross mean earnings and the inverse of the unemployment rate may be more strongly influenced by such development paths, with greater employment generation being negatively associated with the proportion of employment associated with managerial positions. This highlights the importance of including those indicators associated with the welfare of the population as a whole in the WCIR, otherwise greater competitiveness would be skewed towards those regions that pursue policies and courses of development associated with labour shedding.

As discussed above, there is no single route to competitiveness due to the

Table 4.4 Correlations between managers per 1,000 employees and other WCIR indicators

	Pearson correlation coefficient	*Spearman rank correlation coefficient*
Per capita private equity investment	***0.255*** (0.000)	***0.091*** (0.034)
Internet hosts	***0.171*** (0.000)	***0.202*** (0.000)
Employment in instrumentation and electrical machinery	***0.143*** (0.001)	***0.205*** (0.000)
Employment in high-tech services	***0.117*** (0.006)	0.054 (0.212)
Employment in automotive and mechanical engineering	0.073 (0.088)	***0.157*** (0.000)
Labour productivity	0.013 (0.763)	–0.058 (0.177)
Expenditures on primary and secondary education	–0.004 (0.926)	–0.064 (0.136)
Secure servers	–0.006 (0.890)	***–0.144*** (0.001)
Expenditures on higher education	–0.025 (0.558)	–0.033 (0.435)
Employment in biotechnology and chemicals	–0.037 (0.393)	0.063 (0.139)
Expenditures on R&D performed by government	–0.046 (0.286)	–0.072 (0.091)
Broadband access	–0.061 (0.155)	***–0.099*** (0.020)
Mean gross monthly earnings	***–0.113*** (0.008)	***–0.156*** (0.000)
Economic activity rate	***–0.136*** (0.001)	***–0.105*** (0.014)
Number of patents registered	***–0.221*** (0.000)	***–0.209*** (0.000)
Expenditures on R&D performed by business	***–0.225*** (0.000)	***–0.263*** (0.000)
Unemployment rates	***–0.225*** (0.000)	***–0.258*** (0.000)
Employment in IT and computer manufacturing	***–0.275*** (0.000)	***–0.134*** (0.002)

Notes: Correlations significant at the 5 per cent level are in bold italics. *p*-values in parenthesis differing underlying resources and institutions present within individual regions, which limits the value of trying to fully replicate development in successful regions (Asheim, 2002; Ewers and Malecki, 2010). Therefore, whilst a higher level of managerial inputs is likely to positively influence the competitiveness of regions, the overall share of employment accounted for by these positions will differ depending on the particular development path a region pursues.

Finally, as shown by Figure 4.10, there is a negative relationship present between the unemployment rate and GDP per capita. However, the line of best fit explains very little of the variation in the level of development experienced by a region. The wealthiest regions have generally avoided the highest and most extreme levels of unemployment, with the capital region of Belgium, Région de Bruxelles-Capitale, perhaps the exception. Although this region is the second most competitive of all regions on the WCIR, the nature of its industrial makeup involves less labour-intensive sectors, so that whilst possessing a GDP per capita of just over $70,000 it also has an unemployment rate of 16.9 per cent. Overall, however, regions with lower and moderate levels of unemployment ranging from 4 to 12 per cent also have GDP per capita levels with a considerable range. For example, both Bihar in India and San Jose in the US have unemployment rates of approximately 11 per cent, but the GDP per capita of the Indian region is only $1,287, whilst San Jose enjoys a GDP per capita of $80,105. However, it should be noted that although unemployment has been associated with lower levels of happiness (Frey and Stutzer, 2002; Clark, 2003; Shields *et al.*, 2009), Belgium

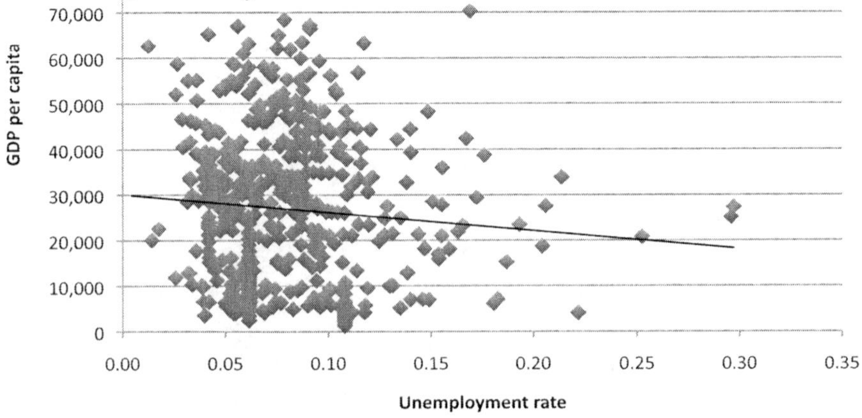

Figure 4.10 Relationship between the unemployment rate and GDP per capita (US$)

enjoys relatively high levels of happiness as captured by a wide variety of well-being measures, such as the Cantril Ladder scales, which requires respondents to evaluate their lives from the worst to best possible (15th of 156) and average life satisfaction (23rd of 129 countries) (Helliwell *et al.*, 2012).

Concluding remarks

This chapter has explored the link between WCIR measures of economic development and economic development as captured using the 'traditional' GDP per capita measure. With the exceptions of unemployment and employment within managerial positions, significant positive relationships are found for all indicators. However, the strength of these positive relationships is relatively weak in many cases. This is consistent with Lall's (2000) assessment that there are multiple routes to development, which, although containing common components such as the creation of human capital and close contact to world markets, will vary considerably in their detail. In particular, regions will vary as to the stage of economic development they have attained, which will often be related to their geospatial location. The following chapter, therefore, focuses on analysing regional competitiveness from the perspective of different stages of economic development.

Note

1 The Russian region of Nenets Autonomous Okrug has been removed from the analysis. This region is an extreme outlier, located in the extreme north of the country on the Barents Sea, it has a population of just over 40,000 according to the Russian 2010 census, but has a rapidly developing oil and gas industry accounting for much of the industrial activity within the region leading to a GDP per capita of over $210,000.

5 Regional competitiveness and stages of development

As indicated in Chapter 4, the structural features of regional economies and their societies, especially those features that determine the competitiveness of a region, will evolve through time and are likely to display a degree of path dependence (Boschma and Frenken, 2006; Martin and Sunley, 2006). Given the quite different development histories of European and North American economies, particularly compared with BRIC countries and Middle Eastern economies where growth rates have been much more rapid in recent years, it is logical to expect that regions within these broad groupings will differ substantially in the sources of their competitiveness. Following on from Chapter 4, this chapter analyses the sources of competitiveness across continental blocs, as well as encompassing an analysis based on the particular stage of economic development that nations have reached. This facilitates a more in-depth analysis of the different drivers of regional competitiveness across the globe.

Although it is clear that there have been large increases in the competitiveness of many regions within emerging economies, the majority of these regions still lag behind the strongest performing North American and European regions. This means that when comparing the components of the WCIR it is useful to consider the relative contribution of the individual competitiveness components to a region's (or group of regions) overall competitiveness. In order to achieve this, the competitiveness contributions stemming from each of the four components are compared. The difference between a region's performance and the mean average component score is scaled by the standard deviation of the overall average of the four components to provide an indication of the relative contribution of the individual components:

$$Contr_{j,i} = \frac{C_{j,i} - \bar{C}_i}{\sigma_{\bar{C}_i}}$$

Where: $C_{j,i}$ is the value of component j for a group of regions i

$\bar{C}_i$ is the average of the components for a group of regions i

$\sigma_{\bar{C}_i}$ is the standard deviation of the average of components for a group of regions i.

The relative contributions are estimated for each of the four components according to four groups of regions: Europe, North America, BRIC, and the Middle East. The relative contributions are calculated for all regions in each of the groups, and also for the sub-samples of the top ten regions in each of regional groups. This allows comparisons to be made between the most competitive regions in the groups and the average in order to determine if these are atypical of their regional group.[1]

Analysis by regional group

Table 5.1 presents the contributions of the four components for each of the regional groups along with the absolute values of the components. On average, all four components tend to have greater values for the European and North American regions than the BRIC and Middle Eastern regional groups. However, it is also worth noting the extent to which the most competitive regions in the BRIC and Middle Eastern economies have caught up with the European and North American averages. For example, the ten strongest performing BRIC

Table 5.1 Absolute and relative contributions by individual components of the WCIR

			5th-wave knowledge capital	4th-wave knowledge capital	Outputs/ outcomes	Knowledge sustainability
Europe	Absolute value	Average	0.15	0.28	–0.00	0.30
		Average Top 10	1.18	0.82	1.05	1.44
	Contribution	Average	–0.06	0.20	–0.38	0.25
		Average Top 10	0.25	–1.30	–0.30	1.35
North America	Absolute value	Average	0.09	0.00	0.71	1.12
		Average Top 10	1.07	0.82	1.37	1.51
	Contribution	Average	–1.18	–1.44	0.70	1.92
		Average Top 10	–0.50	–1.54	0.74	1.29
BRIC	Absolute value	Average	–0.27	–0.18	–0.51	–0.68
		Average Top 10	0.44	0.34	0.53	0.26
	Contribution	Average	0.42	0.71	–0.31	–0.82
		Average Top 10	0.13	-0.15	0.41	–0.38
Middle East	Absolute value	Average	–0.46	–0.55	–0.12	–0.38
		Average Top 10	–0.31	–0.31	0.42	–0.32
	Contribution	Average	–0.27	–0.57	0.84	–0.01
		Average Top 10	–0.59	–0.60	1.81	–0.62

regions have, on average, higher 5th-wave knowledge capital levels than either the European and North American groups of regions as a whole, along with similar patterns for other components with the exception of the knowledge sustainability. However, it should be noted that expenditure on higher education, in particular, has been rapidly increasing in many of these emerging economies, as has the international standing of their universities (Looney, 1994; Cooper, 2006; Ewers and Malecki, 2010). Therefore, this knowledge sustainability gap may well erode in coming years. In order to 'leapfrog' to a post-industrial economy without an industrial phase regions such as those in the Gulf States may require a further concentration on finance- and arts-based education, rather than the traditional route of pursuing science and engineering education, as a means of promoting economic diversification (Schoales, 2006). Governments of the nations in the BRIC and Middle Eastern regional groups also have a long history of sponsoring their students to study overseas, which is not only a limited source of skilled personnel, but in some cases actually results in talent migration that will impinge on competitiveness gains (Marginson, 2006).

Turning to the contributions made by the individual components, the differences are easier to observe using a graphical representation. Figure 5.1 shows the relative contributions of each of the four components for the regional groups when considered as a whole. Overall, it is noticeable that each regional group displays quite different contribution patterns. Europe appears to rely more heavily on the 4th-wave knowledge capital associated with activities and inputs such as R&D spending and high levels of human capital (Huggins and Izushi, 2007).

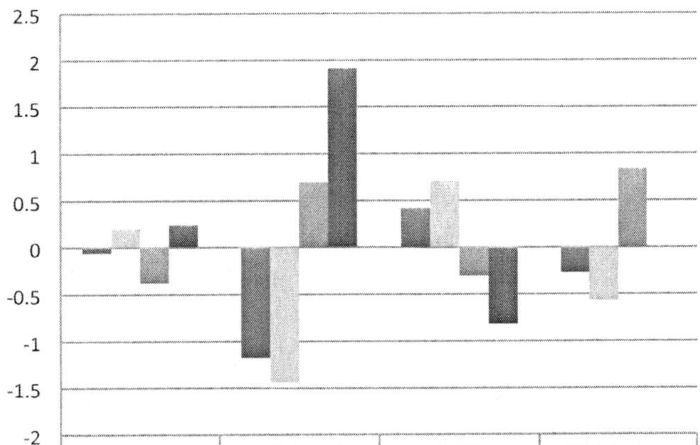

	Europe	North America	BRIC	Middle East
5th-wave knowledge capital	-0.06	-1.18	0.42	-0.27
4th-wave knowledge capital	0.2	-1.44	0.71	-0.57
Outputs/Outcomes	-0.38	0.7	-0.31	0.84
Knowledge sustainability	0.25	1.92	-0.82	-0.01

Figure 5.1 Relative contribution of the WCIR components

Within Europe, knowledge sustainability is also a contributor to regional competitiveness, with many of the top performing regions having had a university presence for hundreds of years. Consistent with a degree of path dependency, the current basis for the competitiveness of European regions continues to be based around the educational and research contributions of these institutions. North American regions display a similarly large contribution from knowledge sustainability, whilst the contributions are relatively low for both the BRIC and Middle Eastern region groups. North America also sees relatively high contributions from output and outcome measures, such as labour productivity. Whilst the knowledge-based sectors associated with 5th-wave knowledge capital account for a much larger proportion of the average workforce in European and North American regions (Table 5.1), the relatively recent emergence of many of these sectors means that the competitiveness of these regions does not appear to be built around their presence.

Overall, it is clear that knowledge sustainability factors make a relatively small contribution to the competitiveness of BRIC regions. The success of these regions in climbing up the competitiveness table appears to be based more around the development of 4th- and 5th-wave knowledge capital.

It is clear from this analysis that the contributions of the WCIR components varies considerably across regional groups, which in many cases are consistent with their historic development and evolution. However, it should be remembered that there will also be heterogeneity within these regional groups.

Figure 5.2 shows the relative contributions of the four components, but this time restricted to the top ten regions in each grouping. Some of the patterns are consistent with the all-region analysis; for example, the relatively high contribution in Europe and North America from knowledge sustainability. However, in Europe 5th-wave knowledge capital is also a relatively high contributor in the most competitive regions. Given the histories and success of regions such as the East of England with its Cambridge biotechnology cluster (Martin and Sunley, 2011a), it is perfectly understandable to expect that the most successful regions will be those that have the most capability in combining their traditional strengths with emerging sources of competitiveness. In the most successful BRIC regions, 4th-wave knowledge capital plays a smaller role in promoting competitiveness than it does across all regions in this group.

Analysis by national stage of development

Although grouping nations is informative in the sense that such nations and their continental blocs may possess similar cultural traits, and pursue similar patterns of development, there is also likely to be considerable variation within these groups, not only between nations, but also within nations. For example, the BRIC regions will differ between the resource-rich Russian regions and the large Chinese agglomerations. This section of the chapter considers the extent to which regions can be grouped by their national stage of development.

Initially, regional competitiveness is analysed based on the stage of economic

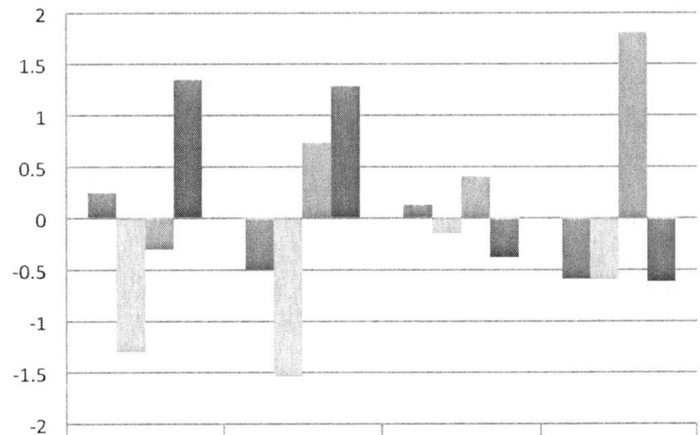

	Europe	North America	BRIC	Middle East
5th-wave knowledge capital	0.25	-0.5	0.13	-0.59
4th-wave knowledge capital	-1.3	-1.54	-0.15	-0.6
Outputs/Outcomes	-0.3	0.74	0.41	1.81
Knowledge sustainability	1.35	1.29	-0.38	-0.62

Figure 5.2 Relative contribution of the WCIR components for the top ten regions in each group

development of the nation in which they are located. The stage of development used here is the World Economic Forum's typology presented in its *Global Competitiveness Report* (World Economic Forum, 2012), which is based on Michael Porter's (1990) original conception. This approach places nations into three main stages of development, along with two intermediate transition stages between these main stages. The three main stages of development are: *Factor*, *Efficiency*, and *Innovation* driven economies. Factor-driven economies compete on the basis of their factor endowments, such as their natural resources and plentiful supplies of cheap labour. Firm production relies on low prices to make sales, based on low costs. In the efficiency-driven stage, wage costs are likely to rise, with the main route to achieving competitiveness being increases in efficiency, particularly within the labour force and through the use of established technology. In the final innovation stage of development, wage levels increase further, with competitiveness primarily resulting from the benefits of creating new products and production processes.

The World Economic Forum (2012) uses two variables to determine the stage of national development. The most influential of these is GDP per capita, with nations allocated to a particular stage of development based on the GDP per capita group they fall into. However, as a further determinant of whether a nation is at the factor-driven stage of development, the percentage of exports (goods and services) associated with mineral goods is explored. Those nations in which mineral exports account for 70 per cent or more of total exports using a five-year average are classed as factor-driven economies regardless of their GDP per capita level.

Table 5.2 presents the GDP per capita ranges used by World Economic Forum (2012) and the stage of economic development for nations in which WCIR-ranked regions are located. The WCIR regions are largely in nations in the innovation-driven stage of development. However, it is also apparent that the WCIR has regions representing all stages of national development, with there being a considerable number of regions located within economies that are in the transition phase between efficiency- and innovation-driven states, as shown by Figure 5.3. In total, slightly more than a quarter of regions are found in the group representing the transition between efficiency- and innovation-driven economies, with Russian and Brazilian regions falling into this group. Those regions not having reached the point of starting the transition to becoming an innovation-driven economy make up the remainder and are, therefore, dealt with as one group.

Table 5.3 indicates that the average competitiveness of regions is higher for those regions located in nations classed as more developed, which is the case regardless of whether the mean or median average is examined. It is logical that regions within the transition phase of development display a lower standard deviation for their competitiveness scores, as this group is captured by a smaller GDP per capita range than the innovation driven countries. The least developed group of nations (consisting of those that have not yet entered into the transition phase to become innovation driven) display a higher variation in regional competitiveness than those in transition phase, reflecting the fact that whilst some of these are

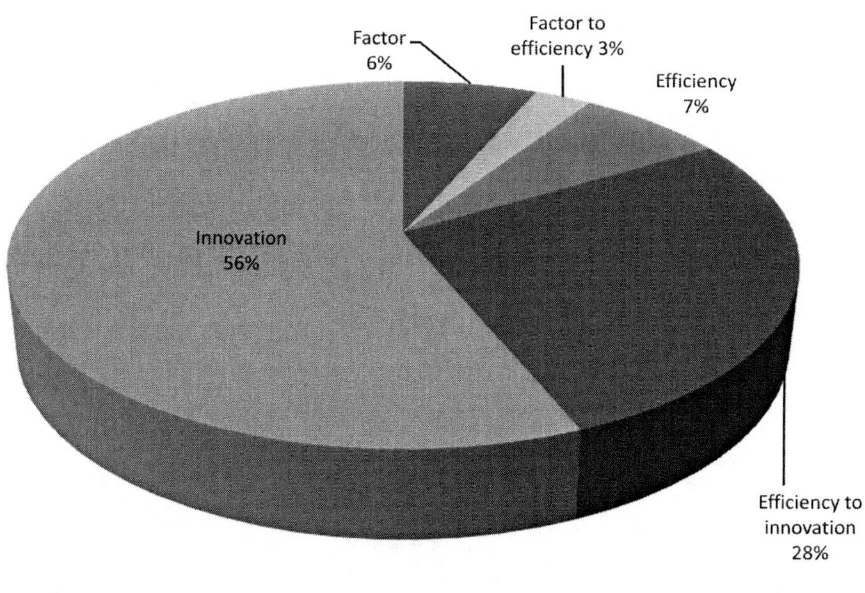

Figure 5.3 Distribution of regions by national stage of development

Table 5.2 Nations included in the WCIR by stage of development

	Factor driven	*Transition from factor to efficiency driven*	*Efficiency driven*	*Transition from efficiency to innovation driven*	*Innovation driven*
GDP per capita range (US$)	< 2,000	2,000–2,999	3,000–8,999	9,000–17,000	> 17,000
Number of nations	1	3	4	9	34
Number of regions	35	15	39	150	307
	India	Kuwait Qatar Saudi Arabia	Bulgaria China Colombia Romania	Brazil Estonia Hungary Kazakhstan Latvia Lithuania Poland Russia Turkey	Australia Austria Belgium Canada Cyprus Czech Republic Denmark Finland France Germany Greece Hong Kong Iceland Ireland Israel Italy Japan Korea Luxembourg Malta Netherlands New Zealand Norway Portugal Singapore Slovakia Slovenia Spain Sweden Switzerland Taiwan UAE UK US

Note: Based on World Economic Forum (2012)

now efficiency driven, others are still – at least in part – factor-oriented economies.

Table 5.3 Regional competitiveness by national stage of development

	Not in transition to innovation driven	*In transition to innovation driven*	*Innovation driven*
Mean average	11.9	48.1	150.9
Median	–1.8	43.4	147.3
Standard deviation	51.4	32.8	61.1
Maximum	216.5	250.9	360.0
Minimum	–50.3	–9.8	–8.7
Range	266.8	260.7	368.7
Upper quartile	24.5	62.1	182.9
Lower quartile	–22.2	24.8	115.8
Inter quartile range	46.7	37.3	67.1
Skewness	2.0	2.1	0.2
Kurtosis	4.7	9.7	0.6

Overall, there is a strikingly large range in competitiveness scores found for regions within a particular stage of development group. In all three stages of development the range of regional competitiveness scores is in excess of 250, and although the minimum and maximum values increase with stage of development, there is little difference in the least competitive region within the group of transition nations (the Chechen Republic in Russia, WCIR –9.79) and that in the innovation-driven nations (Canarias in Spain, WCIR –8.72).

As previously indicated, the most competitive regions of the world are drawn from an increasingly wider variety of nations, and Figure 5.4 emphasizes this by highlighting the extent to which there is overlap between the three stages of development. The large ranges in regional competitiveness across the three groups mean that there are regions from nations that are yet to make it to the transition phase, as well as those in the transition phase that are more competitive than the lowest ranked regions within the innovation-driven economies. For example, Shanghai and Beijing, with WCIR scores of 216.5 and 214.2, rank above all regions in transition phase with the exception of Nenets Autonomous Okrug in Russia. This shows that although nations such as China as a whole may be rated as only moderately successful in terms of their competitiveness (29th out of 144) by studies such as the World Economic Forum's Global Competitiveness Index (World Economic Forum, 2012), or even uncompetitive in the case of Russia (67th), individual regions within these nations perform much more strongly. At the same time, some nations with low national competitiveness rankings according to the Global Competitiveness Report, such as Brazil (48th), may lack a leading region; for example Distrito Federal in Brazil achieves a WCIR score of 111.13 ranking it only 250th.

Reflecting the rapid growth of Asian hotspots, the Xinhua-Dow Jones International Financial Centers Development Index in 2011 (CFC Holding

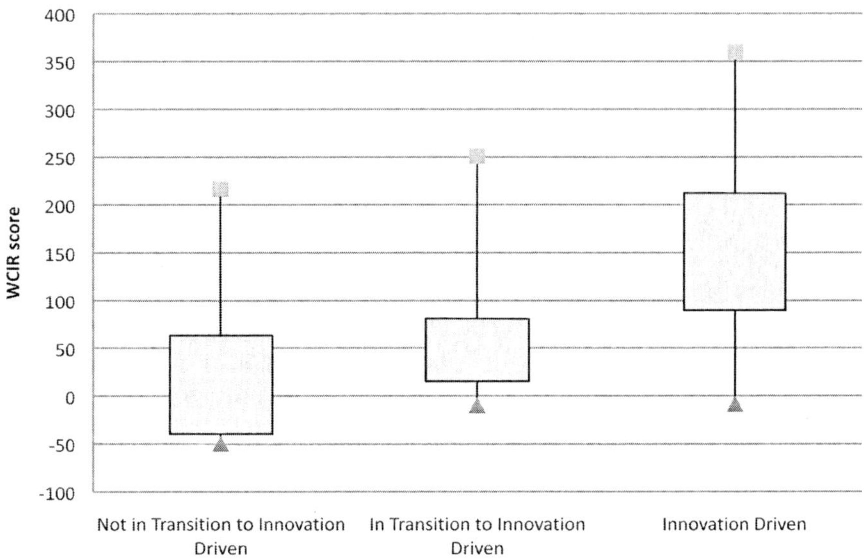

Figure 5.4 Distribution of regional competitiveness by national stage of development (shaded boxes represent those WCIR scores within 1 standard deviation of the mean)

Company and CME Group, 2011) ranks Shanghai within the top ten financial centres for four of its five measures: financial markets; growth and development; industrial support; and services. Only in terms of the broader general environment measure, which includes elements concerning the economic environment, political environment and openness, does Shanghai fall outside the top ten, although it is still ranked 19th of the 45 financial centres covered. It is this 'economic environment' measure that perhaps best accounts for broader competitiveness beyond the financial industry and is therefore more reflective of the WCIR measures. Figure 5.4 does indicate, however, that in those nations that are either pre-transition or undergoing the transition phase, more competitive regions are the exceptions to the rule. This is confirmed by the positive skewness statistics presented in Table 5.3, although it does not detract from the fact that there is considerable overlap in the competitiveness of regions within nations at all three stages of development.

These patterns are consistent with studies that find functional networks based around specific technologies to be international in nature (Foray, 2004), and which do not necessarily require innovative firms to be located in regions with strong national economies (Jaffe and Trajtenberg, 2002). Even where production requires greater spatial proximity of specialized labour forces and suppliers, production may not require a significantly high level of national development, given that the geographical proximity required is on a much smaller scale, as identified by the literature on agglomeration economies (van Oort, 2004) and clusters (Porter, 2000). Regions can increasingly attract skilled labour internationally, providing they are open and integrate foreign workers (Florida, 2002b; Raunio, 2007).

If regions in less developed nations continue to become more open economies, there is no reason to consider that they cannot continue to improve their competitiveness. Once a region begins to develop successful innovative firms, this process becomes reinforcing, with the prospect of agglomeration economies in the form of knowledge spillovers encouraging other knowledge-based enterprises to locate in the same location, further enhancing the knowledge spillovers present (Koo, 2005). This confirms the suggestion that in the modern globalized world, where global knowledge pipelines are equally as important as local sources (de Bruijn and van Oort, 2007), the national stage of development may become less relevant in defining the economic trajectory of regions. Instead, what may play a pivotal role is the extent to which international linkages with the world's most competitive regions are formalized (Saxenian, 2002; Huggins and Thompson, 2014).

Table 5.4 and Figure 5.5 show the absolute and relative contributions made to competitiveness by the four regional competitiveness components according to the stage of national development. Understandably, the average absolute values for the four components are higher in those regions situated in the more highly developed nations. The maximum and minimum values indicate that the highest values for regions in nations that have not entered the transition phase to becoming innovation driven are higher than those found in those regions with the lowest value for each component in innovation-driven countries. This reaffirms the case that in a globalized economy the most competitive regional economies are not necessarily located in the most highly developed nations as a whole.

Table 5.4 Absolute and relative contributions by individual components of the WCIR

		5th-wave knowledge capital	*4th-wave knowledge capital*	*Outputs/ outcomes*	*Knowl. sustain.*
Not in transition to innovation driven	Average absolute value	–0.50	–0.41	–0.72	–0.77
	Maximum absolute value	1.84	1.60	1.26	0.55
	Minimum absolute value	–0.81	–1.09	–2.07	–1.14
	Contribution	0.27	0.55	–0.34	–0.48
Transition to innovation driven	Average absolute value	–0.23	–0.15	–0.41	–0.61
	Maximum absolute value	1.04	0.60	3.44	1.40
	Minimum absolute value	–0.73	–0.74	–1.28	–1.01
	Contribution	1.13	1.80	–0.56	–2.37
Innovation driven	Average absolute value	0.26	0.19	0.41	0.52
	Maximum absolute value	2.86	2.20	2.49	2.46
	Minimum absolute value	–0.70	–0.62	–2.03	–1.11
	Contribution	–0.21	–0.37	0.16	0.42

Note: Knowl. sustain. = Knowledge sustainability.

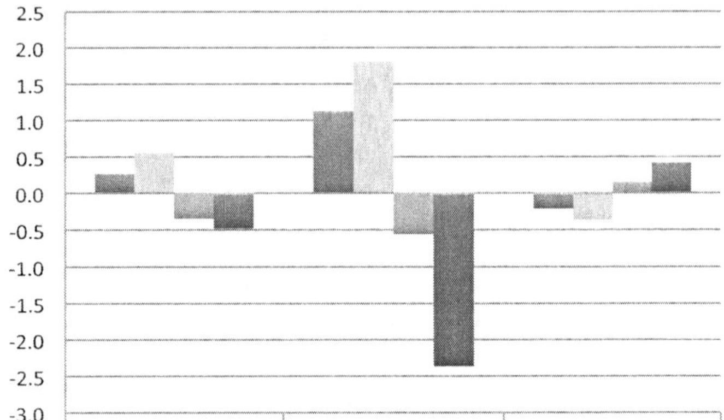

	Not In Transition to Innovation Driven	Transition to Innovation Driven	Innovation Driven
5th-wave knowledge capital	0.27	1.13	-0.21
4th-wave knowledge capital	0.55	1.80	-0.37
Outputs/Outcomes	-0.34	-0.56	0.16
Knowledge sustainability	-0.48	-2.37	0.42

Figure 5.5 Relative contribution of the WCIR components for each development group

The relative contributions for the four components provide an understanding of how regions have developed their overall competitiveness position, and the extent to which regions within nations at different stages of development are relying on particular components to improve their competitiveness. The difference in average contribution between those regions located in innovation-driven countries and the other regional groups is quite striking. In particular, those regions in the less highly developed nations appear to show more reliance on 5th- and 4th-wave knowledge capital sources. The innovation-driven nations are home to regions that place a higher level of reliance on sustainability. They are also better at converting their advantages into positive outcomes for their population in terms of higher labour productivity, gross earnings, and lower unemployment. As such, outcomes are also likely to be of importance in attracting talented staff (Ferguson *et al.*, 2007; Sasser, 2010). This greater emphasis on outcomes is likely to further increase sustainability, although, as Zheng *et al.* (2008) note, skills shortages in East Asian high-growth economies may still become an acute problem for regions and their firms in coming years.

Regions outside of the most developed nations have tended to pursue a pattern of development that relies more on drawing further knowledge from global pipelines, rather than developing it indigenously from scratch (Mathews, 2001). This may allow emerging regions to rapidly develop industries that provide 4th- and 5th-wave knowledge capital, especially by using policies to attract foreign direct investment (Wang and Lee, 2007).

Figure 5.6 shows that for those regions in nations starting the transition to becoming innovation driven there is a strong link between employment in industries associated with 4th-wave knowledge capital, such as mechanical engineering, and the automotive industry and the overall WCIR score. No such pattern is obvious for those regions in innovation-driven economies where there is less reliance on 4th-wave knowledge capital for competitiveness. This is understandable given that in many emerging economies these industries have become important for stimulating economic growth, particularly as these activities have migrated away from more advanced economic centres (Huggins and Izushi, 2007).

Similarly, when considering industries such as the IT and computer manufacturing sectors associated with 5th-wave knowledge capital, the link between employment in these sectors and overall competitiveness is again present for those regions in transition nations (Figure 5.7). Accessing knowledge through these sources, especially through the utilization of mechanisms such as FDI, is likely to allow regions in less developed countries to catch up considerably (Temple, 1999). However, as scholars such as Cohen and Levinthal (1990) and Lemoine and Ünal Kesenci (2004) have outlined, this will have limited potential without sufficient absorptive capacity.

Figure 5.8 shows that whilst there is some evidence of government spending on R&D rising with the level of national economic development, there are still many regions in innovation-driven nations with lower R&D spending per capita

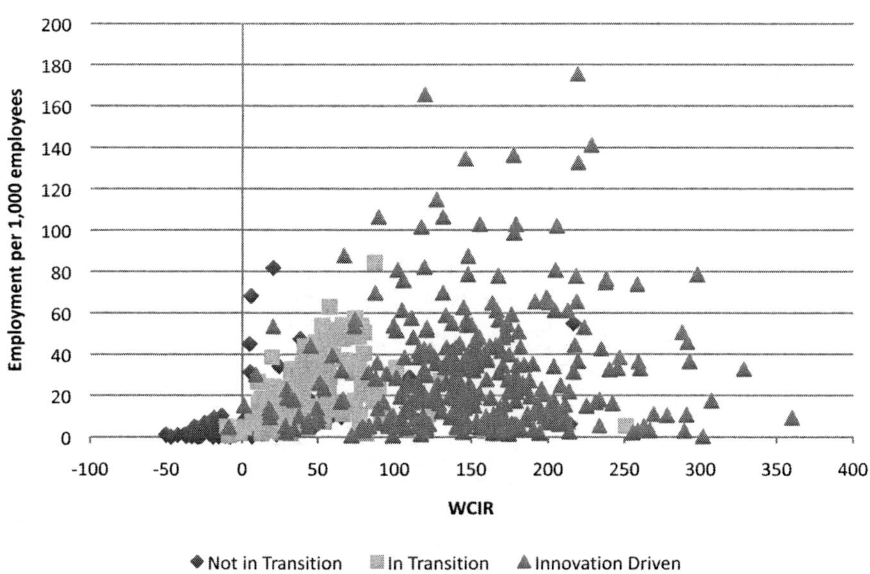

Figure 5.6 Employment in mechanical engineering and automotive industries per 1,000 employees by stage of development and WCIR

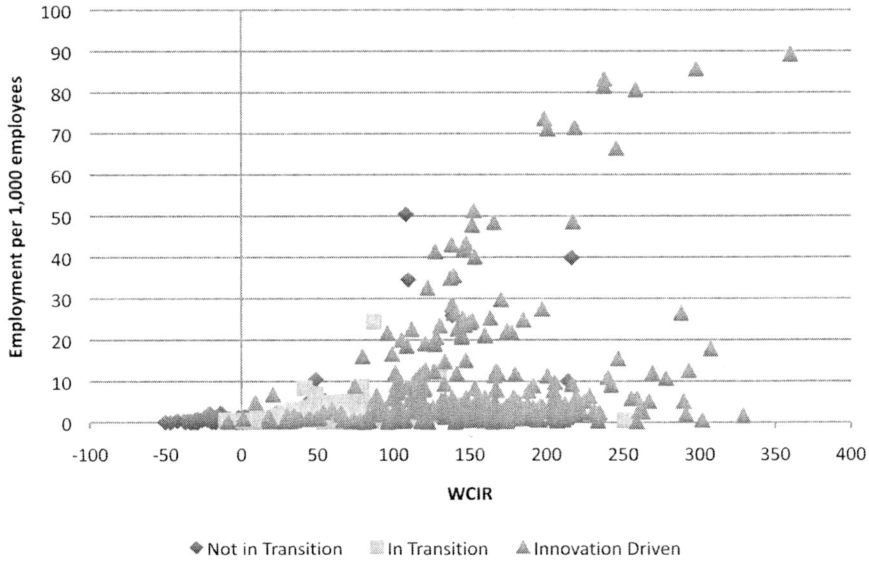

Figure 5.7 Employment in IT and computer manufacturing per 1,000 employees by stage of development and WCIR

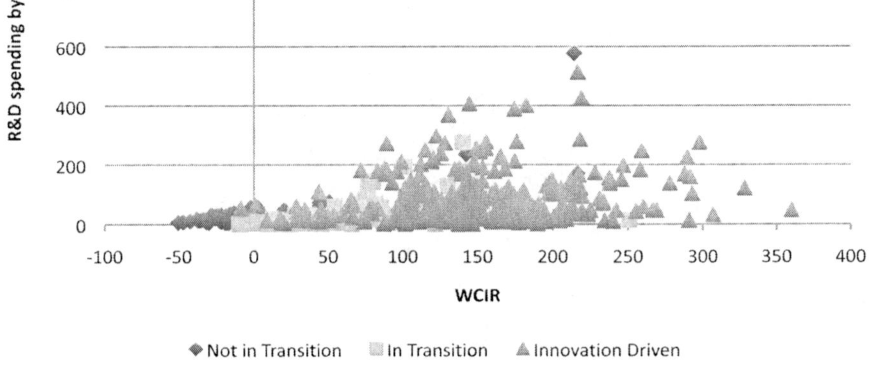

Figure 5.8 Government R&D spending per capita by stage of development and WCIR

than those regions in transition nations. Many regions have either chosen or not been able to increase R&D expenditure to the levels seen in innovation-driven economies. One explanation proposed for R&D activity being lower in lagging or less developed economies is the 'regional innovation paradox' (Oughton *et al.*, 2002). This paradox suggests that, whilst lagging regions require more spending to promote innovation (such as government R&D spending), firms and other actors in these regions are weaker at absorbing these funds effectively, in part due to other industrial policies that direct funds to more successful regions. This means that regional policymakers in lagging regions may not be able to pursue this pattern of encouraging R&D expenditure to achieve growth (Lewison, 1991). When considering private sector R&D spending (Figure 5.9) a clear link between such spending and competitiveness is found for regions in innovation-driven economies, which is likely to result in higher levels of regional GDP per capita (Howells, 2005).

Finally, Table 5.5 presents the Spearman rank correlation coefficients for the four indicators discussed above with the overall WCIR score for the regions grouped by their nation's level of development. It is clear that with the exception of employment in IT and computer manufacturing, the 4th- and 5th-wave knowledge capital indicators show a much greater link with competitiveness for those regional groups not belonging to innovation-driven economies. It is also noticeable that there is a strong link between competitiveness and R&D expenditure per capita across regions in non-innovation-driven nations.

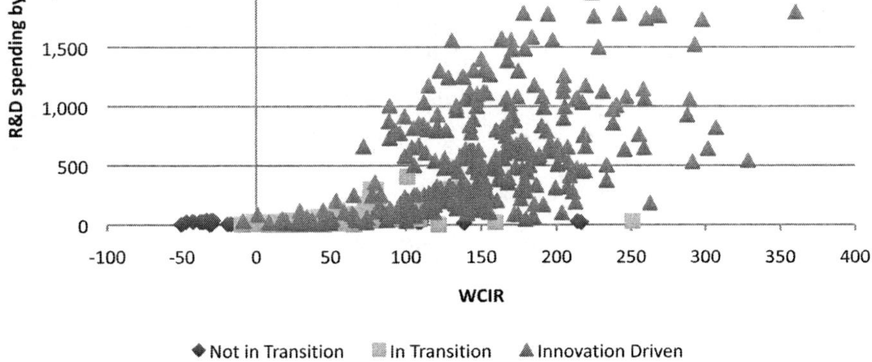

Figure 5.9 Private sector R&D spending per capita by stage of development and WCIR

Table 5.5 Correlation between 4th- and 5th-wave knowledge capital indicators and WCIR

	Employment in automotive and mechanical engineering[a]	*Employment in IT and computer manufacturing*[a]	*Per capita expenditures on R&D performed by government*	*Per capita expenditures on R&D performed by business*
All (N = 546)	0.517 (0.000)	0.789 (0.000)	0.375 (0.000)	0.542 (0.000)
Not in transition (N = 89)	0.190 (0.074)	0.554 (0.000)	0.671 (0.000)	0.576 (0.000)
In transition (N = 150)	0.564 (0.000)	0.560 (0.000)	0.446 (0.000)	0.530 (0.000)
Innovation driven (N = 307)	0.167 (0.003)	0.582 (0.000)	0.121 (0.033)	0.229 (0.000)

Notes: Spearman rank correlation coefficients, p-values in parenthesis.
[a] Per 1,000 employees.

Concluding remarks

This chapter has shown that in a globalized economic environment, regional competitiveness differences are not always related to national or geospatial characteristics, with regions undertaking economic change and evolution that is more related to their position within a global network of regions. Technological progress has clearly impacted on this network development with improvements in ICT facilitating new modes of knowledge exchange, heightening the propensity to penetrate international markets. Indeed, the apparent limits of globalization (Storper, 1992) are being stretched by new spaces of knowledge flow and the emergence of new regional centres. These knowledge bases are the primary spatial architecture underlying systems of innovation, and the interesting issue, which is the focus of the next chapter, is that this architecture is subject to evolutionary forces, with new key regional knowledge bases emerging around the globe as other more mature bases move into a period of decline.

Note

1 In subsequent chapters the same methodology is employed to identify the relative contribution of the competitiveness components across a range of regional groupings.

6 Regional evolution and waves of growth

The evolution of a regional economy and its competitiveness capacity may involve multiple independent trajectories through which different sets of resources and capabilities evolve together. However, there is a dearth of evidence concerning how these trends are occurring across the globe. This chapter seeks to present evidence, based on the WCIR variables, in relation to the recent development of the globe's most productive regions from the viewpoint of their growth trajectories, and the particular form of growth they are experiencing. The aim is to uncover the underlying structure of the changes in knowledge-based resources, capabilities and outputs across regions, in order to offer an analysis of these regions according to an uncovered set of key trends. From these trends the chapter identifies that regions are experiencing differing 'waves of growth' related to their overall economic evolution.

A number of theories, including agglomeration, industrial districts and clusters, as well as innovation systems, attempt to explain the way in which productive resources are combined and productivity is enhanced within a regional economy. In general, these concepts suggest a number of factors, such as industry structure, firm type and the geographical range of external economies, to explain regional economic evolution, with all of them highlighting the multiple trajectories that regions may follow in their development (Markusen, 1996; Phelps and Ozawa, 2003; Iammarino and McCann, 2006). Yet, while a large number of extant empirical studies resting on these theories are informative and useful in their own right, they are not always without shortcomings in light of the aim of uncovering an underlying structure of economic evolution and development across regions. For instance, a significant number of studies are designed to account for a specific dependent variable, such as GDP as a measure of economic output, or patents as a measure of innovation. This is typically achieved through the identification of a linear combination of other variables, which maximizes the proportion of the variance of the dependent variable they seek to explain. However, such accounting is different in its purpose and results from approaches that seek to identify a set of commonalities across variables. When variables represent the growth of resources, capabilities and outputs of regional innovation systems and economies, the commonalities identified across these variables may suggest processes of co-evolution across regions.

A further limitation of many extant studies is the lack of a common framework and dataset that is applicable to an analysis of regions across the globe. Empirical findings on innovation systems are typically initially generated on the basis of regions selected from a particular nation or continental bloc, rather than a fuller global coverage, resulting in a lack of harmony in terms of the frameworks employed, or the capability to provide regional comparisons that uncover regional trends across the globe (Doloreux and Parto, 2005). This chapter seeks to go some way to overcoming this particular shortcoming by examining the globe's most productive regions. This facilitates a better understanding of the connections between knowledge-based development and the fundamentals of economic development, such as job creation, at a regional level (Vivarelli and Pianta, 2000; Döpke, 2001).

The co-evolution of resources, capabilities and outputs

Based on the view of a region as an interlinked system, innovation systems theory proposes the co-evolution of its components (Freeman, 2002; Borrás, 2004; Heidenreich, 2004). However, there is little evidence concerning the key dimensions through which a region's resources, capabilities and outputs evolve together. Doloreux and Parto (2005) find that studies of regional innovation systems are typically designed either to offer 'snapshots' of individual regional innovation systems, or to specify desirable factors and mechanisms for promoting innovation through a comparison of regions. Surveying approximately 200 studies of regional innovation systems, Carlsson (2006) finds that slightly more than half are empirically oriented, focusing mostly on a particular region or multiple regions, with more than half of the empirical studies focusing solely on regions within Europe. A significant proportion of early studies are qualitative case studies that aim to provide a narrative on the intangible dimension of knowledge circulation and learning (Doloreux and Parto, 2005). More recently, a growing body of literature takes a quantitative approach, such as a knowledge production function model, to investigate regional innovation systems (Fritsch, 2002; Bilbao-Osorio and Rodríguez-Pose, 2004; Buesa *et al.*, 2006, 2010; Crescenzi *et al.*, 2007; Rodríguez-Pose and Crescenzi, 2008).

The aim of these studies is to account for a specific variable selected *a priori*, such as patents or GDP, and to examine the effects of variables representing innovation system characteristics. In these studies, variables are often measured only at one point in time, thus failing to show change over time. Such analyses are different in their aims and findings from approaches seeking to identify the co-evolution of the key components of regional economic systems. An exception to this is a recent study of four selected knowledge-based sectors across German regions by Buerger *et al.* (2012), who investigate the co-evolution of patents, R&D and employment, analysing panel data for these three variables with a vector autoregression model. The study finds that past innovation growth, as measured by patents, is associated with the subsequent growth of employment in certain sectors, suggesting that, in these sectors: the employment gains of innovators are greater than the losses of non-innovators; and, the labour-saving effects of process innovations are compensated for by other positive effects resulting from these innovations. However, the study focuses on a relatively small number of variables in selected knowledge-based sectors, leaving their relationships with other less knowledge-intensive sectors unexplored. Furthermore, the study concerns regions in a single nation. This latter point of limited regional coverage is shared by most qualitative case studies examining a single or only a few regions, as well as econometric studies that examine regions in a single nation (Buesa *et al.*, 2006), in Europe (Fritsch, 2002; Bilbao-Osorio and Rodríguez-Pose, 2004; Rodríguez-Pose and Crescenzi, 2008; Buesa *et al.*, 2010) or in Europe and the US (Crescenzi *et al.*, 2007).

There is, therefore, a gap in the literature in terms of identifying the co-evolution of regional economic system components at a global level. In order to achieve this, the analysis presented here seeks to combine theories of knowledge production and innovation systems (Fritsch, 2002; Cooke, 2004; Buesa *et al.*, 2006, 2010) with the wider economic systems underlying the production of goods and services, allowing an examination of the interrelationships among these components at a regional level. In particular, the impact of knowledge-based sectors upon the rest of their regional economy is likely to be influenced by how closely the former is tied to more traditional, less knowledge-intensive economic activity within the region through knowledge spillovers, as well as through input–output linkages and the multiplier effects of demand creation (Adams, 1990; Rodríguez-Pose and Crescenzi, 2008).

Data and analysis

The analysis reported in this chapter covers a subset of 117 regions included by the WCIR for which data are available for the 19 WCIR indicators plus GDP per capita at two time points, 2000/01 and 2010/11, or equivalent years. The analysis utilizes the compound annual growth rates across these two time periods. Of the 117 regions contained in the dataset there are 54 representatives from North America, 41 from Europe, and 22 from Asia and Pacific. Of the North American regions, 48 are US and 6 are Canadian. Among the Asian and Pacific regions, there are 7 Chinese regions (Taiwan is also included separately), 9 Japanese regions, and 3 Australian regions, as well as New Zealand and Singapore (a list of the regions covered by the analysis is presented in Appendix 3).

As the annual compound growth rates of the 20 indicators may overlap with one another, factor analysis is utilized to reduce the original set of variables into a smaller number of composite variables called ‘factors’. Each factor is a latent dimension underlying the original set of variables, presented as a condensed statement of the relationships between them. Furthermore, the position of a region in each dimension is given as a score called a factor score. The factors identified are orthogonal with one another and accordingly factor scores are uncorrelated across factors. With the use of the Anderson–Rubin method of estimation, factor scores have a mean of zero and a standard deviation of one. As for the extraction of factors and the rotation of a factor matrix, the maximum likelihood method and the varimax method are utilized. The maximum likelihood method provides the best statistical procedure as a goodness-of-fit test of the factor model (Gorsuch, 1983).

In the factor analysis, four variables—the growth rates for gross domestic product (GDP) per capita, public expenditures on primary and secondary education, secure servers, and broadband access—are dropped as they are found to conform to Heywood case variables. In factor analysis, the variance of each variable is divided into the variable's unique variance and the rest explained by latent factors. A Heywood case refers to the appearance of a negative estimate of the unique variance or the convergence of an estimate to zero, which is practically implausible. This computational anomaly often arises from the presence of one or more high correlations of variables and the attempt to extract more factors than are present (Bartholomew and Knott, 1999).

After these variables are removed, a reliable set of factors is obtained using the Schwarz (1978) method to determine the number of factors. A goodness-of-fit test of the factor model obtains a chi-squared value of 196.06 and a significance value of 0.00, showing a highly satisfactory level. Utilizing the factor score of each region, cluster analysis is then undertaken to establish a grouping of regions. Cluster analysis is the most commonly used technique for identifying groups of homogeneous objects within the population. This is achieved by maximizing the homogeneity of objects within the clusters, while also maximizing the heterogeneity between the clusters. Similarity between regions is defined by the Euclidian distance using their factors scores as coordinates. For a hierarchical clustering algorithm the average linkage procedure is adopted. The number of clusters is decided by examining changes in the agglomerative coefficients (Hair *et al.*, 2010).

Growth rates

The average growth rates of the 117 regions for the 20 indicators and their averages by nation or continental bloc – the US, Europe, Canada, Australia, Japan, and China – are shown in Table 6.1. When the averages of the regions are examined, per capita GDP reaches an annual growth rate of 4.18 per cent. The majority of this growth comes from the growth of labour productivity, which shows an annual growth of 2.95 per cent, whilst the rest derives from the growth of labour force participation relative to the total population. Economic activity rates grew at an annual rate of 1.25 per cent. In contrast, the employment rate dropped by 0.24 per cent on average. Thanks to the growth of labour productivity, mean gross monthly earnings grew at an annual rate of 5.67 per cent. However, the number of managers per 1,000 employees declined by 1.30 per cent annually, most likely due to the reduction of middle managers through the delayering of corporate hierarchies.

In terms of knowledge creation, the number of patents registered per 1,000 inhabitants grew by 11.39 per cent annually, which is an indication of a number of factors including changes made in patenting regimes in the 1990s and tactics

Table 6.1 Average compound annual growth rates of 20 variables from 2000/01 to 2010/11 or equivalent (percentage)

	US regions	*Canadian regions*	*European regions*	*Australian regions*	*Japanese regions*	*Chinese regions*	*All regions*
Gross domestic product per inhabitant	3.64	4.18	4.15	4.35	3.66	7.60	4.18
Labour productivity	2.39	2.63	3.46	3.07	1.88	4.89	2.95
Mean gross monthly earnings	7.20	4.68	5.53	1.62	6.97	–2.40	5.67
Economic activity rate	0.99	–0.04	0.21	0.42	1.92	10.09	1.25
Employment rate	–0.50	0.04	–0.15	0.14	0.07	0.06	–0.24
Number of managers [a]	–2.57	–6.52	2.00	5.17	–1.32	–11.89	–1.30
Number of patents registered [c]	2.00	5.09	10.78	13.66	26.88	59.84	11.39
Per capita expenditures on R&D performed by government	–30.31	–9.17	8.41	–1.22	13.95	–7.13	–9.20
Per capita expenditures on R&D performed by business	6.43	5.51	5.63	19.93	5.97	15.14	7.13
Employment in instrumentation and electrical machinery [a]	–5.79	0.70	17.22	–0.81	–1.72	19.13	4.78
Employment in automotive and mechanical engineering [a]	–8.49	–4.96	6.54	3.65	–2.13	16.60	–0.53
Employment in biotech and chemicals [a]	–4.07	0.90	–1.40	–12.50	–1.50	10.67	–2.05
Employment in IT and computer manufacturing [a]	–9.66	–20.94	–3.90	0.44	–2.82	16.64	–5.55
Employment in high-tech services [a]	–0.72	4.97	2.25	14.50	–2.31	29.17	2.77
Per capita public expenditures on primary and secondary education	7.36	2.69	6.23	6.91	–5.34	7.18	5.75
Per capita public expenditures on higher education	8.03	11.24	6.17	5.22	2.56	35.78	8.76
Venture capital ($ per capita)	–9.72	5.38	8.14	36.41	2.59	193.05	12.71
Internet hosts [b]	10.45	15.80	31.11	27.07	27.90	337.03	39.44
Secure servers [c]	15.70	18.76	35.19	27.84	28.96	317.60	42.55
Broadband access [b]	19.12	12.75	24.69	26.14	12.66	37.98	21.47

Notes: [a] Per 1,000 employees; [b] per 1,000 inhabitants; [c] per 1 million inhabitants.

of patent harvesting employed by a growing number of corporations, as well as a deepening of the knowledge economy. As for the inputs of knowledge creation, per capita expenditures on R&D performed by government dropped by 9.20 per cent annually, reflecting recent austerity measures taken by governments in many nations and regions. By contrast, per capita expenditures on R&D performed by business continued to grow, with an average annual growth rate of 7.13 per cent.

Changes in employment in high-technology industries vary significantly across the five sectors examined. The growth of employment in instrumentation and electrical machinery was the fastest, showing an annual growth rate of 4.78 per cent, followed by 2.77 per cent for high-tech services. By contrast, the other three sectors exhibit a decline in their employment per 1,000 employees. IT and computer manufacturing was hit the hardest with a decline of 5.55 per cent annually. This was followed by biotechnology and chemicals which declined by 2.05 per cent and automotive and mechanical engineering by 0.53 per cent.

As for public educational expenditures per inhabitant, expenditures on higher education grew by 5.75 per cent, whilst expenditures on primary and secondary education showed a more modest growth of 2.77 per cent annually. The amount of private equity investment, or venture capital, per inhabitant grew by 12.71 per cent annually, second only to the three ICT infrastructure indicators – internet hosts, secure servers, and broadband access – which showed the fastest rates of growth, 39.44 per cent, 42.55 per cent, and 21.47 per cent, respectively.

Against this overall picture, regions in the US, Europe, Canada, Australia, Japan, and China present differentiated patterns of growth. In terms of per capita GDP, the growth performance of Chinese regions is spectacular with an average rate of 7.60 per cent, which is in stark contrast to the rest of the regions analysed. Five Chinese regions – Beijing, Jiangsu, Tianjin, Shandong, and Guangdong – are in the top 10 of the fastest growing economies along with Singapore, British Columbia, Bratislavský kraj, Ontario, and Estonia. In contrast, regions in the US, Canada, Europe, Australia, and Japan grew at nearly half of the average rate achieved by Chinese regions. The slowest-growing regions are predominantly US, with six regions (Buffalo-Niagara Falls, Rochester, Grand Rapids-Wyoming, Richmond, Louisville, and Sacramento–Arden-Arcade–Roseville) ranking in the bottom 10, along with Alberta, Quebec, Saskatchewan, and Emilia-Romagna. Of these, Buffalo-Niagara Falls, Rochester, and Alberta have shown a fall in per capita GDP.

Productivity, earnings, and activity rates

Labour productivity growth has been most pronounced among Chinese regions, showing an average rate of 4.89 per cent. However, the gap with the rest of the regions, particularly European regions, is smaller than the gaps observed in per capita GDP growth. This is in large part due to a significant proportion of GDP growth in Chinese regions deriving from the inflow of labour from other parts of the nation, which is shown by the fast pace of growth in Chinese economic participation rates. For the rest of the regions analysed, European and Australian regions have shown relatively fast growth rates, whilst Japanese regions showed the slowest pace. The fastest rate of labour productivity growth was recorded by Bratislavský kraj and Praha, two central eastern European regions, with the rest of the top 10 regions consisting of Tianjin, Région de Bruxelles-Capitale, Singapore, London, Beijing, Shandong, Tokyo, and Estonia. By contrast, the bottom 10 regions include seven US regions (Buffalo-Niagara Falls, Rochester, Hartford-West Hartford-East Hartford, Richmond, Grand Rapids-Wyoming, San Antonio, and Sacramento–Arden-Arcade– Roseville), two Dutch regions (Noord-Nederland and Zuid-Nederland), and one Japanese region (Kanagawa).

Earnings growth shows a significantly different pattern from those of per capita GDP and labour productivity growth. Chinese regions have experienced a decline of 2.40 per cent annually, whilst the other nations or continental blocs have shown a positive average growth, with the US and Japanese regions in particular showing a strong performance. Latvia and Estonia are the best performers on this indicator, followed by five US regions (Salt Lake City, Houston-Sugar Land-Baytown, Nashville-Davidson–Murfreesboro–Franklin, Milwaukee-Waukesha-West Allis, and Virginia Beach-Norfolk-Newport News), two Japanese regions (Kanagawa and Kyoto), and Etelä-Suomi in Finland. The bottom 10 regions are dominated by Chinese regions (Beijing, Guangdong, Tianjin, Shanghai, and Zhejing), along with Israel, Taiwan, Sydsverige (Sweden), and two Australian regions (Victoria and New South Wales).

Changes observed in economic activity rates are relatively small with the exception of the Chinese regions. As mentioned earlier, the strong performance of the Chinese regions in GDP growth comes from the influx of the labour force into leading regions from other parts of the nation, resulting in a significant increase in economic activity rates in these regions. All seven Chinese regions are ranked in the top 10, followed by three US regions (Virginia Beach-Norfolk-Newport News, Miami-Fort Lauderdale-Miami Beach, and San Antonio). The Canadian and European regions are weak performers, on average, on this indicator.

Of the 117 regions analysed, 20 regions suffered a fall in economic activity rate, with the great majority of them being located in Europe and Canada. In particular, six regions in the Nordic nations (Västsverige, Stockholm, Småland med Öarna, and Sydsverige in Sweden, Etelä-Suomi in Finland, and Norway) rank in the bottom 10 regions, along with Ontario and three US regions (Cleveland-Elyria-Mentor, Salt Lake City, and Milwaukee-Waukesha-West Allis).

Across the 20 indicators, employment rates show the smallest change in percentage terms. The annual rate of change ranges from 0.14 per cent in the Australian regions to –0.50 per cent in the US regions. The largest improvement on this indicator is made by Israel (0.55 per cent), with Berlin (0.52 per cent) and Bratislavský kraj (0.34 per cent) being the second and third best performers. These are followed by Singapore, Schleswig-Holstein, Quebec, Osaka, Niedersachsen, Zhejing, and Western (Australia). The bottom 10 regions on this indicator consist of seven US regions (Las Vegas-Paradise, Detroit-Warren-Livonia, Sacramento–Arden-Arcade–Roseville, Tampa-St. Petersburg-Clearwater, Hartford-West Hartford-East Hartford, Charlotte-Gastonia-Concord, and

Jacksonville), two Spanish regions (Comunidad de Madrid and Noreste), and Southern and Eastern in Ireland. Las Vegas-Paradise, Comunidad de Madrid, and Southern and Eastern (Ireland) suffered an annual rate of at least –1.00 per cent.

Human capital and innovation

The number of managers per 1,000 employees is another indicator in which the Chinese regions showed the weakest performance, followed by the Canadian, US, and Japanese regions. The fall in the Chinese regions is most likely due to the massive inflow of labour across regions, which filled newly-created low-level, non-managerial positions. By contrast, the fall in the Canadian, US, and Japanese regions appears to derive from the flattening of corporate organizational hierarchies, which cut back middle management positions. Against the trend, the European and Australian regions exhibit an increase overall, with the top 10 regions being predominantly European, including Saarland, Schleswig-Holstein, Nordrhein-Westfalen, and Niedersachsen in Germany, Lazio and Emilia-Romagna in Italy, Småland med Öarna (Sweden), Switzerland, Région de Bruxelles-Capitale, and Lithuania. The bottom 10 regions include four Chinese regions (Tianjin, Shanghai, Guangdong, and Jiangsu) along with West-Nederland, Bratislavský kraj, Közép-Magyarország, Île de France, and Noreste and Comunidad de Madrid.

Growth rates for patent registrations show that Chinese regions have seen the greatest improvement. The fastest ten growth rates include seven Chinese regions, followed by three Japanese regions: Aichi; Toyama; and Tochigi. In contrast, North American regions achieved the slowest average growth. With the exception of London, which suffered the fastest pace of decline (–3.72 per cent), the bottom 10 regions are dominated by North American regions, including Memphis, Nashville-Davidson–Murfreesboro–Franklin, Indianapolis, Columbus, Cincinnati-Middletown, Cleveland-Elyria-Mentor, and Milwaukee-Waukesha-West Allis in the US, and Manitoba and British Columbia in Canada, all of which have seen a fall on this indicator.

In terms of R&D expenditures, those regions in receipt of the biggest increases in R&D expenditures performed by government are regions in Japan and Europe. The top three regions are Swedish (Småland med Öarna, Sydsverige, and Västsverige), followed by four Japanese regions (Shiga, Kyoto, Toyama, and Shizuoka), Zuid-Nederland in the Netherlands, Noreste in Spain, and Singapore. Conversely, US, Canadian, and the Australian regions have seen a dilution of government R&D investment. In particular, the drop in government R&D investment was large in the US regions, which occupy the bottom 10 positions (Hartford-West Hartford-East Hartford, Kansas City, Buffalo-Niagara Falls, Rochester, Minneapolis-St. Paul-Bloomington, St. Louis, Pittsburgh, Seattle-Tacoma-Bellevue, Louisville, and Las Vegas-Paradise).

As for R&D investment by businesses, the Australian and Chinese regions have seen by far the strongest growth on the whole, with the biggest growth occurring in Western Australia and Victoria in the former, and Shandong, Jiangsu,

Zhejing, and Tianjin in the latter. The other top 10 regions are Estonia, Singapore, Raleigh-Cary, and Alberta. Across all regions, eight have seen a drop in business R&D investment, including Baltimore-Towson and Seattle-Tacoma-Bellevue in the US, Ontario and Manitoba in Canada, Kanagawa and Osaka in Japan, Bratislavský kraj in the Slovak Republic, and Beijing in China. Västsverige and Stockholm in Sweden are the other two in the bottom 10 regions, showing only a marginal increase.

Industrial development

As shown by Table 6.1, there is significant volatility in employment change across the knowledge-based sectors. In the instrumentation and electrical machinery sector, Chinese and European regions have seen strong growth, with the top 10 spots occupied by Jiangsu, Zhejing, and Shandong (China), Estonia, Ostösterreich (Austria), Lazio (Italy), Stockholm (Sweden), Région de Bruxelles-Capitale (Belgium), Etelä-Suomi (Finland), and Zuid-Nederland (Netherlands). In contrast, a significant proportion of US and Japanese regions have seen a decline in these sectors. With the exception of Switzerland, all the bottom 10 regions are located in the US, consisting of Memphis, Louisville, Baltimore-Towson, Nashville-Davidson–Murfreesboro–Franklin, St. Louis, Atlanta-Sandy Springs-Marietta, Charlotte-Gastonia-Concord, San Antonio, and Kansas City.

In the automotive and mechanical engineering sector, the majority of regions have seen a decline in employment as a proportion of total regional employment. Those regions showing growth are predominantly European and Chinese, with the top 10 regions including Zhejing, Jiangsu, Shandong, and Guangdong in China, as well as Bratislavský kraj, Stockholm, Västsverige, Région de Bruxelles-Capitale, Saarland, and Norway. As for the regions that have been hit hardest, Beijing is the worst with an annual change of –23.54 per cent. Aside from the Chinese capital, those regions suffering the fastest pace of decline are predominantly US, including Washington-Arlington-Alexandria, Nashville-Davidson–Murfreesboro–Franklin, Louisville, Atlanta-Sandy Springs-Marietta, St. Louis, San Jose-Sunnyvale-Santa Clara, Columbus, Buffalo-Niagara Falls, and Kansas City.

In a similar vein, less than one third of regions have seen proportional employment growth in the biotechnology and chemicals sectors. Chinese regions are the best performers in this sector, with Jiangsu, Shandong, Zhejing, and Guangdong ranking in the top 10. Canadian regions also gain in these sectors, with Saskatchewan and Manitoba in the top 10 positions. Although the average growth of the US and European regions is negative, some have performed well, with Région de Bruxelles-Capitale, Saarland, Minneapolis-St. Paul-Bloomington, and Île de France occupying the other top 10 spots. Of those regions which have seen a fall in employment in these sectors, the worst 10 include seven US regions (Richmond, Virginia Beach-Norfolk-Newport News, Charlotte-Gastonia-Concord, Columbus, Nashville-Davidson–Murfreesboro–Franklin, Rochester, and San Antonio), two Australian (New South Wales and Victoria), and New Zealand.

As mentioned earlier, of the five knowledge-based sectors, IT and computer manufacturing was hit hardest in terms of the share of employment, with only 24 regions showing positive growth rates. Regions in China gained most, which gives a strong indication of the extent to which employment has become increasingly concentrated in key locations. The top 10 regions include four Chinese regions (Jiangsu, Shandong, Zhejing, and Guangdong) along with Jacksonville and Louisville, Saarland, Switzerland, Taiwan, and Praha. Over 30 regions have witnessed a double-digit fall in employment share in percentage terms annually. Of these, those hit hardest include Virginia Beach-Norfolk-Newport News, Nashville-Davidson–Murfreesboro–Franklin, Baltimore-Towson, Sacramento–Arden-Arcade–Roseville, Charlotte-Gastonia-Concord, Houston-Sugar Land-Baytown, and San Antonio in the US, as well as Saskatchewan, Manitoba, and Zuid-Nederland.

As for high-tech services, the regions analysed are relatively evenly split into those 57 regions that have gained and those 60 that have lost in terms of employment share. The pattern is somewhat surprising, as one might expect more widely spread growth resulting from the increased deindustrialization of advanced regional economies. However, growth in the offshoring of high-technology services in many advanced regions appears to have dampened employment growth. Of the former group, 13 regions have seen double-digit growth annually. The top 10 includes five Chinese regions (Zhejing, Shandong, Tianjin, Shanghai, and Guangdong) and three Australian regions (New South Wales, Western, and Victoria), as well as Région de Bruxelles-Capitale and Switzerland. The worst performing regions are Vlaams Gewest, Shiga, and Kanagawa, followed by two Dutch regions (Noord-Nederland and West-Nederland), four US regions (Chicago-Naperville-Joliet, San Antonio, Atlanta-Sandy Springs-Marietta, and Houston-Sugar Land-Baytown), and Lombardia in Italy.

Knowledge sustainability and finance

In terms of growth in public expenditure on primary and secondary education, the great majority of the analysed regions recorded an increase, led by Irish, Chinese, and US regions. The top 10 regions include Southern and Eastern (Ireland), Shandong, Jiangsu, Zhejing, Orlando-Kissimmee, Washington-Arlington-Alexandria, Phoenix-Mesa-Scottsdale, and Las Vegas-Paradise, as well as Latvia and Singapore, which all have recorded double-digit annual growth rates. By contrast, only 12 regions have seen a fall in this indicator, including three Chinese regions (Beijing, Tianjin, and Guangdong) and all nine Japanese regions analysed.

In a similar vein, except for five regions, all analysed regions recorded an increase in expenditure on higher education. The fastest growth is shown by Chinese and Canadian regions, with all seven Chinese regions and Ontario ranking in the top 10, along with Southern and Eastern (Ireland) and Praha. As for those regions experiencing falls in expenditure, they include Buffalo-Niagara

Falls, Rochester, Scotland, Israel, and Latvia. These regions are followed by Switzerland, New York-Northern New Jersey-Long Island, Seattle-Tacoma-Bellevue, Westösterreich (Austria), and Emilia-Romagna, which have all shown only a marginal increase in expenditure.

Growth in private equity investment shows a significant contrast between Chinese regions and US regions. It is clear that the biggest growth has occurred in Chinese regions, which occupy the top seven spots in the rankings, followed by Taiwan, New South Wales, and Victoria in Australia. In the US, the traditional heartland of venture capital, most regions have seen a fall in levels of such capital investment. Of the all regions analysed, 30 regions have shown a double-digit decline in percentage terms, with only two regions (Latvia and Bratislavský kraj) being outside the US. Those US regions that have seen the largest falls include Hartford-West Hartford-East Hartford, Louisville, Orlando-Kissimmee, Jacksonville, Tampa-St. Petersburg-Clearwater, Miami-Fort Lauderdale-Miami Beach, Memphis, Phoenix-Mesa-Scottsdale, Milwaukee-Waukesha-West Allis, and Las Vegas-Paradise.

Finally, for the three ICT infrastructure indicators, Chinese regions have made the greatest strides in ICT development. In particular, the Chinese regions have achieved a three-digit growth in percentage terms in internet host per capita and secure servers per capita, dominating the top 10 rankings. They are followed by Bratislavský kraj, Praha, and Lithuania in the growth of internet hosts, and by Bratislavský kraj, Praha, and Taiwan in the growth of secure servers. European, Australian, and Japanese regions have shown modest growth in both internet hosts and secure servers, occupying middle positions in the rankings. In contrast, US and Canadian regions show a slower rate of growth. The bottom 10 regions include two Canadian regions (Manitoba and Saskatchewan) and eight US regions (San Antonio, Buffalo-Niagara Falls, Tampa-St. Petersburg-Clearwater, Grand Rapids-Wyoming, Rochester, Detroit-Warren-Livonia, Jacksonville, and Louisville). Such findings may be expected given that many US and Canadian regions already possess high levels of connectivity.

The growth of broadband access is led by the Chinese regions, although their growth rates are more comparable with those shown by European and Australian regions. The top 10 spots are populated by Chinese and European (mostly Central European) regions, including Beijing, Shanghai, Guangdong, and Zhejing in China, and Bratislavský kraj, Praha, Southern and Eastern (Ireland), Közép-Magyarország, and Lithuania in Europe, as well as Ontario. In Europe, Swedish regions are anomalies to this trend, with Småland med Öarna, Sydsverige, and Västsverige occupying three of the bottom 10 spots. In addition, Japanese and Canadian regions have shown weak growth in the diffusion of broadband access. Aside from the three Swedish regions, Manitoba, Saskatchewan, Kanagawa, and Kyoto enter the list of the bottom 10 regions. Taiwan, Israel, and Singapore are also in the bottom 10 list.

Waves of growth: Factor analysis

Utilizing the results of the factor analysis, the original variables are reduced to three factors, each of which represents a unique combination of the original variables. The three identified factors explain 64.50 per cent of the total variance, a satisfactory level, given the fact that more than 100 regions are included, with the subsequent analysis focusing on those variables with a loading of ±0.40 (Gorsuch, 1983).

As shown by Table 6.2, Factor 1 indicates a close association between the growth of high-tech services employment, internet hosts, venture capital, patent registration, and public expenditures on higher education. Growth in economic activity rates and falls in mean gross monthly earnings rates are also significantly loaded on this factor. This factor is labelled 'Fifth-wave Growth' as it indicates a close association between ICT-based service growth, growth in knowledge outputs, and growth in key knowledge-based investments.

Table 6.2 Factor loadings of the variables

	1 (5th-wave growth)	*2 (3rd- and 4th-wave growth)*	*3 Government-led (3rd-wave growth)*
Labour productivity	0.20	0.22	0.20
Mean gross monthly earnings	***–0.69***	0.11	–0.24
Economic activity rate	***0.80***	***0.45***	–0.18
Employment rate	0.20	0.14	***0.52***
Number of managers [a]	–0.33	–0.11	0.33
Number of patents registered [c]	***0.65***	***0.53***	0.20
Per capita expenditures on R&D performed by government	0.00	0.12	***0.73***
Per capita expenditures on R&D performed by business	0.22	0.34	0.03
Employment in instrumentation and electrical machinery [a]	0.06	***0.54***	***0.64***
Employment in automotive and mechanical engineering [a]	0.12	***0.68***	***0.60***
Employment in biotech and chemicals [a]	0.12	***0.75***	0.11
Employment in IT and computer manufacturing [a]	0.29	***0.50***	0.21
Employment in high tech services [a]	***0.57***	0.36	0.21
Per capita public expenditures on higher education	***0.73***	0.36	–0.15
Venture capital ($ per capita)	***0.93***	0.13	0.19
Internet hosts [b]	***0.90***	***0.42***	0.08

Notes: Factor loadings greater than 0.40 or lower than –0.40 are shown in bold italics.
[a] Per 1,000 employees; [b] per 1,000 inhabitants; [c] per 1 million inhabitants.

Based on Nikolai Kondratieff's work (1926, 1935) on the cycle of major economic crises at approximately half-century intervals, Joseph Schumpeter (1939) wrote that each of the 'long waves' of economic development starts with a new group of innovations, which results in the creation of new industries. According to this long-wave theory, the first Kondratieff wave was based on iron and cotton industries, spanning the period 1785–1842. This is followed by the second wave (1843–1897) with steel, machine tools, and shipbuilding as its key industries. The twentieth century includes two waves: the third wave (1896–1947) based on automotive, electrical engineering, and chemicals; and the fourth wave (1948–) for which growth was propelled by electronics, computers, communications, aerospace, and producer services (Hall and Preston, 1988). Whilst the timing of the fourth wave's end and the fifth wave's beginning remains open to debate, ranging from the early 1990s to around the turn of the century, there is much agreement as to the central role played by the digital revolution and the internet as the enabling innovation underpinning the fifth wave, creating a large increase in informational service jobs, as well as new infrastructural network development (Hall and Preston, 1988; Wymbs, 2004; Devezas *et al.*, 2005; Linstone and Devezas, 2012).

The close association identified between employment in high-tech services and internet hosts, as well as private equity investment capital, signifies the newest wave of economic development. Also, the association with patents strengthens its representation as a fifth wave, especially as patents are found to grow during a long-wave upswing (Korotayev *et al.*, 2011). Of course, our analysis cannot be said to infer causality, but at an exploratory level it does suggest that across this cohort of leading regions in both established and emerging economies the trajectory of knowledge-based service sectors and patents generally moves in the same direction as growth in venture capital, as well as investment in ICT infrastructure and higher education, chiming with the propositions of innovation systems theory.

The second factor mainly represents employment growth in the four knowledge-intensive manufacturing sectors and growth in patent registration, with growth in internet hosts and economic activity rates also marginally loaded. We label this factor 'Third- and Fourth-wave Growth', as those manufacturing sectors represent leading industries in the third and fourth waves. As for the third factor, highly loaded variables include growth in R&D expenditures performed by business and employment in automotive and mechanical engineering, as well as instrumentation and electrical machinery. Growth in employment rates (namely, a decline in the unemployment rate) is also significantly loaded on this factor. We call this factor 'Government-led Third-wave Growth', suggesting a close association between public R&D spending growth and growth in third wave manufacturing sectors. The loading for employment rate growth may also be interpreted as a sign of an interventionist approach taken by government in job creation and its association with the older generation of knowledge-intensive manufacturing sectors.

Waves of growth: Cluster analysis

Following the factor analysis, cluster analysis is undertaken to identify groups of regions. Regions within a group are close to one another according to the distance defined by their factor scores. Figures 6.1 and 6.2 show the identified 13 groups of regions in three-dimensional space consisting of the three factors. Chinese regions are clearly set apart from the rest of the regions in terms of their extremely high values for Fifth-wave Growth. Furthermore, the Chinese regions show much wider variations in their values for the Third- and Fourth-wave Growth than the rest of the regions. As a result, each of the seven Chinese regions forms a cluster of its own.

By construct, the Fifth-wave Growth and the Third- and Fourth-wave Growth are necessarily orthogonal, with their values showing no correlation. However, in Figure 6.1, the Chinese regions show a pattern of negative association between the Fifth-wave Growth and the Third- and Fourth-wave Growth. In a similar vein, the negative association is replicated among the rest of the regions as well, meaning that those regions showing faster growth in high-tech service employment, venture capital, and public expenditure on higher education tend to exhibit slower growth, or even falls, in employment in the four knowledge-intensive manufacturing industries.

In the close-up section of Figure 6.1, which focuses on the distribution of non-Chinese regions, a few clusters are identified at the opposite corners, with a three-region cluster of New South Wales, Victoria, and Taiwan and a single-region cluster of Nashville-Davidson–Murfreesboro–Franklin in the right-hand bottom, and a two-region cluster of Estonia and Latvia in the left-hand top. As for the rest of the non-Chinese regions, although there is a significant overlap, US regions tend to be situated in the right-hand bottom, with European regions in the left-hand top, and Japanese regions occupying the middle ground.

The US and European regions are clearly separated in terms of Government-led Third-wave Growth, as shown by Figure 6.2. All US regions, except for Nashville-Davidson–Murfreesboro–Franklin and Salt Lake City, form a cluster situated at the bottom, along with Saskatchewan (Canada) and Kanagawa (Japan). There is an independent cluster of three Swedish regions (Småland med Öarna, Västsverige, and Sydsverige) situated at the top, with the rest of the regions forming another large cluster, consisting mainly of European, Japanese, and Canadian regions. Clearly the two large clusters are differentiated in terms of Government-led Third-wave Growth, with the European cluster showing faster growth than the US cluster.

Four key findings emerge from the results. First, there is a spread of knowledge-based resources in the form of human capital formation, knowledge production, and entrepreneurial investment, as well as overall economic growth in GDP and labour productivity, in regional economies within China. In the three key growth trends identified, Chinese regions stand out from the rest in terms of Fifth-wave and Third- and Fourth-wave Growth. In terms of the Fifth-wave Growth, all seven Chinese regions grew at a faster pace than the rest of the regions analysed.

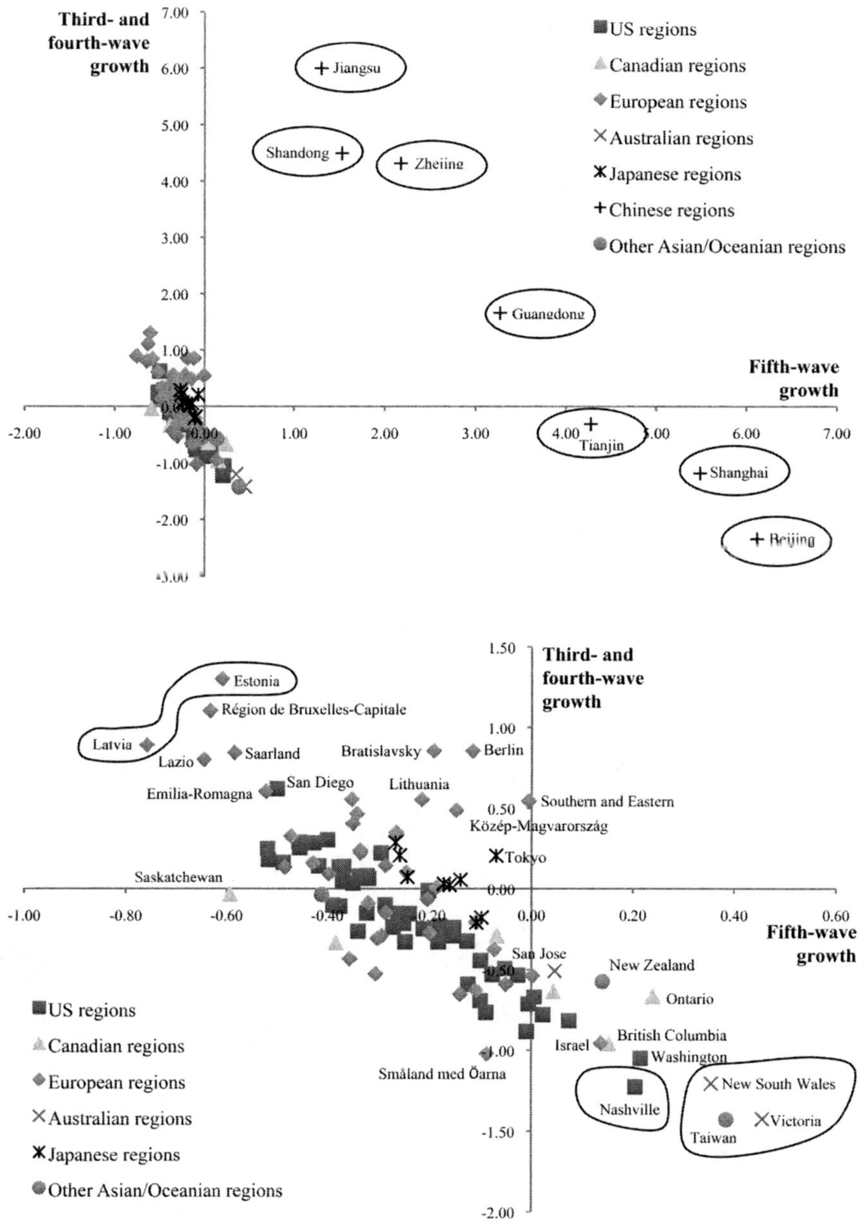

Figure 6.1 Regions and waves of growth

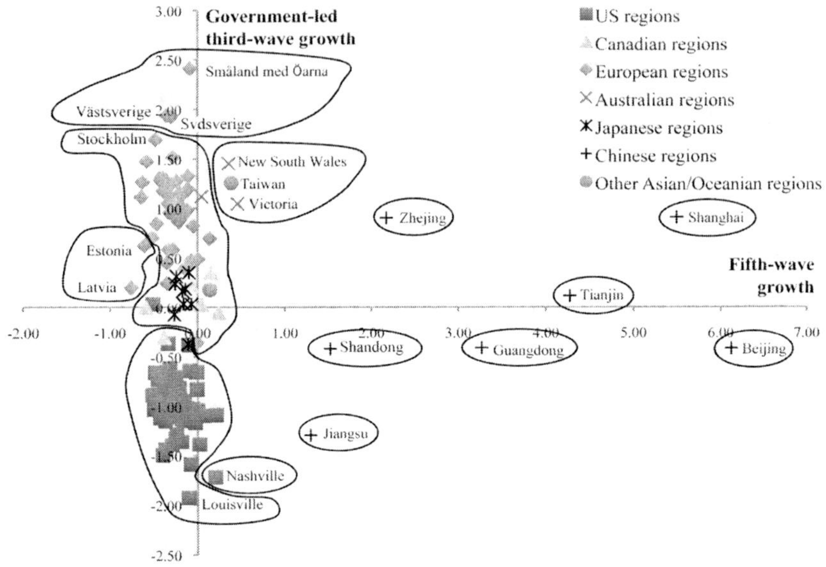

Cluster 1: Beijing
Cluster 2: Shanghai
Cluster 3: Tianjin
Cluster 4: Guangdong
Cluster 5: Zhejing
Cluster 6: Shanghai
Cluster 7: Shandong
Cluster 8: New South Wales, Victoria (Australia), Taiwan
Cluster 9: Nashville-Davidson–Murfreesboro–Franklin (US)
Cluster 10: Atlanta-Sandy Springs-Marietta, Austin-Round Rock, Baltimore-Towson, Boston-Cambridge-Quincy, Buffalo-Niagara Falls, Charlotte-Gastonia-Concord, Chicago-Naperville-Joliet, Cincinnati-Middletown, Cleveland-Elyria-Mentor, Columbus, Dallas-Fort Worth-Arlington, Denver-Aurora, Detroit-Warren-Livonia, Grand Rapids-Wyoming, Greensboro-High Point, Hartford-West Hartford-East Hartford, Houston-Sugar Land-Baytown, Indianapolis, Jacksonville, Kansas City, Las Vegas-Paradise, Los Angeles-Long Beach-Santa Ana, Louisville, Memphis, Miami-Fort Lauderdale-Miami Beach, Milwaukee-Waukesha-West Allis, Minneapolis-St. Paul-Bloomington, New York-Northern New Jersey-Long Island, Orlando-Kissimmee, Philadelphia-Camden-Wilmington, Phoenix-Mesa-Scottsdale, Pittsburgh, Portland-Vancouver-Beaverton, Raleigh-Cary, Richmond, Rochester, Sacramento–Arden-Arcade–Roseville, San Antonio, San Diego-Carlsbad-San Marcos, San Francisco-Oakland-Fremont, San Jose-Sunnyvale-Santa Clara, Seattle-Tacoma-Bellevue, St. Louis, Tampa-St. Petersburg-Clearwater, Virginia Beach-Norfolk-Newport News, Washington-Arlington-Alexandria (US), Saskatchewan (Canada), Kanagawa (Japan)
Cluster 11: Salt Lake City (US), Alberta, British Columbia, Manitoba, Ontario, Quebec (Canada), Région de Bruxelles-Capitale, Vlaams Gewest (Belgium), Baden-Württemberg, Bayern, Berlin, Hessen, Niedersachsen, Nordrhein-Westfalen, Saarland, Schleswig-Holstein (Germany), Noreste, Comunidad de Madrid (Spain), Île de France, Centre-Est (France), Southern and Eastern (Ireland), Emilia-Romagna, Lazio, Lombardia (Italy), Noord-Nederland, West-Nederland, Zuid-Nederland (Netherlands), Ostösterreich, Westösterreich (Austria), Etelä-Suomi (Finland), Stockholm (Sweden), Eastern, London, Scotland, South East (UK), Bratislavsky (Slovak Republic), Közép-Magyarország (Hungary), Praha (Czech Republic), Lithuania, Norway, Switzerland, Israel, Western (Australia), Aichi, Kyoto, Osaka, Shiga, Shizuoka, Tochigi, Tokyo, Toyama (Japan), New Zealand, Singapore
Cluster 12: Sydsverige, Västsverige, Småland med Öarna (Sweden)
Cluster 13: Estonia, Latvia

Figure 6.2 Fifth-wave growth and government-led third-wave growth

Among the more established regions, many of those showing relatively strong performance in terms of Fifth-wave Growth are located around the Pacific Rim, such as Victoria, New South Wales, Taiwan, and New Zealand, indicating that they enjoy an opportunity for the offshoring of labour-intensive operations to China, as well as robust demand from within the Chinese economy. As for Third- and Fourth-wave Growth, again, four of the seven Chinese regions (Jiangsu, Shandong, Zhejing, and Guangdong) grew faster than all the non-Chinese regions. Across the non-Chinese regions, those showing the strongest performance are to a large extent concentrated in Eastern Europe, including Estonia, Latvia, Bratislavský kraj, Praha, Lithuania, and Közép-Magyarország. Overall, a continued shift of knowledge-based resources and capabilities to the East can be observed, or what can be termed the globalization of knowledge-based development.

Second, a bipolar development can be observed with regard to Fifth-wave Growth on the one hand and Third- and Fourth-wave Growth on the other. As mentioned earlier, Fifth-wave Growth and Third- and Fourth-wave Growth are orthogonal, with their values showing no association. This means that, at the global scale, a region's position on Fifth-wave Growth shows no indication of its position on Third- and Fourth-wave Growth, and vice versa. However, as shown in Figure 6.1, when the Chinese regions and the non-Chinese regions are divided into two separate groups, we observe in each of the groups a close negative association between the values for Fifth-wave Growth and Third- and Fourth-wave Growth, meaning that a region with faster growth in high-tech service employment and venture capital formation tends to show slower growth (or a faster fall) in knowledge-intensive manufacturing employment, and vice versa. Whilst the speed at which this development has taken place is much faster within the Chinese regions, what is common between the two groups of regions is growing sector specialization in either high-tech services accompanied by venture capital formation, or knowledge-intensive manufacturing.

Third, sector specialization emerges as one of the three key trends by which the economic evolution and growth patterns of leading regions across the globe are differentiated. In addition to the first two factors, the third factor concerns employment change in Third-wave manufacturing industries, automotive and mechanical engineering, as well as instrumentation and electrical machinery. Within this Government-led Third-wave Growth, two large clusters – the US-centric cluster and the Europe-centric cluster – are identified, along with a few much smaller clusters at the fringe.

Fundamentally, the superstructure identified by the analysis is based on sector specialization, and is in contrast to an observation from an earlier period at the turn of the new century. In an earlier study covering the period from 2001/02 to 2004/05 (Huggins and Izushi, 2013), it is found that the key trends differentiating the globe's most productive regions are not sector employment change but a commonality between GDP growth, gross monthly earnings, and business R&D, as well as labour market growth. This change in the identified factors may indicate that leading regions have been in the process of repositioning themselves in the global value chain through sector specialization, in response to the major shocks including the bursting of the dotcom bubble in 2001 and the more recent Lehman shock in 2008.

Last, but not least, the factor analysis presented above does not suggest the insignificance of labour productivity growth as an indicator of knowledge-based growth. In Table 6.2, labour productivity is conspicuously not loaded on any of the three factors strongly. However, this means that labour productivity growth is not associated with any one of the three diverging sector employment changes alone, but it is to a great extent evenly associated with all three sector employment changes. Technical progress appears to have taken place in each of the sectors associated with the three factors, and by design the factor analysis identifies commonalities orthogonal to, or independent of, each other, resulting in labour productivity not being strongly loaded on any of the factors. In a similar vein, the growth of private R&D expenditure is not loaded strongly on any of the three factors, although an analysis regressing labour productivity growth shows that it is closely associated with the growth of private R&D expenditure.

Concluding remarks

It is widely observed that the global geography of innovation is rapidly evolving. This chapter presents evidence concerning the contemporary evolution of the globe's most productive regions, uncovering the underlying structure and co-evolution of knowledge-based resources, capabilities and outputs across these regions. The analysis identifies three key trends by which the economic evolution and growth patterns of regions are differentiated – namely Fifth-wave Growth, Third- and Fourth-wave Growth, and Government-led Third-wave Growth. Overall, spectacular knowledge-based growth in leading Chinese regions is evident, highlighting a continued shift of knowledge-based resources to Asia. In addition, a superstructure is observed at the global scale, consisting of two separate continuums that explicitly distinguish Chinese regions from the rest in terms of regional growth trajectories.

7 The competitiveness of European regions

The rapidly changing pattern of regional competitiveness across the globe, as captured by the WCIR indicators, has been explored in previous chapters, making it clear that many regions outside the Western economies of Europe and North America are increasingly coming to the fore. The analysis presented in the preceding chapters provide a potential explanation for the perceived troubles experienced by the European regions, which are viewed as lagging their counterparts in the US (Gardiner *et al.*, 2004). In general, the evolutionary nature of regional development is considered to have made it difficult for many European regions to adapt sufficiently to the accelerating process of globalization (Camagni and Capello, 2012).

For some European regions, the process of increased international trade and the move to a global supply chain has created opportunities, with these regions possessing the resources, and following a path of development, that has allowed them to utilize the outsourcing process to their own advantage (Affuso *et al.*, 2011). Other regions within Europe, however, have suffered as their strengths have been less suited to institutional change, which has further weakened their prospects (Sacchetti and Tomlinson, 2009). Nevertheless, studies have shown that it is possible to overcome the difficulties imposed by prior economic development, to re-emerge and regain competitiveness (Power *et al.*, 2010), implying that the outlook for struggling European regions need not be as bleak as is sometimes portrayed.

This chapter concentrates upon the competitiveness of the European regions surveyed by the WCIR. An analysis of the components of the WCIR helps to facilitate an understanding of which European regions are best placed to exploit the new global economy that will emerge from the financial crisis, as well as insights into those regions that are struggling to re-establish their position.

The chapter provides an overview of the most and least competitive European regions covered by the WCIR. In order to understand the extent to which regions have been able to withstand, or otherwise, the economic buffeting from the financial crisis of 2007, those regions displaying the greatest changes in competitiveness ranking since 2008 are explored. The chapter also examines the differing nature of the regions within Europe based on the underlying components of the WCIR. As with the previous chapter, this analysis seeks to better understand the evolutionary nature of European regions, particularly in relation to the regional development policies adopted at a national and supranational level.

Patterns and change in European regional competitiveness

Although studies have often suggested that European economies are struggling to retain their competitiveness within the global economy (Denis *et al.*, 2005; Reiner, 2010; Koschatzky and Stahlecker, 2010), the WCIR indicates that for the most competitive European regions the rise of East Asian and BRIC economies has not undermined their competitiveness. In particular, Western and Central European regions contribute 27 per cent of the top 30 most competitive regions in both the 2008 and the 2014 WCIR surveys. This suggests that there is no evidence of the leading European regions losing their position. As noted above, this may reflect the ability of some regions to adapt and move to a globalized supply chain (Affuso *et al.*, 2011). However, this need not be the case across Europe or even for all regions within individual European nations.

In this chapter the definition of European regions excludes the Russian regions, which will be discussed in more depth within the separate chapter on BRIC nations. Similarly, although aspiring for European Union membership, Turkey is analysed along with the Middle Eastern regions (in a number of respects, Turkey does not represent a perfect fit in either group). This leaves 140 regions spread across 30 nations to consider.[1] The pattern of regional competitiveness within Europe is presented in Figure 7.1, which shows both the WCIR score for the 140 regions and their overall ranking across all the regions covered by the WCIR.

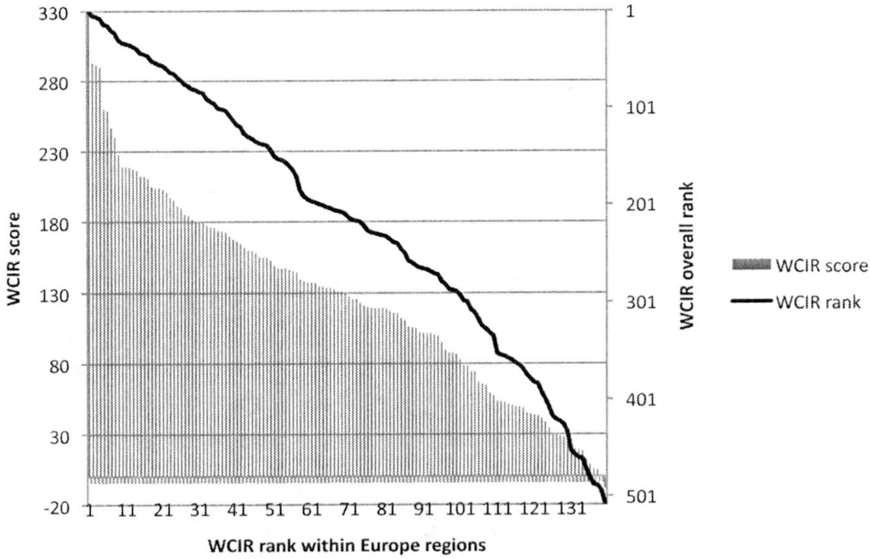

Figure 7.1 Regional competitiveness across Europe

Clearly, the pattern of regional competitiveness scores in Europe is not one of gradual decline from the most competitive region to the least competitive. There are some ranges where the competitiveness of regions changes quite rapidly. For instance, the nine most competitive regions are atypical of the other top 20 European regions. At the other end of the competitiveness spectrum, there appears to be an accelerated decline in competitiveness once the 95th European region (Vzhodna Slovenija in Slovenia) is reached. Some of these differences are likely to reflect groups of specific types of regions within nations; for example, capital cities or economically dominant core regions. Alternatively, they may also reflect different groupings of nations, such as between those regions in Western European nations, which have enjoyed long-term membership of the European Union and access to its structural funds.

To put the competitiveness of European regions into the context of the whole sample of regions included in the WCIR, Table 7.1 provides some summary statistics for this regional group. The European sample, which is dominated by innovation-driven economies, has an average WCIR score of 126.7. This relatively low mean score is a reflection of the large range of regional competitiveness present within Europe. Although Région de Bruxelles-Capitale in Belgium is the second most competitive region covered by the WCIR, two regions, Sur and Canarias in Spain, are within the 50 least competitive regions covered by the WCIR. This means that the WCIR score and ranks for European regions have ranges of 337.2 index points and 506 places, respectively. The negative kurtosis statistic is suggestive of more extreme WCIR scores in the European sample than might be expected. There is also some evidence of a positive skew in both measures. In terms of the WCIR score, this reflects the atypical nature of the most competitive European regions noted above, which have much higher WCIR scores than the rest of Europe. The positive skew in European WCIR ranks suggests that there is a long tail of relatively less competitive European regions.

As shown by Table 7.2, of the top 20 European regions, 17 are in the 50 most competitive regions globally. In total, 12 nations are represented by the regions in the top 20. Understandably, all the nations covering the most competitive regions are classed as possessing innovation-driven national economies according to the World Economic Forum (2012) definition. The most competitive regions fall into

Table 7.1 Summary statistics for WCIR across European regions

	WCIR score	*WCIR rank*
Mean average	126.7	218
Median	128.6	213
Maximum	328.5	2
Minimum	–8.7	508
Range	337.2	506
Skewness	0.232	0.286
Kurtosis	–0.283	–0.887

Table 7.2 Twenty most competitive European regions

WCIR Europe rank	*European region*	*Nation*	*WEF stage of development*	*WCIR score*	*WCIR world rank*
1	Région de Bruxelles-Capitale	Belgium	Innovation driven	328.5	2
2	Stockholm	Sweden	Innovation driven	292.8	6
3	Norway	Norway	Innovation driven	291.3	7
4	Luxembourg	Luxembourg	Innovation driven	289.5	9
5	Hovedstaden	Denmark	Innovation driven	260.3	15
6	Île de France	France	Innovation driven	259.1	16
7	Etelä-Suomi	Finland	Innovation driven	246.7	21
8	Switzerland	Switzerland	Innovation driven	240.1	24
9	Baden-Württemberg	Germany	Innovation driven	228.1	31
10	Zuid-Nederland	Netherlands	Innovation driven	219.6	34
11	Västsverige	Sweden	Innovation driven	219.6	35
12	Bremen	Germany	Innovation driven	219.0	36
13	Hamburg	Germany	Innovation driven	218.2	38
14	Praha	Czech Republic	Innovation driven	216.7	40
15	London	UK	Innovation driven	212.9	45
16	Hessen	Germany	Innovation driven	212.8	46
17	West-Nederland	Netherlands	Innovation driven	211.0	48
18	Bayern	Germany	Innovation driven	205.6	53
19	Östra Mellansverige	Sweden	Innovation driven	204.7	55
20	Sydsverige	Sweden	Innovation driven	204.3	57

Notes: WEF = World Economic Forum.

a number of different categories. Three of the regions reflect small advanced nations, with these three region-states displaying some similarities, such as a high degree of specialism in certain sectors. However, these sectors differ, with Luxembourg and Switzerland having a considerable presence in the financial services sectors, whilst Norway has benefited from its access to North Sea oil and gas. A second group of regions are associated with the capital regions of larger nations including: Île de France, Praha and London. In many regards, these advanced service-oriented economies are likely to have similarities with Luxembourg and Switzerland. However, Germany (5 regions), Sweden (4 regions) and the Netherlands (2 regions) contribute more than one region each. It should be noted that no nation has more than one representative region in the ten most competitive European regions.

Overall, North West Europe contributes the greatest number of competitive European regions. Of the big four European economies, only Germany achieves more than a single region in the top 20. France's second highest ranked region, Centre-Est, is the 45th most competitive European region, whilst the second highest ranked region in the UK is the South East of England region surrounding London, which is ranked 24th. This is likely to be a reflection of the path-dependent nature of regional development, where particular national systems lead to a greater regional concentration of economic activity, such as in the UK, whilst others, such as those in Sweden and Germany, lead to a more evenly or widely distributed pattern of economic activity (Combes and Overman, 2004), and therefore a larger number of competitive regions. However, Clifton *et al.* (2012) find mixed evidence for this when considering the distribution of the creative class in both Sweden and the UK.

At the other end of the spectrum, Table 7.3 presents the 20 least competitive European regions, with there being an overrepresentation of regions in less fully developed national economies such as Romania and Bulgaria, which the World Economic Forum (2012) class as being efficiency driven, with these nations largely concentrating on large-scale manufacturing production, rather than the knowledge creation seen in innovation-driven economies. However, 11 of the 20 least competitive European regions included are located within national economies that are classed as innovation driven. It is clear, therefore, that uneven regional development within European regions remains an enduring challenge (Eriksson and Hansen, 2013). The more peripheral regions of some of the most developed national economies are continuing to struggle due to accessibility

Table 7.3 Twenty least competitive European regions

WCIR Europe rank	*European region*	*Nation*	*WEF stage of development*	*WCIR score*	*WCIR world rank*
121	Départements d'outre-mer	France	Innovation driven	44	384
122	Calabria	Italy	Innovation driven	44	385
123	Alföld és Észak	Hungary	Transition eff. to inn.	41	394
124	Macroregiunea patru	Romania	Efficiency driven	39	401
125	Região Autónoma da Madeira	Portugal	Innovation driven	34	409
126	Centro	Spain	Innovation driven	30	419
127	Região Autónoma dos Açores	Portugal	Innovation driven	29	422
128	Nisia Aigaiou, Kriti	Greece	Innovation driven	29	424
129	Lithuania	Lithuania	Transition eff. to inn.	28	427
130	Macroregiunea unu	Romania	Efficiency driven	25	435
131	Stredné Slovensko	Slovakia	Innovation driven	20	454
132	Region Wschodni	Poland	Transition eff. to inn.	20	458
133	Kentriki Ellada	Greece	Innovation driven	19	461
134	Voreia Ellada	Greece	Innovation driven	18	462
135	Latvia	Latvia	Transition eff. to inn.	13	473
136	Východné Slovensko	Slovakia	Innovation driven	9	482
137	Macroregiunea doi	Romania	Efficiency driven	5	489
138	Severna i iztochna	Bulgaria	Efficiency driven	5	490
139	Sur	Spain	Innovation driven	1	495
140	Canarias	Spain	Innovation driven	–9	508

Notes: Transition eff. to inn. = Transition efficiency to innovation driven.
WEF = World Economic Forum.

issues and the lack of an entrepreneurial culture, even where knowledge-based institutions such as universities are present (Makkonen, 2012). France is one example of the prevalence of regional uneven development, whereby Île de France is one of the most competitive European regions (ranked 6th), while at the same time the Départements d'outre-mer region is classed as one of the least competitive (ranked 121st).

Geographically, the least competitive regions are mostly a mixture of Eastern Europe and Mediterranean economies. Studies as far back as Weber (1930) suggest that a cultural element may play a role in the differing economic success experienced by Northern and Southern European nations, although the inability to often separate institutions and culture has made such sweeping conclusions problematic.

A number of the innovation-driven nations with less competitive regions are those that have been particularly strongly hit by the Eurozone sovereign debt crisis, such as Greece and Spain. However, as Figure 7.2 indicates, there is little evidence to suggest that the majority of European regions have seen a considerable loss of competitiveness due to the financial crisis relative to their counterparts. The main exception to this is Iceland, which had achieved a high level of competitiveness on the back of its rapidly expanding financial services sector, which grew disproportionately large relative to its economy as a whole (OECD, 2009; Ólafsson and Pétursson, 2010). The collapse of the Icelandic banking system has seen a large decrease in both absolute and relative regional competitiveness. However, the next largest decrease in competitiveness ranking is found in the East of England in the UK. This region, which has strengths in the

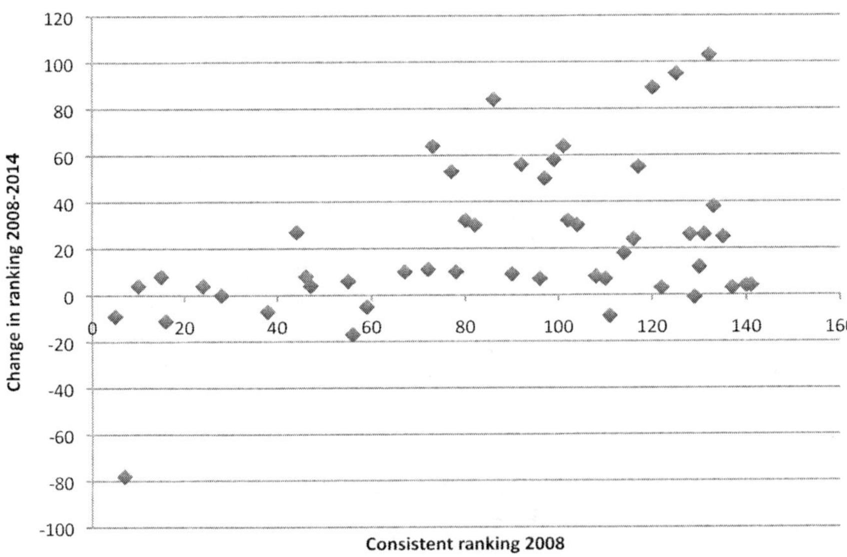

Figure 7.2 WCIR consistent ranking in 2008 and change in rank 2008–2014

biotechnology and ICT sectors based around the University of Cambridge (Cooke and Huggins, 2003), saw a decline in its ranking of 17 places, falling from 56th in 2008 to 73rd in 2014.

Of those Mediterranean nations that have suffered the greatest difficulties, it is possible to examine the experience of the Spanish and Italian regions included across both years. In Spain, the capital region of Communidad de Madrid fell nine places to be ranked 120th, whilst the Noreste region saw little change shedding one place to 130th. These changes in rank are relatively small compared with those that may have been expected, which suggests that contrary to the fears of some policymakers (Gardiner *et al.*, 2004), European regions have actually maintained their competitiveness relatively well compared to many regions in other continental blocs. Similarly, the three Italian regions covered by both surveys all increased their consistent ranking by at least seven places. Lombardia experienced the largest rise to 81st in 2014, a rise of 9 places on its 2008 rank. It appears, therefore, that the resilience of these regions is fairly strong.

Overall, the evidence suggests that, with the exception of Iceland and the East of England, the inter-linkages required to achieve a high level of competitiveness have not been acquired at the expense of the reduced adaptability that will ultimately lead to decline (Pouder and St John, 1996). Although it may at first appear a surprise to find that the East of England has been one of the regions to suffer the greatest decline in competitiveness, some of these problems may relate to capacity constraints associated with infrastructure availability, which Simmie *et al.* (2006) suggest have become evident in the region in recent years. More generally, a lack of adaptability is a continuing danger faced by successful regions, and the clusters within them, as they become locked in to particular technologies or processes (Ter Wal and Boschma, 2011) or to dominant firms, which through reduced competition lose their growth orientation, making regional economies vulnerable to large external shocks (Martin and Sunley, 2011b).

Table 7.4 outlines those regions experiencing the largest positive and negative changes in their rankings over the two time periods. Confirming the results presented in Figure 7.2, only eight European regions saw their ranking fall, whilst all top ten European regions experiencing the greatest rises in competitiveness ranking did so by more than 50 places, which is likely to have been at the expense of a number of US regions. The robustness and resilience of the German economy is apparent, with German regions accounting for six of the top ten regions enjoying the largest increases in consistent ranking. These regions include Bremen and Hamburg, which both rose by more than 90 places to be ranked 36th and 38th in the overall WCIR for 2014. Bremen traditionally relied on port activities and heavy industry such as shipbuilding, but with the decline of these activities it has become more technology- and innovation-focused, whilst maintaining its role as a major port and enjoying the benefits of Germany's export growth (Power *et al.*, 2010).

Other big regional climbers are found in the Benelux countries, as well as London in the UK. London is clearly one of the world's leading financial centres, and it is interesting to find that such regions appear to be more robust and resilient

Table 7.4 Regions experiencing the largest increases and decreases in consistent ranking 2008–2014

2014 overall rank	*European region*	*Nation*	*Consistent rankings (regions included in both 2008 and 2014 only)*		
			2014 rank	*2008 rank*	*Change*
36	Bremen	Germany	29	132	103
38	Hamburg	Germany	30	125	95
40	Praha	Czech Republic	31	120	89
2	Région de Bruxelles-Capitale	Belgium	2	86	84
9	Luxembourg	Luxembourg	9	73	64
46	Hessen	Germany	37	101	64
53	Bayern	Germany	41	99	58
45	London	UK	36	92	56
83	Nordrhein-Westfalen	Germany	62	117	55
31	Baden-Württemberg	Germany	24	77	53
300	Estonia	Estonia	134	137	3
35	Västsverige	Sweden	28	28	0
261	Noreste	Spain	130	129	–1
86	Oost-Nederland	Netherlands	64	59	–5
57	Sydsverige	Sweden	45	38	–7
218	Comunidad de Madrid	Spain	120	111	–9
16	Île de France	France	14	5	–9
34	Zuid-Nederland	Netherlands	27	16	–11
102	East of England	UK	73	56	–17
121	Iceland	Iceland	85	7	–78

to the shocks associated with the financial crisis than those regions that are more reliant on the 'real economy'. The other European region showing impressive increases in relative competitiveness is the capital of the Czech Republic, Praha. Whilst Brussels and Luxembourg have both improved their relative positions, Oost-Nederland and Zuid-Nederland are two of the very few European regions to actually see a decline in their relative competitiveness in the recent period. Sweden contributes four of the top 20 most competitive European regions, but Västsverige and Sydsverige have both experienced poor performance relative to other regions. In these regions, policy emphasis has been placed on boosting entrepreneurship and innovation along with attempting to regenerate problematic urban areas in a sustainable manner.

The anatomy of European regional competitiveness

Chapter 5 outlined the relative contributions of the WCIR components for Europe and noted that, unlike some groups of regions, there is a more balanced contribution from the individual components towards the overall competitiveness level achieved. However, there is a larger contribution from the knowledge sustainability component, which is linked to the long-term development of higher education in many regions throughout Europe. This appears to be particularly the case for those regions that are more competitive, although it is unclear whether this pattern is consistent for all regions in Europe. Given the evidence presented in the preceding section, which showed that the most competitive regional economies tend to be located in Northern and Western Europe, it is of interest to determine whether or not there is a significant difference in the sources of competitiveness associated with these regions. In other words, do differing initial conditions and influences, such as culture and institutions, lead to different forms of regional development and sources of regional competitiveness.

Breaking the European regions into quartiles by their level of competitiveness yields an initial impression of the patterns present in the competitiveness components (Table 7.5). As noted above, knowledge sustainability makes the greatest contribution for the most competitive regions in Europe, but once outside the most competitive regions, 4th-wave knowledge capital associated with industries such as mechanical and electrical engineering and traditional R&D activities becomes the biggest influence on average competitiveness. This is suggestive of a split between those regions that have invested heavily in their education sectors and digital infrastructure and other European regions. With the exception of the most competitive regions, the outputs and outcomes component contributes the least, on average, towards overall competitiveness.

To observe the differing relative importance of the four components, Figure 7.3 presents the relative contributions of each component. It is again clear that for less competitive regions there is a greater reliance on 4th-wave knowledge capital, and whilst knowledge sustainability remains important, it is not as dominant as it is in the most competitive regions. What is most striking is the falling importance of the outputs and outcomes component. This component is one of the least important components for all groups of European regions, but it becomes even less important as competitiveness decreases. Put simply, this implies that European regions are relatively weak in converting their inputs into raised productivity and greater employment and income.

An alternative method of grouping nations and their regions is suggested by the 'varieties of capitalism' approach (Hall and Soskice, 2001), which argues that

Table 7.5 Absolute contribution of competitiveness components for European regions by quartiles

	5th-wave knowledge capital	*4th-wave knowledge capital*	*Outputs/ outcomes*	*Knowl. sustain.*	*WCIR*
1st quartile	0.75	0.63	0.69	1.10	216.6
2nd quartile	0.28	0.43	0.24	0.39	149.5
3rd quartile	–0.05	0.27	–0.09	0.00	104.8
4th quartile	–0.36	–0.23	–0.85	–0.29	35.9

Note: Knowl. sustain. = Knowledge sustainability.

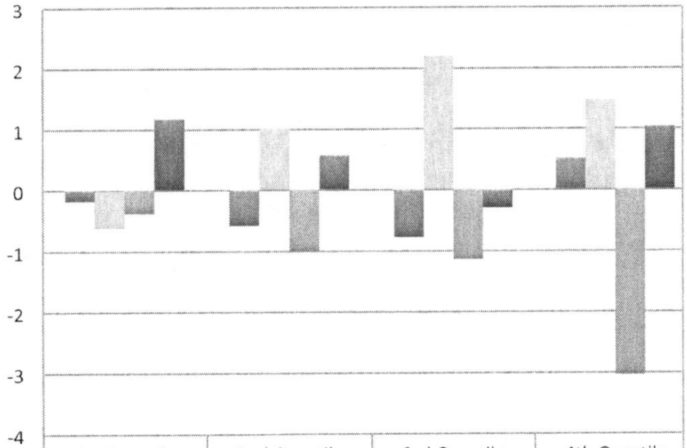

	1st Quartile	2nd Quartile	3rd Quartile	4th Quartile
5th-wave knowledge capital	-0.18	-0.58	-0.77	0.52
4th-wave knowledge capital	-0.62	1.01	2.20	1.48
Outputs/Outcomes	-0.38	-1.00	-1.13	-3.04
Knowledge sustainability	1.18	0.57	-0.30	1.04

Figure 7.3 Relative contribution of WCIR components by quartiles across European regions

differing institutions develop to match the activities undertaken in an economy. This provides those activities with a comparative advantage, which leads to institutions co-evolving to further support these activities. The literature normally regards most continental European economies as Coordinated Market Economies (CME), whereby strategic interaction between firms and other actors such as trade unions is used to coordinate activities. The UK and other Anglo-Saxon nations are perceived to possess more Liberal Market Economies (LME), whereby markets coordinate activities of firms and other actors.

Attempts to operationalize these concepts and to categorize nations have produced conflicting results. Hall and Gingerich (2009) use an approach based around labour relations and corporate governance measures that finds three main groups in Europe: the liberal market economies of the UK and the Republic of Ireland; the coordinated market economies of northern Europe and Scandinavia (Austria, Belgium, Denmark, Finland, Netherlands, Germany, Norway, Sweden); and the more southern economies where corporate governance is more internal, but labour relations are more fractured and weak (France, Italy, Portugal and Spain). Kenworthy (2006) applies a similar 'cooperation' measure based on qualitative assessments of relations between a variety of actors developed in Hicks and Kenworthy (1998), and obtains a similar grouping of nations.[2] Utilizing a combination of the comparative capitalism approach and economic performance, Casey (2009) generates a similar grouping of nations, although Greece is included in the Mediterranean group, whilst Austria, France and Iceland do not fit into any of the groups comfortably.

Geffen and Kenyon (2006) suggest that such categorizations must be treated with a degree of scepticism, as their use of cluster analysis often finds that nations change groups between different time periods. Bearing this caveat in mind, for the analysis presented in Table 7.6, European regions are split into three 'varieties of capitalism' groups as a means of examining the sources of competitiveness across these groups: Coordinated Market Economies (CME) – Northern and Mediterranean; Liberal Market Economies (LMEs); and Dependent Market Economies (DMEs). Given the particular issue of categorizing regions in France, the Mediterranean group is examined both with and without the French regions. Eastern Europe has had less attention paid to it in this regard, and Nölke and Vliegenthart (2009) suggest that a fourth grouping of Dependent Market Economies (DME) reliant on external financing has emerged, including the Czech Republic, Hungary, Poland and the Slovak Republic, which have similar institutions. Studies have also recognized that other Eastern European and Baltic states display considerable differences in the form of capitalism they have established (Nölke and Vliegenthart, 2009; Adam *et al.*, 2009). Therefore, these states and the nations highlighted by Nölke and Vliegenthart (2009) are included in the analysis as a separate group referred to as Dependent Market Economies (DMEs).

In general, the results are compatible with the theory predicted by the varieties of capitalism literature, the coordinated market (CME) and liberal market (LME) approaches are neither better nor worse than one another (Hall and Soskice, 2001), with there appearing to be very little difference in the overall competitiveness of regions across the Northern CME group and the LME group of regions. These two groups of regions are both more competitive than the WCIR average and the average for the European regions (European WCIR average = 126.7). The average competitiveness is a little higher for the Northern CME group, which can be linked with the suggestion that the compatibility and complementarity of institutions with the economic activities undertaken in these regions is greater, compared with those in the Mediterranean and Eastern

Table 7.6 Absolute contribution to competitiveness by components of WCIR by 'varieties of capitalism'

	5th-wave knowledge capital	*4th-wave knowledge capital*	*Outputs/ outcomes*	*Knowl. sustain.*	*WCIR*
Northern CME	0.47	0.51	0.49	0.90	187.0
Mediterranean CME	–0.13	–0.01	–0.18	0.04	89.6
Mediterranean CME (excluding France)	–0.23	–0.06	–0.25	–0.03	79.0
LME	0.60	0.51	0.09	0.45	160.3
DME	–0.02	0.40	–0.46	–0.30	86.0

Notes: Knowl. sustain. = Knowledge sustainability.
CME = Coordinated Market Economies.
LME = Liberal Market Economies.
DME = Dependent Market Economies.

European regions where institutions are weaker or less well developed (Hall and Gingerich, 2009; Nölke and Vliegenthart, 2009). The inclusion or exclusion of French regions in this group has little effect on the results obtained. As might be expected, outputs and outcomes appear more important for the competitiveness of Northern CME regions, whilst 5th-wave knowledge capital appears to be favoured by the institutions associated with LME regions.

Figure 7.4 makes the differences clearer through an illustration of relative contributions. Those regions within the LME group show the lowest relative contribution from outputs and outcomes. This is consistent with studies that have criticized the Anglo-Saxon form of capitalism for generating higher levels of inequality and less even distribution of economic growth. Instead, the Market Coordination Mechanism favours the development of both 4th- and 5th-wave knowledge capital. The Northern CME regions, on the other hand, have followed a pattern of development that places a greater emphasis on the development of inputs in the form of skilled labour through the education system (Bouvet, 2010). The Mediterranean CME group follow a similar pattern, but with knowledge sustainability playing a weaker role than in the Northern CME regions. As suggested by Nölke and Vliegenthart (2009), the reliance on outside resources has seen competitiveness in DME regions drawn more from 4th-wave knowledge capital, which is likely to reflect the investments being made by actors from other regions in these economies.

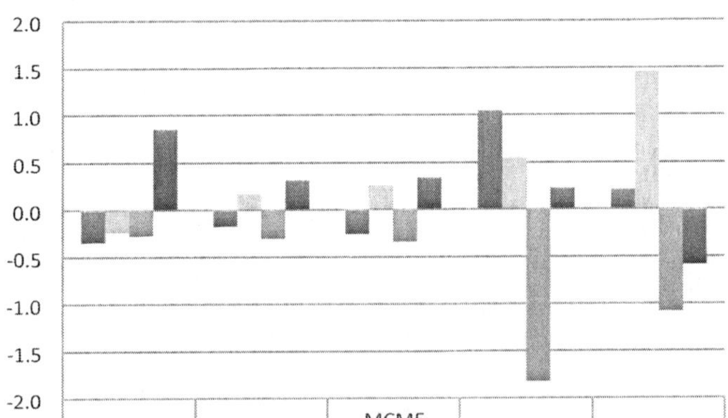

	NCME	MCME	MCME (excluding France)	LME	DME
5th-wave knowledge capital	-0.34	-0.18	-0.26	1.05	0.21
4th-wave knowledge capital	-0.24	0.17	0.26	0.55	1.46
Outputs/Outcomes	-0.28	-0.31	-0.34	-1.82	-1.08
Knowledge sustainability	0.86	0.32	0.34	0.23	-0.59

Figure 7.4 Relative contribution to competitiveness by components of WCIR by 'varieties of capitalism'

Concluding remarks

Although there have been concerns about a loss of competitiveness within Europe relative to both the US and other emerging competitors, the WCIR indicates that on average European regions have retained their competitiveness. However, this competitiveness is not evenly spread across Europe, which means that convergence policies at both a national and supra-national scale should continue to have importance (Petrakos *et al.*, 2011). A particular concern for policymakers is the relative inability of European regions to convert their strengths in 4th- and 5th-wave knowledge capital and knowledge sustainability into improved standards of living, and a key challenge for Europe's regions is to transfer more of their human and knowledge capital assets into tangible gains in the form of higher productivity rates and greater wealth generation.

Notes

1 The 30 nations included in the chapter's analysis are Austria, Belgium, Bulgaria, Cyprus, Czech Republic, Denmark, Estonia, Finland, France, Germany, Greece, Hungary, Iceland, Ireland, Italy, Latvia, Lithuania, Luxembourg, Malta, Netherlands, Norway, Poland, Portugal, Romania, Slovakia, Slovenia, Spain, Sweden, Switzerland, and United Kingdom.

2 The relationships examined include: firms in different industries, unions, state and interest groups, firms and investors, firms and suppliers, competing firms, labour and management, workers, functional departments in firms.

8 The competitiveness of North American regions

International studies of national competitiveness have frequently identified the US as one of the most competitive national economies (World Economic Forum, 2012). Furthermore, particular regions within the US, such as San Jose-Sunnyvale-Santa Clara (better known as Silicon Valley) are often used as exemplars of successful and competitive regions (Saxenian, 1994). However, North America, is clearly not without its own peripheral and less competitive regions. In addition, some of the time series data presented in previous chapters suggest that many US regions are losing competitiveness relative to regions in other developed nations. Combined with the threat from regions within emerging economies, there is a real risk that with the exception of a few truly globally competitive regions, many US regions will find it harder to continue to grow and maintain the standard of living currently enjoyed by their populations.

Following on from the preceding chapter on the competitiveness of European regions, this chapter concentrates on analysing the North American regions covered by the WCIR survey, consisting of 102 North American regions, with 12 of these being Canadian provinces and territories and the remaining 90 North American metropolitan statistical areas.

Patterns and change in North American regional competitiveness

The pattern of competitiveness across North American regions is similar in some ways to that found in Europe, with the most competitive regions displaying very high levels of competitiveness, but as one moves down the rankings of the index the scores drop dramatically before flattening off (Figure 8.1). The overall distribution of regional competitiveness is similar to that found both in Europe and the WCIR sample of regions as a whole, and, as shown by Figure 8.2, there is a bell-shaped distribution of regional competitiveness.

A significant proportion of North American regions exhibit competitiveness levels in the 106 to 219 WCIR score range, indicating above regional competitiveness at the global level. Indeed, as shown by Table 8.1, North American regions are comfortably more competitive than the WCIR global regional average, with a WCIR average score of 170.5. Regional competitiveness levels range

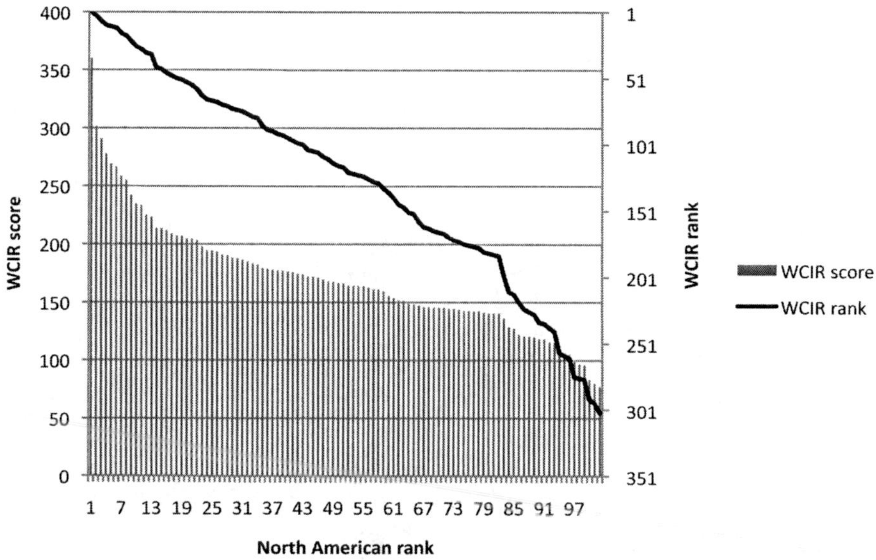

Figure 8.1 Regional competitiveness across North America

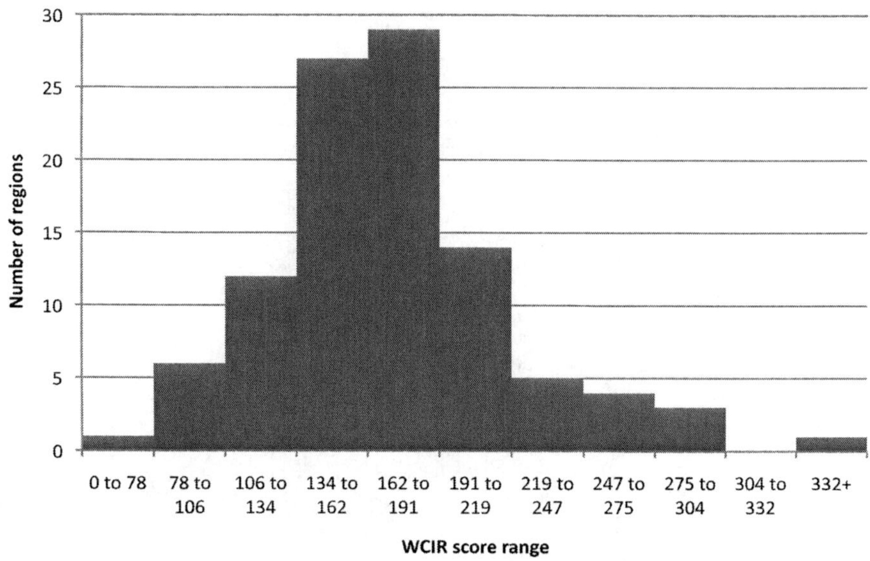

Figure 8.2 Distribution of regional competitiveness scores across North America

Table 8.1 Summary statistics for WCIR across North American regions

	WCIR score	*WCIR rank*
Average	170.5	129
Median	165.5	120
Maximum	360.0	1
Minimum	77.7	303
Range	282.3	302
Skewness	0.95	0.39
Kurtosis	1.82	–0.67

from 77.7 for the US region Cape Coral-Fort Myers in Florida to 360.0 for San Jose-Sunnyvale-Santa Clara in California. This means that even the lowest ranked North American region is still only just outside the top 300 regions. As indicated by Figure 8.2, there is a positive skew in the distribution of the competitiveness scores, indicating that the most competitive North American regions are further from the typical North American region than the least competitive regions.

The most competitive regions in North America are presented in Table 8.2. Within the top 20 North American regions there are 17 regions in the US and

Table 8.2 Twenty most competitive regions in North America

WCIR North America rank	*North American region*	*Nation/ area*	*WCIR score*	*WCIR World rank*
1	San Jose-Sunnyvale-Santa Clara, CA	US/West	360.0	1
2	Washington-Arlington-Alexandria, DC-VA-MD-WV	US/South	301.7	4
3	Bridgeport-Stamford-Norwalk, CT	US/North East	290.9	8
4	Boston-Cambridge-Quincy, MA-NH	US/North East	278.0	11
5	Oxnard-Thousand Oaks-Ventura, CA	US/West	269.1	12
6	San Francisco-Oakland-Fremont, CA	US/West	266.7	13
7	Baltimore-Towson, MD	US/South	258.7	17
8	Durham-Chapel Hill, NC	US/South	255.4	19
9	San Diego-Carlsbad-San Marcos, CA	US/West	242.2	23
10	Hartford-West Hartford-East Hartford, CT	US/North East	234.7	27
11	Yukon	Canada	233.6	29
12	Los Angeles-Long Beach-Santa Ana, CA	US/West	225.1	32
13	Seattle-Tacoma-Bellevue, WA	US/West	223.5	33
14	New York-Northern New Jersey-Long Island, NY-NJ-PA	US/North East	213.9	43
15	Ontario	Canada	213.7	44
16	Worcester, MA	US/North East	211.9	47
17	Des Moines-West Des Moines, IA	US/Midwest	209.0	49
18	Salt Lake City, UT	US/West	207.5	51
19	Northwest Territories and Nunavut	Canada	207.2	52
20	Minneapolis-St. Paul-Bloomington, MN-WI	US/Midwest	204.9	54

three from Canada. The highest ranked Canadian region is the sparsely populated Yukon territories, which is the 11th most competitive North American region, and ranked 29th globally. Along with the Northwest Territories and Nunavut (19th most competitive North American region, overall WCIR rank of 52), Yukon is a relatively remote region located in the far North of Canada. Both Yukon and Northwest Territories and Nunavut have advantages in terms of mineral wealth and, in Yukon's case, oil and gas reserves (Yukon Economic Development, 2006; Industry, Tourism and Investment, 2011; Government of Nunavut, 2012). Yukon also has one of the most highly qualified populations in Canada, with high levels of labour market participation (Yukon Economic Development, 2006). The third of the Canadian regions in the top 20 North American regions is Ontario (WCIR score 213.7, ranked 44th), which bears more similarity to the most competitive regions in the US. It contains two of Canada's larger agglomerations, Ottawa, the capital, and Toronto, the largest city.

The most competitive regions in North America are located in the US, with many of the leading regions associated with highly successful universities such as Stanford University (*Times Higher Education* ranked 2nd) in San Jose-Sunnyvale-Santa Clara; and both Harvard University (*Times Higher Education* ranked 4th) and Massachusetts Institute of Technology (*Times Higher Education* ranked 5th) in Boston-Cambridge-Quincy.[1] Washington-Arlington-Alexandria, the second most competitive region in North America, accrues significant advantages by being the capital of the world's largest national economy. In this respect, Bridgeport-Stamford-Norwalk is perhaps an outlier having neither a top 10 global university nor being a political centre. However, it does have a strong financial services centre and is the home of significant venture capital investment.

Among the 20 most competitive regions there is representation from four areas associated with the US Census Bureau regional divisions: seven regions from the West; five regions from the North East; three regions from the South; and two regions from the Midwest. Of the most competitive regions in the West of the US, four are drawn from California. However, it is clear that within a global environment, competitive regions need not be geographically proximate to other competitive regions, with the other two West US regions in the top 20 being Seattle-Tacoma-Bellevue (WCIR score 223.5, ranked 33rd overall) in Washington state, with a strong computer software and aerospace presence, and Salt Lake City (WCIR score 207.5, ranked 51st) in Utah. Salt Lake City's economy and competitiveness is driven by firms engaged in high-technology manufacturing, especially speciality chemicals, automotive parts, and aerospace (Economic Development Corporation of Utah, 2013).

A number of the most competitive regions in the North East of US such as Hartford (WCIR score 234.7, ranked 27th) have developed a strong presence in the financial sector, particularly insurance. In the most competitive regions in the South, economic success was originally built on manufacturing, such as steel in Baltimore-Towson and tobacco and textiles in Durham-Chapel Hill, but their economies have increasingly become more high-technology service-led, with one of Durham's biggest resources being IBM's software laboratory in the Research

Triangle Park, a facility intended to attract research oriented businesses (Weddle *et al.*, 2006).

The least well-represented area of the US in the North American top 20 regions is the Midwest, with only Des Moines-West Des Moines (the 17th most competitive North American region, WCIR score 209.0, ranked 49) and Minneapolis-St. Paul-Bloomington (20th most competitive North American region, WCIR score 204.9, ranked 54) represented. Minneapolis-St. Paul-Bloomington is the third largest metropolitan area in the Midwest after Chicago-Naperville-Elgin and Detroit-Warren-Dearborn, with a US Census Bureau population of 3.4 million. It has strengths in the medical device manufacturing industry (Tijuana Economic Development Corporation, 2011), whilst Des-Moines has a strong financial services sector with many insurance companies based in the city.

It is notable that a number of Canadian regions are classed amongst the least competitive in North America (Table 8.3). These regions frequently have economies with an overrepresentation in agriculture, forestry and fishery. Although these sectors will continue to provide a source of employment into the future, economic growth is likely to be restricted, particularly if issues of sustainability and the environment are taken into account (Timoney and Lee, 2001). Similarly, a number of agricultural-based regions in Florida in the South of the

Table 8.3 Twenty least competitive North American regions

WCIR North America rank	*North American region*	*Nation/ area*	*WCIR score*	*WCIR World rank*
83	El Paso, TX	US/South	136.6	200
84	Charleston-North Charleston-Summerville, SC	US/South	128.9	212
85	Palm Bay-Melbourne-Titusville, FL	US/South	127.5	214
86	Nashville-Davidson–Murfreesboro–Franklin, TN	US/South	122.5	220
87	Scranton–Wilkes-Barre, PA	US/North East	120.9	225
88	Augusta-Richmond County, GA-SC	US/South	120.6	227
89	Orlando-Kissimmee-Sanford, FL	US/South	120.1	229
90	Manitoba	Canada	118.8	235
91	Chattanooga, TN-GA	US/South	118.4	236
92	Jacksonville, FL	US/South	116.0	239
93	Knoxville, TN	US/South	115.5	242
94	Miami-Fort Lauderdale-Pompano Beach, FL	US/South	107.6	258
95	Prince Edward Island	Canada	106.4	260
96	Tampa-St. Petersburg-Clearwater, FL	US/South	105.5	262
97	Las Vegas-Paradise, NV	US/West	99.0	276
98	Nova Scotia	Canada	97.0	277
99	Newfoundland and Labrador	Canada	96.1	278
100	North Port-Bradenton-Sarasota, FL	US/South	83.6	293
101	New Brunswick	Canada	80.3	296
102	Cape Coral-Fort Myers, FL	US/South	77.7	303

US are found among the least competitive regions in North America, and whilst some of the larger regions are beginning to redevelop, in order to replace prior strengths, such as dairy farming in Jacksonville (WCIR score 116.0, ranked 239), this has been more difficult for those areas with smaller agglomerations and weak infrastructure.

Across the least competitive regions in North America, both the North East and West of the US are represented, which as indicated above, are also the two areas of the US that dominate the 20 most competitive regions. In the West of the US, Las Vegas's (WCIR score 99.0, ranked 276) strength in the leisure industry may have come at a cost, as much of the employment created consists of low-paid and low-skilled service occupations. The question faced by Las Vegas is whether it can maintain its competitive advantage in these industries as other regions in the US seek to develop counter-attractions. Scranton–Wilkes-Barre (WCIR score 120.9, ranked 225), in the North East of the US, may, in some respects, have even greater difficulties than Las Vegas. Whilst Las Vegas retains its position as a leading tourist destination, Scranton-Wilkes-Barre's original prosperity lay in the coal mining industry. With the decline in coal as a fuel source it has lost many of its advantages. In addition, public-sector-driven recovery may prove difficult, with Scranton City perceived to be close to economic bankruptcy (Harris, 2012).

The above examination of the most and least competitive regions in North America has revealed that most areas have both highly competitive and less competitive regions. For example, although the Southern states are found to be large contributors to the list of the least competitive regions, Washington-Arlington-Alexandria and Durham-Chapel Hill are both within the most competitive North American regions, as well making the list of the top 20 regions globally. On average, however, regions in the West of the US display the highest level of competitiveness, followed by the North East US regions (Table 8.4). Furthermore, Canadian regions are less competitive than those in the US, with there being significant competitiveness disparities across regions in Canada. Those regions with either natural advantages provided by the resources available, or containing the most important cities in terms of size or political power, are highly competitive, whilst others lacking these advantages tend to lag and show less growth capacity. Similarly, in the Southern US regions there has been an ongoing decline in the manufacturing industries that were previously relied upon for prosperity. For some regions, developments such as the Research Triangle

Table 8.4 Average regional competitiveness by nation/area

Nation/area	*WCIR score*	*WCIR rank*
Canada	148.1	170
US/North East	198.6	85
US/Midwest	173.0	108
US/West	202.3	85
US/South	155.6	157

Park in Durham-Chapel Hill have been successful and created a strong knowledge economy presence. For other regions, however, there has been less evidence of this kind of economic regeneration.

In order to investigate which North American regions have seen the greatest changes in relative competitiveness, Tables 8.5 and 8.6 contrast the ranks achieved on the WCIR for 2008 and 2014 using a consistent sample of regions in both analyses. As shown by Table 8.5, the reduced competitiveness of North American regions is immediately evident. Only seven regions retain their ranking in 2008 or improve on it by 2014. The largest climber is the Canadian region of Ontario, followed by Alberta. Although Ontario has faced declining employment in traditional industries such the automotive sector, it has important high technology clusters that have often developed from higher education institutions, government defence research laboratories and previous telecom companies such as Nortel (Wolfe, 2010). This has attracted engineers, researchers and managers to the region (Wolfe and Gertler, 2006), which has led to the generation of many spinouts over the years (Wolfe, 2010).

Table 8.5 Best performing regions as per changes in relative competitiveness 2008 to 2014 (based on a consistent sample of regions)

2014 overall rank	*North American region*	*Nation/area*	*Ranks using consistent sample*		
			2014 rank	*2008 rank*	*Change*
44	Ontario	Canada	35	74	39
76	Alberta	Canada	56	65	9
12	Oxnard-Thousand Oaks-Ventura, CA	US/West	12	18	6
4	Washington-Arlington-Alexandria, DC-VA-MD-WV	US/South	4	9	5
17	Baltimore-Towson, MD	US/South	15	19	4
51	Salt Lake City, UT	US/West	40	42	2
1	San Jose-Sunnyvale-Santa Clara, CA	US/West	1	1	0
167	British Columbia	Canada	107	106	–1
59	Houston-Sugar Land-Baytown, TX	US/South	46	43	–3
32	Los Angeles-Long Beach-Santa Ana, CA	US/West	25	21	–4
11	Boston-Cambridge-Quincy, MA-NH	US/North East	11	6	–5
8	Bridgeport-Stamford-Norwalk, CT	US/North East	8	3	–5
23	San Diego-Carlsbad-San Marcos, CA	US/West	19	13	–6
19	Durham-Chapel Hill, NC	US/South	16	8	–8
146	Quebec	Canada	98	89	–9

As outlined by studies such as Feldman *et al.* (2005) and Carlsson (2006), often the collapse of a major employer is required to release enough skilled workers to push a cluster to the next level of development, through the creation of a second generation of firms. In the case of Ontario, the bankruptcy of Microsystems International Ltd. (MIL) appears to have been the catalyst for this kind of development (Harrison *et al.*, 2004). Interestingly, Wolfe (2010) attributes the success of this cluster in terms of its economic resilience to strong institutions of civic governance.

As with those North American regions displaying the greatest resilience, the regions displaying the greatest falls in competitiveness are drawn from all parts of the continent. As shown by Table 8.6, a number of the regions suffering the largest declines in competitiveness are those associated with heavy industry such as Providence-New Bedford-Fall River in the North East of the US, which has relied on primary metal production as its largest export good (International Trade Administration, 2012). Such regions are likely to have benefited from the commodities boom prior to the global slowdown, but this was only likely to have been a blip in the decline of such industries, and these regions will need to seek new ways of utilizing the skills and expertise present within other industries.

Table 8.6 Worst performing regions as per changes in relative competitiveness 2008 to 2014 (based on a consistent sample of regions)

2014 overall rank	*North American region*	*Nation/area*	*Ranks using consistent sample*		
			2014 rank	*2008 rank*	*Change*
153	Akron, OH	US/Midwest	101	68	–33
220	Nashville-Davidson–Murfreesboro–Franklin, TN	US/South	121	87	–34
124	Raleigh-Cary, NC	US/South	87	53	–34
235	Manitoba	Canada	123	88	–35
174	St. Louis, MO-IL	US/Midwest	111	76	–35
163	Louisville/Jefferson County, KY-IN	US/South	104	63	–41
90	Milwaukee-Waukesha-West Allis, WI	US/Midwest	67	26	–41
75	Rochester, NY	US/North East	55	12	–43
171	Atlanta-Sandy Springs-Marietta, GA	US/South	109	62	–47
182	Phoenix-Mesa-Glendale, AZ	US/West	114	66	–48
117	Colorado Springs, CO	US/West	83	34	–49
118	Greensboro-High Point, NC	US/South	84	35	–49
110	Detroit-Warren-Livonia, MI	US/Midwest	78	25	–53
134	Buffalo-Niagara Falls, NY	US/North East	93	33	-60
137	Providence-New Bedford-Fall River, RI-MA	US/North East	94	22	–72

Other regions have struggled as fiscal problems have cut public sector spending, such as Colorado Springs in the West of the US, which is heavily reliant on the defence industry. However, such regions may be in a better position to recover in the longer run, as the defence industry represents a large supply of skilled researchers and engineers who can be utilized within the high-technology industries that already exist in the region.

The nature of regional competitiveness in North America

The preceding section has indicated that there are clear differences in competitiveness across North America. In particular, regions in the West and North East of the US are found to be more competitive than those in the South of the US. With this in mind, this section seeks to understand how the reliance on the WCIR components in North America differs across regions. In Table 8.7 the absolute contribution of the different components of the WCIR for regions delineated by level of competitiveness is shown. In general, the pattern of absolute contribution to competitiveness appears to be fairly similar across regions regardless of their overall level of competitiveness. Comparing regions based on their level of overall competitiveness, the stand out component is 5th-wave knowledge capital, with there being a more consistent decline in the other three components from the most to the least competitive regions.

In order to highlight more clearly the most important sources of competitiveness for each group of regions, the relative contributions of each component are presented in Figure 8.3. Combining the evidence in both Table 8.7 and Figure 8.3, it is clear that North American regions as a whole owe much of their competitiveness to the output and outcomes and knowledge sustainability components. These components contribute more to competitiveness in all groups of North American regions than the 4th and 5th-wave knowledge capital components. The disparities in the size of relative contributions for the first quartile regions, compared to the second and third quartile regions, reflects the relatively high variation in competitiveness. For the fourth quartile regions the relative contributions are closer for each component due to the absolute contribution of outputs/outcomes and knowledge sustainability falling at a faster rate than 4th-

Table 8.7 Absolute contribution of competitiveness components for North American regions by quartiles

	5th-wave knowledge capital	*4th-wave knowledge capital*	*Outputs/ outcomes*	*Knowl. sustain.*
1st quartile	0.7	0.5	1.1	1.5
2nd quartile	0.0	0.0	0.8	1.3
3rd quartile	–0.1	–0.2	0.6	1.1
4th quartile	–0.2	–0.3	0.3	0.7

Note: Knowl. sustain. = Knowledge sustainability.

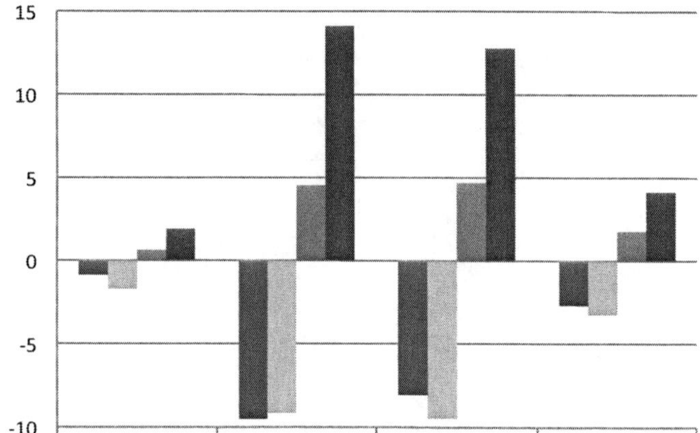

	1st Quartile	2nd Quartile	3rd Quartile	4th Quartile
5th-wave knowledge capital	-0.89	-9.52	-8.06	-2.69
4th-wave knowledge capital	-1.72	-9.16	-9.46	-3.26
Outputs/Outcomes	0.66	4.55	4.71	1.79
Knowledge sustainability	1.94	14.13	12.81	4.16

Figure 8.3 Relative contribution of WCIR components by quartiles across North American regions

and 5th-wave knowledge capital. Nevertheless, a striking feature of the analysis is the similarity in the sources of competitiveness for North American regions regardless of their overall rates of competitiveness. This can be compared to Figure 7.3 in the previous chapter, which examined the relative contributions of the four WCIR components for the European regions, finding a far greater range of competitiveness contributions across regions.

One possible explanation for the differences found across European regions are the differences in the institutions that have developed within specific European nations to support economic activity undertaken within these regions, in particular the extent to which nations function as either Coordinated Market Economies (CME) or Liberal Market Economics (LME). The analysis presented in Chapter 7 found that when placed in particular groups based on their national systems, European regions display different contributions in terms of the underlying components of the WCIR. These differences partly reflect the different cultures and institutions that underpin the national political-economic systems within which the regions are based. However, in North America it is argued that both the US and Canada is represented by a Liberal Market Economy (LME) political-economic system (Hall and Gingerich, 2009), meaning that regional differences associated with national systems are not immediately apparent. Therefore, in order to further determine whether a similar pattern exists, the crude groupings of North American regions into the US Census Bureau divisions are utilized, as shown by Table 8.8. Given the differing historical strengths in

Table 8.8 Absolute contribution to competitiveness by WCIR components in North American regions by area/nation

Nation/ area	*5th-wave knowledge capital*	*4th-wave knowledge capital*	*Outputs/ outcomes*	*Knowl. sustain.*
Canada	0.3	–0.2	0.3	0.9
US/North East	0.2	0.2	0.9	1.3
US/Midwest	–0.1	0.0	0.8	1.3
US/West	0.5	0.2	0.8	1.3
US/South	–0.1	–0.1	0.7	1.0

Note: Knowl. sustain. = Knowledge sustainability.

industry (North East) and agriculture (South) it may be envisaged that some differences in the relative contribution of the WCIR components will be present even with the long history of Federal government.

Across the four US areas and Canada, the component with the greatest contribution to competitiveness for North American regions is knowledge sustainability, in which Canada lags behind all four groups of regions in the US, although only marginally so in the case of the South US regions. More generally, regional competitiveness in Canada appears to be less well suited to directly influencing the economic well-being of their populations at large, and although the competitiveness of Canadian regions is above the global average, it could be argued that to some extent more of Canada's regions have followed a 'lower road' to competitiveness compared to the majority of US regions (Malecki, 2004).

Regions in the West and North East of the US generally have similar contributions from the different components of competitiveness, with the largest difference being the greater investment in 5th-wave knowledge capital in the West US regions. Given the economic dominance and long running success of regions such as San Jose-Sunnyvale-Santa Clara (WCIR score 360.0, ranked 1st) in developing clusters in high technology, especially that associated with computing and ICT, this is to be expected. However, it should be remembered that Silicon Valley is just one example, and the North East has its own equivalent in the Boston Route 128 cluster (Dorfman, 1983; Saxenian, 1994; Wonglimpiyarat, 2006). The success of this cluster helped to propel Boston-Cambridge-Quincy's competitiveness and its ranking as the fourth most competitive region in North America (WCIR score 278.0, ranked 11th). Nevertheless, whilst both the San Jose-Sunnyvale-Santa Clara and Boston-Cambridge-Quincy clusters are world leaders in their fields, within the western US area there are a number of additional regions that also possess high levels of 5th-wave knowledge capital.

As can be seen from Table 8.9, when considering the top 10 North American regions by 5th-wave knowledge capital, the West US regions are overrepresented with five of the top 10. In addition to San Jose-Sunnyvale-Santa Clara, four other regions located in California are also included. Foremost is Oxnard-Thousand Oaks-Ventura (WCIR score 269.1, ranked 12th), which has a particular strength

Table 8.9 North American regions with high levels of 5th-wave knowledge capital

North American region	*Area/nation*	*5th-wave knowledge capital*	*WCIR score*	*WCIR rank*
San Jose-Sunnyvale-Santa Clara, CA	US/West	2.9	360.0	1
Yukon	Canada	2.8	233.6	29
Oxnard-Thousand Oaks-Ventura, CA	US/West	2.4	269.1	12
Durham-Chapel Hill, NC	US/South	1.5	255.4	19
Boston-Cambridge-Quincy, MA-NH	US/North East	1.2	278.0	11
San Francisco-Oakland-Fremont, CA	US/West	1.0	266.7	13
San Diego-Carlsbad-San Marcos, CA	US/West	0.9	242.2	23
Worcester, MA	US/North East	0.9	211.9	47
Northwest Territories and Nunavut	Canada	0.7	207.2	52
Los Angeles-Long Beach-Santa Ana, CA	US/West	0.7	225.1	32

in Biotechnology and Chemicals with 40.2 people per 1,000 employees in these sectors. San Francisco-Oakland-Fremont, San Diego-Carlsbad-San Marcos and Los Angeles-Long Beach-Santa Ana also make the top 10 with strengths in high-technology service employment and a strong private venture capital industry to support entrepreneurial activity.

In contrast, in the North East US only Worcester (WCIR score 211.9, ranked 49th) appears in the top 10 North American regions alongside Boston-Cambridge-Quincy. Worcester draws on high-technology services for its 5th-wave knowledge capital, alongside an extremely high level of venture capital investment per capita, which at US$376.6 per capita, exceeds that of Boston-Cambridge-Quincy (US$346.4 per capita), Los Angeles-Long Beach-Santa Ana (US$315.2 per capita) and San Jose-Sunnyvale-Santa Clara (US$314.5 per capita). Indeed, Worcester actually has the 7th highest private venture capital investment per capita in the world. However, the general pattern indicates that whilst some regions in the North East of the US possess strengths in 5th-wave knowledge capital, they are relatively isolated compared to the larger number of clusters of this type in the West of the US.

Both Tables 8.8 and 8.9 indicate that whilst Canadian regions struggle with regard to the output and outcome component of competitiveness, they do perform well in absolute terms with regard to the 5th-wave knowledge capital component. Two Canadian regions appear in the top 10 regions for 5th-wave knowledge capital in North America: Yukon; and Northwest Territories and Nunavut. In both cases this reflects exceptionally high employment densities in high-technology services (341.0 and 131.8 people per 1,000 employees, respectively). These clusters are relatively small compared to those in the US regions, but the small population sizes of the Canadian regions means that these sectors are disproportionately important in these regions.

The absolute contributions of the four components to competitiveness across the regional groupings indicate that 5th-wave knowledge capital may show the most significant variation. Figure 8.4 presents the relative contributions to

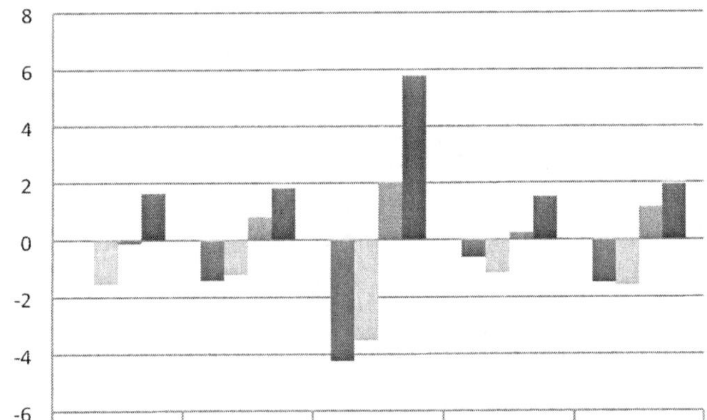

	Canada	US/North East	US/Midwest	US/West	US/South
5th-wave knowledge capital	0.01	-1.42	-4.23	-0.62	-1.49
4th-wave knowledge capital	-1.54	-1.22	-3.53	-1.17	-1.59
Outputs/Outcomes	-0.12	0.82	1.97	0.26	1.15
Knowledge sustainability	1.65	1.83	5.79	1.53	1.93

Figure 8.4 Relative contribution of WCIR components to the competitiveness of North American regions by area/nation

observe whether or not there is any evidence of this. Across the North American regions it is generally clear that strong school and university systems, along with an advanced digital infrastructure, ensure that knowledge sustainability is the largest contributor to regional competitiveness regardless of area or nation. As noted above, US regions perform well on the outputs and outcomes component, which may reflect a system based on the high geographical mobility of the labour force (Bentivogli and Pagano, 1999), where competition for the most skilled and creative workers may be even more important (Florida, 2005) than for other regions such as those in Europe (Favell, 2008; Martin-Brelot *et al.*, 2010). Overall, 5th-wave knowledge capital plays the third or fourth most important role for the US regions in terms of competitiveness, even in West US where more regions have strengths in this component. Only for the Canadian regions is the 5th-wave knowledge capital component marginally more important than the output and outcomes component.

Concluding remarks

It is clear that North America continues to be home of some of the globe's most competitive regions. Silicon Valley remains at the summit, followed by a range of other economically advanced and leading regions, especially on the western and eastern seaboards. However, there remains significant differentiation in competitiveness across regions, manifested by an economic divide within the continent –

although not on the scale to which such divides exist in multination Europe. Furthermore, in aggregate terms, North American regions are seeing their global competitiveness continue to come under pressure as regions in Europe, Asia-Pacific, and the BRIC nations challenge for the investment, resources and subsequent economic activity associated with twenty-first-century growth.

Note

1 The numbers in parentheses represent the 2012/13 world universities ranking of the *Times Higher Education*: www.timeshighereducation.co.uk/world-university-rankings/2012-13/world-ranking.

9 The competitiveness of BRIC regions

One of the greatest changes in the global economy over the last 20 years has been the rise of the BRIC – Brazil, Russia, India, and China – economies (O'Neal, 2001). These nations, with their huge populations and in some cases access to plentiful natural resources, have reshaped world trade patterns (Watt, 2006; Havlik *et al.*, 2009; Ogrean and Herciu, 2010; De Castro, 2012). Although there is some distance between the current situation and the potential for these economies to influence different markets for goods and services, it is clear that few global businesses and policymakers consider it wise to ignore these economies.

In general, as labour costs rise, global manufacturing chains will move to other nations to gain access to lower labour costs (Yang, 2009). For regions within the BRIC economies this is even more important, as individual regions face the prospect of losing economic activity to other regions within the same nation. This may be where alternative locations offer lower unskilled labour costs (Zhang *et al.*, 2012), or where other regions provide better access to global knowledge pipelines (Yang, 2009). In light of this, as labour costs have risen in the BRIC regions, the knowledge economy has become a more important element of their continuing economic prosperity. Although cutting-edge innovative outcomes may be relatively sparse, the level of investment in developing innovation capabilities is rapidly changing the nature of many BRIC regional economies (Altenburg *et al.*, 2008). Nevertheless, in most cases the current level of regional competitiveness remains considerably below that of regions within Europe and North America. However, as indicated in Chapter 5, a smaller number of leading regions within the BRIC economies are now achieving levels of competitiveness comparable with their Western counterparts.

This process of competitiveness improvement has been partly driven by the increasing importance of the knowledge economy, the goods and services created, and the technologies available (Powell and Snellman, 2004). Although there is an expectation in some quarters that new technologies allow faster codification and transfer for data, reducing the importance of geography (Cairncross, 1997), there is little evidence that the world is moving towards a spaceless economy (Longhi, 2005). Contrary to the expectations highlighted by some previous works (Friedman, 2005), location and the clustering of firms to allow networking appears to be as, if not more, important given the types of goods and services being produced (Brandt *et al.*, 2009). The civic relations that develop in a region can allow a whole region to retain its competitiveness, but proximity is required for many of these relationships to develop (Lorenzen, 2007). This means that agglomeration economies and the knowledge spillovers associated with clusters ensure location remains an important economic development factor (Fan and Scott, 2003; Yusuf and Nabeshima, 2005; Kauffman and Kumar, 2007).

For regions within the BRIC economies, other changes have also ensured that they are better able to compete with Western regions. Moves toward greater offshoring and globalized supply chains have increased the importance of accessing not just local knowledge from within the cluster, but also knowledge through global pipelines (Bathelt *et al.*, 2004; Maskell *et al.*, 2006). As such, firms have been found to place a greater importance on network partners outside their own region (Huggins and Johnston, 2010). Maurer and Ebers (2006) indicate that whilst firms can manage their networks, this is often a daunting and investment-heavy task. However, it is also a necessary task if firms and their regions are to avoid becoming locked in to particular technologies or processes (Gerschenkron, 1962; Uzzi, 1997), and many BRIC regions have caught up by investing in, accessing and utilizing technology, knowledge and information developed elsewhere (Mathews, 2001; Lewis, 2007). However, this is moderated by the fact that the ability to use external knowledge is related to the existing regional knowledge base (Teece, 1998).

With their competitiveness built on institutions associated with accessing and modifying knowledge from elsewhere, it could be argued that regions in BRIC economies are actually better placed than some traditionally competitive regional economies in more developed national economies (Hitt *et al.*, 2005). However, to retain a regional competitive advantage, firms must have the dynamic capabilities to continue to learn and progress toward the technological frontier (Teece, 1998). This means that an approach of simultaneously searching for technology to transfer, alongside the indigenous development of innovation capabilities, is potentially the most effective route toward competitiveness enhancement (Fu and Zhang, 2011), particularly where existing technologies may not be appropriate for the emerging economy context (Fu *et al.*, 2011). On the other hand, it has been argued that regions in Russia and China, in particular, have struggled to throw off a top-down approach, which has inhibited the effective utilization of existing and developing innovation resources (Narula and Jormanainen, 2008).

In general, BRIC nations are not necessarily disadvantaged, and there is evidence of their leading regions displacing regions from more advanced economies, but at this point in time only a relatively small number of regions have achieved higher levels of competitiveness. As indicated in earlier chapters, Chinese and Russian regions have generally been more successful than their Indian and Brazilian counterparts in increasing their competitiveness. Furthermore, the resources and approaches that have led to increased competitiveness have also been seen to differ between regions in these quite different economies. This chapter, therefore, investigates the competitiveness of regions within the BRIC economies, considering not only where regions have been successful in increasing their competitiveness and how this has been achieved, but also why other regions within the same or different nations have been less successful.

Patterns of regional competitiveness within the BRIC nations

The BRIC nations are clearly quite different from one another, with their original grouping based entirely on their potential to dominate the global economy in the medium term, given their large populations and access to other resources (O'Neal, 2001). However, in some respects this grouping has the potential to develop into a self-fulfilling prophecy, with the BRIC nations now holding joint coordination meetings (Ogrean and Herciu, 2010). Although their aggregate economies are large, their current stage of development has meant that their position within the knowledge economy has only recently been established and recognized (Tseng, 2009). Chapter 5 noted that the leading regions within the BRIC economies are now beginning to reach levels of competitiveness previously associated with only the more traditional economic centres in Western economies. Within this section the pattern of competitiveness across BRIC regions will be explored.

Although the BRIC nations as a whole have enjoyed considerable growth in recent years (Lin and Rosenblatt, 2012), with the exception of Russia, these economies have started from a relatively low level of GDP per capita and human capital (Cooper, 2006). This means that the levels of competitiveness and variation across the BRIC regions are of considerable interest in terms of understanding how this development will manifest itself in future years. Table 9.1 indicates that the average level of competitiveness in the BRIC regions, represented by a WCIR score of 39.7, is well below that of the global average (WCIR = 100). The median BRIC region also has a ranking of 393rd, which means that the typical BRIC region is positioned within the lower half of WCIR regions.

The BRIC regions, however, are no different to the European and North American regions in the sense that they are highly diverse in terms of the spread of regional competitiveness. The highest ranked region, Nenets Autonomous Okrug in Russia, actually appears in the top 20 most competitive regions across

Table 9.1 Summary statistics of BRIC regions' competitiveness

	WCIR score	*WCIR rank*
Average	39.7	394
Median	41.8	393
Maximum	250.9	20
Minimum	–46.9	545
Range	297.8	525
Skewness	1.1	–0.8
Kurtosis	3.2	1.5

the index as a whole (WCIR ranked 20th). On the other hand, the least competitive region, Bihar in India, is the second least competitive region across the WCIR rankings (WCIR ranked 545th), with only Nariño in Colombia having a lower level of competitiveness. This results in a range of 525 ranking places, which is slightly wider than Europe (506 places) as well as representing a much greater variation than is found in North America (302 places). This is understandable, especially as the World Economic Forum's definition of 'stage of development' indicates that national BRIC economies are categorized as being at three different stages of development. Whilst Russia and Brazil are perceived to be in the transition stage between efficiency-driven and innovation-driven economies, China is not perceived to have started this transition, remaining efficiency-driven. India remains a factor-driven economy, so whilst potentially overtaking China in future years in terms of population, it has seen its development lag behind that of the other BRIC nations.

As with the European and North American regions, there is evidence of a positive skew in the distribution of regional competitiveness in the BRIC economies. As shown by Figure 9.1, the most competitive regions in the BRIC economies are extreme outliers compared to the level of competitiveness seen for other regions. The top 17 BRIC regions appear to be atypical of the other BRIC regions, for which there are more gradual changes in the level of competitiveness between these regions and their overall rankings. This may be suggestive of extreme uneven development and the potential for rapidly increasing regional disparities evolving within the BRIC economies.

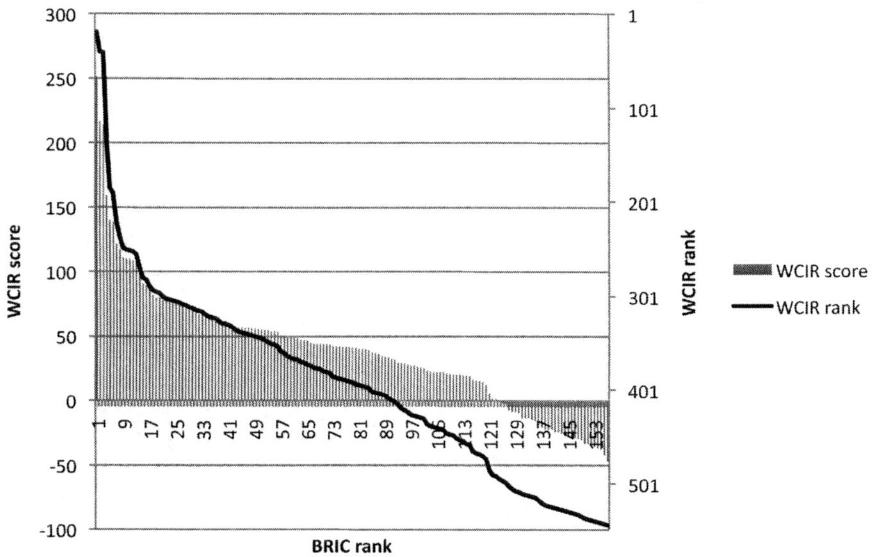

Figure 9.1 Regional competitiveness across BRIC regions

The most competitive 20 BRIC regions are presented in Table 9.2. Consistent with the less than natural grouping of BRIC economies, the most competitive regions within these economies display vastly varying characteristics. Only India is not represented in the top 20 regions, with the most competitive Indian region being Goa, which is only the 69th BRIC region by level of competitiveness, with a WCIR score of 44.4. This is well below the global regional average level of competitiveness, meaning that Goa ranks only 379th overall. With regard to the other three nations, the policies pursued to adopt more market-oriented approaches are likely to lead to further regional inequalities, particularly where resources from neighbouring regions are sucked into growth poles (Myrdal, 1957; Fu, 2008). As such, those regions with concentrations of resources associated with export-led growth are likely to further enhance their positions (Haddad and Hewings, 2001).

Of the top 20 BRIC regions, 11 are located in Russia, seven are in China (including Hong Kong), and three in Brazil. The large number of Russian regions reflects a number of factors; in particular, compared with the other BRIC nations, Russia developed a stronger knowledge economy much earlier, with centres of excellence already well established (Watkins, 2003). This is manifested by the appearance of large cities with research institutes such as Moscow (WCIR score 140.1, ranked 186th) and St Petersburg (WCIR score 101.0, ranked 271st) in the top 20, which has allowed Russia to generate more patent applications than other BRIC nations (Tseng, 2009). However, Moscow and St Petersburg are in fact only

Table 9.2 Twenty most competitive BRIC regions

WCIR BRIC rank	*BRIC region*	*Nation*	*WCIR score*	*WCIR World rank*
1	Nenets Autonomous Okrug	Russia	250.93	20
2	Shanghai	China	216.50	41
3	Beijing	China	214.21	42
4	Chukotka Autonomous Okrug	Russia	159.49	135
5	Moscow	Russia	140.06	186
6	Tianjing	China	138.68	192
7	Yamalo-Nenets Autonomous Okrug	Russia	121.72	222
8	Hong Kong	Hong Kong	117.13	238
9	Distrito Federal	Brazil	111.13	250
10	Zhejiang	China	110.20	252
11	Jiangsu	China	109.78	253
12	Khanty-Mansi Autonomous Okrug-Yugra	Russia	108.99	254
13	Guangdong	China	108.21	257
14	Saint Petersburg	Russia	101.03	271
15	Sakhalin Oblast	Russia	91.16	282
16	Santa Catarina	Brazil	89.61	284
17	São Paulo	Brazil	86.28	291
18	Magadan Oblast	Russia	81.76	295
19	Nizhny Novgorod Oblast	Russia	79.98	297
20	Novgorod Oblast	Russia	79.84	298

the 3rd and 6th most competitive Russian regions, which is partly a reflection of the impact of the global commodities boom that put a number of the more remote sparsely populated regions such as Nenets (WCIR score 250.9, ranked 20th) and Chukotka (WCIR score 159.5, ranked 135th) in strong positions.

The appearance of Chinese regions in the top 20 represents the extent to which these regions have not only developed industrially since the Chinese economy started to undertake capitalist reforms in the late 1970s, but also the fact that they have advanced to such an extent that policymakers in European regions are increasingly concerned about being overtaken in the knowledge economy stakes by these regions (Havlik *et al.*, 2009; Groot *et al.*, 2011). It is worth noting that Hong Kong was already an international financial centre under British rule (Schenk, 2001), and has continued to develop in this direction, while its reliance on manufacturing has continued to decline, resulting in manufacturing-related producer services becoming more economically important (Tao and Wong, 2002). However, in terms of competitiveness it has now been surpassed by the Beijing, Shanghai and Tianjing regions. These regions are home to some of China's leading research institutions. Beijing possesses education institutions, such as Peking University (*Times Higher Education* ranked 46th) and Tsinghua University (*Times Higher Education* ranked 52nd) which are both ranked within the top 60 universities in the world.[1] Shanghai has traditionally been one of the more open regions of China, and this has continued, with a large number of Taiwanese ICT businesses locating in the region.

Guangdong, another Chinese region in the top 20 BRIC regions (WCIR score 108.21, ranked 257th), started from a lower point and utilized an export-driven approach based around the supply of cheap labour (Eng, 1997; Wang and Meng, 2004). The success of Shanghai and the broader Yangtze River Delta, on the other hand, is based more on the agglomeration economies and knowledge spillovers associated with the region (Huggins *et al.*, 2013). Although enjoying high levels of growth through its integration with the segmented global production system, Guangdong gained less in terms of technology transfer from earlier foreign investments, due to the low-skilled assembly nature of much of the work (Lemoine and Ünal-Kesenci, 2004).

De Vries *et al.* (2012) provide an explanation for the lesser presence of Brazilian regions in the top 20. Their disaggregation of the growth of the BRIC nations finds that the reallocation of labour between sectors has contributed to growth in the other three BRIC nations more so than in Brazil. The highest ranked Brazilian region is Distrito Federal, which includes the capital city Brasilia. The other two Brazilian regions to enter the 20 most competitive BRIC regions are Santa Catarina, located on the coast in the South of the country, and São Paulo, also located in the South. Both of these regions have a WCIR score less than that associated with the average for all regions included in the WCIR (Santa Catarina, WCIR score 89.6, ranked 284th; São Paulo, WCIR score 86.3, ranked 291st). Santa Catarina has a strong manufacturing base with an electromechanical cluster in the city of Joinville, located in the north east of the state (Meyer-Stamer, 1998). São Paulo is one of the most financially developed regions of Brazil (Bittencourt, 2010). The region is the location of many of the headquarters of Brazil's largest corporations and financial services firms, where a relatively high proportion of these firms have listings on international stock markets (Wójcik and Burger, 2010).

Turning to the 20 least competitive regions within the BRIC countries, it is perhaps no surprise that all are located in India given the national economy's factor-driven stage of development. All Indian regions display a WCIR score more than a single standard deviation below the average of all the WCIR regions (Table 9.3). This is a reflection of the extent to which India continues to lag behind Chinese regions in making investments in innovative capacity that will allow it to develop its knowledge economy (Altenburg *et al.*, 2008). This is not to say that all Indian regions are less competitive, with Goa (WCIR score 44.4; overall ranked 379th; BRIC ranked 69th), and Daman and Diu (WCIR score 20.5; overall ranked 453rd; BRIC ranked 111) outperforming a number of Brazilian and Russian regions included in the WCIR.

Interestingly, even with success stories such as the Bangalore IT cluster, the Karnataka region only achieves a WCIR score of –20.97 and ranking of 522. D'Costa (2011) suggests that the success of such clusters is currently strictly limited to a small middle class. The influence of the Indian class structure on the education system, which perpetuates the pattern of economic success, continues to result in limited opportunities for the wider Indian public to benefit (Reed, 2008; D'Costa, 2011). It may, therefore, not be wise to hope that the development of the more successful Indian regions will spread to neighbouring regions. The

Table 9.3 Twenty least competitive BRIC regions

WCIR BRIC rank	*BRIC region*	*Nation*	*WCIR score*	*WCIR World rank*
138	Gujarat	India	–22.22	524
139	Mizoram	India	–22.49	525
140	Arunachal Pradesh	India	–22.50	526
141	Lakshadweep	India	–24.52	527
142	Sikkim	India	–24.62	528
143	West Bengal	India	–25.75	529
144	Manipur	India	–27.40	530
145	Nagaland	India	–28.13	531
146	Uttarakhand	India	–28.80	532
147	Tripura	India	–28.87	533
148	Jharkhand	India	–29.67	534
149	Meghalaya	India	–30.43	536
150	Orissa	India	–33.10	538
151	Chattisgarh	India	–33.39	539
152	Rajasthan	India	–34.18	540
153	Madhya Pradesh	India	–35.61	541
154	Assam	India	–36.82	542
155	Jammu and Kashmir	India	–37.85	543
156	Uttar Pradesh	India	–42.40	544
157	Bihar	India	–46.90	545

Chinese experience has been that government investment and intervention has actually weakened the prospects of its lagging central and western regional economies (Groenewold *et al.*, 2010). This suggests that similar interventions by the Indian authorities to boost economic growth in poorer regions indirectly through supporting the most competitive regions on the global stage are probably unlikely to succeed due to the lack of appropriate institutional trickle-down and spreading mechanisms.

In general, the growth and development of the national economies of Brazil, China, India and Russia, along with their prospects for future growth, have been highlighted by studies such as Herd and Dougherty (2007). However, it is unclear to what extent individual regions have improved their competitiveness to allow them to compete with more the traditionally developed European and North American regional economies. Only a small number of the BRIC regions were included in the 2008 index drawn from China and India. However, as these are some of the largest regions, it is still informative to examine the extent to which these regions have improved their competitiveness ranking in 2014 when compared with a consistent sample of other regions (Table 9.4).

Of the 11 BRIC regions appearing in both years of analysis only the established economic centre of Hong Kong shows no increase in rank. This confirms the findings of other studies that have noted the rise of the BRIC economies. When contrasted with a common group of regions appearing in both the 2008 and 2014 WCIR analysis, it is the dominant Chinese regions that show huge increases in their competitiveness. Shanghai has risen over 95 places in the consistent rankings from 127th in 2008 to 32nd in 2014. Beijing has also seen a similar leap in performance from 123rd to 33rd in the consistent WCIR rankings. This is likely to reflect the connections that both these regions have to the international knowledge economy community.

Table 9.4 Changes in rankings of BRIC regions 2008–2014 (based on a consistent sample of regions)

2014 overall rank	*BRIC region*	*Nation*	*Consistent sample for 2008 and 2014*		
			2014 rank	*2008 rank*	*Change in rank*
41	Shanghai	China	32	127	95
42	Beijing	China	33	123	90
192	Tianjin	China	117	134	17
253	Jiangsu	China	127	139	12
252	Zhejiang	China	126	138	12
257	Guangdong	China	128	136	8
350	Shandong	China	135	142	7
512	Andhra Pradesh	India	139	145	6
509	Maharashtra	India	138	143	5
522	Karnataka	India	140	144	4
238	Hong Kong	Hong Kong	124	124	0

In the case of Shanghai, this region operates most strongly through the private sector (Wu, 2007), with it being particularly successful in drawing in Western FDI and diffusing this technology throughout the region (Gan, 2003; Fu, 2008). This investment has tended to be more advanced than in other regions (Gan, 2003), which has aided the diffusion of technology and knowledge. State-owned enterprises and their employees have also had long-established relationships with private enterprises in Shanghai, providing technical expertise and close customer–supplier relationships (Wei *et al.*, 2007). Furthermore, as Li (2009) notes, Shanghai's universities are more reliant on the private sector for funding, necessitating a more commercial perspective.

Beijing is more government controlled, with its state-owned enterprises providing employees with high levels of remuneration (Zhao, 2002). Wu (2007), however, highlights the competition being generated by the private sector for skilled staff. In terms of global knowledge pipelines, Beijing, with its world-recognized research-intensive universities, has often been found to provide a link from the Chinese academic community to the wider global science and technology communities (Liefner and Hennemann, 2011). This public sector-led engagement is also evident in the high levels of government investment in research institutions and enterprises in the Beijing region (Wu, 2010; Scherngell and Hu, 2011). In addition, the preferred route for commercializing university research is through University Owned Technology Enterprises (UOTE) rather than the traditional Western university spinout model, which is being more widely adopted elsewhere in China (Kroll and Liefner, 2008).

It is interesting to note that the increase in competitiveness enjoyed by China's two leading regions is not evident to the same extent in the other Chinese regions. Ke (2010) suggests that there is more evidence of spreading effects in the Eastern China. However, although all Chinese regions improved their rankings, the disproportionate increases in competitiveness enjoyed relative to other regions suggests that these two growth poles are beginning to suck in resources from other regions more than neighbouring regions are enjoying spillovers from connectivity with more successful regions.

The three Indian regions that can be compared over the six-year period have enjoyed an increase in their rankings. However, they lag behind the Chinese regions in terms of improvement in relative competitiveness. It has been suggested that part of India's underperformance is due to it being less willing to open its economy to international firms (Herd and Dougherty, 2007). Whereas Chinese regions have built much of their success on exploiting and diffusing international knowledge and technology rapidly, the Indian approach to foreign enterprise has been much more protectionist (Herd and Dougherty, 2007).

The nature of regional competitiveness in the BRIC economies

As the previous section highlighted, there is much more heterogeneity across BRIC regions compared with their European or North American counterparts. This could be expected to lead to quite different sources of competitiveness being drawn upon by the most and least competitive regions. As shown in Chapter 5, the WCIR components that make the largest relative contribution are those associated with 5th-wave knowledge capital and outputs and outcomes. However, as noted above, it is unlikely that this will be the case for all four nations within the group, or even all regions within individual nations, as not all regions have enjoyed the same magnitude of growth.

Table 9.5 presents the average absolute contributions of the four components for the BRIC regions when split by quartiles of competitiveness. The most competitive quartile of BRIC regions have a competitiveness score that places them just below the average for all regions included in the WCIR. This reflects the fact that although these regions have developed quickly, with the exception of Russian regions, they have started from a low base (Cooper, 2006). Furthermore, the increase in competitiveness and associated economic growth has not been distributed evenly across the BRIC regions (Fedorov, 2002; Kolenikov and Shorrocks, 2005; Ma, 2006; Fleisher *et al.*, 2010; D'Costa, 2011; Freguglia and Menezes-Filho, 2012).

Although these regions have invested large amounts in their education systems, particularly their universities (Yuan, 2011), they still score below the average regional level for the knowledge sustainability component (average = 0). The continued investment in knowledge sustainability is likely to be of growing importance as the BRIC regions begin to lose their cost advantage (Mok, 2009; Yang *et al.*, 2010). Regions are likely to enjoy high returns from investment in university education compared to earlier stages of education, reflecting the changes taking place within the BRIC economies as knowledge-based development takes a more prominent role (Carnoy *et al.*, 2012). Nevertheless, given the large populations of the BRIC nations, it will take a considerable period of time to achieve levels of human capital equivalent to those regions in more developed nations (de Araujo, 2012; Chattopadhyay and Mukhopadhyay, 2013). This suggests that uneven development will continue, with the more successful BRIC regions drawing in skilled labour from other regions.

The most competitive BRIC regions are, on average, beginning to achieve output/outcome component scores similar to the WCIR sample average. This is likely to reflect not only the growing knowledge economies within leading

Table 9.5 Absolute contribution to competitiveness by WCIR components in BRIC regions

	5th-wave knowledge capital	*4th-wave knowledge capital*	*Outputs/ outcomes*	*Knowl. sustain.*	*WCIR*
1st quartile	0.16	0.18	–0.05	–0.31	99.1
2nd quartile	–0.14	–0.07	–0.47	–0.67	50.2
3rd quartile	–0.41	–0.32	–0.55	–0.69	27.7
4th quartile	–0.70	–0.49	–0.98	–1.06	–18.6

Note: Knowl. sustain. = Knowledge sustainability.

regions, but also the boom in natural resources that has aided a number of Russian regions, in particular, to boost productivity (Ahrend, 2012). The drop to the second quartile of regions is quite sharp, further indicating the unevenness of development.

Indigenous and foreign investments in certain industries have led to increased competitiveness in terms of 4th- and 5th-wave knowledge capital for the leading group of BRIC regions. This is reflected by the fact that such regions are beginning to dominate not only trade in more basic products, but also trade associated with more advanced goods and services (Gouvea *et al.*, 2013). However, only the most competitive BRIC regions have scores for these components approaching the sample average, although unlike the output and outcome measure, this stronger performance stretches to the second quartile.

The absolute contribution figures suggest that 4th- and 5th-wave knowledge capital are providing the greatest contribution to competitiveness in the BRIC regions. In order to make this more visible, Figure 9.2 presents the relative contributions of the four components of the WCIR. As suggested by the absolute contributions, 4th- and 5th-wave knowledge capital provide the largest relative contribution for BRIC regions regardless of their overall level of competitiveness. The 4th-wave knowledge capital factor is the most important component overall, and in many cases this knowledge capital is likely to have been initially imported from other nations (Chen *et al.*, 2010), although regions in China and India, in particular, have made efforts to develop their own indigenous R&D presence in these areas (Li *et al.*, 2013). Predictably, given the speed with which many BRIC

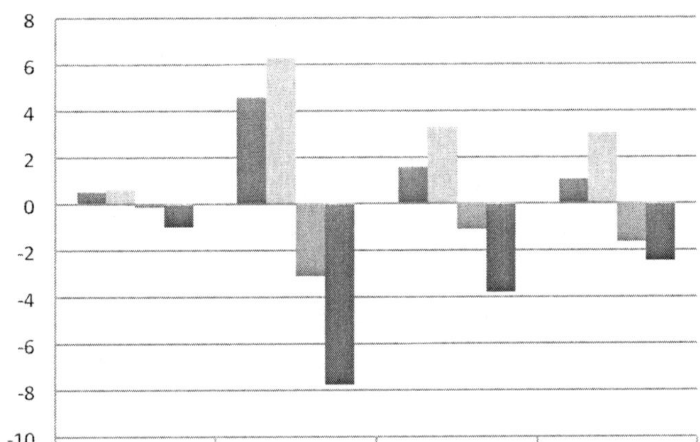

	1st Quartile	2nd Quartile	3rd Quartile	4th Quartile
5th-wave knowledge capital	0.54	4.59	1.60	1.07
4th-wave knowledge capital	0.62	6.28	3.31	3.03
Outputs/Outcomes	-0.15	-3.10	-1.10	-1.64
Knowledge sustainability	-1.00	-7.77	-3.80	-2.46

Figure 9.2 Relative contribution of WCIR components to the competitiveness of BRIC regions

economies have grown and increased their competitiveness, the sustainability component has the lowest relative contribution.

Overall, the most competitive BRIC regions are clearly atypical of the BRIC bloc of regions as a whole, and draw their competitiveness from a number of different sources. This means that the relative contributions of the four components show much less variation for the 1st quartile of BRIC regions than other groups after scaling.

As the BRIC regions do not have the same tradition of connections and strong trade relationships as North American and European regions, it is of interest to examine how the regions belonging to each BRIC nation differs in terms of the average contributions made by the four components of the WCIR. Table 9.6 presents the average absolute contributions for the four components by BRIC nation. Of the regions included, the average competitiveness of the Chinese regions is by far the highest, and is close to the overall average for the WCIR sample. The Russian and Brazilian regions are below the whole sample average, but still lead the Indian regions by a considerable margin. The Chinese regions stand out as having an average absolute contribution from 4th- and 5th-wave knowledge capital above the WCIR sample average. The Chinese regions also, on average, have the best outputs and outcomes, and knowledge sustainability. In part, this reflects the exclusion of some less competitive Chinese regions from the sample.

On average, the Russian regions have the second highest 4th-wave knowledge capital, outputs and outcomes, and knowledge sustainability scores. However, it is the Brazilian regions that have the second highest absolute contribution from 5th-wave knowledge capital. Commentators such as Watkins (2003) and Cooper (2006) have noted that the Russian economy, whilst having a tradition of scientific research along with the existence of knowledge economy infrastructure, has overly relied on natural resources for its economic prosperity. This means that Brazilian regions may begin to close the gap with the Russian regions in the future, as they build their own knowledge infrastructure. However, a number of Brazilian regions also have an abundance of natural resources and, as scholars such as Leamer (1999) and Sachs and Warner (2001) suggest, there can be a curse – the 'resource curse' – from such natural wealth, as investments in more sustainable routes to competitiveness are ignored. It is interesting to note that patent

Table 9.6 Absolute contribution to competitiveness by WCIR components in BRIC regions by nation

	5th-wave knowledge capital	*4th-wave knowledge capital*	*Outputs/ outcomes*	*Knowl. sustain.*	*WCIR*
Brazil	–0.15	–0.31	–0.57	–0.61	39.6
China	0.22	0.32	–0.14	–0.37	100.8
India	–0.67	–0.46	–1.00	–1.11	–19.2
Russia	–0.22	–0.08	–0.34	–0.57	55.7

Note: Knowl. sustain. = Knowledge sustainability.

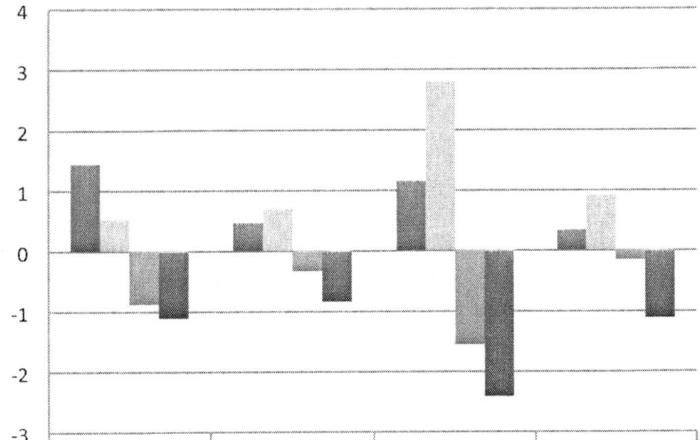

	Brazil	China	India	Russia
5th-wave knowledge capital	1.45	0.47	1.16	0.35
4th-wave knowledge capital	0.53	0.70	2.80	0.92
Outputs/Outcomes	-0.88	-0.33	-1.55	-0.15
Knowledge sustainability	-1.11	-0.84	-2.41	-1.11

Figure 9.3 Relative contribution of WCIR components to the competitiveness of BRIC regions by nation

counts in both Russia and Brazil rose rapidly from the early 1990s, but levelled off at the turn of the millennium, whilst patent counts in China and India have continued to increase (Tseng, 2009).

Figure 9.3 presents the average relative contributions for the BRIC regions. What is notable is that although having quite different traditions and resources, there is a very similar pattern across all four nations. In general, the 4th- and 5th-wave knowledge capital components are over-contributing, whilst output and outcomes, and knowledge sustainability are under-contributing. Although many of the Russian regions appearing in the top 20 BRIC regions are highly reliant on natural resources for their competitiveness overall, the output and outcome component makes a smaller relative contribution than the 4th- and 5th-wave knowledge capital. The one difference in the pattern of relative contributions is that found for Brazil. As noted above, Brazil has developed strengths in 5th-wave knowledge capital, leading to this component having the greatest relative contribution, on average, as opposed to 4th-wave knowledge capital in the case of regions in the other BRIC nations.

Concluding remarks

This chapter has sought to disaggregate the global rise of the BRIC economies to a regional level in order to understand the patterns and nature of changing competitiveness trajectories in these emerging economies. It is clear that leading Chinese regions are to some extent a breed apart in terms of the rapid rates of development occurring in these locations. In particular, these go far beyond that seen in India and most of Brazil. The regional analysis of the Russian regions shows that some locations possess massive competitive strength in terms of natural resources, whilst others are continuing to convert to more knowledge-based regional economies. In the coming years, it will be interesting to see how these regions fare when compared to the newly emerging regional knowledge-bases in the Middle East, which are the focus of the next chapter.

Note

1 The numbers in parentheses represent the 2012/13 world universities ranking of the *Times Higher Education*: www.timeshighereducation.co.uk/world-university-rankings/2012-13/world-ranking.

10 The competitiveness of Middle Eastern regions

This chapter explores the extent to which Middle Eastern regions have generated relatively high or low levels of competitiveness. Whilst many Middle Eastern regions may owe some of their competitiveness to the natural advantages of oil reserves, as is the case for some of the Russian regions examined in Chapter 9, for others their competitiveness has been achieved through other means. In general, many Middle Eastern regions are quite different from the majority of the regions covered by the WCIR. Their small size and high degree of autonomy means that many of the regions are effectively independent states. A further difference is that, for some, their governments are not necessarily regarded as democratic political economies. This is likely to influence the policies and approaches that are pursued. For example, there is a danger that governments will propose routes to competitiveness that lead to self-enrichment (Schwarz, 2008; Brach, 2009). However, there is also the potential to pursue more active and direct policies to achieve higher levels of competitiveness for the benefit of the entire population (Collier and Hoeffler, 2009), particularly through the use of sovereign wealth funds and state-owned corporations (Harris, 2009).

Middle Eastern nations and their regions have been characterized by some as 'rentier states' (Brach, 2009), whereby a rent-seeking culture characterized by traits such as a large welfare deadweight loss, a perception of the market as rewarding the rich and well-connected, and a focus on rent capture rather than innovation (Krueger, 1974), is likely to hold back regional competitiveness. As Rodrik *et al.* (2004) find, institutions are often more important than geography and trade integration for economic development, and it is quite conceivable that the unique political economy of Middle Eastern regions will have profound effects on both their overall competitiveness and also the sources of this competitiveness.

Patterns of regional competitiveness within the Middle East

As noted above, many Middle Eastern regions have advantages associated with natural resources. However, whilst this can boost the output and outcome component of the WCIR, through artificially high labour productivity and employment, these same resources may hold back the development of other components of competitiveness as the population develops a 'feeling of entitlement' (Leamer, 1999; Auty, 2007). As a result, a number of Middle Eastern regions are within nations that fit with Beblawi and Luciani's (1987) definition of the rentier state, whereby a considerable proportion of government income is linked to the exploitation of natural resource wealth rather than tax receipts. This reduces obligations to tax payers and the constraints they face when determining where to spend income (Anderson, 1987). Furthermore, Middle Eastern regions have traditionally been constrained by their climate (Brach, 2009) and human capital resources (Ewers, 2013). Historically, Middle Eastern regions have formed parts of larger empires, as well as being treated as colonies by Western powers in the early- and mid-twentieth century, with independence only being acquired relatively recently (Owen, 2004). This may have directly limited their economic development and opportunities to increase their level of competitiveness. Indirectly, the governance structures developed after independence are to a large degree also influenced by the previous Western powers (Louis, 1984; Owen, 2004), which again may have limited development.

Although neo-classical growth theories such as the Solow (1957) model assume that output is a function of capital and labour, studies have found that only a small proportion (roughly one third) of the difference in growth rates between East Asian nations and those in other regions, such as Latin America, can be explained by differences in labour and capital accumulation (World Bank, 1993). The implication is that it is not just the extent to which investments are made, but also the means by which they are made (Auty, 2007). Linked to this, studies such as Bisat *et al.* (1997) and Nabli and Véganzonès-Varoundakis (2007) have found that investments in physical and human capital have not been matched by improvements in total factor productivity within the Middle East. This has often seen such resource-rich economies fall behind their counterparts (Auty, 2001).

All of the above factors make it no surprise to find that the average level of regional competitiveness in the Middle East is relatively low, with a WCIR score of 39.1 and a median ranking of 411th (Table 10.1). This is below the average competitiveness found for the BRIC regions in Chapter 9, average WCIR score of 39.7 (even though an economy such as India is still heavily influenced by its agrarian sector (D'Costa, 2011)).

Table 10.1 Summary statistics of Middle Eastern regions' competitiveness

	WCIR score	*WCIR rank*
Average	39.1	388
Median	31.7	411
Maximum	168.8	111
Minimum	–21.8	523
Range	190.6	412
Skewness	1.8	–1.2
Kurtosis	4.1	1.5

The range of regional competitiveness is also low compared to that found for the North American, European and BRIC regions, although it is still more than two standard deviations of the underlying indicators. This pattern of regional competitiveness across the Middle East is illustrated by Figure 10.1, with the most competitive three regions exhibiting significantly higher levels of competitiveness than the other regions.

Considering those Middle Eastern regions that are the most competitive, they clearly possess a range of differing economic characteristics (Table 10.2). A number are small oil-rich states such as Kuwait and Qatar, while others are regions of larger countries that include the capital city or other large agglomerations, such as Al-Riyadh and Istanbul. The most competitive region included in the Middle Eastern analysis is Israel (WCIR score 168.8, ranked 111th). This is, perhaps, of little surprise as Israel has long had trade ties to Europe and North America (Baier and Bergstrand, 2007; Munin, 2010). An absence of natural resources has ensured that Israel has achieved competitiveness through different routes to many of the Middle Eastern regions. In particular, it has established a considerable presence in high-technology-based sectors (Rosenberg, 2010), and Almor (2011) provides examples of how small high-technology firms within Israel have continued to prosper following the economic downturn of 2008, largely due to their flexibility, innovative nature and export orientation. Breznitz (2013) also notes the success of small innovative firms within Israel, although doubt is cast on the sustainability of clusters based purely on the innovation phase of the production cycle. It is suggested that for continued regional growth access to firms across the different stages of production will be required (Breznitz, 2013).

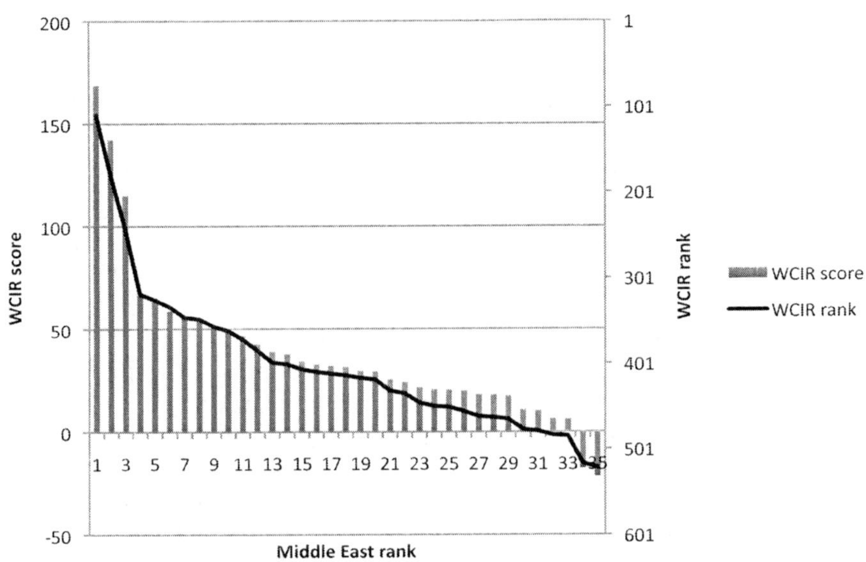

Figure 10.1 Regional competitiveness across Middle Eastern regions

Table 10.2 Ten most competitive Middle Eastern regions

WCIR Middle East rank	*Middle East region*	*Nation*	*WCIR score*	*WCIR World rank*
1	Israel	Israel	168.75	111
2	Qatar	Qatar	142.33	181
3	Kuwait	Kuwait	114.95	244
4	Abu Dhabi	United Arab Emirates	66.44	320
5	Al-Riyadh	Saudi Arabia	65.43	327
6	Eastern Region	Saudi Arabia	58.95	335
7	Istanbul	Turkey	55.48	347
8	Al-Qaseem	Saudi Arabia	55.40	349
9	East Marmara	Turkey	52.22	358
10	Dubai	United Arab Emirates	50.40	363

Alongside Israel are the oil-rich small states of Qatar (WCIR score 142.3, ranked 181st) and Kuwait (WCIR score 115.0, ranked 244th). These regions are the only ones to achieve a level of competitiveness above the WCIR sample average of 100. Many of the other relatively competitive regions are those found in central and eastern Saudi Arabia and the United Arab Emirates, each of which has high levels of oil reserves. The difficulty faced by these regions is the extent to which they can maintain or further develop their competitiveness in a manner that is not so fully reliant on these reserves (Kingdom of Saudi Arabia Ministry of Economy and Planning, 2004; Simmons, 2005; Brach, 2009; Alshumaimri *et al.*, 2010).

Auty (2007) outlines three key factors that may help ensure that natural resource wealth is used in a manner that is sustainable and will ultimately increase competitiveness. First, the establishment of an offshore capital fund set up to capture the rent associated with natural resources and reduce the potential for rent seeking behaviour. Second, the use of rents from natural resource wealth to be made in an open and transparent manner, as a means of limiting rent seeking; and third, the establishment of an organization with responsibility for assessing the most effective alternative uses of capital funds.

Abu Dhabi in the United Arab Emirates, the fourth most competitive Middle Eastern region (WCIR score 66.4, ranked 320th), is one of the regions that has most strongly embraced the sovereign wealth fund approach. Its most important capital fund, the Abu Dhabi Investment Authority, was initiated in 1976 and is estimated to have US$627 billion of assets under management (Sovereign Wealth Fund Institute, 2012). However, as noted above, it is important that these capital funds are not only present, but also well designed and transparent, otherwise there is a danger of a lack of public spending control (Davis *et al.*, 2001), resulting in further rent seeking occurring (Auty, 2007).

The Emirate of Dubai also appears in the top 10 Middle Eastern regions (WCIR score 50.4, ranked 363rd), and although it is below the average for the whole WCIR sample, it is fast positioning itself as a significant financial centre (Cheung, 2010). However, the danger of investment in domestic infrastructure in Dubai is that it is often capital intensive and provides less benefit for the population as a whole. As such, Dubai's overseas investments may be just as important and a more efficient use of resources until the economy has further developed its competitiveness (Auty, 1990).

As is the case for many larger nations, there is variation in the competitiveness across Middle Eastern regions, with there being an identifiable core and periphery (Krugman, 1991, 2011). In the same way that many of the most competitive regions owe their competitiveness to the 'luck' of considerable natural resources or agglomeration, the least competitive regions are those that nature has not favoured in the same manner. In the case of Turkey, Istanbul has a population in excess of 13 million and enjoys considerable agglomeration effects, with the adjacent region of East Marmara further benefiting from spillover effects. In general, studies have found a split between the more successful west and less successful east of Turkey (Ersoy and Taylor, 2012).

Table 10.3 indicates that the majority of the least competitive regions are located in the two largest Middle Eastern nations included in the sample: Saudi Arabia (five regions) and Turkey (three regions). The least competitive Saudi Arabian regions are located in the north (Northern Borders, Al-Jouf, Tabouk) or south (Jazan and Najran) away from the main oil producing areas of the nation. The lagging regions of Turkey are the less densely populated regions in the east of the country. The differing governance mechanisms and institutions of the Middle Eastern states are visible here. For instance, although the Saudi regions differ greatly in terms of their access to natural resources, there are not the same disparities in competitiveness present as there are between the regions of the US, for example, or some of the European and BRIC nations, particularly Russia and China. In the case of Saudi Arabia, whilst a more centralized managed economy may not allow leading regions to achieve the level of competitiveness that could

Table 10.3 Ten least competitive Middle Eastern regions

WCIR Middle East rank	*Middle East region*	*Nation*	*WCIR score*	*WCIR World rank*
26	Najran	Saudi Arabia	19.98	457
27	Ras Al - Khaimah	United Arab Emirates	18.21	463
28	Tabouk	Saudi Arabia	18.16	464
29	Fujairah	United Arab Emirates	17.60	466
30	Middle East Anatolia	Turkey	10.88	478
31	Southeast Anatolia	Turkey	10.34	480
32	Northeast Anatolia	Turkey	6.39	485
33	Al-Jouf	Saudi Arabia	6.25	486
34	Jazan	Saudi Arabia	–17.86	518
35	Northern Borders	Saudi Arabia	–21.84	523

be reached with freer markets, this approach does potentially provide more freedom to redistribute resources (Collier and Hoeffler, 2009), which may prevent the development of large disparities between regions.

In terms of achieving the maximum level of national welfare, such an approach may have benefits (Brun *et al.*, 2002). However, it may also have long-term consequences, particularly where a high-rent approach is taken and governments move away from wealth creation to rent redistribution. A further outcome of this approach is that it may not lead to increased industrialization, which would absorb labour and reduce poverty, but an economy within which the civil service becomes over-expanded (Auty, 2007). This leads to a bureaucratic regional economy within which physical (Auty and Kiiski, 2001), human (Birdsall *et al.*, 2001), and social capital (Woolcock *et al.*, 2001) are accumulated more slowly. Unfortunately, such a system is largely self-sustaining (Acemoglu *et al.*, 2011), and there have been calls for greater autonomy to be given to provinces, which reflects growing dissatisfaction with corruption and the mismanagement of regional development projects (Al-Rasheed, 2013). This helps to explain the relatively low average competitiveness of the Middle Eastern regions identified in Table 10.1, even with the advantages many enjoy. In the case of economies such as Turkey, the weaker regions in the east of the nation have suffered further difficulties in the form of terrorist activities that have hindered investment and limited competitiveness (Öcal and Yildirim, 2010; Derin-Gure, 2011).

Brach (2009) uses the Heritage Foundation's 'Index of Economic Freedom' (Miller *et al.*, 2013) as a proxy for economic institutions in order to link such institutions and economic development. No equivalent measure is available at the regional level, but Table 10.4 reports the national Index of Economic Freedom measures for the relevant nations in 2013. There seems to be evidence to suggest that a number of the Middle Eastern regions are developing stronger economic institutions, and it might be expected that, along with the other developments discussed above, this will lead to competitiveness improvements in future years. Qatar and the regions of the United Arab Emirates appear to be best positioned to move beyond their dependence on natural resource wealth (Cevik, 2011). In the case of Kuwait, although it is one of the most competitive Middle Eastern regions, it may struggle to utilize its mineral wealth in an efficient manner to

Table 10.4 Economic Freedom Index 2013

Nation	*World rank (N = 177)*	*2013 Score*
Qatar	27	71.3
United Arab Emirates	28	71.1
Israel	51	66.9
Kuwait	66	63.1
Turkey	69	62.9
Saudi Arabia	82	60.6

Source: Miller *et al.* (2013)

maintain or increase its competitiveness. In the case of Turkish regions, they are less likely to be influenced by the resource curse, but weak economic institutions may also hinder their ability to improve their competitiveness in future years.

The nature of competitiveness in Middle Eastern regions

In general, the most competitive regions in the Middle East are those that have developed beyond their traditional reliance on natural resource exploitation, and diversified their economies toward high-technology manufacturing or advanced service-based sectors. Those regions within the Middle East that are the least competitive tend to be the more peripheral regions, which lack natural resource wealth and do not possess a large urban agglomeration. In some cases these regions are reliant on the better resourced regions for their level of welfare, particularly through the subsidized supply of goods (Silva *et al.*, 2013).

Table 10.5 divides regions into those with above or below median Middle Eastern regional competitiveness in order to examine in more detail the nature of competitiveness differences. Overall, it is clear that both the relatively more competitive (WCIR score 64.5) and less competitive (WCIR score 15.1) regions in the Middle East display levels of competitiveness below the average for the WCIR sample and, as the analysis in the preceding section showed, these figures to some extent hide the overall variation in competitiveness levels, with Israel, Qatar and Kuwait displaying much higher levels of competitiveness than the majority of the remaining regions.

The one component that differs little between the most and least competitive Middle Eastern regions is that of knowledge sustainability. For both sets of regions the mean average of this component is well below the average for the overall sample of regions. In fact, successful Middle Eastern regions, such as Dubai and Abu Dhabi in the United Arab Emirates, are highly reliant on foreign labour for the continued development of their industries (Toledo, 2011). This is consistent with studies that have found much of the growth in the Middle East to be associated with physical capital accumulation, rather than human capital (Abu-Qarn and Abu-Bader, 2007). As such, knowledge absorption from foreign companies has been relatively low (UNDP, 2003), and there seems to be little evidence that the relevant infrastructure and investment is being made in the

Table 10.5 Absolute contributions to competitiveness by WCIR components in more and less competitive Middle Eastern regions

	5th-wave knowledge capital	*4th-wave knowledge capital*	*Outputs/ outcomes*	*Knowl. sustain.*	*WCIR*
More competitive	–0.30	–0.32	0.14	–0.49	64.5
Less competitive	–0.53	–0.68	–0.55	–0.54	15.1

Note: Knowl. sustain. = Knowledge sustainability.

knowledge sustainability component of development. In the case of education, however, it should be noted that whilst investment may be significant as a whole, it is not always distributed effectively (World Bank, 2007). Ibourk and Amaghouss (2012) suggest that less affluent nations often display high levels of education inequality, so that benefits from increased investment in education are largely received by a relatively rich minority of the population. There are also suggestions that universities are not providing graduates with the skills required by the private sector (Achoui, 2009).

The most competitive regions clearly have higher levels of 4th- and 5th-wave knowledge capital, although crucially this component remains below the global average. This suggests that whilst attempts have been made by a number of regions to diversify their economies, these efforts have not been wholly successful. For a number of these resource-rich economies, the inability to reduce their dependence on their staple product may again be associated with the potential for rent-seeking activities. Olson (1982) outlines how those associated with mineral extraction will potentially limit the adoption of new innovations and technologies through political pressure to protect their own positions. In contrast to a number of the BRIC regions, which have been able to adopt and adapt foreign technologies to establish considerable stocks of 4th- and 5th-wave knowledge capital, efforts in most Middle Eastern regions have been less apparent.

One fundamental explanation for this lack of knowledge-upgrading lies with the weak private sector found in these economies. The private sector of many of the Middle Eastern regions is dependent on state patronage rather than entrepreneurship, with it being poorly connected to the global economy, which limits its ability to adopt new technologies and exploit economies of scale (Malik and Awadallah, 2013). Indeed, in some Middle Eastern nations changes in productivity rates are found to be negatively associated with economic growth (Abu-Qarn and Abu-Bader, 2007). The exception to this is Israel, which is found to enjoy increases in total factor productivity (TFP) resulting from investments in new technology. In comparison, much of the economic growth experienced in Turkey is attributable to investments in physical capital, with a negative contribution from productivity growth, and a small contribution from improvements in human capital. This is not to say that economic development in nations such as China is entirely due to increases in productivity, as increases in physical and human capital also dominate for most East Asian nations, but efficiency improvements from technological advancements are also present (Krugman, 1994b), and may play a more important role for nations achieving higher levels of development (Collins and Bosworth, 1996).

Where new industries have been established, evidence of their success is not universal. For instance, Ersoy and Taylor (2012) suggest that there may be a negative relationship between the presence of knowledge workers and growth in Turkey. However, the dependent variable in their analysis is change in the unemployment rate, which means there is a danger of reverse causality. The success and higher remuneration in such industries may attract labour to the region, which the knowledge industries are unable to absorb, at least in the short term.

Consistent with this, there has been a marked migration from regions in the east to those in the west of the country in recent years (Kırdar and Saracoğlu, 2008; Yildirim *et al.*, 2009).

Attempts to rectify the deficiencies in both 4th-wave knowledge capital and knowledge sustainability are notable in some economies, such as Saudi Arabia's investment in infrastructure and the development of global knowledge links for its universities; for example, the establishment of the King Abdullah University of Science and Technology in the Saudi Arabian region of Makkah Al-Mokarramah (Fischer, 2008).

In general, Middle Eastern regions often possess considerable resources, but they are struggling to increase their competitiveness. Only the most successful regions enjoy component scores above the whole sample average, and then only for the output and outcomes component. Figure 10.2 presents the relative contributions of the components in order to identify the main sources of competitiveness for each group. The relative contributions confirm the importance that the output and outcome component plays in increasing the competitiveness of the more successful regions. Knowledge sustainability, in particular, is far below the level that might be expected given the amount of available wealth in these regions. For the less competitive regions, the relative contribution of the 5th-wave knowledge capital, outputs and outcomes, and knowledge sustainability components are most apparent, and it is in terms of the

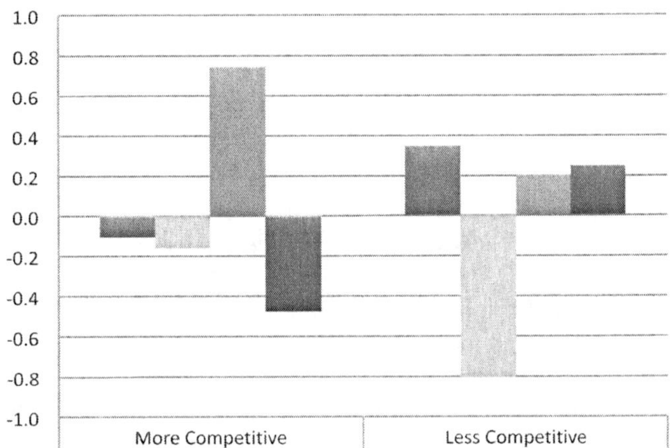

	More Competitive	Less Competitive
5th-wave knowledge capital	-0.11	0.35
4th-wave knowledge capital	-0.16	-0.80
Outputs/Outcomes	0.75	0.20
Knowledge sustainability	-0.48	0.25

Figure 10.2 Relative contribution of WCIR components to the competitiveness of Middle East regions

4th-wave knowledge capital where the less competitive Middle Eastern regions lag most. This contrasts strongly with the results found for the BRIC regions, which have utilized 4th-wave knowledge capital, often imported from other nations, to boost their competitiveness (Chen *et al.*, 2010).

Regional development policies in the Middle East

The policies pursued by Middle Eastern regions to encourage economic development have not necessarily followed the approaches utilized by other regions at the same stage of development. With the exceptions of regions within Saudi Arabia, Turkey and Israel, it could be argued that Middle Eastern regions are attempting to leap-frog industrialization in order to develop knowledge-based economies that could be described in Western terms as post-industrial (Ewers and Malecki, 2010). Some of the policies being utilized in Middle Eastern regions have taken a 'if you build it, they will come' approach, such as the development from scratch of Jubail in the northeast of Saudi Arabia (Clary and Karlin, 2011). This is a tricky proposition since the competitiveness of a knowledge-based service sector is often built upon the demand for professional services by key parts of the manufacturing sector (Guerrieri and Meliciani, 2005). This becomes self-sustaining once a competitive position is reached, as the service sector itself also becomes one of the main customers for services. Reaching this point, however, without an existing manufacturing sector may be harder. Many Middle Eastern regions have the rent from oil production to finance investments, but choosing the most effective and appropriate investments to make is the bigger problem (Auty, 2007). In order to address this, policy efforts are being made to enhance lagging knowledge sustainability and 4th- and 5th-wave knowledge capital. However, the traditional approach of paying for the population to study abroad has not been entirely successful, with funding not always linked to studying courses that are appropriate for the type of knowledge-based services economy that Middle Eastern regions are seeking (Looney, 1994).

Acknowledging the unsustainable nature of economies based on the exploitation of natural resources, Al-Riyadh in Saudi Arabia is one of a number of regions to invest heavily in educational and research infrastructure, such as the King Saud University (Onsman, 2011). The first Saudi Arabian mixed-gender higher-education institution, the King Abdullah University of Science and Technology (KAUST), was also recently established in Makkah Al-Mokarramah (Clary and Karlin, 2011). Alongside the high investment in domestic educational resources, the Saudi Arabian authorities have also attempted to accelerate the process through policies such as the King Abdullah Foreign Scholarship Program, which funds its population to study in Western universities. The programme's scale is apparent in the fact that Saudi Arabia has the highest proportion of its population across all nations studying internationally (Clary and Karlin, 2011).

Other regions in the Middle East have followed a slightly different path, with one approach being to encourage Western universities to establish campuses and 'knowledge cities' through the use of subsidies, such as the Education City in

Qatar or International Academic City in Dubai (Krieger, 2008). However, these investments have little direct input from their parent universities, so that effectively just a brand is being sold (Lewin, 2008). This may explain why attempts to increase the education of the indigenous population of many regions, as a means of improving participation rates in the growing knowledge intensive sectors, have not been entirely successful, with managers in the United Arab Emirates often being reluctant to recruit from the national population due to a distrust of indigenous capabilities and work-readiness (Al-Ali, 2007).

In an attempt to mirror the success of university science park regions, such as Silicon Valley (Saxenian, 1994) and the Research Triangle Park (Link and Scott, 2003; Weddle *et al.*, 2006) in the US region of Durham-Chapel Hill, the Riyadh Techno Valley Park has been developed at King Saud University (Alshumaimri *et al.*, 2010). The science park aims to boost the skills and abilities of university staff and students as knowledge workers, as well as enabling greater knowledge and technology transfer with private sector businesses. The park is intended to focus primarily on those sectors perceived to have the greatest potential for boosting productivity in industries related to chemical technology and materials; biological, agriculture and environmental technologies; and information and communication technologies. In many ways, Saudi Arabia is leading the way with such investments, with the majority of universities in Middle Eastern regions continuing to function primarily as education and training institutions, with little emphasis on research activity (Weir, 2007).

Attempts to foster more diversified knowledge-based economies have been the focus of policies in Abu Dhabi, with the objective being to provide sustainable employment for the region's population (Davidson, 2009). Encouraging young workers to take jobs in the private sector is difficult, with the alternative of highly paid and relatively low-effort public-sector jobs stemming from a culture of entitlement (Leamer, 1999). As noted above, managers of private firms are wary of the engagement of local individuals, and in order to integrate United Arab Emirate nationals into the private-sector workforce policies requiring quotas have been utilized (Al-Ali, 2007). However, the lack of motivation means that even when employed there are still difficulties of fostering the indigenous workforce to achieve higher levels of productive effort (Marcel, 2006). Kuran (2004) suggests that Islamic institutions have hindered the development of an enterprise sector, constraining the ability to harness the knowledge and technology accessed through policies devised to drive indigenous innovation (Dodgson, 2000). Ewers and Malecki (2010) suggest that there is a need to promote greater interaction between local regional firms and foreign affiliates to boost knowledge transfer. Indeed, even the most competitive Middle Eastern regions, such as Dubai, are failing to provide appropriate mechanisms to boost interactions between universities, foreign firms and domestic firms (Ferretti and Parmentola, 2007).

Ross (2008) suggests that ensuring there is a clear agreement as to how mineral wealth will be utilized and distributed is important and, where possible, should be established before extraction occurs, in order to avoid potential conflict. This provides a difficult conundrum in relation to the design of sovereign wealth funds. Auty (2007) highlights the need for funds to be transparent, with the investment decision-making processes being required to consider all available options, both domestic and international. However, whilst rules on the proportion of rent absorbed by a capital fund, and the categories on which it is spent, reduces the potential for political interference, it can also prevent adjustment when revenues change over time and previous spending plans are no longer appropriate. Davis *et al.* (2001) question the viability of sovereign wealth funds, given the ability of governments to circumnavigate the fiscal discipline that such funds are intended to impose. Where funds have a stabilization function they are intended to prevent overspending in periods of high oil revenues and expensive borrowing in periods of falling oil revenues. Stabilization can be undermined where funds are earmarked for certain types of off-budget spending, which may have long term ramifications where recurring expenditure will appear in future budgets. Whilst the saving function of funds is intended to ensure that oil revenues are available for future generations, the problem is that a government can always borrow to finance flows into the fund, resulting in no additional saving actually occurring.

Concluding remarks

This chapter has analysed the competitiveness of a range of regions across Middle Eastern economies. It has shown that whilst there are a small number of globally competitive regions, most still have some way to go before they move into the higher competitiveness echelons. Despite much investment in regions in economies such as Saudi Arabia and the United Arab Emirates, these regions still perform below the global average. However, it is still early days in terms of these regions reaping the competitiveness rewards of such investments, and time will tell whether or not these investments achieve their apparent promise. Furthermore, it is clear that the complexities of the political economies of the nations within which these regions are located, especially the role of sovereign wealth funds, adds a significant dimension in terms of the efficiency and effectiveness of the link between investment and competitiveness. It will, therefore, be interesting to monitor changes in Middle Eastern regional competitiveness in comparison with both the more western and eastern politico-economic regimes in coming years.

11 Regional competitiveness benchmarking and policymaking

Previous chapters of this book have largely focused on analysing and benchmarking the global competitiveness of regions based on their revealed 'performance' across a range of related metrics. This chapter suggests that such performance measurement should form part of a suite of regional benchmarking exercises that also cover the benchmarking of the processes and institutions underlying the functioning of regional economic systems, as well as the public policies that impact on regional economic performance. In essence, it is argued that regional competitiveness benchmarking exercises should employ a '3P' methodology encompassing the performance, process, and policy contexts as a means of providing a rounded assessment and evaluation of the economic development trajectories of regions.

The concept of benchmarking first came to prominence in the corporate sector, initially in Japan and then adopted by firms such as Rank Xerox, as a means of identifying and learning from 'best-in-class' practices or products from elsewhere (Underwood, 2002; Murphy, 2005). Benchmarking is a process whereby firms look beyond their boundaries as a means of learning and stimulating innovation. However, there is no singular accepted definition of benchmarking, but it is generally considered to be a method of making improvements by making comparisons, and learning the lessons these comparisons generate (Boxwell, 1994).

In general, regional benchmarking has become a feature of policymaking and facilitated learning processes that seek to understand regional contexts in more depth and promote improved regional competitiveness outcomes. This chapter analyses the concept of regional benchmarking and its links with regional policymaking processes. It develops a typology of regional benchmarking exercises and regional benchmarkers, and reviews the related literature. In particular, prevailing critical discourse in this area has often highlighted the distinctiveness of regional environments as limiting the utility of what is considered 'copy-and-paste' and 'one-size-fits-all' policymaking, as regional stakeholders purport to transfer perceived 'best practice' from one region to another (Asheim, 1997, 2002; Boschma, 2004; Turok, 2004; Bristow, 2005; Hospers, 2005, 2006; Wink, 2007).

This discourse has usually analysed regional benchmarking as a generic concept or methodology, rather than focusing on the variety and evolution of differing forms of benchmarking. This evolution has occurred as regional policymaking has begun to shift from processes undertaken principally on an intra-regional basis to one that is also integrating processes based on inter-regional learning activities (Bathelt *et al.*, 2004; Hassink, 2007). At a political level the proliferation of benchmarking efforts is considered by some to be intrinsically linked to new governance structures rooted in a culture of accountability and audit (Greene *et al.*, 2007). These issues have resulted in benchmarking becoming a highly contested concept and practice across academic and policymaking boundaries.

Policy context

From the perspective of regional policymaking, benchmarking forms part of processes concerned with learning by comparing, whereby regions seek to measure the performance, activities and policies of their competitors (Rose, 1993; Malecki, 2007). The political drive underlying the push towards the development of benchmarking as a policy instrument has varied across the world. In the US, for example, regional benchmarking exercises have tended to be undertaken by independent think-tanks and academics, who have essentially played an 'ideas-mongering' role (Rose, 1993) in seeking to measure and understand apparent new modes of regional economic development, or unilaterally by particular regions.

In Europe, regional benchmarking activity has become more prevalent due to the adoption by the European Union of a new mode of governance across a wide range of policy areas. The 'Open Method of Coordination' (OMC) is an institutional innovation utilized by the European Union to promote a switch from governance models based on a top-down regulatory approach to those based on mutual learning and the identification and transfer of so-called 'best practice' (Lundvall and Tomlinson, 2002; Arrowsmith *et al.*, 2004).

Emerging from the Lisbon Summit, with its objective of making the European Union a highly competitive and dynamic knowledge-based economy, the OMC explicitly promotes benchmarking activities as a key means of catalysing economic and social development across the European Union and tracking its progress (De La Porte *et al.*, 2001; Kaiser and Prange, 2004). This has resulted in benchmarking becoming central to the European Union's approach to coordinating economic and social policy, with increased importance given to the development of benchmarking activities and exercises in the formulation of policy in a number of fields, including competitiveness, innovation, and regional policymaking (Lundvall and Tomlinson, 2002; Arrowsmith *et al.*, 2004; Room, 2005). The OMC is closely aligned to the concept of learning-by-monitoring, which consists of coordination through goal-setting, linking the performance of cooperating parties – monitoring – to discussions of how to improve operations in light of this performance (learning), i.e. it links the evaluation of performance to the reassessment of goals (Sabel, 1996). Interestingly, in the context of the OMC, the focus on benchmarking stemmed from recommendations produced by Europe's corporate sector, i.e. the European Round Table of Industrialists (ERT, 1996).

The Lisbon agenda and its drive for improved competitiveness and a shift towards a knowledge-based economy has become central to regional policy agendas (Kitson *et al.*, 2004; Malecki, 2004; Bristow, 2005). Regional benchmarking is also a key thread of the European Commission's Mutual Learning Platform, which was established in 2005 to define policies to make regional innovation more effective, with the European Commission funding a number of regional benchmarking projects across the European Union (European Commission, 2006). The focus the OMC gives to methods of transferring best practice has led many to criticize benchmarking efforts, particularly regional benchmarking, due to the perceived limitations of trying to replicate and copy activities from elsewhere (Asheim, 1997, 2002; Boschma, 2004; Hospers, 2005, 2006). However, as is argued in more detail below, regional benchmarking efforts are not merely copy-and-paste instruments, but a means of providing a stimulus for thinking about, and engaging in, new ways of development (Bessant and Rush, 1999; Arrowsmith *et al.*, 2004).

Many regional strategy-building and development initiatives contain some form of benchmarking component. This is most common in establishing or furthering regional economic or innovation strategies where there is often an attempt to identify 'competitor' or 'exemplar' regions (Martin, 2005). Even though every region operates in a distinct economic environment with a distinct institutional endowment, a region can compare itself with others in order to assess the suitability of its strategy, and whether or not current policy is addressing the right problems and actors (Sabel, 1996). Such comparison or benchmarking most often incorporates a broad analysis of 'key performance indicators' across these regions, as well as possibly more qualitative evidence on the structure, economic and social, of these regions and their policy framework (Charles and Benneworth, 1999; Petty, 2005; Parkinson and Karecha, 2006). In most instances, such benchmarking is carried out at arm's length, with there being little or no direct engagement with the benchmarked regions, although in recent years there has been an increasing focus on inter-regional learning processes and collaboration across regions (Ketels and Sölvell, 2005; Johannesson *et al.*, 2006).

It is argued by some that benchmarking activities merely result in the unsuccessful imitation of the regional 'hardware', such as science and research parks, existing in competitor or leading regions (Boschma, 2004; Hospers, 2005, 2006) rather than 'software' such as networks and knowledge-exchange mechanisms. It is the case that there is often little to distinguish the visions, missions, and objectives contained within the strategies of different regions. Many are generic and anodyne in their content, resulting in the production of vacuous strategy and policy documents. Whether or not such an outcome is the result of the use of benchmarking, the ineffective implementation of benchmarking and/or its results, or is unconnected to benchmarking, is unclear.

The relative newness of regional benchmarking techniques and regional-level strategy-building processes in many contexts are factors that form part of the regional learning process. There is little to suggest that approaches excluding a benchmarking element would produce more effective strategy building, particularly as the continuous emergence of 'competitor regions' means that it is extremely difficult to sustain regional competitiveness based solely on the knowledge created and shared within a region (Hospers, 2005; Malecki, 2007).

Benchmarking exercises have the potential to form part of the toolbox of instruments available to regional policymakers. They are able to contribute to policymaking in three broad ways: delineating and monitoring regional economic development and its progress; facilitating the exchange and gathering of knowledge on regional practices and policies; and promoting the image and attractiveness of regional economies. While the first two functions are at the crux of the link between regional benchmarking and policymaking, the third aspect refers to the role benchmarking can play in contributing to the collective exercise of image building, as well as the communication component of the process for making transparent the awareness of a region about its own assets and competitive position (Bellini and Landabaso, 2007) or 'being good' and letting it be known (Malecki and Hospers, 2007).

Types of regional benchmarking and benchmarkers

Evidence suggests that at a firm level corporate benchmarking has proved to be an evolutionary practice developing from relatively simplistic 'reverse engineering' – comparing the characteristics, functionality, and performance of competitive offerings – to increasingly sophisticated modes of 'process benchmarking', 'strategic benchmarking', and 'network benchmarking' (Ahmed and Rafiq, 1998; Kyrö, 2003). As the modes of benchmarking become more sophisticated, the more they are typified by increasingly intensive and systematic learning (Kyrö, 2003).

Similarly, regional benchmarking is developing upon its own evolutionary path, progressing from quite simplistic forms to more complex modes (Luque-Martínez and Munöz-Leiva, 2005). These modes can be classified into three groups based on the focus of each benchmarking exercise: *performance benchmarking* – based on a comparison of metrics portraying the relevant characteristics of benchmarked regions; *process benchmarking* – based on a comparison of the structures, institutions, and systems constituting the practices and functioning of benchmarked regions; and *policy benchmarking* – based on a comparison of the types of public policy considered to influence the nature of the practices and subsequently the characteristics of benchmarked regions.

As regional benchmarking becomes more sophisticated, it builds on the preceding modes, i.e. it is difficult to undertake regional process benchmarking without first undertaking a performance benchmarking exercise, and similarly policy benchmarking usually builds upon the findings of process benchmarking exercises.

Alongside these three types of regional benchmarking, there is also the issue of who undertakes the benchmarking exercise, i.e. who or what is the benchmarker? Regional benchmarkers generally consist of one of the following: *independent benchmarkers* – external benchmarkers such as academics, consultants, or financial and business institutions that have no particular affiliation to one or more of the benchmarked regions; *single-region benchmarkers* – the authority/authorities or stakeholders attached to the objectives and orientation of the benchmarking exercise in one of the benchmarked regions; and *multi-region benchmarkers* – the authority/authorities or stakeholders attached to the objectives and orientation of the benchmarking exercise in more than one of the benchmarked regions.

These types also echo the evolution of corporate benchmarking whereby multi-region benchmarkers resemble the relatively new phenomenon of network benchmarking involving companies sharing experiences in order to alleviate mutual or common problems (Huggins, 2000; Kyrö, 2003). Table 11.1 provides a summary of the various potential permutations relating to both the form of benchmarking and type of benchmarker.

Table 11.1 Summary of types of regional benchmarking and regional benchmarkers

	Types of regional benchmarker		
	Independent benchmarkers	*Single region benchmarkers*	*Multi region benchmarkers*
Performance benchmarking	Metrics-based comparison of characteristics, undertaken by regionally external organizations	Metrics-based comparison of characteristics, undertaken by authorities / stakeholders representing one region	Metrics-based comparison of characteristics, undertaken by authorities / stakeholders representing more than one region
Process benchmarking	Structures, institutions and systems comparison of practices, undertaken by regionally external organizations	Structures, institutions and systems comparison of practices, undertaken by authorities / stakeholders representing one region	Structures, institutions and systems comparison of practices, undertaken by authorities / stakeholders representing more than one region
Policy benchmarking	Comparison of the public policies influencing processes and performance, undertaken by regionally external organizations	Comparison of the public policies influencing processes and performance, undertaken by authorities / stakeholders representing one region	Comparison of the public policies influencing processes and performance, undertaken by authorities / stakeholders representing more than one region

Performance benchmarking

Performance benchmarking is by far the most prevalent type of regional benchmarking, rapidly increasing as the focus of regional development policy has been drawn to the concepts of regional competitiveness and regional knowledge economies (Cooke, 2002c; Huggins, 2003; Malecki, 2007). Performance benchmarking provides 'comparative statics' in the form of regional league tables and ranks that seek to measure, analyse, and compare relative performance (Rose, 1993; Bristow, 2005). As this book has argued, the policy emergence of the knowledge economy has resulted in regional economies becoming defined by competitiveness metrics such as research and development expenditure, patent applications, the production of intangible goods, education levels, specialization in high-technology and knowledge-based sectors, and science and technology investment (Malecki, 2004; Raab and Kotamraju, 2006; Cooke, 2007; Huggins and Izushi, 2007). In general, the purpose of regional performance benchmarking is to ascertain how certain regions, or a particular region, are performing based on an identified set of metrics representing a particular set of regional characteristics (Erickek and Watts, 2003).

The choice of regions against which to benchmark will depend on the type of regional benchmarker. Independent benchmarkers will usually seek to benchmark the performance of a relatively high number of regions chosen against specific criteria, such as location (for example, regions in particular parts of the world) or underlying economic structure (for example, high economic performers, lagging regions, or regions in transition). Single-region benchmarkers may choose regions against which to benchmark themselves based on criteria relating to economic commonality or similarity, i.e. those regions in one's 'class' (Luque-Martínez and Munöz-Leiva, 2005; Iurcovich *et al.*, 2006); or they may choose regions they identify as being 'aspirational', i.e. regions whose economic fortunes they wish to emulate. Multi-region benchmarking usually consists of comparing the performance of a group of regions that are also seeking to improve cooperation and linkage between themselves, although the set of benchmark regions need not necessarily be restricted to those involved in the multi-region benchmark network.

Multi-region benchmarking also tends to incorporate process and policy benchmarking. The choice of regions against which to benchmark should involve 'searching the globe selectively' (Rose, 1993) to ensure not only are the objectives of the performance benchmarking exercise met, but also that these regions are appropriate candidates for resulting process or policy benchmarking exercises. Performance benchmarking may be a one-off activity (Iurcovich *et al.*, 2006), but is usually undertaken on a periodic basis, such as annually or biennially, as a means of assessing how a set of regions are adapting and adjusting to ever-changing market, technological, and competitive conditions (Martin, 2005). One of the key features of performance benchmarking is the ability to make comparisons across regions over time (Luque-Martínez and Munöz-Leiva, 2005).

Regional performance benchmarking has increased rapidly since the late

1990s, with many exercises and studies concentrating on comparing indicators related to regional competitiveness, economic development, innovation, and the conversion towards a knowledge-based economy. Alongside exercises undertaken by independent benchmarkers there has been considerable growth in the number of performance benchmarking exercises undertaken by single regions.

Performance benchmarking exercises, including those undertaken by independent, single-region or multi-regional benchmarkers, seek to make a connection with regional policymaking. However, the impact on regional policymaking is restricted to making a systematic analysis of regional strengths, weaknesses, and potential in relation to the performance of a defined set of preselected comparator regions. Therefore, performance benchmarking is an important first component of regional policymaking activities, but one which needs to incorporate process and policy benchmarking in order to provide high-value policy learning.

Process benchmarking

While performance benchmarking provides the comparative statics facilitating a baseline understanding of how regions differ, it does not provide the comparative dynamics facilitating an understanding of practices or policy learning (Rose, 1993). For instance, regional innovation metrics are not sufficient to analyse regional innovation systems (Zabala-Iturriagagoitia *et al.*, 2007). However, both process and policy benchmarking are far less evident forms of regional benchmarking. In terms of regional competitiveness, the challenge for the benchmarker is to identify those factors that best reveal the sources of competitiveness, which it is not always possible to do from existing metrics.

An example of the progression from performance to process and policy benchmarking might be as follows. A performance benchmarking exercise finds that Region *A* is highly dependent on its higher education sector for its knowledge creation and research and development investments. A subsequent process benchmarking exercise finds that in Regions *B*, *C*, and *D*, which are also highly dependent on their higher education system, knowledge-transfer systems are more adept at creating greater commercializable outputs. The obvious extension of this process is that Region *A* seeks to understand why Regions *B*, *C*, and *D*'s systems are superior. It would not necessarily be the objective of Region *A* to impose any of the knowledge-transfer systems in place in the other regions. Instead, a process benchmarking exercise could be used to inform policymakers of whether or not it is a credible strategic option to tackle the low level of commercialization. It may well be the case that the relative ineffectiveness of the knowledge-transfer system is due to the unsuitability of the knowledge created by the higher education sector for commercialization.

A more appropriate feature of Region *A*'s policy framework would be either to seek to generate more commercializable knowledge within other sectors in the region or to propose to alter or extend the type of knowledge the higher education sector creates. Alternatively, if it is considered that changes to Region *A*'s knowledge-transfer system are required then policy benchmarking can be used to assess the applicability of transferring related policies, or components of such policies, from other regions. This highlights that regional benchmarking is not necessarily a means of facilitating the direct transfer of practices, but of enabling a broader level of learning concerning the appropriateness of particular forms of intervention. In particular, process benchmarking aims to discriminate between what is specific, incidental or exceptional to and among benchmarked regions (Entrikin, 1991; Rota and Vanolo, 2006). Rose (1993) draws an important distinction between policy innovation (the relatively risky adoption of a novel idea) – due to the lack of transferable policies from elsewhere – and policy learning (less risky lessons that draw on the experiences of what was once an innovation elsewhere).

While performance benchmarking can be considered as a form of regional stocktaking, process benchmarking is based upon the insights into what makes processes effective and efficient (Iurcovich *et al.*, 2006). Process benchmarking is necessarily based more on qualitative data and information than performance benchmarking. However, most regional benchmarking exercises still tend to focus on gathering quantitative data, as its collection is less resource intensive (Rota and Vanolo, 2006). Process benchmarking provides the shift away from characteristics that are relatively easy to measure to learning about less tangible systems and practices (Lundvall and Tomlinson, 2002; Malecki, 2007).

Process benchmarking resembles Lundvall and Tomlinson's (2002) concept of systemic benchmarking, whereby practices and the relations between them are compared among different systems using a variety of analytical tools and methodologies. As Lundvall and Tomlinson (2002) suggest, the aim is not necessarily to search for best practice, but to improve a system's performance by the contemplation of another system's features. Where process benchmarking exercises have been undertaken, they have usually followed or occurred in tandem with performance measurement exercises. For instance, the benchmarking study of 'Competitive European Cities' commissioned by the UK government incorporated process benchmarking through a qualitative review of the economic and social infrastructure in the benchmarked cities (Parkinson *et al.*, 2004).

Policy benchmarking

Policy benchmarking is part of the policy-learning process, which Rose (1993) refers to as searching experience and lessons across space. Its role is to help 'find' policies and strategies that may usefully inform future policy building in the region(s) undertaking the search. In this respect, it is a starting point to a policy-learning process that might subsequently seek to use policies adopted in comparator or aspirational regions to copy, adapt, synthesize, establish hybrids or inspire future policies in the searching region (Rose, 1993). Without regional benchmarking the searching experience is liable to be a rather random process. Prospective evaluation of whether a policy has the potential to be transferred in some form involves 'bounded speculation', consisting of the appraisal of a chain of reasoning (Rose, 1993). In a regional sense, the chain, or continuum, from performance to process and regional policy benchmarking contains this reasoning. Regional policy benchmarking is a relatively new form of benchmarking used to understand and evaluate alternative policy options, supplying policymakers with examples of interventions from other regions, including the financial, legal, and regulatory aspects of such interventions (Iurcovich *et al.*, 2006).

In recent years the European Union has funded a set of projects principally concerned with regional policy benchmarking, whereby a network of European regions undertake a multi-region benchmarking exercise utilizing one or more of a number of methodologies such as quantitative and qualitative assessment, case studies, workshops, exchange visits, and study tours. The aim of this benchmarking is to systematically analyse the impact of policies across the benchmarked regions and exchange policy practices considered to have the potential to inform policymaking in other benchmark regions. This form of inter-regional policymaking potentially adds the most powerful dimension to the utilization of regional benchmarking, encompassing the continuum across performance, process and policy benchmarking modes, as well as being undertaken by a multi-regional benchmarker allowing performance, practices, and policies to be compared across those regions seeking cooperation and increased linkage. Benchmarking of this kind can establish commonalities and complementarities across regions forming the basis of future collaboration (Luque-Martínez and Munöz-Leiva, 2005).

Regional policymaking and benchmarking

There are those who suggest that the impact of regional benchmarking exercises on the regional policymaking community is limited or even negative (Asheim, 1997, 2002; Boschma, 2004; Wink, 2007). Greene *et al.* (2007) argue that regional benchmarking explains very little beyond the obvious, and forms part of a new political rationality comprising of a shift in market economies towards an audit culture and a wider neoliberal approach to economic governance. Others argue that while regional performance benchmarking exercises often attract substantial media attention and provoke public debate, they conceal more than they reveal because they are snapshots frozen in time (Cortright and Mayer, 2004).

However, the more fundamental criticism of regional benchmarking concerns the premise that it is founded on facilitating imitation rather than a deeper form of policy learning. Benchmarking is considered by some to be intrinsically flawed as a policy-learning mechanism as its aim of attempting to export so-called 'best-practice' policies from one region to another is not only extremely difficult to achieve, due to the specificity of regional contexts, but also results in the copying and imitation of policies inappropriate to the policy-receiving region (Asheim, 1997, 2002; Boschma, 2004; Hospers, 2005, 2006; Wink, 2007).

The apparent downside, therefore, of regional benchmarking is considered to be its propensity to stimulate the serial reproduction and replication of the same ideas from place to place, with the outcome being 'one-size-fits all' policymaking and 'identikit' regional strategies (Malecki, 2004; Bristow, 2005; Howells, 2005; Tödtling and Trippl, 2005). By investing in the same or similar technologies and infrastructure and copying apparent best practice, regions are considered to 'undermine their potential competitive advantage and should not be surprised that in the end a painful regional shake-out will occur' (Hospers, 2005: 453).

Clearly, the effective transfer and implementation of policy from one region to another is problematic (Lundvall and Tomlinson, 2002; Malecki, 2007). However, standardization rather than uniqueness across borders characterizes most areas of public policy, which suggests that it is not impossible (Rose, 1993). As Cooke (2002c: 6) argues, the contention that policy accomplishment cannot be transferred across borders 'belies economic history and denies human ingenuity'. Nevertheless, further disdain of the validity and utility of regional benchmarking exercises is based on the view that a lack of spatial comparability across regions renders such exercises as being limited to making performance comparisons, rather than methods for facilitating policy transfer (Turok, 2004; Greene *et al.*, 2007; Malecki, 2007). It is this notion of copying and imitation through policy transfer that is misleadingly associated with benchmarking exercises undertaken at the regional level. Whereas corporate benchmarking may be undertaken purely to imitate, regional benchmarking conforms more to the learning and improvement aspects of such exercises.

Regional benchmarking exercises facilitate an understanding of how this might be best enhanced, with performance, process, and policy benchmarking playing complementary roles. The concept of benchmarking as it has been applied in the corporate sector, and its use by some firms to identify and directly imitate innovations from elsewhere (Dattakumar and Jagadeesh, 2003), needs to be differentiated from regional benchmarking. Due to a whole range of regional specificities and context (Boschma, 2004), the aim of regional benchmarking exercises is to produce a targeted policy framework for future development, and not the direct imitation of polices or practices implemented in other regions.

While the corporate community uses benchmarking to provide an external perspective on improving processes and performance measures within the internal value chain of firms, which is likely to be relatively well defined (Kyrö, 2003), regional benchmarking is concerned with assisting regions in identifying regional value chains and then supporting improvements. Most corporate managers generally understand their operational model and the source and performance of the value created by their firms. Due to the complexity of regional environments, policymaking in most regions has yet to evolve to the stage where there is this level of understanding (Bellini and Landabaso, 2007). Therefore, benchmarking, through comparative analysis, assists this understanding by providing regions with intelligence on their operational model and their performance in comparison with other regions. This establishes a platform for a targeted policy framework, rather than producing an isomorphic process of policy transfer (Lagendijk and Cornford, 2000; Radaelli, 2000).

As Rose (1993: 22) argues, 'a lesson can conclude with a positive endorsement or be negative, warning of difficulties in imitating what is done elsewhere'. In general, benchmarking has led to increasingly sophisticated policymaking, and informs an understanding of systemic change within regions (Malecki, 2007). However, much activity has been restricted to performance benchmarking, rather than the types of multi- and inter-regional policy and process benchmarking with the potential to make the deepest contribution to policy learning. This lack of progression from performance benchmarking is an aspect that Arrowsmith *et al.* (2004) find common across benchmarking activities in most policy fields. In general, regional policy-learning activities remain more confined to local and intra-regional, rather than inter-regional, learning (Sabel, 1996; Bathelt *et al.*, 2004; Hassink, 2007). The relative lack of external and inter-regional awareness within the regional strategy-building process arises mainly as a result of structural weaknesses within this process.

The political economy of many regions is such that the development of economic and innovation strategies targeted at improving competitiveness have a tendency toward intra-regional processes (Hassink and Lagendijk, 2001; Roberts and Benneworth, 2001). Whilst policymakers within regional development agencies and authorities may be tasked with establishing, furthering, and evaluating these strategies, the process itself is usually undertaken through a networked polity (Ansell, 2000). This consists of a wide range of stakeholder groups within a region that have a position, which may be formal or informal, in the policy-making process (Rose, 1993). The process is based on widespread consultation and engagement with a broad spectrum of regional and local institutions, which may represent differing or conflicting interests.

Often, undertaking an effective benchmarking exercise can prove problematic when there are potentially conflicting policy goals and polarized factions seeking to promote different agendas (Arrowsmith *et al.*, 2004; Malecki, 2007). Nevertheless, the engagement of these stakeholders is important from three perspectives. First, without engagement it is less likely that these groups will agree to the policies recommended. Second, these institutions, especially local authorities, may be important financiers and implementers of the actions arising from the strategies. Third, these stakeholders are a crucial source of localized and regionalized learning, bringing with them a wealth of experience concerning the issues and problems regions face, as well as the scope for particular forms of intervention.

The third perspective is clearly a very necessary component of the regional policymaking process, with localized learning resulting from an embedded monitoring of the evolution of a region, impacting on the mind-set of the particular interests represented (Morgan, 1997; Lagendijk, 1999). Such learning, however, is double-edged since it may correctly diagnose problems of relevance to policy-making, but provide an incorrect prognosis of the potential for appropriate solutions. For example, an ongoing, common and difficult experience for regional policymakers concerns decisions regarding future support for industries and sectors that are in long-term decline and offer low value added. The perspective of local interest groups and stakeholders is often one where the apparent solution is publicly funded financial assistance in a bid to revive the competitiveness of the local or regional sector. While such local responses are understandable, they are a result of learning based on an outlook conditioned by the path dependency and 'lock-in' a region has experienced (Hassink and Lagendijk, 2001; Boschma, 2004; Martin and Sunley, 2006).

Such conditioning constrains the scope, innovativeness, and future appropriateness of the interventions proposed and lobbied for by these institutions. This is not to insinuate that processes of local engagement or intra-regional learning be cast aside in favour of unilateral policymaking by regional development agencies and authorities. It is to suggest that there is a requirement for future regional policymaking to be based on a more equitable balance between inter- and intra-regional learning processes. Inter-regional learning based on benchmarking provides a means for regions to 'de-lock' themselves by building their adaptive capacities and creating new paths (Martin and Sunley, 2006).

If inter-regional learning processes such as benchmarking are of importance for effective policymaking, why is there still such a dominance of the intra-regional approach? One answer is resource requirement. As Rose (1993) highlights, problems in implementing policies, particularly at the local and regional level, often arise due to a lack of adequate financial resources. To undertake a regional benchmarking exercise that goes beyond arm's-length approaches requires substantial resources in terms of the time and finance required to facilitate study visits, international data collection, and the development of appropriate reporting and analytical tools. On the other hand, intra-regional learning processes are usually already embedded within the policymaking infrastructure of a region through a variety of routes, such as the boards of regional agencies and authorities, and therefore require far less resource to activate.

Alongside appropriate resource allocation, multi-level governance structures and the relationship between regional and national policymaking (and, in Europe, European Union-level policymaking) can constrain effective policy development (Giordano and Roller, 2003; Greene *et al.*, 2007). In most regions, particularly in Europe, regional policymaking is required to be set within an overarching national policy framework. Although such frameworks are predominantly a sensible approach for ensuring regional coherence across nations, it has a limiting effect on regional policymaking. Principally, these limitations concern the mechanisms by which consensus is built around regional policies, with the role of regional policymakers often reduced to attempting to align local interests within the parameters set by a national framework. As a consequence of efforts to operate within a system of multi-level policymaking, the capacity to engage in horizontal inter-regional learning is limited (Benz and Eberlein, 1999; Gertler and Wolfe, 2004).

Within the European Union, the European Commission has responded to these limiting effects by introducing a range of initiatives, such as those previously cited, aimed at facilitating inter-regional policy benchmarking. However, such 'top-down' benchmarking and policy-learning initiatives run the risk of casting a further shadow of coercion over regions (Arrowsmith *et al.*, 2004; Malecki,

2007). As Malecki (2007) indicates, this approach differs from regional benchmarking initiatives in the US, which usually consist of either independent or single-region benchmarkers, with the downside being potential restrictions on the capacity for policy learning. In summary, regional policymaking, especially that relating to innovation, is intrinsically difficult to manage due to the requirements for high levels of institutional cooperation, constraints on available financial resources, and complex governance systems involving intergovernmental relations, both upwards (in the form of national government and the European Union) and downwards (in the form of municipalities and provincial governments) (Sabel, 1996; Bellini and Landabaso, 2007).

All these aspects impact on the potential effectiveness of benchmarking as a policymaking instrument. However, even if they are surmountable, some consider that the ethics and the 'darker side' (Arrowsmith *et al.*, 2004) underlying benchmarking exercises calls into question their promotion. Greene *et al.* (2007: 15) express 'fundamental concerns about the ethics and value of these studies in both an academic and policy context'. Of key concern is the possibility of the results of benchmarking exercises being utilized by stakeholders to gain legitimacy for preconceived beliefs or proposals for action, rather than stimulating new ideas or policy innovation (Bristow, 2005; Boland, 2007). Boland (2007), for example, is sceptical of single-region benchmark exercises that are outsourced to high-profile 'academic consultants', which Boland considers is often a strategy utilized by those regional policymakers commissioning the exercise to exert a direct influence on policy formation.

Whilst there is undoubtedly some merit to these concerns, the means by which certain interest groups seek to advance their views and beliefs is an issue common to the field of policymaking per se. From the perspective of the link between regional policymaking and benchmarking, while (performance) benchmarking exercises have often been restricted to identifying the symptoms of regional weaknesses and failure, new models are seeking to pinpoint the poor developmental capacities underlying these symptoms (Morgan, 1997).

Despite the backlash from those in the academic community who consider benchmarking to be a crude and over-simplistic means of achieving regional policy objectives, it is forming an increasingly critical tool for policymakers and is rapidly becoming more methodologically sophisticated (Di Nicola *et al.*, 2004). As Bellini and Landabaso (2007) argue, there is an enduring divide between academics and regional planners, which has meant that academic theory had tended to be diagnostic rather than providing planners with an effective and pragmatic way to improve their policymaking.

Lesson-drawing, as Rose (1993) suggests, is a return to the original notion of social science, which is both comparative and theoretical, and while policy cannot be expected to be fully fungible across regions, total blockage should not be expected either. It is clear that if a region uses a benchmarking exercise to try to re-create Silicon Valley through copycat behaviour, it is undoubtedly doomed to fail (Hospers, 2005, 2006). Most regional benchmarking efforts, however, are shifting away from the imitation of 'best practices' and the unattainable search for an 'optimal' development model (Boschma, 2004) toward the adaptation of good practices and more reflective policymaking.

Although the days of regional policymaking based on 'high-tech fantasies' (Massey *et al.*, 1992) are not fully behind us, more efforts are being made to understand the processes that make operations such as science parks and business incubators effective (Huggins and Izushi, 2007). For instance, the inter-regional benchmarking exercises supported by the European Commission are clearly seeking to understand the softer more intangible factors underlying regional competitiveness, such as networks and social capital. The European Commission is also attempting to connect benchmarking with other modes of policy intelligence gathering such as foresight exercises (Howells, 2005; Iurcovich *et al.*, 2006).

Knowing and measuring how other regions are doing, as Malecki (2007: 645) argues, 'seems to be a prerequisite for membership among competitively advantaged regions'. However, if the evolution of regional benchmarking is to be successful, current benchmarking efforts must only be a starting point. The recurring paradox of regional benchmarking exercises is that while it is paramount to understand practices and policies related to soft, rather than to hard, infrastructure and intangibles such as networks, knowledge-transfer mechanisms, and social capital, there are few metrics and tools available to enable such benchmarking. Bellini and Landabaso (2007: 247), for example, point to the benefits of benchmarking regional social capital, arguing that 'we need to learn how to measure social capital in different regions and to monitor its evolution over time'.

Concluding remarks

The rapidity with which regional benchmarking projects have grown is clearly related to a perceived necessity to make sense of the seemingly dramatic shifts occurring in the structure of regional economies, as knowledge and innovation become the bedrocks of competitiveness. Critics suggest that regional benchmarking is a flawed technique since it does not allow regions to see themselves in a manner that is meaningful or constructive to policy formulation. Such criticism fails to take account of the variety and rapid development of regional benchmarking systems. Instead, it largely draws on well-worn arguments regarding problems in transferring policy from one context and environment to another. Although these issues are certainly of high relevance to regional benchmarking, the future challenge for benchmarking is broader.

While each region has a unique combination of competitiveness requirements, globalization is necessitating heightened interaction and linkage, which will require regions to increasingly pool and consolidate their competitive strengths as a means of eradicating their weaknesses. Without effective benchmarking, regions are unlikely to have the prerequisite competitive intelligence to engage in these processes of global connection. As Dattakumar and Jagadeesh (2003: 176) find in their review of benchmarking activity in the corporate sector: quite often, the benchmarking concept is understood to be an act of imitating or copying. But in reality this proves to be a concept that helps innovation rather than imitation.

The growth of regional benchmarking has formed a component of the drive towards new forms of governance that impact on regions, but which have been accompanied by a bottom-up push from regions themselves to engage in such exercises. The extent to which such exercises are the result of the embedding of an audit culture in governance structures is questionable. In a globalized world, where regions must increasingly look externally in order to understand their role, benchmarking represents more a form of 'foreign policy', allowing regions the opportunity to see themselves in a wider context (Malecki, 2004). Such activities are still relatively embryonic, with much regional benchmarking to date limited to performance benchmarking exercises. This, in turn, has constrained the impact of such exercises on policymaking, which have been hampered by both political and financial factors.

It will be instructive to understand the type of regional benchmarking that emerges in the future. There is a growing emphasis in both the business and policy worlds on 'real-time benchmarking', especially as a result of increased global security and financial risks. The globalization of production and knowledge means that regional policymakers already have innate difficulties in maintaining up-to-date intelligence to inform relevant policymaking. Regional benchmarking data has notoriously long time lags, particularly compared with national exercises, and more development is required in this area. Such development inevitably has financial and intellectual resource implications, which may lead to a benchmarking divide between core and peripheral regions, compounding the very problems regional policy is seeking to alleviate. This is the essence of the learning region discourse, whereby the open and connected create virtuous circles of dynamism and growth, and the isolated and disconnected vicious circles of stagnancy and mediocrity.

12 Conclusions

This book has argued that locational competition has shifted to the international stage, with regions being key geographical units for understanding changing patterns of global economic development. The notion of regional competitiveness is a means of understanding differences in rates of economic development across regions, as well as their future economic growth prospects. Initiatives such as the World Competitiveness Index of Regions (WCIR) seek to provide a more spatially nuanced understanding of global competitiveness than national measures of international competitiveness, with regional competitiveness focused explicitly on the microeconomic determinants of regional development and growth. Economic development, especially at the regional level, remains a relatively fuzzy concept with no standard or accepted means of conceptualizing or measuring it. The concept of regional competitiveness provides a means for both conceptualization and measurement based on the understood key levers and drivers of growth within a twenty-first-century global economy.

As well as empirically framing the underlying tenets of regional competitiveness, it has been argued that regional competitiveness is both allied to, and an extension of, regional growth theories, with a key factor in achieving such growth likely to be the possession of a critical stock of firms that are able to generate knowledge, entrepreneurs, and innovations in developing sectors and markets, and ultimately new jobs. Regional competitiveness, therefore, is predicated on the presence of conditions that enable firms to compete in their chosen markets, and on the value that these firms generate being captured by the respective region. This view is consistent with endogenous approaches to regional development that are focused on factors such as human capital, education, and innovation systems, with regional competitiveness occurring only when sustainable growth is achieved at labour (wage) rates that enhance overall standards of living. Although some commentators have criticized the regional competitiveness discourse because of the connotations of head-to-head winner-takes-all battles, the concept is far more closely related to a notion of regions comparing and contrasting themselves as a means of improving.

The growing theoretical support for the concept of localized competition lends considerable weight to the use and importance of competitiveness theory and measurement at the regional, rather than the national, level. This is not to dismiss the fact that, in some circumstances, a region remains a somewhat arbitrary level of analysis. Nevertheless, the use of sub-national regional spatial units brings us much closer in line with the nature of competition and the appropriate role of government in economic development activity. Policymakers are increasingly seeking to improve the economic performance of the regions for which they have responsibility, and the competitiveness discourse, and the theoretical and empirical basis upon which it is constructed, offers a route for policymakers to understand further the most viable options for removing economic unevenness.

As the global economy continues to open up, the barriers constraining the international mobility of capital and labour will become further reduced. The increased global mobility of the factors of production across regions heightens the significance of benchmarking and understanding the competitiveness of regions within this global context. Further work, however, is required, particularly in terms of integrating the role of institutions and institutional enablers – discussed below – into regional competitiveness models. This suggests that alongside the competitiveness performance measures outlined in this book, there is a need to examine in more depth the processes that allow regional economic systems to function effectively, as well as the policies that can support this functioning. In this regard, there is scope to further develop techniques related to process benchmarking, based on a comparison of the structures and systems constituting the practices and functioning of regions, as well as policy benchmarking, based on a comparison of the types of public policy considered to influence the nature of these practices and, subsequently, the characteristics of regions.

In recent years, concepts concerning institutions, resilience and well-being have gained prominence in bids to better explain uneven development. In the following sections each of these concepts are discussed with regard to the connection with regional competitiveness theory, with the chapter concluding by offering some thoughts on future public policy intervention in less competitive regions, especially in emerging economies.

Institutions

Although regions seek greater competitiveness, there are clearly different routes to achieving growth and prosperity (Kitson *et al.*, 2004; Malecki, 2007; Huggins and Thompson, 2010). Some of these routes are likely to be more attractive for some regions than others. However, whether or not regions are truly free to choose their economic development paths, or whether past history dictates the future potential of an economy is another question. The evolutionary school of economic geography suggests that regional development is likely to be determined, at least to some extent, by past histories (Boschma, 2004; Bristow, 2005; Boschma and Frenken, 2006; Martin and Sunley, 2006; Huggins, 2010b). Regions that are tightly bound in their structures and networks may not be able to move to alternative development paths, so when hit by exogenous shocks, they are unable to escape from a declining competitiveness spiral (Martin and Sunley, 2006; Huggins and Izushi, 2007). These factors have ramifications for regions, especially in the long term, as activities taken to increase competitiveness may have hidden costs in terms of the welfare of the population, which may compromise future competitiveness, particularly if key workers cannot be retained (Florida *et al.*, 2011; Mellander *et al.*, 2011).

The evolutionary nature of regional economic development may further limit a region's ability to move away from industries associated with providing a low contribution to regional competitiveness. Institutional theorists suggest that a key means of escaping a downward evolutionary economic trajectory is through the development of efficient institutions that facilitate effective economic development (North, 1990, 2005; Acemoglu *et al.*, 2005; Acemoglu and Robinson, 2012). Institutions are considered to consist of the underlying rules of the game relating to factors such as the incentives to: save and invest; embrace competition, innovation and technological development; along with the presence and structure of property rights, markets, unbiased systems of law and regulation, and the provision of public services (Acemoglu and Robinson, 2012).

In effect, institutions, in the shape of both the tangible and intangible characteristics constituting the political economy of regions and nations and the functioning of their economic systems, are either enablers or constrainers on competitiveness. Institutional enablers are the conditions and factors that facilitate competitiveness by creating an environment that is conducive for firms to operate at their optimum level. These enablers principally encompass the institutions that support economic actors in taking advantage of perceived opportunities. Whilst some of these institutions are fixed across nations, such as law, regulation, and property rights, others, such as the embracement of competition and innovation, are clearly subject to regional differentiation. Enabling institutions will take account of regional contextual factors, with complementary institutions developing through repeated interactions. Constraining institutions may limit the directions in which a regional economy can develop in the future. Therefore, choices that push places towards the development of a particular set of institutions over another may influence competitiveness in the long term. Regions with institutions conducive to enabling economic development are likely to increase their competitiveness by attracting investment, skills, and talent. Some examples include: effective rule of law, which allows commercial activity to be efficient; the ease of doing business; government initiatives; and ultimately, the perceptions of businesses and individuals in a region.

In order to better understand the nature of regional economic systems and their competitive performance, it is useful to add institutions to the fundamental competitiveness model presented in Figure 2.2. More specifically, as shown by Figure 12.1, it would seem appropriate to consider the institutions that facilitate or impede the extent to which the inputs of regional economic systems are effectively transferred in to high-value outcomes. Similarly, there is a need to consider how institutions enable the transfer of economic outputs into high-grade outcomes, as manifested by regional standards of living. Institutions also play a role in ensuring that the wealth underpinning standards of living replenishes the inputs of the regional economic system.

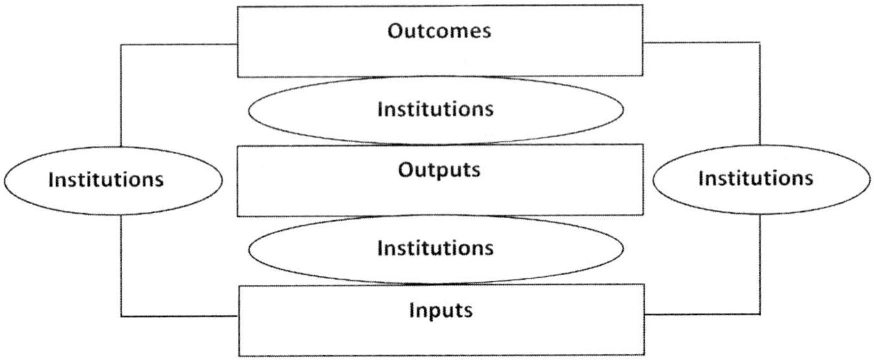

Figure 12.1 Addressing the role of institutions in the regional competitiveness framework

In a series of works, Rodríguez-Pose, Storper, and their colleagues (Storper, 2005, 2008; Rodríguez-Pose and Storper, 2006; Storper *et al.*, 2007; Farole *et al.*, 2011; Rodríguez-Pose, 2013) have developed the framework of community – which appears to represent a spatially localized notion of institutions – and society – which conversely represents spatially broader institutions – in order to better place institutionalist approaches central to regional economic development. In the process, this framework highlights the importance of the geographical context when examining institutional models of growth. Both community and society are considered to influence economic development through the expectations and incentives provided to economic agents (Farole *et al.*, 2011). However, as the authors acknowledge, how these effects vary across regions and localities is little understood, excepting that community and society effects are likely to reinforce one another (Farole *et al.*, 2011).

As Storper and Scott (2009: 148) put it when seeking to identify where city growth comes from:

> Our own argument is that the key to this question can be found in the spatial logic of productive activity and that individual choices about residential location are profoundly shaped by the possibilities and constraints created by this situation.

Therefore, the functioning of a region becomes a dynamic trait, rather than a static one, with the competitiveness of a region also being mediated by an external chances element (Veenhoven, 2009), whereby a region's resources and institutions determine their environmental fit. Furthermore, internal chances (Veenhoven, 2009), through flexible well-suited institutions, ensure that a region maintains its external chances, through the ability to adapt and create the resilience required to endure external shocks.

Resilience

For Simmie and Martin (2010), it is avoiding rigidities from interconnectedness within a region that best ensures its resilience. For instance, regions in advanced national economies with heritages of heavy industry may struggle to adapt to external shocks, and where competitiveness is lost, these regions may still place more reliance on development opportunities where negative externalities, such as those related to the environment, are more prevalent. This is more likely to be the case where economic resilience is low and regions are unable to adapt and adjust. One explanation for the differing levels of resilience displayed across regions concerns the extent to which a strong regional system of innovation is present (Christopherson *et al.*, 2010) which, like competitiveness, is likely to be underpinned by an embedded, vibrant, and generally innovative and entrepreneurial economy (Wennekers and Thurik, 1999; Audretsch and Thurik, 2001; Aoyama, 2009).

In the sphere of economics, resilience is seen as the ability to return to equilibrium or move between equilibria, but the social sciences have tended to link the term more to adaptability and evolutionary economics. From a policy perspective, the latter view is likely to be of more use as resilience is not restricted to the capability to rebound from a shock, but also considers the actions taken in the lead up to the shock and how this influences the ability to rebound. Another perspective views resilience as the capability to withstand shocks. This can be determined by the sensitivity to a shock, with those economies that are less influenced by shocks being more likely to recover (Simmie and Martin, 2010).

Resilience effectively has three properties in the socio-ecological context of regional economies: the extent to which change can be experienced without the loss of structure; the degree to which an economy can reorganize; and the degree to which it can create and sustain a capacity to learn and adapt (Thornton, 1999; Begley and Tan, 2001; Hudson, 2010; Thornton *et al.*, 2011). Of course, it would be wrong to consider the resilience of regional economies in isolation, since the extent to which resilience develops and changes is likely to be influenced by the actions of neighbouring economies and factors such as national policies (Bristow, 2010; Christopherson *et al.*, 2010).

A key challenge in examining regional resilience is that such resilience can only be put to the test in periods of difficulty. This means that future economic success cannot be based on current success. To address this, Martin and Sunley (2011a) conceptualize resilience through an adaptive cycle model, and although economies may benefit from increased knowledge flows and accumulation as connectedness increases (Garofoli, 2002), connectedness where it progresses too far can lead to collective lock in (Ter Wal and Boschma, 2011). It is important, therefore, that sufficient adaptability and flexibility are retained; otherwise, there is a danger that highly specialized regional economies can enter a release phase where firms are rapidly lost from the economy (Peterson, 2000). This can then lead to a large decline in community welfare and well-being.

Well-being

The ultimate aim of regional policymaking should be to increase the well-being of the population residing within regions (Easterlin, 1974; Huggins and Thompson, 2012). It is not, though, always evident that policymaking related to achieving competitiveness improvements fully considers the extent of the outcomes concerning issues of well-being. In basic terms, improved economic performance should not be sought at the expense of a population's welfare. For instance, it is possible to improve productivity by cutting back on labour inputs and competing on price through lower remuneration; however, the end effect of this may be reduced standards of living and lower long-term competitiveness. Although a number of alternative measures of regional competitiveness have been developed, often attempting to incorporate outcome factors such as average wages and levels of unemployment (for reviews see Martin, 2005; Huggins, 2010b), they do not fully encapsulate the broader measures of the well-being of the citizens residing in a particular region.

Emerging research is beginning to examine the link between competitiveness and well-being, with the results suggesting that, in general, higher levels of regional competitiveness are associated with higher levels of well-being (Huggins and Thompson, 2012). Regions with relatively low competitiveness are more likely to suffer from negative externalities, which are also associated with lower levels of well-being. This means that when seeking to maximize the well-being and welfare of a region's population, competitiveness measures are a reasonable guide to the extent of success. In general, the key features of the well-being of places have a strong symbiotic association with the prevailing socioeconomic business culture, defined as encompassing competitiveness-related traits such as entrepreneurship, innovation, risk taking, and more generally, collective aspirations, motivations, and opportunity development. However, whether or not these relationships are necessarily sustainable in an evolutionary sense is less clear (Huggins and Thompson, 2012).

From a policymaking perspective, it is crucial that future formulations pay more attention to the dynamic link between competitiveness and well-being at the regional level. Economic development, social cohesion, welfare, and environmental policies must become better integrated if they are to build sustainable local communities. Policymakers have for many years recognized the link between social and community development and economic development. Most development strategies at a regional level, therefore, provide an understanding of how policy initiatives related to improving social inclusion can facilitate wider economic development in relation to a number of core strands, including community development. There is, however, little underlying policy research that seeks to integrate these strands to provide a cohesive framework for understanding how the social condition of particular regions and their communities impinges on economic development trajectories and vice versa.

This suggests the requirement for a fundamental rethinking of the organization and governance of regional policymaking. As new concepts and measures of this social condition emerge, they will offer a significant opportunity to better understand not only the well-being of places but also the social welfare aspects of policy intervention. In future, these aspects must play a stronger role in policy-making at the regional level.

Public policy

As has been shown, there are significant regional competitiveness divides across the globe, and for the less competitive regions, especially in emerging economies, evidence suggests there is a need for stronger regional leadership (Huggins and Strakova, 2012). The leadership of regional networks will be critical for economic development in less competitive regions in order to enable the creation and accessibility of regional knowledge resources. Also, levers such as venture capital may be attracted if the level of dynamism is increased through regional collaboration and international trading.

In order to improve regional competitiveness, a more integrated approach to development is likely to be required that combines support and advisory services through the innovation process, and promotes sector-specific support policy focused on regional firms. Future regional competitiveness and innovation policies should be designed to fulfil both 'quantitative' and 'qualitative' targets to improve the overall organization of regional economic and innovation systems. Quantitative developments will manifest themselves through the changing role of different actors in the innovation process, as well as through encouraging the development and strengthening of networks between them. Clearly, an important step in lagging regions is to convince firms, intermediaries and knowledge creators that competitiveness and innovation investments have to be accepted as important factors affecting their medium- and long-run growth. In such a regional economic context, it has to be made transparent that the trade-off between short-run economic performance (related to the cost–benefit ratio) and long-run economic development is almost unavoidable.

More qualitative development should be targeted at organizations such as universities, which are traditionally viewed as a source of human capital and only secondarily as a source of useful knowledge. As far as the education system is concerned, a further next step may be redesigning the curricula in order to better meet corporate demand, since national education systems are often not flexible enough to adapt to a continuously changing technological and economic environment. This barrier can be partly alleviated at the regional level by engaging educational bodies and firms in the joint development of specialized courses.

In less competitive regions there is undoubtedly a requirement to implement awareness-raising activities across both the public and the private sectors concerning the importance of intellectual property right protection (patents, copyrights and trademarks), particularly as a means of levering risk capital and promoting competitiveness and innovation. More generally, firm-level requirements, such as access to various forms of resources and capital, may only be facilitated through systemic changes in the regional socioeconomic business culture within which firms are positioned and operate. This differs from more competitive regions where firms may face barriers to resource access despite relatively progressive cultural attributes. As indicated by Figure 12.2, strong effective regional leadership and coordination is a basic necessity when ensuring the success of these policies, echoing the focus placed on such factors by the endogenous school of regional development (Maillat, 1998a, 1998b; Garofoli, 2002; Vázquez-Barquero, 2007).

In many ways the problems and barriers found in less competitive regions in emerging economies – a lack of innovation culture and resource restrictions – and the potential solutions – cluster development and the integration of universities into the regional economic infrastructure – resonate with those that are apparent in the less competitive regions of more advanced national economies (Harding *et al.*, 2007; Rutten and Boekema, 2007; Huggins *et al.*, 2008b; Huggins and Johnston, 2009). In the case of emerging regions, however, the policy learning curve remains relatively steep and is coupled with an industrial structure dominated by traditional sectors and activities. There is often a lack of regional-level awareness of the importance of innovation as a means of competing, alongside an innovation culture that does not fully promote or foster technological and entrepreneurial learning. A key part of this culture relates to 'risk-taking', with many regional stakeholders – both public and private – still averse to investing time and resources in knowledge and innovation.

Future development may rely on alleviating a continuing gap between the scientific community and the business community. At present there is likely to be a lack of transparency concerning mutual learning benefits and also disjointed systems of business support, with little regional emphasis in terms of either

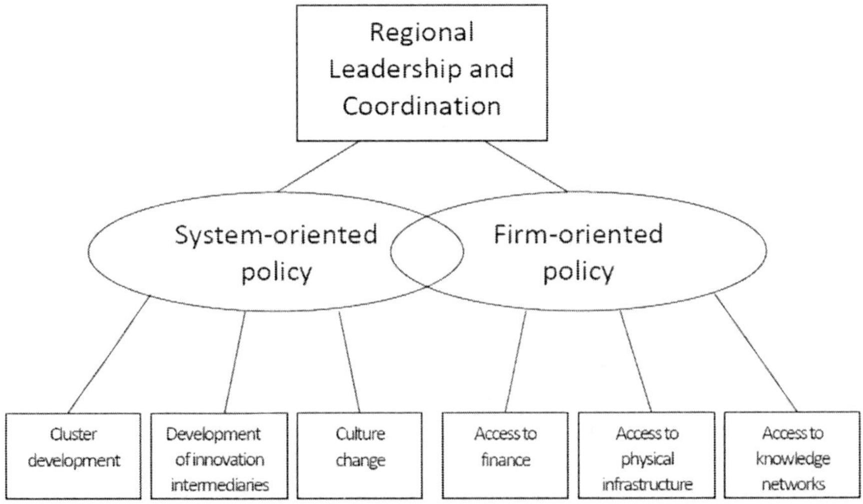

Figure 12.2 Economic development priorities in emerging regions

strategy or delivery (resulting in an apparent lack of demand for services). A lack of awareness of the potential value of intellectual property, and the lack of an institutional legal framework to manage and protect this property, further hinders knowledge-based development.

Nevertheless, emerging regions will continue to upgrade towards more knowledge-based economies through sustained exposure to international practices in other regions, particularly through regionally focused projects, such as those supported by the European Commission (Huggins, 2010b). Such efforts contribute to establishing a competitive and innovative culture amongst economic actors relevant for creating an awareness of the trends in the globalizing economy and the place of regions in this process. Much of the focus of intervention, however, has been on metropolitan regions and cities, with little emphasis on more rural regions and hinterlands. Whilst this focus fits with the challenges facing rapidly growing city-regions, strategic thinking is also required to take account of the potential for the rise of counter-urbanization (Shucksmith *et al.*, 2009), as negative externalities such as congestion, high office prices, or lack of quality space, and negative perceptions of the urban environment (coupled with improved physical and virtual connectivity) push a certain strata of society to favour more accessible and higher quality-of-place rural areas (Huggins and Clifton, 2011). While the gains of the urban renaissance are visible in many economies, issues relating to negative externalities and well-being bring into question the long-term sustainability of ongoing urbanization. The realization that new technology can help break down geographic boundaries, with knowledge-based economic activity offering rural areas an opportunity to become less constrained by an overdependence on traditional activities, needs to be more readily permeated through national and regional policymaking machinery.

At a wider level, efforts are required to promote cultural change toward innovation and entrepreneurship, especially among the community of young scientists and future human capital, including school students. Clearly, this is a long-term process, but policy agendas seeking to facilitate such change are emerging, with some governments introducing initiatives into the education system at a number of levels (Huggins and Williams, 2009). Finally, regional economic development policies, and the manner in which such policies are implemented, form part of the way in which regions learn, and regional collaboration initiatives clearly inform this learning (Huggins, 2010b). Therefore, regional policy should encourage cumulative learning through networking activities that will have a positive effect not only on economic actors, but regional societies as a whole.

Appendix 1

Regions analysed by the World Competitiveness Index of Regions (WCIR)

European regions

Ostösterreich, Austria
Südösterreich, Austria
Westösterreich, Austria
Région de Bruxelles-Capitale, Belgium
Région Wallonne, Belgium
Vlaams Gewest, Belgium
Severna i iztochna Bulgaria, Bulgaria
Yugozapadna i yuzhna tsentralna Bulgaria, Bulgaria
Cyprus
Jihovýchod, Czech Republic
Jihozápad, Czech Republic
Moravskoslezsko, Czech Republic
Praha, Czech Republic
Severovýchod, Czech Republic
Severozápad, Czech Republic
Stredni Cechy, Czech Republic
Stredni Morava, Czech Republic
Hovedstaden, Denmark
Midtjylland, Denmark
Nordjylland, Denmark
Sjælland, Denmark
Syddanmark, Denmark
Estonia
Åland, Finland
Etelä-Suomi, Finland
Itä-Suomi, Finland
Länsi-Suomi, Finland
Pohjois-Suomi, Finland
Bassin Parisien, France
Centre-Est, France
Départements d'outre-mer, France
Est, France
Île de France, France
Méditerranée, France
Nord – Pas-de-Calais, France
Ouest, France
Sud-Ouest, France
Baden-Württemberg, Germany
Bayern, Germany
Berlin, Germany
Brandenburg, Germany
Bremen, Germany
Hamburg, Germany
Hessen, Germany
Mecklenburg-Vorpommern, Germany
Niedersachsen, Germany
Nordrhein-Westfalen, Germany
Rheinland-Pfalz, Germany
Saarland, Germany
Sachsen, Germany
Sachsen-Anhalt, Germany
Schleswig-Holstein, Germany
Thüringen, Germany
Attiki, Greece
Kentriki Ellada, Greece
Nisia Aigaiou, Kriti, Greece
Voreia Ellada, Greece
Alföld és Észak, Hungary
Dunántúl, Hungary
Közép-Magyarország, Hungary

Iceland
Border, Midland and Western, Ireland
Southern and Eastern, Ireland
Abruzzo, Italy
Basilicata, Italy
Calabria, Italy
Campania, Italy
Emilia-Romagna, Italy
Friuli-Venezia Giulia, Italy
Lazio, Italy
Liguria, Italy
Lombardia, Italy
Marche, Italy
Molise, Italy
Piemonte, Italy
Provincia Autonoma Bolzano, Italy
Provincia Autonoma Trento, Italy
Puglia, Italy
Sardegna, Italy
Sicilia, Italy
Toscana, Italy
Umbria, Italy
Valle d'Aosta, Italy
Veneto, Italy
Latvia
Lithuania
Luxembourg
Malta
Noord-Nederland, Netherlands
Oost-Nederland, Netherlands
West-Nederland, Netherlands
Zuid-Nederland, Netherlands
Norway
Region Centralny, Poland
Region Pólnocno-Zachodni, Poland
Region Pólnocny, Poland
Region Poludniowo-Zachodni, Poland
Region Poludniowy, Poland
Region Wschodni, Poland
Continente, Portugal
Região Autónoma dos Açores, Portugal
Região Autónoma da Madeira, Portugal
Macroregiunea unu, Romania
Macroregiunea doi, Romania
Macroregiunea trei, Romania
Macroregiunea patru, Romania
Arkhangelsk Oblast, Russia
Astrakhan Oblast, Russia
Belgorod Oblast, Russia
Bryansk Oblast, Russia
Chechen Republic, Russia
Chuvash Republic, Russia
Ivanovo Oblast, Russia
Kabardino-Balkar Republic, Russia
Kaliningrad Oblast, Russia
Kaluga Oblast, Russia
Karachay-Cherkess Republic, Russia
Kirov Oblast, Russia
Komi Republic, Russia
Kostroma Oblast, Russia
Krasnodar Krai, Russia
Kursk Oblast, Russia
Leningrad Oblast, Russia
Lipetsk Oblast, Russia
Mari El Republic, Russia
Moscow Oblast, Russia
Moscow, Russia
Murmansk Oblast, Russia
Nenets Autonomous Okrug, Russia
Nizhny Novgorod Oblast, Russia
Novgorod Oblast, Russia
Orenburg Oblast, Russia
Oryol Oblast, Russia
Penza Oblast, Russia
Perm Krai, Russia
Pskov Oblast, Russia
Republic of Adygea, Russia
Republic of Bashkortostan, Russia
Republic of Dagestan, Russia
Republic of Ingushetia, Russia
Republic of Kalmykia, Russia
Republic of Karelia, Russia
Republic of Mordovia, Russia
Republic of North Ossetia-Alania, Russia
Republic of Tatarstan, Russia
Rostov Oblast, Russia
Ryazan Oblast, Russia

Saint Petersburg, Russia
Samara Oblast, Russia
Saratov Oblast, Russia
Smolensk Oblast, Russia
Stavropol Krai, Russia
Tambov Oblast, Russia
Tula Oblast, Russia
Tver Oblast, Russia
Udmurt Republic, Russia
Ulyanovsk Oblast, Russia
Vladimir Oblast, Russia
Volgograd Oblast, Russia
Vologda Oblast, Russia
Voronezh Oblast, Russia
Yaroslavl Oblast, Russia
Bratislavský kraj, Slovakia
Stredné Slovensko, Slovakia
Východné Slovensko, Slovakia
Západné Slovensko, Slovakia
Vzhodna Slovenija, Slovenia
Zahodna Slovenija, Slovenia
Canarias, Spain
Centro, Spain
Comunidad de Madrid, Spain
Este, Spain
Noreste, Spain
Noroeste, Spain
Sur, Spain
Mellersta Norrland, Sweden
Norra Mellansverige, Sweden
Östra Mellansverige, Sweden
Övre Norrland, Sweden
Småland med öarna, Sweden
Stockholm, Sweden
Sydsverige, Sweden
Västsverige, Sweden
Switzerland
East Midlands, UK
East of England, UK
London, UK
North East, UK
North West, UK
Northern Ireland, UK
Scotland, UK
South East, UK
South West, UK
Wales, UK
West Midlands, UK
Yorkshire and The Humber, UK

North American regions

Alberta, Canada
British Columbia, Canada
Manitoba, Canada
New Brunswick, Canada
Newfoundland and Labrador, Canada
Northwest Territories & Nunavut, Canada
Nova Scotia, Canada
Ontario, Canada
Prince Edward Island, Canada
Quebec, Canada
Saskatchewan, Canada
Yukon, Canada
Akron, OH, US
Albany-Schenectady-Troy, NY, US
Albuquerque, NM, US
Allentown-Bethlehem-Easton, PA-NJ, US
Atlanta-Sandy Springs-Marietta, GA, US
Augusta-Richmond County, GA-SC, US
Austin-Round Rock-San Marcos, TX, US
Bakersfield-Delano, CA, US
Baltimore-Towson, MD, US
Baton Rouge, LA, US
Birmingham-Hoover, AL, US
Boise City-Nampa, ID, US
Boston-Cambridge-Quincy, MA-NH, US
Bridgeport-Stamford-Norwalk, CT, US
Buffalo-Niagara Falls, NY, US

Cape Coral-Fort Myers, FL, US
Charleston-North Charleston-Summerville, SC, US
Charlotte-Gastonia-Rock Hill, NC-SC, US
Chattanooga, TN-GA, US
Chicago-Joliet-Naperville, IL-IN-WI, US
Cincinnati-Middletown, OH-KY-IN, US
Cleveland-Elyria-Mentor, OH, US
Colorado Springs, CO, US
Columbia, SC, US
Columbus, OH, US
Dallas-Fort Worth-Arlington, TX, US
Dayton, OH, US
Denver-Aurora-Broomfield, CO, US
Des Moines-West Des Moines, IA, US
Detroit-Warren-Livonia, MI, US
Durham-Chapel Hill, NC, US
El Paso, TX, US
Grand Rapids-Wyoming, MI, US
Greensboro-High Point, NC, US
Greenville-Mauldin-Easley, SC, US
Harrisburg-Carlisle, PA, US
Hartford-West Hartford-East Hartford, CT, US
Honolulu, HI, US
Houston-Sugar Land-Baytown, TX, US
Indianapolis-Carmel, IN, US
Jackson, MS, US
Jacksonville, FL, US
Kansas City, MO-KS, US
Knoxville, TN, US
Lancaster, PA, US
Las Vegas-Paradise, NV, US
Little Rock-North Little Rock-Conway, AR, US
Los Angeles-Long Beach-Santa Ana, CA, US
Louisville/Jefferson County, KY-IN, US
Madison, WI, US
Memphis, TN-MS-AR, US
Miami-Fort Lauderdale-Pompano Beach, FL, US
Milwaukee-Waukesha-West Allis, WI, US
Minneapolis-St. Paul-Bloomington, MN-WI, US
Nashville-Davidson–Murfreesboro–Franklin, TN, US
New Haven-Milford, CT, US
New Orleans-Metairie-Kenner, LA, US
New York-Northern New Jersey-Long Island, NY-NJ-PA, US
North Port-Bradenton-Sarasota, FL, US
Oklahoma City, OK, US
Omaha-Council Bluffs, NE-IA, US
Orlando-Kissimmee-Sanford, FL, US
Oxnard-Thousand Oaks-Ventura, CA, US
Palm Bay-Melbourne-Titusville, FL, US
Philadelphia-Camden-Wilmington, PA-NJ-DE-MD, US
Phoenix-Mesa-Glendale, AZ, US
Pittsburgh, PA, US
Portland-South Portland-Biddeford, ME, US
Portland-Vancouver-Hillsboro, OR-WA, US
Providence-New Bedford-Fall River, RI-MA, US
Raleigh-Cary, NC, US
Richmond, VA, US
Rochester, NY, US
Sacramento–Arden-Arcade–Roseville, CA, US
Salt Lake City, UT, US
San Antonio-New Braunfels, TX, US
San Diego-Carlsbad-San Marcos, CA, US
San Francisco-Oakland-Fremont, CA, US
San Jose-Sunnyvale-Santa Clara, CA, US

Scranton–Wilkes-Barre, PA, US
Seattle-Tacoma-Bellevue, WA, US
St. Louis, MO-IL, US
Syracuse, NY, US
Tampa-St. Petersburg-Clearwater, FL, US
Toledo, OH, US
Tulsa, OK, US
Virginia Beach-Norfolk-Newport News, VA-NC, US
Washington-Arlington-Alexandria, DC-VA-MD-WV, US
Wichita, KS, US
Worcester, MA, US

Asia and Pacific regions

Australian Capital Territory, Australia
New South Wales, Australia
Northern Territory, Australia
Queensland, Australia
South Australia, Australia
Tasmania, Australia
Victoria, Australia
Western Australia, Australia
Beijing, China
Chongqing, China
Fujian, China
Guangdong, China
Hubei, China
Jiangsu, China
Liaoning, China
Shandong, China
Shanghai, China
Tianjing, China
Zhejiang China
Hong Kong
Andaman & Nicobar Islands, India
Andhra Pradesh, India
Arunachal Pradesh, India
Assam, India
Bihar, India
Chandigarh, India
Chattisgarh, India
Dadra & Nagar Haveli, India
Daman & Diu, India
Delhi, India
Goa, India
Gujarat, India
Haryana, India
Himachal Pradesh, India
Jammu & Kashmir, India
Jharkhand, India
Karnataka, India
Kerala, India
Lakshadweep, India
Madhya Pradesh, India
Maharashtra, India
Manipur, India
Meghalaya, India
Mizoram, India
Nagaland, India
Orissa, India
Puducherry, India
Punjab, India
Rajasthan, India
Sikkim, India
Tamil Nadu, India
Tripura, India
Uttar Pradesh, India
Uttarakhand, India
West Bengal, India
Aichi, Japan
Akita, Japan
Aomori, Japan
Chiba, Japan
Ehime, Japan
Fukui, Japan
Fukuoka, Japan
Fukushima, Japan
Gifu, Japan
Gunma, Japan
Hiroshima, Japan
Hokkaido, Japan
Hyogo, Japan
Ibaraki, Japan
Ishikawa, Japan

Iwate, Japan
Kagawa, Japan
Kagoshima, Japan
Kanagawa, Japan
Kochi, Japan
Kumamoto, Japan
Kyoto, Japan
Mie, Japan
Miyagi, Japan
Miyazaki, Japan
Nagano, Japan
Nagasaki, Japan
Nara, Japan
Niigata, Japan
Oita, Japan
Okayama, Japan
Okinawa, Japan
Osaka, Japan
Saga, Japan
Saitama, Japan
Shiga, Japan
Shimane, Japan
Shizuoka, Japan
Tochigi, Japan
Tokushima, Japan
Tokyo, Japan
Tottori, Japan
Toyama, Japan
Wakayama, Japan
Yamagata, Japan
Yamaguchi, Japan
Yamanashi, Japan
Akmola, Kazakhstan
Aktobe, Kazakhstan
Almaty city, Kazakhstan
Almaty, Kazakhstan
Astana city, Kazakhstan
Atyrau, Kazakhstan
East, Kazakhstan
Karaganda, Kazakhstan
Kostanai, Kazakhstan
Kyzylorda, Kazakhstan
Mangistau, Kazakhstan
Nord, Kazakhstan
Pavlodar, Kazakhstan
South, Kazakhstan
West, Kazakhstan
Zhambyl, Kazakhstan
Busan, Korea
Chungbuk, Korea
Chungnam, Korea
Daegu, Korea
Daejeon, Korea
Gangwon, Korea
Gwangju, Korea
Gyeongbuk, Korea
Gyeonggi, Korea
Gyeongnam, Korea
Incheon, Korea
Jeju, Korea
Jeonbuk, Korea
Jeonnam, Korea
Seoul, Korea
Ulsan, Korea
New Zealand
Altai Krai, Russia
Altai Republic, Russia
Amur Oblast, Russia
Chelyabinsk Oblast, Russia
Chukotka Autonomous Okrug, Russia
Irkutsk Oblast, Russia
Jewish Autonomous Oblast, Russia
Kamchatka Krai, Russia
Kemerovo Oblast, Russia
Khabarovsk Krai, Russia
Khanty-Mansi Autonomous Okrug-Yugra, Russia
Krasnoyarsk Krai, Russia
Kurgan Oblast, Russia
Magadan Oblast, Russia
Novosibirsk Oblast, Russia
Omsk Oblast, Russia
Primorsky Krai, Russia
Republic of Buryatia, Russia
Republic of Khakassia, Russia
Sakha (Yakutia) Republic, Russia
Sakhalin Oblast, Russia
Sverdlovsk Oblast, Russia
Tomsk Oblast, Russia
Tuva Republic, Russia

Tyumen Oblast, Russia
Yamalo-Nenets Autonomous Okrug, Russia
Zabaykalsky Krai, Russia
Singapore
Taiwan

Middle Eastern regions

Israel
Kuwait
Qatar
Al-Baha, Saudi Arabia
Al-Jouf, Saudi Arabia
Al-Madinah Al-Monawarah, Saudi Arabia
Al-Qaseem, Saudi Arabia
Al-Riyadh, Saudi Arabia
Aseer, Saudi Arabia
Eastern Region, Saudi Arabia
Hail, Saudi Arabia
Jazan, Saudi Arabia
Makkah Al-Mokarramah, Saudi Arabia
Najran, Saudi Arabia
Northern Borders, Saudi Arabia
Tabouk, Saudi Arabia
Aegean, Turkey
Central Anatolia, Turkey
East Black Sea, Turkey
East Marmara, Turkey
Istanbul, Turkey
Meditterranean, Turkey
Middle East Anatolia, Turkey
Northeast Anatolia, Turkey
Southeast Anatolia, Turkey
West Anatolia, Turkey
West Black Sea, Turkey
West Marmara, Turkey
Abu Dhabi, UAE
Ajman, UAE
Dubai, UAE
Fujairah, UAE
Ras Al – Khaimah, UAE
Sharjah, UAE
Umm Al – Quwain, UAE

South American regions

Acre, Brazil
Alagoas, Brazil
Amapá, Brazil
Amazon, Brazil
Bahia, Brazil
Ceará, Brazil
Distrito Federal, Brazil
Goiás, Brazil
Holy Spirit, Brazil
Maranhão, Brazil
Mato Grosso do Sul, Brazil
Mato Grosso, Brazil
Minas Gerais, Brazil
Para, Brazil
Paraíba, Brazil
Paraná, Brazil
Pernambuco, Brazil
Piauí, Brazil
Rio de Janeiro, Brazil
Rio Grande do Norte, Brazil
Rio Grande do Sul, Brazil
Rondônia, Brazil
Roraima, Brazil
Santa Catarina, Brazil
São Paulo, Brazil
Sergipe, Brazil
Tocantins, Brazil
Antioquia, Colombia
Atlántico, Colombia
Bogotá, D.C., Colombia
Bolívar, Colombia
Boyacá, Colombia
Caldas, Colombia
Caquetá, Colombia

Cauca, Colombia
Cesar, Colombia
Córdoba, Colombia
Cundinamarca, Colombia
Huila, Colombia
Magdalena, Colombia
Meta, Colombia
Nariño, Colombia
Norte de Santander, Colombia
Quindio, Colombia
Risaralda, Colombia
Santander, Colombia
Sucre, Colombia
Tolima, Colombia
Valle del Cauca, Colombia

Appendix 2

Key WCIR data sources

Data sources

Agency for Science, Technology and Research (www.a-star.edu.sg/)
Australian Bureau of Statistics (www.abs.gov.au/)
Bank of Korea (www.bok.or.kr)
Bureau of Economic Analysis (www.bea.gov/)
Bureau of Labor Statistics (www.bls.gov)
Canada's Venture Capital and Private Equity Association (CVCA) (www.cvca.ca/)
Census and Statistics Department (The Government of the Hong Kong Special Administrative Region) (www.censtatd.gov.hk/)
Census of India (http://censusindia.gov.in)
Central Bureau of Statistics (www1.cbs.gov.il)
CIA World FactBook (www.cia.gov/library/publications/the-world-factbook/)
Controller General of Patents Designs and Trademarks, Department of Industrial Policy and Promotions, Ministry of Commerce and Industry (Government of India) (www.ipindia.nic.in/)
DANE (www.dane.gov.co)
Department of Education, Ministry of Human Resource Development (http://mhrd.gov.in/)
Department of Education, Yukon Government (2010) Education (www.finance.gov.yk.ca)
Department of Finance, Province of New Brunswick (2009) Main Estimates 2010–2011 (www.gnb.ca/)
Directorate General of Employment and Training, Ministry of Labour and Employment (India) (http://dget.gov.in/)
Dutta, S. and Mia, I. (2011) The Global Information Technology Report 2010-2011, (INSEAD) World Economic Forum (www3.weforum.org/docs/WEF_GITR_Report_2011.pdf)
Education Bureau (The Government of the Hong Kong Special Administrative Region) (www.edb.gov.hk)
Estadisticas del Sector Educativo, Ministerio de Educacion Nacional (http://menweb.mineducacion.gov.co)
European Venture Capital Association (EVCA) (www.evca.eu)

Eurostat (http://epp.eurostat.ec.europa.eu/)
Hensei Economic Census 2009 – Statistics Bureau, Director-General for Policy Planning and Statistical Research and Training Institute (www.stat.go.jp/)
India Venture Capital Association (2011) The Fourth Wheel: Private Equity in the Indian Corporate Landscape, Grant Thornton and IVCA (http://indiavca.org/pdf/The-Fourth-Wheel-a-Grant-Thornton-Report-.pdf)
INSEAD – PWC (2011) Brazilian Private Equity: Moving Centre Stage, Faculty and Research Working Paper, INSEAD (www.insead.edu/facultyresearch/research/doc.cfm?did=48210)
Instituto Brasileiro de Geografia e Estatística (www.ibge.gov.br)
Instituto Nacional de Estudos e Pesquisas Educacionais Anísio Teixeira (http://portal.inep.gov.br)
International Labour Organization (www.ilo.org)
International Monetary Fund – World Economic Outlook (www.imf.org)
Inter-Union Department of Statistics and Socio-Economic Studies (www.dieese.org.br)
IVC Research Centre (www.ivc-online.com)
Japan Patent Office (www.jpo.go.jp)
Korea Venture Capital Association (www.kvca.or.kr/)
Korean Intellectual Property Office (www.kipo.go.kr)
Labour Bureau Chandigarh, Ministry of Labour and Employment (http://labourbureau.nic.in/)
Latin American Venture Capital Association (2011) Scorecard 2011: The Private Equity and Venture Capital Environment in Latin America (http://lavca.org/)
Luk and Fung (2008/09) Country Q&A Hong Kong, Private Equity, (www.practicallaw.com)
McKinsey & Company (2011) Private equity Asia-Pacific: Rebounds, glocalization, and other tales (www.mckinsey.com)
Ministry of Education, Science and Technology (http://english.mest.go.kr)
Ministry of Employment and Labor (www.moel.go.kr/)
Ministry of Manpower (www.mom.gov.sg)
Ministry of Statistics and Programme Implementation (http://mospi.nic.in)
Ministry of Statistics and Programme Implementation (MOSPI) (http://mospi.nic.in)
National Science Foundation (www.nsf.gov)
National Statistics, Republic of China (Taiwan) (http://eng.stat.gov.tw/)
National Venture Capital Association (www.nvca.org) (PricewaterhouseCoopers/National Venture Capital Association MoneyTree™ Report, Data: Thomson Reuters)
New Zealand Venture Capital Association and Ernst & Young (2010) New Zealand Private Equity and Venture Capital Monitor, Ernst & Young New Zealand (www.nzvca.co.nz/content/NZ_PEVC_Monitor_Full_year_2010.pdf)
OECD (2011), OECD Communications Outlook 2011, OECD Publishing
OECD Statistics (http://stats.oecd.org)
Rea (2009) Government Expenditure and Revenue in New Zealand: A Brief

Overview, *Policy Quarterly* (5)3, 58–67. (http://ips.ac.nz/publications/files/99f91186d74.pdf)
Réseaux IP Européens (RIPE) Network Coordination Centre (www.ripe.net/info/stats/hostcount2/hostcount/stats/pl/2010-12/2.html)
Reserve Bank of India (www.rbi.org.in)
ROSPATENT – Federal Service for Intellectual Property (www.rupto.ru/)
Russian Federation Federal State Statistics Service (www.gks.ru)
Russian Post Office (www.russianpost.ru/rp/company/ru/home)
RVCA (2010) Russian private equity and venture capital market review 2010, Russian Venture Capital Association, St. Petersburg, Russia. (www.rvca.ru/upload/files/lib/RVCA-yearbook-2011.pdf)
Santa Consultants (2010) Private Equity in Turkey (www.collerinstitute.com/Content/pdf/Private%20Equity%20in%20Turkey_Santa.pdf)
Singapore Economic Development Board (www.edb.gov.sg)
Statistics Bureau, Director-General for Policy Planning and Statistical Research and Training Institute (www.stat.go.jp/)
Statistics Canada (www.statcan.gc.ca)
Statistics Iceland (www.statice.is/)
Statistics Korea (http://kostat.go.kr)
Statistics New Zealand (www.stats.govt.nz/)
Statistics Norway (www.ssb.no)
Statistics Singapore (www.singstat.gov.sg/)
Study in Korea (www.studyinkorea.go.kr/)
Swiss Statistics (www.bfs.admin.ch)
Taiwan Venture Capital Association (www.tvca.org.tw/en/)
Thomson Reuters (2011) Private Equity Market Activity in Quebec and Canada in 2010 (http://canadavc.com/files/public/Reseau%20Capital_02-11_%20English.pdf)
TurkStat (Turkish Statistical Institute) (www.turkstat.gov.tr)
US Department of Education, National Center for Education Statistics (http://nces.ed.gov/)
UNESCO Institute for Statistics (http://stats.uis.unesco.org/)
United States Census Bureau (www.census.gov/)
University Grants Commission (www.ugc.ac.in/)
World Bank (http://databank.worldbank.org)
World Intellectual Property Organization (www.wipo.int)

Appendix 3

Regions analysed in Chapter 6

North America

Atlanta-Sandy Springs-Marietta, US
Austin-Round Rock, US
Baltimore-Towson, US
Boston-Cambridge-Quincy, US
Buffalo-Niagara Falls, US
Charlotte-Gastonia-Concord, US
Chicago-Naperville-Joliet, US
Cincinnati-Middletown, US
Cleveland-Elyria-Mentor, US
Columbus, US
Dallas-Fort Worth-Arlington, US
Denver-Aurora, US
Detroit-Warren-Livonia, US
Grand Rapids-Wyoming, US
Greensboro-High Point, US
Hartford-West Hartford-East Hartford, US
Houston-Sugar Land-Baytown, US
Indianapolis, US
Jacksonville, US
Kansas City, US
Las Vegas-Paradise, US
Los Angeles-Long Beach-Santa Ana, US
Louisville, US
Memphis, US
Miami-Fort Lauderdale-Miami Beach, US
Milwaukee-Waukesha-West Allis, US
Minneapolis-St. Paul-Bloomington, US
Nashville-Davidson—Murfreesboro–Franklin, US
New York-Northern New Jersey-Long Island, US
Orlando-Kissimmee, US
Philadelphia-Camden-Wilmington, US
Phoenix-Mesa-Scottsdale, US
Pittsburgh, US
Portland-Vancouver-Beaverton, US
Raleigh-Cary, US
Richmond, US
Rochester, US
Sacramento–Arden-Arcade–Roseville, US
Salt Lake City, US
San Antonio, US
San Diego-Carlsbad-San Marcos, US
San Francisco-Oakland-Fremont, US
San Jose-Sunnyvale-Santa Clara, US
Seattle-Tacoma-Bellevue, US
St. Louis, US
Tampa-St. Petersburg-Clearwater, US
Virginia Beach-Norfolk-Newport News, US
Washington-Arlington-Alexandria, US
Alberta, Canada
British Columbia, Canada
Manitoba, Canada
Ontario, Canada
Quebec, Canada
Saskatchewan, CanadaRégion de Bruxelles-Capitale, Belgium

Europe

Vlaams Gewest, Belgium
Baden-Württemberg, Germany
Bayern, Germany
Berlin, Germany
Hessen, Germany
Niedersachsen, Germany
Nordrhein-Westfalen, Germany
Saarland, Germany
Schleswig-Holstein, Germany
Estonia
Noreste, Spain
Comunidad de Madrid, Spain
Île de France, France
Centre-Est, France
Southern and Eastern, Ireland
Emilia-Romagna, Italy
Lazio, Italy
Lombardia, Italy
Latvia
Lithuania
Noord-Nederland, Netherlands
West-Nederland, Netherlands
Zuid-Nederland, Netherlands
Ostösterreich, Austria
Westösterreich, Austria
Etelä-Suomi, Finland
Småland med Öarna, Sweden
Stockholm, Sweden
Sydsverige, Sweden
Västsverige, Sweden
Eastern, UK
London, UK
Scotland, UK
South East, UK
Norway
Switzerland
Bratislavsky, Slovak Republic
Közép-Magyarország, Hungary
Praha, Czech Republic
Israel

Asia and Oceania

New South Wales, Australia
Victoria, Australia
Western, Australia
Aichi, Japan
Kanagawa, Japan
Kyoto, Japan
Osaka, Japan
Shiga, Japan
Shizuoka, Japan
Tochigi, Japan
Tokyo, Japan
Toyama, Japan
New Zealand
Singapore
Taiwan
Beijing, China
Guangdong, China
Jiangsu, China
Shandong, China
Shanghai, China
Tianjin, China
Zhejing, China

References

Abu-Qarn, A. S. and Abu-Bader, S. (2007) Sources of growth revisited: evidence from selected MENA countries, *World Development*, 35(5), 752–71.

Acemoglu, D. and Zilibotti, F. (2001) Productivity differences, *Quarterly Journal of Economics*, 116(2), 563–606.

Acemoglu, D. and Robinson, J. A. (2012) *Why Nations Fail: The Origins of Power, Prosperity, and Poverty*, New York: Crown Publishers.

Acemoglu, D., Johnson, S. and Robinson, J. A. (2005) Institutions as a fundamental cause of long-run growth, in Aghion, P. and Durlauf, S. (eds), *Handbook of Economic Growth: Vol. 1A*, Amsterdam, The Netherlands: North-Holland, 385–472.

Acemoglu, D., Ticchi, D. and Vindigni, A. (2011) Emergence and persistence of inefficient states, *Journal of the European Economic Association*, 9(2), 177–208.

Achoui, M. M. (2009) Human resource development in Gulf countries: an analysis of the trends and challenges facing Saudi Arabia, *Human Resource Development International*, 12(1), 35–46.

Acs, Z. J., Audretsch, D. B. and Evans, D. S. (1994) Why does the self-employment rate vary across countries and over time?, *CEPR Discussion Paper*, #871.

Acs, Z. J., Anselin, L. and Varga, A. (2002) Patents and innovation counts as measures of regional production of new knowledge, *Research Policy*, 31(7), 1069–85.

Acs, Z. J., Desai, S. and Hessels, J. (2008) Entrepreneurship, economic development and institutions, *Small Business Economics*, 31(3), 219–34.

Adam, F., Kristan, P. and Tomšič, M. (2009) Varieties of capitalism in Eastern Europe (with special emphasis on Estonia and Slovenia), *Communist and Post-Communist Studies*, 42(1), 65–81.

Adams, J. D. (1990) Fundamental stocks of knowledge and productivity growth, *Journal of Political Economy*, 98(4), 673–702.

Affuso, A. Capello, R. and Fratesi, U. (2011) Globalization and competitive strategies in European vulnerable regions, *Regional Studies*, 45(5), 657–75.

Aghion, P. and Howitt, P. (1998) *Endogenous Growth Theory*, Cambridge, MA: MIT Press.

Agrawal, A. and Henderson, R. (2002) Putting patents in context: exploring knowledge transfer from MIT, *Management Science*, 48(1), 44–60.

Ahmed, P. K. and Rafiq, M. (1998) Integrated benchmarking: a holistic examination of select techniques for benchmarking analysis, *Benchmarking for Quality Management and Technology*, 5, 225–42.

Ahrend, R. (2012) Understanding Russian regions' economic performance during periods of decline and growth: an extreme bound analysis approach, *Economic Systems*, 36(3), 426–43.

Aiginger, K. (2006) Competitiveness: from a dangerous obsession to a welfare creating ability with positive externalities, *Journal of Industry, Competition and Trade*, 6(2), 161–77.

Al-Ali, J. (2007) Emiratisation: drawing UAE nationals into their surging economy, *International Journal of Sociology and Social Policy*, 28(9/10), 365–79.

Almor, T. (2011) Dancing as fast as they can: Israeli high-tech firms and the Great Recession of 2008, *Thunderbird International Business Review*, 53(2), 195–208.

Al-Rasheed, M. (2013) Saudi Arabia: local and regional challenges, *Contemporary Arab Affairs*, 6(1), 28–40.

Alshumaimri, A., Aldridge, T. and Audretsch, D. B. (2010) The university technology transfer revolution in Saudi Arabia, *Journal of Technology Transfer*, 35(6), 585–96.

Altenburg, T., Schmitz, H. and Stamm, A. (2008) Breakthrough? China's and India's transition from production to innovation, *World Development*, 36(2), 325–44.

Amin, A. (1999) An institutionalist perspective on regional economic development, *International Journal of Urban and Regional Research,* 23(2), 365–78.

Anderson, L. (1987) The state in the Middle East and North Africa, *Comparative Politics*, 20(1), 1–18.

Andersson, D. E. (2005) The spatial nature of entrepreneurship, *The Quarterly Journal of Austrian Economics,* 8(2), 21–34.

Andersson, M. and Karlsson, C. (2007) Knowledge in regional economic growth: the role of knowledge accessibility, *Industry and Innovation*, 14, 129–49.

Ansell, C. (2000) The networked polity: regional development in Western Europe, *Governance*, 13, 279–91.

Antonelli, C., Patrucco, P. and Quatraro, A. (2011) Productivity growth and pecuniary knowledge externalities: an empirical analysis of agglomeration economies in European regions, *Economic Geography*, 87, 23–50.

Aoyama, Y. (2009) Entrepreneurship and regional culture: the case of Hamamatsu and Kyoto, Japan, *Regional Studies*, 43(3), 495–512.

Archibugi, D. (1992) Patenting as an indicator of technological innovation: a review, *Science and Public Policy*, 19(6), 357–68.

Archibugi, D. and Filippetti, A. (2011) Is the economic crisis impairing convergence in innovation performance across Europe?, *Journal of Common Market Studies*, 49(6), 1153–82.

Arrowsmith, J., Sisson, K. and Marginson, P. (2004) What can 'benchmarking' offer the open method of co-ordination?, *Journal of European Public Policy*, 11, 311–28.

Arundel, A. (2003) Biotechnology indicators and public policy, *OECD Science, Technology and Industry Working Papers*, #2003/5.

Asheim, B. (1996) Industrial districts as 'learning regions': a condition for prosperity, *European Planning Studies*, 4, 379–400.

Asheim, B. (1997) *Towards a learning based strategy for regional development: structural limits or new possibilities?*, Paper presented at the Regional Studies Conference on 'Regional Frontiers', Frankfurt an der Oder, Germany.

Asheim, B. (2002) Temporary organisations and spatial embeddedness of learning and knowledge creation, *Geographiska Annaler B: Human Geography*, 84(2), 111–24.

Atkinson, R. D. and Gottlieb, P. D. (2001) *The Metropolitan New Economy Index: Benchmarking Economic Transformation in the Nation's Metropolitan Areas.* Washington, DC: Progressive Policy Institute.

Atkinson, R. D. and Correa, D. K. (2007) *The 2007 State New Economy Index: Benchmarking Economic Transformation in the States*, Kansas City, KS: Ewing Marion Kauffman Foundation.

Audretsch, D. B. and Thurik, A. R. (2001) What's new about the new economy? Sources of growth in the managed and entrepreneurial economies, *Industrial and Corporate Change*, 10(1), 267–315.

Audretsch, D. and Keilbach, M. (2004) Entrepreneurship and regional growth: an evolutionary interpretation, *Journal of Evolutionary Economics,* 14(5), 605–16.

Auty, R. M. (1990) *Resource-Based Industrialisation: Sowing the Oil in Eight Exporting Countries*, Oxford: Clarendon Press.

Auty, R. M. (ed.) (2001) *Resource Abundance and Economic Development*, Oxford: Clarendon Press.

Auty, R. M. (2007) Natural resources, capital accumulation and the resource curse, *Ecological Economics*, 61(4), 627–34.

Auty, R. M. and Kiiski, S. (2001) Natural resources, capital accumulation and welfare, in Auty, R. M. (ed.), *Resource Abundance and Economic Development*, Oxford: Oxford University Press, 19–35.

Badinger, H. and Tondl, G. (2002) Trade, human capital and innovation: the engines of European regional growth in the 1990s, in Fingleton, B. (ed.), *European Regional Growth*, Heidelberg, Germany: Springer, 215–40.

Baier, S. L. and Bergstrand, J. H. (2007) Do free trade agreements actually increase members' international trade?, *Journal of International Economics*, 71(1), 72–95.

Baldwin, J. R., Beckstead, D., Brown, W. M. and Rigby, D. L. (2008) Agglomeration and the geography of localization economies in Canada, *Regional Studies*, 42(1), 117–32.

Barkley, D. L. and Dudensing, R. M. (2011) Industrial legacy matters: implications for the development and use of indices of regional competitiveness, *Economic Development Quarterly*, 25(2), 130–42.

Bartholomew, D.J. and Knott, M. (1999) *Latent Variable Models and Factor Analysis*, 2nd edn, London: Arnold.

Basu, S. and Weil, D. N. (1998) Appropriate technology and growth, *Quarterly Journal of Economics*, 113(4), 1025–54.

Bathelt, H., Malmberg, A. and Maskell, P. (2004) Clusters and knowledge: local buzz, global pipelines, and the process of knowledge creation, *Progress in Human Geography* 28(1), 31–56.

Bayo-Moriones, A. and Lera-López, F. (2007) A firm-level analysis of determinants of ICT adoption in Spain, *Technovation*, 27(6/7), 352–66.

Beblawi, H. and Luciani, G. (1987) *The Rentier State*, London: Croome Helm.

Begg, I. (1999) Cities and competitiveness, *Urban Studies*, 36(5/6), 795–810.

Begley, T. M. and Tan, W-L. (2001) The socio-cultural environment for entrepreneurship: A comparison between East Asian and Anglo-Saxon countries, *Journal of International Business Studies*, 32, 537–53.

Bekaert, G., Harvey, C. R. and Lundblad, C. (2001) Emerging markets and economic development, *Journal of Development Economics*, 66(2), 465–504.

Bellini, N. and Landabaso, M. (2007) Learning about innovation in Europe's regional policy, in Rutten, R. and Boekema, F. (eds), *The Learning Region: Foundations, State of the Art, Future*, Cheltenham: Edward Elgar, 231–51.

Benneworth, P. (2004) In what sense "regional development"? Entrepreneurship, underdevelopment and strong tradition in the periphery, *Entrepreneurship and Regional Development*, 16(6), 439–58.

Benneworth, P. and Charles, D. (2005) University spin-off policies and economic development in less successful regions: learning from two decades of policy practice, *European Planning Studies,* 13, 537–57.

Benneworth, P. and Hospers, G.-J. (2007) The new economic geography of old industrial regions: universities as global-local pipelines, *Environment and Planning C*, 25, 779–802.

Bentivogli, C. and Pagano, P. (1999) Regional disparities and labour mobility: the Euro-11 versus the USA, *Labour*, 13(3), 737–60.

Benz, A. and Eberlein, B. (1999) The Europeanization of regional policies: patterns of multi-level governance, *Journal of European Public Policy*, 6, 329–48.

Berger, A. N. and Udell, G. F. (1998) The economics of small business finance: the roles of private equity and debt markets in the financial growth cycle, *Journal of Banking and Finance*, 22(6–8), 613–73.

Bessant, J. and Rush, H. (1999) *Benchmarking Framework Conditions*, Paper (November) for the Benchmarking Co-ordination Office, Brussels, Belgium: European Commission.

Beugelsdijk, S. and Maseland, R. (2011) *Culture in Economics: History, Methodological Reflections and Contemporary Applications*, Cambridge: Cambridge University Press.

Beynon-Davies, P. (2010) eBusiness as a driver for regional development, *Journal of Systems and Information Technology*, 12(1), 17–36.

Bhar, R. and Nikolova, B. (2009) Oil prices and equity returns in the BRIC countries, *World Economy*, 32(7), 1036–54.

Bilbao-Osorio, B. and Rodríguez-Pose, A. (2004) From R&D to innovation and economic growth in the EU, *Growth and Change*, 35(4), 434–55.

Birdsall, N., Pincknety, T. and Sabot, R. (2001) Natural resources, human capital and growth, in Auty, R. M. (ed.), *Resource Abundance and Economic Development*, Oxford: Oxford University Press, 57–75.

Bisat, A., El-Erian, M. and Helbling, T. (1997) Growth, investment, and saving in the Arab economies, *IMF Working Paper*, #WP/97/85.

Bittencourt, M. (2010) Financial development and inequality: Brazil 1985–1994, *Economic Change and Restructuring*, 43(2), 113–30.

Boland, P. (2007) Unpacking the theory-policy interface of local economic development: an analysis of Cardiff and Liverpool, *Urban Studies*, 44, 1019–39.

Borrás, S. (2004) System of innovation theory and the European Union, *Science and Public Policy*, 31(6), 425–33.

Boschma, R. (2004) Competitiveness of regions from an evolutionary perspective, *Regional Studies*, 38(9), 1001–14.

Boschma, R. A. and Frenken, K. (2006) Why is economic geography not an evolutionary science? Towards an evolutionary economic geography, *Journal of Economic Geography*, 6(3), 273–302.

Bouvet, F. (2010) EMU and the dynamics of regional per capita income inequality in Europe, *Journal of Economic Inequality*, 8(3), 323–44.

Boxwell, R. J. (1994) *Benchmarking for Competitive Advantage*, New York: McGraw-Hill.

Boyce, J. R. and Emery, J. C. H. (2011) Is a negative correlation between resource abundance and growth sufficient evidence that there is a "resource curse"?, *Resources Policy*, 36(1), 1–13.

Brach, J. (2009) Technology, political economy, and economic development in the Middle East and North Africa, *Review of Middle East Economics and Finance*, 5(3), Article 1.

Bradley, S. and Taylor, J. (1996) Human capital formation and local economic performance, *Regional Studies*, 30(1), 1–14.

Brandt, A., Hahn, C., Krätke, S. and Kiese, M. (2009) Metropolitan regions in the knowledge economy: network analysis as a strategic information tool, *Tijdschrift voor Economische en Sociale Geografie*, 100(2), 236–49.

Breznitz, S. M. (2013) Cluster sustainability: the Israeli life sciences industry, *Economic Development Quarterly*, 27(1), 29–39.

Bristow, G. (2005) Everyone's a 'winner': problematising the discourse of regional competitiveness, *Journal of Economic Geography*, 5(3), 285–304.

Bristow, G. (2010) Resilient regions: Re-'place'ing regional competitiveness, *Cambridge Journal of Regions, Economy and Society*, 3(1), 153–67.

Brun, J. F., Combes, J. L. and Renard, M. F. (2002) Are there spillover effects between coastal and non-coastal regions in China?, *China Economic Review*, 13(2/3), 161–9.

Buerger, M., Broekel, T. and Coad, A. (2012) Regional dynamics of innovation: investigating the co-evolution of patents, research and development (R&D), and employment, *Regional Studies*, 46(5), 565–82.

Buesa, M., Heijs, J., Pellitero, M. M. and Baumert, T. (2006) Regional systems of innovation and the knowledge production function: the Spanish case, *Technovation*, 26(4), 463–72.

Buesa, M., Heijs, J. and Baumert, T. (2010) The determinants of regional innovation in Europe: a combined factorial and regression knowledge production function approach, *Research Policy*, 39(6), 722–35.

Cairncross, F. (1997) *The Death of Distance*, Boston, MA: HBS Press.

Cairns, A. P. and Meilke, K. D. (2012) Canadian agrifood export performance and the growth potential of the BRICs and Next-11, *Canadian Agricultural Trade Policy and Competitiveness Research Network Working Paper*, #2012-05.

Camagni, R. (2002) On the concept of territorial competitiveness: sound or misleading?, *Urban Studies,* 39, 2395–411.

Camagni, R. and Capello, R. (2010) Macroeconomic and territorial policies for regional competitiveness: an EU perspective, *Regional Science Policy and Practice*, 2(1), 1–19.

Camagni, R. and Capello, R. (2012) Globalization and economic crisis: how will the future of European regions look?, in Capello, R. and Dentinho, T. P. (eds), *Globalization Trends and Regional Development: Dynamics of FDI and Human Capital Flows*, Cheltenham: Edward Elgar, 36–62.

Camagni, R. and Capello, R. (2013) Regional competitiveness and territorial capital: a conceptual approach and empirical evidence from the European Union, *Regional Studies,* 47(9), 1383–402.

Cantner, U., Conti, E. and Meder, A. (2009) Networks and innovation: the role of social assets in explaining firms' innovative capacity, *Jena Economic Research Papers,* #2009-040.

Capello, R. (1999) Spatial transfer of knowledge in high technology milieux: learning versus collective learning processes, *Regional Studies,* 33, 353–65.

Capello, R. and Nijkamp, P. (eds) (2009) *Handbook of Regional Growth and Development Theories*, Cheltenham: Edward Elgar.

Capello, R., Caragliu, A. and Nijkamp, P. (2011) Territorial capital and regional growth: increasing returns in knowledge use, *Tijdschrift voor Economische en Sociale Geografie,* 102(4), 385–405.

Carlino, G. A. and Saiz, A. (2008) City beautiful, *IZA Discussion Paper Series*, #3778.

Carlsson, B. (2006) Internationalization of innovation systems: a survey of the literature, *Research Policy*, 35, 56–67.

Carnoy, M., Loyalka, P., Androushchak, G. and Proudnikova, A. (2012) The economic returns to higher education in the BRIC countries and their implications for higher education expansion, *National Research University Higher School of Economics Research Paper*, #WP BRP 02/EDU/2012.

Carree, M., van Stel, A., Thurik, R. and Wennekers, S. (2002) Economic development and business ownership: an analysis using data of 23 OECD countries in the period 1976–1996, *Small Business Economics*, 19(3), 271–90.

Casey, T. (2009) Mapping stability and change in advanced capitalisms, *Comparative European Politics*, 7(2), 255–78.

Castellacci, F. and Archibugi, D. (2008) The technology clubs: the distribution of knowledge across nations, *Research Policy*, 37, 1659–73.

Castells, M. and Hall, P. (1994) *Technopoles of the World: The Making of Twenty-First Century Industrial Complexes*, London: Routledge.

Cevik, S. (2011) Policy coordination in fiscal federalism: drawing lessons from the Dubai debt crisis, *IMF Working Paper*, #WP/11/147.

CFC Holding Company and CME Group (2011) *Xinhua-Dow Jones IFCD Index Report 2011*, Beijing: CFC Holding Company.

Charles, D. and Benneworth, P. (1999) *The Competitiveness Project: Regional Benchmarking Report*, Newcastle upon Tyne: Centre for Urban and Regional Development Studies, University of Newcastle upon Tyne.

Chaston, I. (2009) Entrepreneurs, intuition, and small-business performance, *JCC: The Business and Economics Research Journal*, 2(1), 37–45.

Chattopadhyay, S. and Mukhopadhyay, R. N. (2013) Embracing the global knowledge economy: challenges facing Indian higher education, in Banerjee, S. and Chakrabarti, A. (eds), *Development and Sustainability: India in a Global Perspective*, New Delhi: Springer, 537–59.

Chen, J., Liu, W., Zhang, Y. and Sheng, Y. (2010) An empirical study on FDI international knowledge spillovers and regional economic development in China, *Frontiers of Economics in China*, 5(3), 489–508.

Chesbrough, H. (2003) *Open Innovation: The New Imperative for Creating and Profiting from Technology*, Boston, MA: Harvard Business School Press.

Cheung, G. C. K. (2010) The 2008–2009 global financial fallout: Shanghai and Dubai as emerging financial powerhouses?, *Asian Politics and Policy*, 2(1), 77–93.

Chinn, M. D. and Fairlie, R. W. (2010) ICT use in the developing world: an analysis of differences in computer and internet penetration, *Review of International Economics*, 18(1), 153–67.

Christopherson, S., Michie, J. and Tyler, P. (2010) Regional resilience: theoretical and empirical perspectives, *Cambridge Journal of Regions, Economy and Society*, 3(1), 3–10.

Claessens, S., Dell'Ariccia, G., Igan, D. and Laeven, L. (2010) Cross-country experiences and policy implications from the global financial crisis, *Economic Policy*, 25(62), 267–93.

Clark, A. E. (2003) Unemployment as a social norm: psychological evidence from panel data, *Journal of Labor Economics*, 21(2), 324–51.

Clark, G. (2007) *World Cities and Economic Development: Case Studies in Economic Strategies to Address Globalisation in Established and Emerging Cities*, Toronto: City of Toronto.

Clary, C. and Karlin, M. E. (2011) Saudi Arabia's reform gamble, *Survival*, 53(5), 15–20.

Clifton, N., Cooke, P. and Hansen, H. K. (2012) Towards a reconciliation of the 'contextless; with the 'space-less'? The creative class across varieties of capitalism: new evidence from Sweden and the UK, *Regional Studies*, 47(2), 201–15.

Cohen, W. and Levinthal, L. (1990) Absorptive capacity: a new perspective on learning and innovation, *Administrative Science Quarterly*, 35(1), 128–52.

Collier, P. and Hoeffler, A. (2009) Testing the neocon agenda: democracy in resource-rich societies, *European Economic Review*, 53(3), 293–308.

Collins, S. M. and Bosworth, B. P. (1996) Economic growth in East Asia: accumulation versus assimilation, *Brookings Papers on Economic Activity*, 1996(2), 135–203.

Combes, P.-P. and Overman, H. G. (2004) The spatial distribution of economic activities in the European Union, in Henderson, J. V. and Thisse, J.-F. (eds), *Handbook of Regional and Urban Economics: Volume 4 Cities and Geography*, 2845–909.

Cooke, P. (1992) Regional innovation systems: competitive regulation in the new Europe, *Geoforum,* 23(3), 365–82.

Cooke, P. (1997) Regions in a global market: the experiences of Wales and Baden Württemberg, *Review of International Political Economy,* 4(2), 349–81.

Cooke, P. (2001) Regional innovation systems, clusters, and the knowledge economy, *Industrial and Corporate Change,* 10, 945–74.

Cooke, P. (2002a) Regional innovation systems: general findings and some new evidence from biotechnology clusters, *Journal of Technology Transfer*, 27(1), 133–45.

Cooke, P. (2002b) Biotechnology clusters as regional, sectoral innovation systems, *International Regional Science Review*, 25(1), 8–37.

Cooke, P. (2002c) *Knowledge Economies*, London: Routledge.

Cooke, P. (2004) Regional innovation systems: an evolutionary approach, in Cooke, P., Heidenreich, M. and Braczyk, H.-J. (eds), *Regional Innovation Systems: The Role of Governance in a Globalised World*, 2nd edn, London: Routledge, 1–18.

Cooke, P. (2007) Regional innovation systems, asymmetric knowledge and the legacies of learning, in Rutten, R. and Boekema, F. (eds), *The Learning Region: Foundations, State of the Art, Future*, Cheltenham: Edward Elgar, 184–205.

Cooke, P. and Huggins, R. (2003) High-technology clustering in Cambridge (UK), in Sforzi, F. (ed.), *The Institutions of Local Development*, Aldershot: Ashgate, 51–72.

Cooke, P., Asheim, B., Boschma, R., Martin, R., Schwartz, D. and Tödtling, F. (eds) (2011) *Handbook of Regional Innovation and Growth*, Cheltenham: Edward Elgar.

Cooper, J. (2006) Of BRICs and brains: comparing Russia with China, India and other populous emerging economies, *Eurasian Geography and Economics*, 47(3), 255–84.

Cortright, J. and Mayer, H. (2004) Increasingly rank: the use and misuse of rankings in economic development, *Economic Development Quarterly*, 18, 34–9.

Courlet, C. and Soulage, B. (1995) Industrial dynamics and territorial space, *Entrepreneurship and Regional Development*, 7, 285–307.

Cox, W. (2013) World's Most Affluent Metropolitan Areas: 2012, www.newgeography.com/content/003420-worlds-most-affluent-metropolitan-areas-2012

Crescenzi, R., Rodríguez-Pose, A., and Storper. M. (2007) The territorial dynamics of innovation: a Europe–United States comparative analysis, *Journal of Economic Geography*, 7(6), 673–709.

Crevoisier, O. and Jeannerat, H. (2009) Territorial knowledge dynamics: from the proximity paradigm to multi-location milieus, *European Planning Studies*, 17, 1223–41.

Czernich, N., Falck, O., Kretschmer, T. and Woessmann, L. (2011) Broadband infrastructure and economic growth, *The Economic Journal*, 121(552), 505–32.

D'Costa, A. P. (2011) Geography, uneven development and distributive justice: the political economy of IT growth in India, *Cambridge Journal of Regions, Economy and Society*, 4(2), 237–51.

Dahlander, L. and Gann, D. M. (2010) How open is innovation?, *Research Policy*, 39, 699–709.

Dasgupta, S. and Singh, A. (2005) Will services be the new engine of Indian economic growth?, *Development and Change*, 36(6), 1035–57.

Dattakumar, S. and Jagadeesh, R. (2003) A review of literature on benchmarking, *Benchmarking: An International Journal*, 10, 176–209.

David, P. A., Hall, B. H. and Toole, A. A. (2000) Is public R&D a complement or substitute for private R&D? A review of econometric evidence, *Research Policy*, 29(4/5), 497–529.

Davidson, C. (2009) Abu Dhabi's new economy: oil, investment and domestic development, *Middle East Policy*, 16(2), 59–79.

Davis, J., Ossowski, R., Daniel, J. and Barnett, S. (2001) Oil funds: problems posing as solutions?, *Finance and Development*, 38(4), 56–9.

De Araujo, A. A. (2012) Access to higher education in Brazil with reference to Prouni, *Higher Education Studies*, 2(1), 32–7.

De Bruijn, P. J. M. and van Oort, F. G. (2007) Connectivity and co-location in innovation processes of Dutch firms, in Cooke, P. and Schwartz, D. (eds), *Creative Regions: Technology, Culture and Knowledge Entrepreneurship*, Abingdon: Routledge, 62–80.

De Castro, T. (2012) Trade cooperation indicators: development of BRIC bilateral trade flows, *International Review of Business Research Papers*, 8(1), 211–23.

De La Porte, C., Pochet, P. and Room, G. (2001) Social benchmarking, policy making and new governance in the EU, *Journal of European Social Policy*, 11, 291–307.

De Meulemeester, J.-L. and Rochat, D. (1995) A causality analysis of the link between higher education and economic development, *Economics of Education Review*, 14(4), 351–61.

DeVol, R. C. (1999) *America's High-Tech Economy: Growth, Development, and Risks for Metropolitan Areas*, Santa Monica, CA: Milken Institute.

DeVol, R., Koepp, R. and Ki, J. (2004) *State Technology and Science Index: Enduring Lessons for the Intangible Economy*, Santa Monica, CA: Milken Institute.

DeVol, R., Bedroussian, A. and Soojung, K. (2007) *Best Performing Cities 2007: Where America's Jobs are Created and Sustained*, Santa Monica, CA: Milken Institute.

De Vries, G. J., Erumban, A. A., Timmer, M. P., Voskoboynikov, I. and Wu, H. X. (2012) Deconstructing the BRICs: structural transformation and aggregate productivity growth, *Journal of Comparative Economics*, 40(2), 211–27.

Denis, C., McMorrow, K., Röger, W. and Veugelers, R. (2005) The Lisbon Strategy and the EU's structural productivity problem, *European Commission Directorate-General for Economic and Financial Affairs Economic Papers*, #221.

Derin-Gure, P. (2011) Separatist terrorism and the economic condition in south-eastern Turkey, *Defence and Peace Economics*, 22(4), 393–407.

Devezas, T. C., Linstone, H. A. and Santos, H. J. S. (2005) The growth dynamics of the Internet and the long wave theory, *Technological Forecasting and Social Change*, 72(8), 913–35.

Di Nicola, P., Mingo, I. and Gareis, K. (2004) *Evaluating Information Society at Regional Level: A Benchmarking Approach*, Brussels, Belgium: European Commission.

Dicken, P. (2007) *Global Shift*, 5th edition, New York: Guilford Press.

Dicken, P., Kelly, P., Olds, K. and Wai-Chung Yeung, H. (2001) Chains and networks, territories and scales: towards a relational framework for analysing the global economy, *Global Networks*, 1(2), 89–112.

Diener, E. and Biswas-Diener, R. (2002) Will money increase subjective well-being?, *Social Indicators Research*, 57(2), 119–69.

Dijkstra, L., Annoni, P. and Kozovska, K. (2011) A New Regional Competitiveness Index:

Theory, Methods and Findings, *European Union Regional Policy Working Paper*, #02/11.

Dodgson, M. (2000) Policies for science, technology and innovation in Asian newly industrializing economies, in Kim, L. and Nelson, R. R. (eds), *Technology, Learning, and Innovation: Experiences of Newly Industrializing Economies*, Cambridge: Cambridge University Press, 229–68.

Doloreux, D. and Parto, S. (2005) Regional innovation systems: current discourse and unresolved issues, *Technology in Society*, 27(2), 133–53.

Döpke, J. (2001) The 'employment intensity' of growth in Europe, *Kiel Working Paper*, #1021.

Dorfman, N. S. (1983) Route 128: the development of a regional high technology economy, *Research Policy*, 12(6), 299–316.

Drejer, I. and Lund Vinding, A. (2007) Searching near and far: determinants of innovative firms' propensity to collaborate across geographical distance, *Industry and Innovation*, 14, 259–75.

Easterlin, R. A. (1974) Does economic growth improve the human lot?, in David, P. A. and Reder, M. W. (eds), *Nations and Households in Economic Growth: Essays in Honor of Moses Abramovitz*, New York: Academic Press, 89–125.

Economic Development Corporation of Utah (2013) *Utah Business and Economic Profile*, Salt Lake City, UT: edcUTAH.

Eng, I. (1997) The rise of manufacturing towns: externally driven industrialization and urban development in the Pearl River Delta of China, *International Journal of Urban and Regional Research*, 21(4), 554–68.

Enright, M. J. and Roberts, B. H. (2001) Regional clustering in Australia, *Australian Journal of Management*, 26, 65–85.

Entrikin, J. (1991) *The Betweenness of Place: Towards a Geography of Modernity*, Baltimore, MD: John Hopkins University Press.

Erickek, G. A. and Watts, B. R. (2003) *An Economic Development Benchmarking System for Rural Michigan*, Kalamazoo, MI: W. E. Upjohn Institute for Employment Research.

Eriksson, R. and Hansen, H. K. (2013) Industries, skills and human capital: how does regional size affect uneven development?, *Environment and Planning A*, 45(3), 593–613.

Ersoy, A. and Taylor, M. (2012) Modelling local and regional economic development in Turkey: a "Curates Egg", *Growth and Change*, 43(4), 615–37.

Essletzbichler, J. and Kadokawa, K. (2010) The evolution of regional labour productivities in Japanese manufacturing, 1968–2004, *Regional Studies*, 44(9), 1189–205.

European Commission (2006) *European Innovation. Newsletter No. 5*, Communication and Information Unit, Enterprise and Industry DG, Brussels: European Commission.

European Commission (2010a) *Lisbon Strategy Evaluation Document*, Brussels: European Commission.

European Commission (2010b) *Europe 2020: A Strategy for Smart, Sustainable and Inclusive Growth*, Brussels: European Commission.

ERT (1996) *Benchmarking for Policy-makers. The Way to Competitiveness, Growth and Job Creation*, Report (October), Brussels: European Round Table of Industrialists.

Ewers, M. C. (2013) From knowledge transfer to learning: the acquisition and assimilation of human capital in the United Arab Emirates and the other Gulf States, *Geoforum*, 46, 124–37.

Ewers, M. C. and Malecki, E. J. (2010) Leapfrogging into the knowledge economy: assessing the economic development strategies of the Arab Gulf States, *Tijdschrift voor Economische en Sociale Geografie*, 101(5), 494–508.

Fagerberg, J. (1996) Technology and competitiveness, *Oxford Review of Economic Policy*, 12(3), 39–51.

Fagerberg, J. and Srholec, M. (2008) National innovation systems, capabilities and economic development, *Research Policy*, 37(9), 1417–35.

Fan, C. C. and Scott, A. J. (2003) Industrial agglomeration and development: a survey of spatial economic issues in East Asia and a statistical analysis of Chinese regions, *Economic Geography*, 79(3), 295–319.

Farole, T., Rodríguez-Pose, A. and Storper, M. (2011) Human geography and the institutions that underlie economic growth, *Progress in Human Geography*, 35(1), 58–80.

Favell, A. (2008) *Eurostars and Eurocities: Free Movement and Mobility in an Integrating Europe*, Oxford: Blackwell.

Fedorov, L. (2002) Regional inequality and regional polarization in Russia, 1990–99, *World Development*, 30(3), 443–56.

Feldman, M. P., Francis, J. and Bercovitz, J. (2005) Creating a cluster while building a firm: entrepreneurs and the formation of industrial clusters, *Regional Studies*, 39(1), 129–41.

Ferguson, M., Ali, K., Olfert, M. and Partridge, M. (2007) Voting with their feet: jobs versus amenities, *Growth and Change*, 33(1), 77–110.

Ferretti, M. and Parmentola, A. (2007) The creation of regional innovation systems in emerging countries: the case of Dubai, *International Journal of Globalisation and Small Business*, 2(2), 137–65.

Fischer, K. (2008) Despite doubts, 3 prominent universities sign deals with a Saudi university, *Chronicle of Higher Education*, 54(27), A22–A23.

Fischer, M. F., Revilla Diez, J., Snickars, F. and Varga, A. (2001) *Metropolitan Systems of Innovation: Theory and Evidence from Three Metropolitan Regions in Europe*, Berlin: Springer.

Fleisher, B., Li, H. and Zhao, M. Q. (2010) Human capital, economic growth, and regional inequality in China, *Journal of Development Economics*, 92(2), 215–31.

Florida, R. (1995) Toward the learning region, *Futures*, 27(5), 527–36.

Florida, R. (2002a) The economic geography of talent, *Annals of the Association of American Geographers*, 92(4), 743–55.

Florida, R. (2002b) *The Rise of the Creative Class, and How It's Transforming Work, Leisure, Community, and Everyday Life*, New York: Basic Books.

Florida, R. (2005) *Cities and the Creative Class*, New York: Routledge.

Florida, R. L. and Kenney, M. (1988) Venture capital, high technology and regional development, *Regional Studies*, 22(1), 33–48.

Florida, R., Mellander, C. and Stolarick, K. (2011) Beautiful places: the role of perceived aesthetic beauty in community satisfaction, *Regional Studies*, 45(1), 33–48.

Foray, D. (2004) *The Economics of Knowledge*, Cambridge, MA: MIT Press.

Fox, R. K. and Treuhaft, S. (2006) *Shared Prosperity, Stronger Regions: An Agenda for Rebuilding America's Older Core Cities*, Oakland, CA: Policy Link.

Freeman, C. (1987) *Technology, Policy, and Economic Performance: Lessons from Japan*, London: Pinter.

Freeman, C. (1994) The economics of technical change, *Cambridge Journal of Economics*, 18, 463–514.

Freeman, C. (2002) Continental, national and sub-national innovation systems: complementarity and economic growth, *Research Policy*, 31(2), 191–211.

Freguglia, R. S. and Menezes-Filho, N. A. (2012) Inter-regional wage differentials with individual heterogeneity: evidence from Brazil, *Annals of Regional Science*, 49(1), 17–34.

Frey, B. S. and Stutzer, A. (2002) What can economists learn from happiness research?, *Journal of Economic Literature*, 40(2), 402–35.

Frieden, R. (2005) Lessons from broadband development in Canada, Japan, Korea and the United States, *Telecommunications Policy*, 29(8), 595–613.

Friedman, T. L. (2005) *The World is Flat: A Brief History of the Globalized World in the 21st Century*, London: Penguin Books.

Fritsch, M. (2002) Measuring the quality of regional innovation systems: a knowledge production function approach, *International Regional Science Review*, 25(1), 86–101.

Fritsch, M. and Schwirten, C. (1999) Enterprise-university cooperation and the role of public research institutions in regional innovation systems, *Industry and Innovation*, 6(1), 69–83.

Fu, X. (2008) Foreign direct investment, absorptive capacity and regional innovation capabilities: evidence from China, *Oxford Development Studies*, 36(1), 89–110.

Fu, X. and Zhang, J. (2011) Technology transfer, indigenous innovation and leapfrogging in green technology: the solar-PV industry in China and India, *Journal of Chinese Economic and Business Studies*, 9(4), 329–47.

Fu, X., Pietrobelli, C. and Soete, L. (2011) The role of foreign technology and indigenous innovation in the emerging economies: technological change and catching-up, *World Development*, 39(7), 1204–12.

Furman, J. L., Porter, M. E. and Stern, S. (2002) The determinants of national innovative capacity, *Research Policy,* 31(6), 899–933.

Gan, C. K. (2003) The relationship between FDI and the development of Shanghai industries, *Shanghai Economy*, 3, 35–9.

Gardiner, B., Martin, R. and Tyler, P. (2004) Competitiveness, productivity and economic growth across the European regions, *Regional Studies*, 38(9), 1045–67.

Garofoli, G. (2002) Local development in Europe: theoretical models and international comparisons, *European Urban and Regional Studies,* 9, 225–39.

Gassmann, O. (2006) Opening up the innovation process: towards an agenda, *R&D Management*, 36, 223–8.

Geffen, D. and Kenyon, T. (2006) Heinz capitalism: how many varieties are there? An empirical re-examination of coordination mechanisms in advanced market economies. Available at SSRN: http://ssrn.com/abstract=1005407.

Gentile-Lüdecke, S. and Giroud, A. (2012) Knowledge transfer from TNCs and upgrading of domestic firms: the Polish automotive sector, *World Development*, 40(4), 796–807.

Gereffi, G. (2009) Development models and industrial upgrading in China and Mexico, *European Sociological Review*, 25(1), 37–51.

Gerschenkron, A. (1962) *Economic Backwardness in Historical Perspective*, Cambridge, MA: Harvard University Press.

Gertler, M. and Wolfe, D. (2004) Local social knowledge management: community actors, institutions and multilevel governance in regional foresight exercises, *Futures*, 36, 45–65.

Gibbs, D. and Tanner, K. (1997) Information and communication technologies and local economic development policies: the British case, *Regional Studies*, 31(8), 765–74.

Giordano, B. and Roller, E. (2003) A comparison of city region dynamics in the UK, Spain and Italy: more similarities than differences?, *Regional Studies*, 37, 911–27.

Giroud, A., Jindra, B. and Marek, P. (2012) Heterogeneous FDI in transition economies: a novel approach to assess the developmental impact of backward linkages, *World Development*, 40(11), 2206–20.

Glaeser, E. L., Kolko, J. and Saiz, A. (2001) Consumer city, *Journal of Economic Geography*, 1(1), 27–50.

Gorsuch, R. L. (1983) *Factor Analysis*, 2nd edn., Hills Dale, NJ: Lawrence Erlbaum Associates.

Gottlieb, P. D. (1994) Amenities as an economic development tool: is there enough evidence?, *Economic Development Quarterly*, 8(3), 270–85.

Gouvea, R., Mahto, R. V. and Montoya, M. J. R. (2013) BRIC national export performance: a portfolio approach, *Journal of Chinese Economic and Business Studies*, 11(1), 47–58.

Government of Nunavut (2012) *Economy*, Iqaluit: Government of Nunavut.

Grant, R. M. (1996) Toward a knowledge-based theory of the firm, *Strategic Management Journal*, 17, 109–22.

Green, A. (1999) Education and globalization in Europe and East Asia: convergent and divergent trends, *Journal of Education Policy*, 14(1), 55–71.

Greene, F. J., Tracey, P. and Cowling, M. (2007) Recasting the city into city-regions: place promotion, competitiveness benchmarking and the quest for urban supremacy, *Growth and Change*, 38, 1–22.

Griliches, Z. (1990) Patent statistics as economic indicators: a survey, *Journal of Economic Literature*, 28(4), 1661–707.

Groenewold, N., Chen, A. and Lee, G. (2010) Inter-regional spillovers of policy shocks in China, *Regional Studies*, 44(1), 81–101.

Groot, S. P. T., de Groot, H. L. F., Lejour, A. M. and Möhlmann, J. (2011) *The rise of the BRIC countries and its impact on the Dutch economy* – Rapport voor het Ministerie van Economische Zaken, The Hague: Lamdbouw en Innovatie, CPB Background Document.

Grossman, G. M. and Helpman, E. (1994) Endogenous innovation in the theory of growth, *Journal of Economic Perspectives*, 8, 23–44.

Guellec, D. and van Pottelsberghe de la Potterie, B. (2004) From R&D to productivity growth: do the institutional settings and the source of funds matter?, *Oxford Bulletin of Economics and Statistics*, 66(3), 353–78.

Guerrieri, P. and Meliciani, V. (2005) Technology and international competitiveness: the interdependence between manufacturing and producers services, *Structural Change and Economic Dynamics*, 16(4), 489–502.

Gylfason, T. (2001) Natural resources, education, and economic development, *European Economic Review*, 45(4–6), 847–59.

Ha, J. and Howitt, P. (2007) Accounting for trends in productivity and R&D: A Schumpeterian critique of semi-endogenous growth theory, *Journal of Money, Credit and Banking*, 39(4), 733–74.

Haddad, E. A. and Hewings, G. J. D. (2001) Trade and regional development: international and interregional competitiveness in Brazil, in Johansson, B., Karlsson, C. and Stough, R. R. (eds), *Theories of Endogenous Regional Growth: Lessons for Regional Policies*, Heidelberg: Springer, 181–208.

Hair, Jr., J. F., Black, W. C., Babin, B. J. and Anderson, R. E. (2010) *Multivariate Data Analysis*, 7th edn., Upper Saddle River, NJ: Pearson.

Hall, P. and Preston, P. (1988) *The Carrier Wave: New Information Technology and the Geography of Innovation 1846–2003*, London: Unwin Hyman.

Hall, P. A. and Soskice, D. (2001) An introduction to varieties of capitalism, in Hall, P. A. and Soskice, D. (eds), *Varieties of Capitalism: The Institutional Foundations of Comparative Advantage*, Oxford: Oxford University Press, 1–68.

Hall, P. A. and Gingerich, D. W. (2009) Varieties of capitalism and institutional complementarities in the political economy: an empirical analysis, *British Journal of Political Science*, 39(3), 449–82.

Hanushek, E. A. and Woessmann, L. (2008) The role of cognitive skills in economic development, *Journal of Economic Literature*, 46(3), 607–68.

Harding, A., Scott, A., Laske, S. and Burtscher, C. (eds) (2007) *Bright Satanic Mills: Regional Development and the Knowledge Economy*, Aldershot: Ashgate.

Harris, J. (2009) Statist globalisation in China, Russia and the Gulf States, *Perspectives of Global Development and Technology*, 8(2/3), 139–63.

Harris, P. (2012) Scranton, Pennsylvania: where even the mayor is on minimum wage, *Observer Newspaper*, 14th July.

Harris, R. G. (2001) The knowledge-based economy: intellectual origins and new economic perspectives, *International Journal of Management Reviews*, 3, 21–40.

Harris, R. G. (2011) Models of regional growth: past, present and future, *Journal of Economic Surveys*, 25, 913–51.

Harrison, R. T., Cooper, S. Y. and Mason, C. M. (2004) Entrepreneurial activity and the synamics of technology-based cluster development: the case of Ottawa, *Urban Studies*, 41(5/6), 1045–70.

Hassink, R. (2007) The learning region: a constructive critique, in Rutten, R. and Boekema, F. (eds), *The Learning Region: Foundations, State of the Art, Future*, Cheltenham: Edward Elgar, 252–71.

Hassink, R. and Lagendijk, A. (2001) The dilemmas of interregional institutional learning, *Environment and Planning C*, 19(1), 65–84.

Hatzichronoglou, T. (1997) Revision of the high-technology sector and product classification, *STI Working Papers*, #2.

Hauser, C., Tappeiner, G. and Walde, J. (2007) The learning region: the impact of social capital and weak ties on innovation, *Regional Studies*, 41, 75–88.

Havlik, P., Stöllinger, R., Pindyuk, O., Hunya, G., Dachs, B., Lennon, C., Poplawski Ribeiro, M., Ghosh, J., Urban, W., Astrov, V. and Christie, E. (2009) EU and BRICs: challenges and opportunities for European competitiveness and cooperation, *Industrial Policy and Economic Reforms Papers*, #13.

Heeks, R. (2010) Do information and communication technologies (ICTs) contribute to development?, *Journal of International Development*, 22, 625–40.

Heidenreich, M. (2004) The dilemmas of regional innovation systems, in Cooke, P., Heidenreich, M. and Braczyk, H.-J. (eds), *Regional Innovation Systems: The Role of Governance in a Globalised World*, 2nd edn, London: Routledge, 363–89.

Helliwell, J., Layard, R. and Sachs, J. (2012) *World Happiness Report*, New York: Earth Institute Columbia University.

Herb, M. (2009) A nation of bureaucrats: political participation and economic diversification in Kuwait and the United Arab Emirates, *International Journal of Middle East Studies*, 41(3), 375–95.

Herd, R. and Dougherty, S. (2007) Growth prospects in China and India compared, *European Journal of Comparative Economics*, 4(1), 65–89.

Hershberg, E., Nabseshima, K. and Yusuf, S. (2007) Opening the Ivory Tower to business: university-industry linkages and the development of knowledge-intensive clusters in Asian cities, *World Development*, 35(6), 931–40.

Hicks, A. and Kenworthy, L. (1998) Cooperation and political economic performance in affluent democratic capitalism, *American Journal of Sociology*, 103(6), 1631–72.

Hitt, M. A., Li, H. and Worthington IV, W. J. (2005) Emerging markets as learning laboratories: learning behaviors of local firms and foreign entrants in different institutional contexts, *Management and Organization Review*, 1(3), 353–80.

Hoekman, J., Frenken, K. and van Oort, F. (2009) The geography of collaborative

knowledge production in Europe, *Annals of Regional Science*, 43, 721–38.
Hollanders, H. (2007) *2006 European Regional Innovation Scoreboard*. Brussels, Belgium: European Commission.
Honohan, P. (2010) *The Irish Banking Crisis: Regulatory and Financial Stability Policy 2003–2008*, Dublin: Central Bank of Ireland.
Hopkins, M., Martin, P., Nightingale, P., Kraft, A. and Mahdi, S. (2007) The myth of the biotech revolution: an assessment of technological, clinical and organisational change, *Research Policy*, 36(4), 566–89.
Hospers, G.-J. (2005) 'Best practices' and the dilemma of regional cluster policy in Europe, *Tijdschrift voor Economische en Sociale Geografie*, 96(4), 452–7.
Hospers, G.-J. (2006) Silicon somewhere? Assessing the usefulness of best practices in regional policy, *Policy Studies*, 27(1), 1–15.
Howcroft, D. (2001) After the goldrush: deconstructing the myths of the dot.com market, *Journal of Information Technology*, 16(4), 195–204.
Howells, J. (2005) Innovation and regional economic development: a matter of perspective?, *Research Policy*, 34(8), 1220–34.
Huang, L., Liu, X. and Xu, L. (2012) Regional innovation and spillover effects of foreign direct investment in China: a threshold approach, *Regional Studies*, 46(5), 583–96.
Hudson, R. (2010) Resilient regions in an uncertain world: wishful thinking or a practical reality?, *Cambridge Journal of Regions, Economy and Society*, 3(1), 11–25.
Huggins, R. (1997) Regional competitive specialization: development agency sector initiatives in Wales, *Area*, 29(3), 241–52.
Huggins, R. (2000) *The Business of Networks: Inter-firm Interaction, Institutional Policy and the TEC Experiment*, Aldershot: Ashgate.
Huggins, R. (2003) Creating a UK competitiveness index: regional and local benchmarking, *Regional Studies*, 37(1), 89–96.
Huggins, R. (2008) The evolution of knowledge clusters: progress and policy, *Economic Development Quarterly*, 22, 277–89.
Huggins, R. (2010a) Forms of network resource: knowledge access and the role of inter-firm networks, *International Journal of Management Reviews*, 12(3), 335–52.
Huggins, R. (2010b) Regional competitive intelligence: benchmarking and policy-making, *Regional Studies*, 44(5), 639–58.
Huggins, R. and Izushi, H. (2002) *World Knowledge Competitiveness Index 2002: Benchmarking the Globe's High-Performing Regions*, Cardiff: Robert Huggins Associates.
Huggins, R. and Izushi, H. (2007) *Competing for Knowledge: Creating, Connecting, and Growing*, London: Routledge.
Huggins, R. and Izushi, H. (2009) Regional benchmarking in a global context: knowledge, competitiveness, and economic development, *Economic Development Quarterly*, 23(4), 275–93.
Huggins R. and Johnston, A. (2009) Knowledge networks in an uncompetitive region: SME growth and innovation, *Growth and Change*, 40, 227–59.
Huggins, R. and Williams, N. (2009) Enterprise and public policy: a review of Labour government intervention in the United Kingdom, *Environment and Planning C: Government and Policy*, 27, 19–41.
Huggins, R. and Johnston, A. (2010) Knowledge flow across inter-firm networks: the influence of network resources, spatial proximity and firm size, *Entrepreneurship and Regional Development*, 22(5), 457–84.
Huggins, R. and Thompson, P. (2010) *UK Competitiveness Index 2010*, Cardiff: Centre for International Competitiveness, UWIC.

Huggins, R. and Clifton, N. (2011) Competitiveness, creativity, and place-based development, *Environment and Planning A*, 43(6), 1341.

Huggins, R. and Izushi, H. (eds) (2011) *Competition, Competitive Advantage, and Clusters: The Ideas of Michael Porter*, Oxford: Oxford University Press.

Huggins, R. and Williams, N. (2011) Entrepreneurship and regional competitiveness: the role and progression of policy, *Entrepreneurship and Regional Development,* 23(9/10), 907–32.

Huggins, R. and Strakova, L. (2012) Knowledge-based economic development in emerging regions: policy issues and implications in the Balkan Peninsula, *Regional Studies*, 46(7), 961–75.

Huggins, R. and Thompson, P. (2012) Well-being and competitiveness: are the two linked at a place-based level?, *Cambridge Journal of Regions, Economy and Society*, 5(1), 45–60.

Huggins, R. and Izushi, H. (2013) Knowledge-based development in leading regions across the globe: an exploratory analysis of the co-evolution of resources, capabilities and outputs, *Urban Studies*, 50(5), 1030–48.

Huggins, R. and Thompson, P. (2014) A network-based view of regional growth, *Journal of Economic Geography*, 14(3), 511–45.

Huggins, R., Izushi, H., Day, J., Emlyn-Jones, N., Liu, J. and Sootarsing, K. (2003) *World Knowledge Competitiveness Index 2003–2004: Benchmarking the Globe's Leading Knowledge Economy Regions*, Cardiff: Robert Huggins Associates.

Huggins, R., Bussell, S., Liu, J., Sootarsing, K., Day, J., Izushi, H. *et al.* (2004) *World Knowledge Competitiveness Index 2004: Benchmarking the Globe's Leading Knowledge Economy Regions*, Cardiff: Robert Huggins Associates.

Huggins, R., Izushi, H. and Davies, W. (2005) *World Knowledge Competitiveness Index 2005*, Pontypridd: Robert Huggins Associates.

Huggins, R., Izushi, H., Davies, W. and Luo, S. (2008a) *World Knowledge Competitiveness Index 2008*, Cardiff: Centre for International Competitiveness.

Huggins, R., Johnston, A. and Steffenson, R. (2008b) Universities, knowledge networks and regional policy, *Cambridge Journal of Regions, Economy and Society*, 1(2), 321–40.

Huggins, R., Johnston, A. and Thompson, P. (2012) Network capital, social capital and knowledge flow: how the nature of inter-organizational networks impacts on innovation, *Industry and Innovation*, 19(3), 203–32.

Huggins, R., Luo, S. and Thompson, P. (2013) The competitiveness of China's leading regions: benchmarking their knowledge-based economies, *Tijdschrift voor Economische en Sociale Geografie*, forthcoming.

Hussain, M. and Faes-Cannito, F. (2008) *Surplus in EU Trade in Services with BRIC Countries in 2006*, Luxembourg: European Commission.

Iammarino, S. and McCann, P. (2006) The structure and evolution of industrial clusters: transactions, technology and knowledge spillovers, *Research Policy*, 35(7), 1018–36.

Ibert, O. (2007) Towards a geography of knowledge creation: the ambivalences between 'knowledge as an object' and 'knowing in practice', *Regional Studies*, 41, 103–14.

Ibourk, A. and Amaghouss, J. (2012) Measuring education inequalities: concentration and dispersion-based approach, *World Journal of Education*, 2(6), 51–65.

IMD (2013) *The World Competitiveness Yearbook*, Lausanne, Switzerland: IMD World Competitiveness Center.

Industry, Tourism and Investment (2011) *Northwest Territories: Economic Review and Outlook*, Yellowknife: Government of Northwest Territories.

ITIF (2012) *The 2012 State New Economy Index: Benchmarking Economic Transformation in the States*, Washington, DC: Information Technology and Innovation Foundation.

International Trade Administration (2012) *Providence-New Bedford-Fall River, RI-MA*, Washington, DC: US Department of Commerce.

Istrate, E. and Nadeau, C. A. (2012) *Global Metro Monitor*, Washington, DC: Brookings Institute.

Iurcovich, L., Komninos, N., Reid, A., Heydebreck, P. and Pierrakis, Y. (2006) *Mutual Learning Platform: Regional Benchmarking Report: Blueprint for Regional Innovation Benchmarking*, Brussels: European Commission.

Jackson, L. F. (1984) Hierarchic demand and the Engle curve for variety, *Review of Economics and Statistics*, 66 (1), 8–15.

Jaffe, A. (1986) Technological opportunity and spillovers of R&D: evidence from firms' patents, profits and market value, *American Economic Review*, 76(5), 984–1001.

Jaffe, A. (1989a) Characterizing the 'technological position' of firms, with application to quantifying technological opportunity and research spillovers, *Research Policy*, 18(2), 87–97.

Jaffe, A. B. (1989b) Real effect of academic research, *American Economic Review*, 79, 957–70.

Jaffe, A. B. and Trajtenberg, M. (2002) *Patents, Citations and Innovations: A Window on the Knowledge Economy*, Cambridge, MA: MIT Press.

Jensen, M. C. (1993) The modern industrial revolution, exit, and the failure of internal control systems, *Journal of Finance*, 68(3), 831–80.

Johannesson, C., Köhlmark, J. and Wiik, H. (2006) *How To Get Further, Faster? Report on the 13 Regions Assets, Experiences and Priorities*, Stockholm: Innovation Society.

Jones-Evans, D. and Thompson, P. (2009) The spatial dispersion of informal investment at a regional level: evidence from the UK, *European Planning Studies*, 17(5), 659–75.

Kaiser, R. and Prange, H. (2004) Managing diversity in a system of multi-level governance: the open method of co-ordination in innovation policy, *Journal of European Public Policy*, 11, 249–66.

Kaldor, N. (1957) A model of economic growth, *The Economic Journal*, 67(268), 591–624.

Kauffman, R. J. and Kumar, A. (2007) Scale and scope externalities in growth of IT industries in India: an agglomeration perspective, Paper presented at the 40th Annual Hawaii International Conference on System Sciences, 3rd-6th January.

Ke, S. (2010) Determinants of economic growth and spread-backwash effects in western and eastern China, *Asian Economics Journal*, 24(2), 179–202.

Keating, M. and Loughlin, J. (eds) (1997) *The Political Economy of Regionalism*, London: Frank Cass & Co Ltd.

Keeble, D., Bryson, J. and Wood, P. (1991) Small firms, business services growth and regional development in the United Kingdom: some empirical findings, *Regional Studies*, 25(5), 439–57.

Kenworthy, L. (2006) Institutional coherence and macroeconomic performance, *Socio-Economic Review*, 4(1), 69–91.

Ketels, C. and Sölvell, Ö. (2005) *State of the Region Report: Competitiveness and Cooperation in the Baltic Sea Region*, Helsinki and Stockholm: Tekes and Vinnova.

Kimenyi, M. S. (2011) Contribution of higher education to economic development: a survey of international evidence, *Journal of African Economies*, 20(Supp. 3), iii3–iii49.

Kingdom of Saudi Arabia Ministry of Economy and Planning (2004) *The Eighth Development Plan 1425-1430H (2005–2009)*, Riyadh: Kingdom of Saudi Arabia Ministry of Economy and Planning.

Kırdar, M. G. and Saracoğlu, D. Ş. (2008) Migration and regional convergence: an empirical investigation for Turkey, *Papers in Regional Science*, 87(4), 545–66.

Kitson, M., Martin, R. and Tyler, P. (2004) Regional competitiveness: An elusive yet key concept?, *Regional Studies*, 38, 991–9.

Klagge, B. and Martin, R. (2005) Decentralized versus centralized financial systems: is there a case for local capital markets?, *Journal of Economic Geography*, 5, 387–421.

Kline, S. J. and Rosenberg, N. (1986) An overview of innovation, in Landau, R. and Rosenberg, N. (eds), *The Positive Sum Strategy: Harnessing Technology for Economic Growth*, Washington, DC: National Academy Press, 275–305.

Kolenikov, S. and Shorrocks, A. (2005) A decomposition analysis of regional poverty in Russia, *Review of Development Economics*, 9(1), 24–46.

Kondratieff, N. D. (1926) Die langen Wellen der konjunktur, *Archiv für Sozialwissenschaft*, 56, 573–609.

Kondratieff, N. D. (1935) The long waves in economic life, *Review of Economic Statistics*, 17(6), 105–15.

Koo, J. (2005) Agglomeration and spillovers in a simultaneous framework, *Annals of Regional Science*, 39(1), 35–47.

Korotayev, A., Zinkina, J. and Bogevolnov, J. (2011) Kondratieff waves in global invention activity (1900–2008), *Technological Forecasting and Social Change*, 78(7), 1280–4.

Koschatzky, K. and Stahlecker, T. (2010) A new challenge for regional policy-making in Europe? Chances and risks of the merger between cohesion and innovation policy, *European Planning Studies*, 18(1), 7–25.

Kozma, R. B. (2005) National policies that connect ICT-based education reform to economic and social development, *Human Technology*, 1(2), 117–56.

Kremer, M. (1998) Patents buyouts: a mechanism for encouraging innovation, *Quarterly Journal of Economics*, 113(4), 1137–67.

Krieger, Z. (2008) Academic building boom transforms the Persian Gulf: Western universities find opportunities as three Arab emirates strive to outdo one another, *Education Digest*, 74(1), 4–10.

Kroll, H. and Liefner, I. (2008) Spin-off enterprises as a means of technology commercialisation in a transforming economy: evidence from three universities in China, *Technovation*, 28(5), 298–313.

Krueger, A. O. (1974) The political economy of the rent-seeking society, *American Economic Review*, 64(3), 291–303.

Krugman, P. (1991) Increasing returns and economic geography, *Journal of Political Economy*, 99(3), 483–99.

Krugman, P. (1994a) Competitiveness: a dangerous obsession, *Foreign Affairs*, 73(2), 28–44.

Krugman, P. (1994b) The myth of Asia's miracle, *Foreign Affairs*, 73(6), 62–78.

Krugman, P. (1999) The role of geography in development, *International Regional Science Review*, 22(2), 142–61.

Krugman, P. (2003) *Growth on the Periphery: Second Wind for Industrial Regions?*, Glasgow: Fraser Allander Institute.

Krugman, P. (2009) Increasing returns in a comparative advantage world, in Stern, R. M. (ed.), *Comparative Advantage, Growth, and the Gains from Trade and Globalization*, Singapore: World Scientific Publishing, 43–51.

Krugman, P. (2011) The new economic geography, now middle-aged, *Regional Studies*, 45(1), 1–7.

Kuran, T. (2004) Why the Middle East is economically underdeveloped: historical mechanisms of institutional stagnation, *Journal of Economic Perspectives*, 18(3), 71–90.

Kyrö, P. (2003) Revising the concept and forms of benchmarking, *Benchmarking: An International Journal*, 10, 210–25.

Laafia, I. (1999) Regional employment in high technology, *Statistics in Focus, Research and Development Theme*, 9(1), Luxembourg: Eurostat.

Lagendijk, A. (1999) The emergence of knowledge-oriented forms of regional policy in Europe, *Tijdschrift voor Economische en Sociale Geografie*, 90, 110–16.

Lagendijk, A. and Cornford, J. (2000) Regional institutions and knowledge: tracking new forms of regional development policy, *Geoforum*, 31(2), 209–18.

Lagendijk, A. and Lorentzen, A. (2007) Proximity, knowledge and innovation in peripheral regions. On the intersection between geographical and organizational proximity, *European Planning Studies*, 15(4), 457–66.

Lall, S. (2000) Technological change and industrialization in the Asian newly industrializing economies: achievements and challenges, in Kim, L. and Nelson, R. R. (eds), *Technology, Learning, and Innovation: Experiences of Newly Industrializing Economics*, Cambridge: Cambridge University Press, 13–68.

Lall, S. (2001a) Competitiveness indices and developing countries: an economic evaluation of the Global Competitiveness Report, *World Development*, 29(9), 1501–25.

Lall, S. (2001b) Comparing national competitive performance: an economic analysis of World Economic Forum's Competitiveness Index, *Queen Elizabeth House Working Paper*, #61.

Lawson, C. and Lorenz, E. (1999) Collective learning, tacit knowledge and regional innovative capacity, *Regional Studies*, 33, 305–17.

Leamer, E. (1999) Effort, wages, and the international division of labor, *Journal of Political Economy*, 107(6), 1127–62.

Leborgne, D. and Lipietz, A. (1988) New technologies, new modes of regulation: some spatial implications, *Environment and Planning D: Society and Space*, 6, 263–80.

Lee, F. C. and Has, H. (1996) A quantitative assessment of high-knowledge industries versus low-knowledge industries, in Howitt, P. (ed.), *The Implications of Knowledge-Based Growth for Micro-Economic Policies*, Calgary: University of Calgary Press, 39–78.

Lee, S. Y., Florida, R. and Acs, Z. J. (2004) Creativity and entrepreneurship: a regional analysis of new firm formation, *Regional Studies*, 38(8), 879–91.

Lemoine, F. and Ünal-Kesenci, D. (2004) Assembly trade and technology transfer: the case of China, *World Development*, 32(5), 829–50.

Lewin, T. (2008) Global classrooms: U.S. universities rush to set up outposts abroad, *New York Times*, 10 February.

Lewis, J. I. (2007) Technology acquisition and innovation in the developing world: wind turbine development in China and India, *Studies in Comparative International Development*, 42 (3/4), 208–32.

Lewis, W. A. (1962) Education and economic development, *International Social Science Journal*, 14(4), 685–99.

Lewison, G. (1991) The scientific outputs of the EC's less favoured regions, *Scientometrics*, 21(3), 383–402.

Li, T., Fu, M. and Fu, X. (2013) Regional technology development path in an open developing economy: evidence from China, *Applied Economics*, 45(11), 1405–18.

Li, X. (2009) China's regional innovation capacity in transition: an empirical approach, *Research Policy*, 38(2), 338–57.

Liefner, I. and Hennemann, S. (2011) Structural holes and new dimensions of distance: the

spatial configuration of the scientific knowledge network of China's optical technology sector, *Environment and Planning A*, 43(4), 810–29.
Lin, J. Y. and Rosenblatt, D. (2012) Shifting patterns of economic growth and rethinking development, *Journal of Economic Policy Reform*, 15(3), 171–94.
Link, A. N. and Scott, J. T. (2003) The growth of Research Triangle Park, *Small Business Economics*, 20(2), 167–75.
Linstone, H. A. and Devezas, T. (2012) Technological innovation and the long wave theory revisited, *Technological Forecasting and Social Change*, 79(2), 414–16.
Longhi, C. (2005) Local systems and networks in the globalisations process, in Quadrin Curzio, A. and Fortis, M. (eds), *Research and Technological Innovation*, Heidelberg: Physica Verlag, 81–108.
Looney, R. (1994) *Manpower Policies and Development in the Persian Gulf Region*, London: Praeger.
Lorenzen, M. (2007) Social capital and localised learning: proximity and place in technological and institutional dynamics, *Urban Studies*, 44(4), 799–817.
Los, B. and Timmer, M. (2005) The 'appropriate technology' explanation of productivity growth differentials: an empirical approach, *Journal of Development Economics*, 77(2), 517–53.
Louis, W. R. (1984) *The British Empire in the Middle East 1945–1951: Arab Nationalism, The United States, and Postwar Imperialism*, Oxford: Oxford University Press.
Lucas, R. E. (1978) On the size distribution of business firms, *Bell Journal of Economics* 9, 508–23.
Lucas, R. E. (1988) On the mechanics of economic development, *Journal of Monetary Economics*, 22(1), 3–42.
Lucidi, F. and Kleinknecht, A. (2010) Little innovation, many jobs: an econometric analysis of the Italian labour productivity crisis, *Cambridge Journal of Economics*, 34, 525–46.
Lundvall, B.-Å. (ed.) (1992) *National Systems of Innovation*, London: Pinter.
Lundvall, B.-Å. (2010) *National Systems of Innovation: Toward a Theory of Innovation and Interactive Learning*, London: Anthem Press.
Lundvall, B.-Å. and Tomlinson, M. (2002) International benchmarking as a policy learning tool, in Rodrigues, M. J. (ed.), *The New Knowledge Economy in Europe: A Strategy for International Competitiveness and Social Cohesion*, Cheltenham: Edward Elgar.
Luque-Martínez, T. and Munöz-Leiva, F. (2005) City benchmarking: a methodological proposal referring specifically to Granada, *Cities*, 22, 411–23.
Ma, A. C. (2006) Geographical location of foreign direct investment and wage inequality in China, *World Economy*, 29(8), 1031–55.
Maillat, D. (1998a) Innovative milieux and new generations of regional policies, *Entrepreneurship and Regional Development,* 10, 1–16.
Maillat, D. (1998b) Interactions between urban systems and localized productive systems: an approach to endogenous regional development in terms of innovative milieu, *European Planning Studies*, 6, 117–29.
Makkonen, T. (2012) Peripheral university region and knowledge-based development: the case of Joensuu, *International Journal of Knowledge-Based Development*, 3(3), 216–33.
Malecki, E. J. (2004) Jockeying for position: what it means and why it matters to regional development policy when places compete, *Regional Studies*, 38(9), 1101–20.
Malecki, E. J. (2007) Cities and regions competing in the global economy: knowledge and local development policies, *Environment and Planning C: Government and Policy*, 25(3), 638–54.

Malecki, E. J. and Hospers, G.-J. (2007) Knowledge and the competitiveness of places, in Rutten, R. and Boekema, F. (eds), *The Learning Region: Foundations, State of the Art, Future*, Cheltenham: Edward Elgar, 143–59.

Malik, A. and Awadallah, B. (2013) The economics of the Arab Spring, *World Development*, 45, 296–313.

Malmberg, A. and Power, D. (2006) True clusters: a severe case of conceptual headache, in Asheim, B., Cooke, P. and Martin, R. (eds), *Clusters and Regional Development: Critical Reflections and Explorations*, London: Routledge, 50–68.

Marcel, V. (2006) *Oil Titans: National Oil Companies in the Middle East*, London: Royal Institute of International Affairs.

Marginson, S. (2006) Dynamics of national and global competition in higher education, *Higher Education*, 52(1), 1–39.

Markusen, A. (1996) Sticky places in slippery spaces: a typology of industrial districts, *Economic Geography*, 72(3), 293–313.

Martin, R. (1989) The growth and geographical anatomy of venture capitalism in the United Kingdom, *Regional Studies*, 23(5), 389–403.

Martin, R. (2005) *Thinking About Regional Competitiveness: Critical issues*, Report Commissioned by the East Midlands Regional Development Agency, Nottingham: East Midlands Regional Development Agency.

Martin, R. and Sunley, P. (2006) Path dependence and regional economic evolution, *Journal of Economic Geography*, 6(4), 395–437.

Martin, R. and Sunley, P. (2011a) Conceptualizing cluster evolution: beyond the life cycle model?, *Regional Studies*, 45(10), 1299–318.

Martin, R. and Sunley, P. (2011b) Regional competitiveness: clusters or dynamic comparative advantage?, in Huggins, R. and Izushi, H. (eds), *Competition, Competitive Advantage, and Clusters: The Ideas of Michael Porter*, Oxford: Oxford University Press, 211–38.

Martin, R., Berndt, C., Klagge, B. and Sunley, P. (2005) Spatial proximity effects and regional equity gaps in the venture capital market: evidence from Germany and the United Kingdom, *Environment and Planning A,* 37(7), 1207–31.

Martin-Brelot, H., Grossetti, M., Eckert, D., Gritsai, O. and Kovács, Z. (2010) The spatial mobility of the 'creative class': a European perspective, *International Journal of Urban and Regional Research*, 34(4), 854–70.

Maskell, P. and Malmberg, A. (1999) The competitiveness of firms and regions: 'Ubiquitification' and the importance of localized learning, *European Urban and Regional Studies*, 6(1), 9–25.

Maskell, P. and Malmberg, A. (2007) Myopia, knowledge development and cluster evolution, *Journal of Economic Geography*, 7(5), 603–18.

Maskell, P., Bathelt, H. and Malmberg, A. (2006) Building global knowledge pipelines: the role of temporary clusters, *European Planning Studies*, 14(8), 997–1013.

Maslow, A. H. (1970) *Motivation and Personality*, New York: Harper and Row.

Mason, C. M. and Harrison, R. T. (2003) Closing the regional equity gap? A critique of the Department of Trade and Industry's Regional Venture Capital Funds initiative, *Regional Studies*, 37(8), 855–68.

Massey, D., Quintas, P. and Wield, D. (1992) *High-Tech Fantasies: Science Parks in Society, Science and Space,* London: Routledge.

Mathews, J. A. (2001) National systems of economic learning: the case of technology diffusion management in East Asia, *International Journal of Technology Management*, 22(5/6), 455–79.

Maurer, I. and Ebers, M. (2006) Dynamics of social capital and their performance implications: lessons from biotechnology start-ups, *Administrative Science Quarterly*, 51(2), 262–92.

Mellander, C., Florida, R. and Stolarick, K. (2011) Here to stay: the effects of community satisfaction on the decision to stay, *Spatial Economic Analysis*, 6(1), 5–24.

Meyer-Stamer, J. (1998) Path dependence in regional development: persistence and change in three industrial clusters in Santa Catarina, Brazil, *World Development*, 26(8), 1495–511.

Miller, T., Holmes, K. R., Feulner, E. J., Kim, A. B., Riley, B. and Roberts, J. M. (2013) *2013 Index of Economic Freedom*, Washington, DC: Heritage Foundation.

Mok, K. H. (2009) The growing importance of the privateness in education: challenges for higher education governance in China, *Compare*, 39(1), 35–49.

Moodysson, J. (2008) Principles and practices of knowledge creation: on the organization of "buzz" and "pipelines" in life science communities, *Economic Geography*, 84, 449–69.

Morgan, K. (1997) The learning region: institutions, innovation and regional renewal, *Regional Studies*, 31, 491–503.

Mowery, D. C. (1998) The changing structure of the US national innovation system: implications for international conflict and cooperation in R&D policy, *Research Policy*, 27(6), 639–54.

Muller, E. and Zenker, A. (2001) Business services as actors of knowledge transformation: the role of KIBS in regional and national innovation systems, *Research Policy*, 30(9), 1501–16.

Munin, N. (2010) A free trade area in services between Israel and the EU: time to move up a gear? *Mediterranean Politics*, 15(1), 81–9.

Murphy, C. (2005) *Competitive Intelligence: Gathering, Analysing and Putting It To Work*, Aldershot: Gower.

Myrdal, G. (1957) *Economic Theory and Underdeveloped Regions*, New York: Harper and Row.

Nabli, M. K. and Véganzonès-Varoundakis, M.-A. (2007) Reform complementarities and economic growth in the Middle East and North Africa, *Journal of International Development*, 19(1), 17–54.

Narayan, P. K. and Smyth, R. (2006) Higher education, real income and real investment in China: evidence from Granger causality tests, *Education Economics*, 14(1), 107–25.

Narula, R. and Jormanainen, I. (2008) When a good science base is not enough to create competitive industries: lock-in and inertia in Russian systems of innovation, *SLPTMD Working Paper Series*, #022.

Navaretti, G. B., Castellani, D. and Disdier, A.-C. (2010) How does investing in cheap labour countries affect performance at home? Firm-level evidence from France and Italy, *Oxford Economic Papers*, 62, 234–60.

Nelson, R. R. (1959) The simple economics of basic scientific research, *Journal of Political Economy*, 49(3), 297–306.

Nölke, A. and Vliegenthart, A. (2009) Enlarging the varieties of capitalism: the emergence of dependent market economies in East Central Europe, *World Politics*, 61(4), 670–702.

Nonaka, I. (1991) The knowledge-creating company, *Harvard Business Review* November-December, 162–71.

Nonaka, I. (1994) A dynamic theory of organizational knowledge creation, *Organization Science* 5(1), 14–37.

North, D. (1990) *Institutions, Institutional Change and Economic Performance*, Cambridge: Cambridge University Press.

North, D. (2005) *Understanding the Process of Economic Change*, Princeton, NJ: Princeton University Press.

North, D. and Smallbone, D. (2000) Innovative activity in SMEs and rural economic development: some evidence from England, *European Planning Studies*, 8, 87–106.

Öcal, N. and Yildirim, J. (2010) Regional effects of terrorism on economic growth in Turkey: a geographically weighted regression approach, *Journal of Peace Research*, 47(4), 477–89.

OECD (1994) *Jobs Study: Evidence and Explanations,* Paris: Organisation for Economic Co-operation and Development.

OECD (1999) *OECD Science, Technology and Industry Scoreboard 1999: Benchmarking Knowledge-Based Economies*, Paris: Organisation for Economic Co-operation and Development.

OECD (2009) *OECD Economics Surveys: Iceland 2009*, Paris: Organisation for Economic Co-operation and Development.

OECD (2010) *PISA 2009 Results: What Students Know and Can Do – Student Performance in Reading, Mathematics and Science* (Volume I). Available at: http://dx.doi.org/10.1787/9789264091450-en

Ogrean, C. and Herciu, M. (2010) Changing the patterns of the global economy: the emergence and evolution of the BRIC countries, *Studies in Business and Economics*, 5(2), 100–10.

Ólafsson, T. T. and Pétursson, T. G. (2010) Weathering the financial storm: the importance of fundamentals and flexibility, *Central Bank of Iceland Working Paper*, #51.

Olson, M. (1982) *The Rise and Decline of Nations: Economic Growth, Stagflation, and Social Rigidities*, New Haven, CT: Yale University Press.

O'Neal, J. (2001) Building better global economic BRICs, *Goldman Sachs Global Economics Paper*, #66.

Onsman, A. (2011) It is better to light a candle than to ban the darkness: government led academic development in Saudi Arabian universities, *Higher Education*, 62(4), 519–32.

Oughton, C., Landabaso, M. and Morgan, K. (2002) The regional innovation paradox: innovation policy and industrial policy, *Journal of Technology Transfer*, 27(1), 97–110.

Owen, R. (2004) *State, Power and Politics in the Making of the Modern Middle East: Third Edition*, London: Routledge.

Parkinson, M. and Karecha, J. (2006) *Cardiff: A Competitive European City, Final Report*, Liverpool: European Institute for Urban Affairs.

Parkinson, M., Hutchins, M., Simmie, J., Clark, G. and Verdonk, H. (2004) *Competitive European Cities: Where Do the Core Cities Stand?*, Report to the Office of the Deputy Prime Minister, London: ODPM.

Pavitt, K. (1982) R&D, patenting and innovative activities: a statistical exploration, *Research Policy*, 11(1), 33–51.

Perkmann, M. (2006) Extraregional linkages and the territorial embeddedness of multinational branch plants: evidence from the South Tyrol region in northeast Italy, *Economic Geography*, 82(4), 421–41.

Peterson, G. (2000) Political ecology and ecological resilience: an integration of human and ecological dynamics, *Ecological Economics*, 35(3), 323–36.

Petrakos, G., Kallioras, D. and Anagnostou, A. (2011) Regional convergence and growth in Europe: understanding patterns and determinants, *European Urban and Regional Studies*, 18(4), 375–91.

Petty, D. (2005) *2005–2006 Great North Opportunity Forecast,* Minneapolis-St. Paul, MN: The Great North Alliance.

Phelps, N. A. and Ozawa, T. (2003) Contrasts in agglomeration: proto-industrial, industrial and post-industrial forms compared, *Progress in Human Geography*, 27(5), 583–604.

Pieterse, J. N. (2011) Global rebalancing: crisis and the East-South turn, *Development and Change*, 42(1), 22–48.

Pike, A., Rodríguez-Pose, A. and Tomaney, J. (2007) What kind of local and regional development and for whom?, *Regional Studies*, 41(9), 1253–69.

Piore, M. J. and Sabel, C. (1984) *The Second Industrial Divide*, New York: Basic Books.

Porter, M. E. (1980) *Competitive Strategy: Techniques for Analyzing Industries and Competitors*, New York: Free Press.

Porter, M. E. (1990) *The Competitive Advantage of Nations*, New York: The Free Press.

Porter, M. E. (1998) *On Competition*, Boston, MA: Harvard Business School Publishing.

Porter, M. E. (2000) Locations, clusters, company strategy, in Clarke, G. L., Feldman, M. P. and Gertler, M. S. (eds), *The Oxford Handbook of Economic Geography*, Oxford: Oxford University Press.

Porter, M. E. and Stern, S. (1999) *The New Challenge to America's Prosperity: Findings from the Innovation Index*, Washington, DC: Council on Competitiveness.

Pouder, R. and St John, C. H. (1996) Hot spots and blind spots: geographical clusters of firms and innovation, *Academy of Management Review*, 21(4), 1192–225.

Powell, W. W. and Snellman, K. (2004) The knowledge economy, *Annual Review of Sociology*, 30, 199–220.

Power, A., Plöger, J. and Winkler, A. (2010) *Phoenix Cities: The Fall and Rise of Great Industrial Cities*, Bristol: Policy Press.

Prahalad, C. K. and Hamel, G. (1990) The core competence of the corporation, *Harvard Business Review*, 68(3), 79–91.

Pred, A. R. and Hagerstrand, T. (1967) *Innovation Diffusion as a Spatial Process*, Chicago: University of Chicago Press.

Raab, R. A. and Kotamraju, P. (2006) The efficiency of the high-tech economy: conventional development indexes versus a performance index, *Journal of Regional Science*, 46, 545–62.

Radaelli, C. (2000) Policy transfer in the European Union: institutional isomorphism as a source of legitimacy, *Governance*, 13, 25–43.

Ranjan, V. and Agrawal, G. (2011) FDI inflow determinants in BRIC countries: a panel data analysis, *International Business Research*, 4(4), 255–63.

Raunio, M. (2007) Creative regions and globalizing social capital: connecting foreign ICT experts to Finnish innovation environments, in Cooke, P. and Schwartz, D. (eds), *Creative Regions: Technology, Culture and Knowledge Entrepreneurship*, Abingdon: Routledge, 40–61.

Ravallion, M. (2001) Growth, inequality and poverty: looking beyond averages, *World Development*, 29(11), 1803–15.

Reed, A. M. (2008) *Human Development and Social Power: Perspective from South Asia*, New York: Routledge.

Regling, K. and Watson, M. (2010) *A Preliminary Report on the Sources of Ireland's Banking Crisis*, Dublin: Government Publications.

Reiner, C. (2010) Brain competition policy as a new paradigm of regional policy: a European perspective, *Papers in Regional Science*, 89(2), 449–61.

Revilla Diez, J. (2002) Metropolitan innovation systems: a comparison between Barcelona, Stockholm, and Vienna, *International Regional Science Review*, 25, 63–85.

Roberts, M. and Setterfield, M. (2010) Endogenous regional growth: a critical survey, in Setterfield, M. (ed.), *Handbook of Alternative Theories of Economic Growth*, Cheltenham: Edward Elgar, 431–50.

Roberts, P. and Benneworth, P. (2001) Pathways to the future? An initial assessment of RDA strategies and their contribution to integrated regional development, *Local Economy*, 16, 142–59.

Rodríguez-Pose, A. (1999) Innovation prone and innovation averse societies: economic performance in Europe, *Growth and Change*, 30, 75–105.

Rodríguez-Pose, A. (2013) Do institutions matter for regional development? *Regional Studies*, 47(7), 1034–47.

Rodríguez-Pose, A. and Storper, M. (2006) Better rules or stronger communities? On the social foundations of institutional change and its economic effects, *Economic Geography*, 82(1), 1–25.

Rodríguez-Pose, A. and Crescenzi, R. (2008) Research and development, spillovers, innovation systems, and the genesis of regional growth in Europe, *Regional Studies*, 42(1), 51–67.

Rodríguez-Pose, A. and Tselios, V. (2010) Inequalities in income and education and regional economic growth in western Europe, *Annals of Regional Science*, 44(2), 349–75.

Rodrik, D. and Subramanian, A. (2004) Why India can grow at 7 per cent a year or more: projections and reflections, *Economic and Political Weekly*, 39(16), 1591–6.

Rodrik, D., Subramanian, A. and Trebbi, F. (2004) Institutions rule: the primacy of institutions over geography and integration in economic development, *Journal of Economic Growth*, 9(2), 131–65.

Rohr-Zänker, R. (2001) How to attract managers and professionals to peripheral regions? Recruitment strategies in the Weser-Ems region, Germany, *European Planning Studies*, 9(1), 47–68.

Romer, P. M. (1986) Increasing returns and long-run growth, *Journal of Political Economy*, 94(5), 1002–37.

Romer, P. M. (1990) Endogenous technological change, *Journal of Political Economy*, 98(5), S71–S102.

Romer, P. M. (1993) Idea gaps and object gaps in economic development, *Journal of Monetary Economics*, 32(3), 543–73.

Romer, P. M. (2007) Economic growth, in Henderson, D. (ed.), *The Concise Encyclopedia of Economics*, Indianapolis, IN: Liberty Fund, 128–31.

Room, G. (2005) Policy benchmarking in the European Union, *Policy Studies*, 26, 117–32.

Rose, R. (1993) *Lesson-Drawing in Public Policy*, Chatham, NJ: Chatham House.

Rosenberg, D. (2010) The Israeli economy: after the financial crisis, new challenges, *Middle East Review of International Affairs*, 14(1), Article 6.

Ross, M. L. (2008) Mineral wealth, conflict, and equitable development, in Bebbington, A. J., Dani, A. A., de Haan, A. and Walton, M. (eds), *Pathways to Equity: Addressing Inequality Traps*, Washington, DC: World Bank.

Rota, F. S. and Vanolo, A. (2006) A critical approach to benchmarking in urban studies, Paper presented at the 'Urban Conditions and Life Chances' conference, University of Amsterdam, Amsterdam, the Netherlands, July 2006.

Rothwell, R. (1994) Towards the fifth-generation innovation process, *International Marketing Review*, 11(1), 7–31.

Rutten, R. and Boekema, F. (eds) (2007) *The Learning Region: Foundations, State of the Art, Future*, Cheltenham: Edward Elgar.

Sabel, C. (1996) Learning-by-monitoring: The dilemmas of regional economic policy in Europe, in Organisation for Economic Co-operation and Development (ed.), *Networks of Enterprises and Local Development: Competing and Co-operating in Local Productive Systems*, Paris, France: OECD.

Sacchetti, S. and Tomlinson, P. R. (2009) Economic governance and the evolution of industrial districts under globalization: the case of two mature European industrial districts, *European Planning Studies*, 17(12), 1837–59.

Sachs, J. D. and Warner, A. M. (2001) The curse of natural resources, *European Economic Review*, 45(4–6), 827–38.

Salter, A. J. and Martin, B. R. (2001) The economic benefits of publicly funded basic research: a critical review, *Research Policy*, 30(3), 509–32.

Samake, I. and Yang, Y. (2011) Low-income countries' BRIC linkage: are there growth spillovers? *IMF Working Paper*, #11/267.

Sasser, A. C. (2010) Voting with their feet: relative economic conditions and state migration patterns, *Regional Science and Urban Economics*, 40(2/3), 122–35.

Saxenian, A. (1994) *Regional Advantage: Culture and Competition in Silicon Valley and Route 128*, Cambridge, MA: Harvard University Press.

Saxenian, A. (2002) The Silicon Valley connection: transnational networks and regional development in Taiwan, China and India, *Science Technology and Society*, 7(1), 117–49.

Schenk, C. R. (2001) *Hong Kong as an International Financial Centre: Emergence and Development 1945–65*, London: Routledge.

Scherngell, T. and Hu, Y. (2011) Collaborative knowledge production in China: regional evidence from a gravity model approach, *Research Studies*, 45(6), 755–72.

Schoales, J. (2006) Alpha clusters: creative innovation in local economies, *Economic Development Quarterly*, 20(2), 162–77.

Schumpeter, J. A. (1934) *The Theory of Economic Development*, Cambridge, MA: Harvard University Press.

Schumpeter, J. A. (1939) *Business Cycles*, New York: McGraw-Hill.

Schwarz, G. (1978) Estimating the dimension of a model, *Annals of Statistics*, 6(2), 461–4.

Schwarz, R. (2008) The political economy of state-formation in the Arab Middle East: rentier states, economic reform, and democratization, *Review of International Political Economy*, 15(4), 599–621.

Scott, A. (1995) The geographic foundations of industrial performance, *Competition and Change*, 1(1), 51–66.

Scott, A. and Storper, M. (2003) Regions, globalization, development, *Regional Studies* 37(6/7), 549–78.

Selwyn, N. and Brown, P. (2000) Education, nation states and the globalization of information networks, *Journal of Education Policy*, 15(6), 661–82.

Shields, M. A., Wheatly Price, S. and Wooden, M. (2009) Life satisfaction and the economic and social characteristics of neighbourhoods, *Journal of Population Economics*, 22(2), 421–43.

Shucksmith, M., Cameron, S., Merridew, T. and Pilcher, F. (2009) Urban-rural differences in quality of life across the European Union, *Regional Studies*, 43(10), 1275–89.

Silva, J., Levin, V. and Morgandi, M. (2013) *Inclusion and Resilience: The Way Forward for Social Safety Nets in the Middle East and North Africa*, Washington, DC: World Bank.

Simmie, J. and Martin, R. (2010) The economic resilience of regions: towards an evolutionary approach, *Cambridge Journal of Regions, Economy and Society*, 3(1), 27–43.

Simmie, J., Carpenter, J., Chadwick, A., Martin, R. and Wood, P. (2006) *State of the*

English Cities: The Competitive Economic Performance of English Cities, London: Department for Communities and Local Government.
Simmons, M. R. (2005) *Twilight in the Desert: The Coming Saudi Oil Shock and the World Economy*, Hoboken, NJ: Wiley.
Solow, R. (1956) A contribution to the theory of economic growth, *Quarterly Journal of Economics,* 70, 65–94.
Solow, R. M. (1957) Technical change and the aggregate production function, *Review of Economics and Statistics*, 39(3), 312–20.
Sölvell, Ö. (2008) *Clusters: Balancing Evolutionary and Constructive Forces*, Stockholm: Ivory Tower Books.
Sovereign Wealth Fund Institute (2012) *SWF Asset Allocation Report 2012*, Las Vegas, NV: SWFI.
Sterlacchini, A. (2008) R&D, higher education and regional growth: uneven linkages among European regions, *Research Policy*, 37(6/7), 1096–107.
Stevenson, B. and Wolfers, J. (2008) Economic growth and subjective well-being: reassessing the Easterlin Paradox, *Brookings Papers on Economic Activity*, Spring, 1–102.
Stimson, R. J., Robson, A. and Shyy, T.-K. (2009) Modeling regional endogenous growth: an application to the non-metropolitan regions of Australia, *Annals of Regional Science*, 43(2), 379–98.
Stimson, R., Stough, R. R. and Nijkamp, P. (eds) (2011) *Endogenous Regional Development: Perspectives, Measurement and Empirical Investigation*, Cheltenham: Edward Elgar.
Stoerring, D. and Dalum, B. (2007) Cluster emergence: a comparative study of two cases in North Jutland, Denmark, in Cooke, P. and Schwartz, D. (eds), *Creative Regions: Technology, Culture and Knowledge Entrepreneurship*, Abingdon: Routledge, 127–47.
Stone, H. B. J. and Ranchhod, A. (2006) Competitive advantage of a nation in the global arena: a quantitative advancement to Porter's diamond applied to the UK, USA and BRIC nations, *Strategic Change*, 15(6), 283–94.
Storper, M. (1992) The limits to globalization: technology districts and international trade, *Economic Geography*, 68(1), 60–93.
Storper, M. (1995) Regional technology coalitions: an essential dimension of national technology policy, *Research Policy*, 24, 895–911.
Storper, M. (1997) *The Regional World: Territorial Development in a Global Economy*, New York: Guilford Press.
Storper, M. (2005) Society, community, and economic development, *Studies in Comparative International Development*, 39(4), 30–57.
Storper, M. (2008) Community and economics, in Amin, A. and Roberts, J. (eds), *Community, Economic Creativity, and Organization*, New York: Oxford University Press, 37–68.
Storper, M. (2009) Roepke lecture in economic geography: regional context and global trade, *Economic Geography*, 85, 1–21.
Storper, M. and Venables, A. J. (2004) Buzz: face-to-face contact and the urban economy, *Journal of Economic Geography*, 4, 351–70.
Storper, M. and Scott, A. J. (2009) Rethinking human capital, creativity and urban growth, *Journal of Economic Geography*, 9(2), 147–67.
Storper, M., Chen, Y.-C. and De Paolis, F. (2002) Trade and the location of industries in the OECD and European Union, *Journal of Economic Geography,* 2, 73–107.
Storper, M., Lavinas, L. and Mercado-Célis, A. (2007) Society, community, and develop-

ment: a tale of two regions, in Polenske, K. (ed.), *The Economic Geography of Innovation*, Cambridge: Cambridge University Press, 310–39.

Swan, T. W. (1956) Economic growth and capital accumulation, *Economic Record*, 32, 334–61.

Tabellini, G. (2010) Culture and institutions: economic development in the regions of Europe, *Journal of the European Economic Association*, 8(4), 677–716.

Takalo, T., Tanayama, T. and Toivanen, O. (2013) Market failures and the additionality effects of public support to private R&D: theory and empirical implications, *International Journal of Industrial Organization*, 31(5), 634–42..

Tao, Z. and Wong, Y. C. R. (2002) Hong Kong: from an industrialised city to a centre of manufacturing-related services, *Urban Studies*, 39(12), 2345–58.

Tappeiner, G., Hauser, C. and Walde, J. (2008) Regional knowledge spillovers: fact or artifact?, *Research Policy*, 37, 861–74.

Teece, D. J. (1998) Capturing value from knowledge assets: the new economy, markets for know-how and intangible assets, *California Management Review*, 40(3), 55–79.

Temple, J. (1999) The new growth evidence, *Journal of Economic Literature*, 37(1), 112–56.

Ter Wal, A. L. J. and Boschma, R. (2011) Co-evolution of firms, industries and networks in space, *Regional Studies,* 45(7), 919–33.

Tewdwr-Jones, M. and Phelps, N. A. (2000) Levelling the uneven playing field: inward investment, interregional rivalry and the planning system, *Regional Studies*, 34(5), 429–40.

Thompson, N. and Ward, N. (2005) *Rural Areas and Regional Competitiveness*, Report to Local Government Rural Network, Newcastle: Centre for Rural Economy, University of Newcastle upon Tyne.

Thompson, P., Williams, R. and Thomas, B. C. (2013) Are UK SMEs with active websites more likely to achieve both innovation and growth?, *Journal of Small Business and Enterprise Development*, 20(4), 934–65.

Thorhallsson, B. and Kirby, P. (2012) Financial crises in Iceland and Ireland: does European Union and Euro membership matter?, *Journal of Common Market Studies*, 50(5), 801–18.

Thornton, P. H. (1999) The sociology of entrepreneurship, *Annual Review of Sociology*, 25, 19–46.

Thornton, P. H., Ribeiro-Soriano, D. and Urbano, D. (2011) Socio-cultural factors and entrepreneurial activity: an overview, *International Small Business Journal*, 29(2), 105–18.

Tijuana Economic Development Corporation (2011) *Tijuana: the Capital for Medical Device Manufacturing*, Tijuna: Tijuna Economic Development Corporation.

Timoney, K. and Lee, P. (2001) Environmental management in resource-rich Alberta, Canada: first world jurisdiction, theory world analogue?, *Journal of Environmental Management*, 63(4), 387–405.

Tödtling, F. and Trippl, M. (2005) One size fits all? Towards a differentiated regional innovation policy approach, *Research Policy*, 34, 1203–19.

Toledo, H. (2011) The political economy of the emiratization in the UAE, *Journal of Economic Studies*, 40(1), 39–53.

Trippl, M., Tödtling, F. and Lengauer, L. (2009) Knowledge sourcing beyond buzz and pipelines: evidence from the Vienna software sector, *Economic Geography*, 85, 443–62.

Tseng, C.-Y. (2009) Technological innovation in the BRIC economies, *Research Technology Management*, 52(2), 29–35.

Tura, T. and Harmaakorpi, V. (2005) Social capital in building regional innovation capability, *Regional Studies*, 39, 1111–25.

Turok, I. (2004) Cities, regions and competitiveness, *Regional Studies*, 38, 1069–83.
Underwood, J. (2002) *Competitive Intelligence*, Oxford: Capstone.
UNDP (2003) *Arab Human Development Report: Building a Knowledge Society* [United Nations Development Programme], New York: United Nations.
Uzzi, B. (1997) Social structure and competition in interfirm networks: the paradox of embeddedness, *Administrative Science Quarterly*, 42(1), 35–67.
Van Oort, F. G. (2004) *Urban Growth and Innovation: Spatially Bounded Externalities in the Netherlands*, Aldershot: Ashgate.
Van Stel, A., Carree, M. and Thurik, R. (2005) The effect of entrepreneurial activity on national economic growth, *Small Business Economics*, 24(3), 311–21.
Vaz, T. D. and Nijkamp, P. (2009) Knowledge and innovation: the strings between global and local dimensions of sustainable growth, *Entrepreneurship and Regional Development*, 21, 441–55.
Vázquez-Barquero, A. (2007) Endogenous development: analytical and policy issues, in Scott, A. J. and Garofoli, G. (eds), *Development on the Ground: Clusters, Networks and Regions in Emerging Economies*, London: Routledge, 23–43.
Veenhoven, R. (2009) Well-being in nations and well-being of nations, *Social Indicators Research*, 91(1), 5–21.
Virkkala, S. (2007) Innovation and networking in peripheral areas: a case study of emergence and change in rural manufacturing, *European Planning Studies*, 15(4), 511–29.
Vivarelli, M. and Pianta, M. (eds) (2000) *The Employment Impact of Innovation: Evidence and Policy*, London: Routledge.
von Hippel, E. (2005) *Democratizing Innovation*, Cambridge, MA: MIT Press.
Walter, J., Lechner, C. and Kellermanns. F. W. (2007) Knowledge transfer between and within alliance partners: private versus collective benefits of social capital, *Journal of Business Research*, 60, 698–710.
Wang, E. C. (2007) R&D efficiency and economic performance: a cross-country analysis using the stochastic frontier approach, *Journal of Policy Modelling*, 29(2), 345–60.
Wang, E. H.-H. (1999) ICT and economic development in Taiwan: analysis of the evidence, *Telecommunications Policy*, 23, 235–43.
Wang, J.-H. and Lee, C.-K. (2007) Global production networks and local institution building: the development of the information-technology industry in Suzhou, China, *Environment and Planning A*, 39(8), 1873–88.
Wang, M. Y. and Meng, X. (2004) Global-local initiatives in FDI: the experience of Shenzhen, China, *Asia Pacific Viewpoint*, 45(2), 181–96.
Watkins, A. (2003) From knowledge to wealth: transforming Russian science and technology for a modern knowledge economy, *World Bank Policy Research Working Paper*, #2974.
Watt, A. (2006) The rise of China as an economic power: what impact on the EU economy and labour markets?, *Transfer: European Review of Labour and Research*, 12(4), 539–62.
Weber, M. (1930) *The Protestant Ethic and Spirit of Capitalism*, London: George Allen and Unwin.
Weddle, R. L., Rooks, E. and Valdecanas, T. (2006) Research Triangle Park: evolution and renaissance, Paper presented at the Internation Assocation of Science Parks World Conference, Helsinki Finland, 6th–9th June.
Wei, Y. D., Li, W. and Wang, C. (2007) Restructuring industrial districts, scaling up regional development: a study of the Wenzhou model, China, *Economic Geography*, 83(4), 421–44.

Weir, D. (2007) Managing knowledge in the Middle East and North Africa, in Hutchings, K. and Mohannak, K. (eds), *Knowledge Management in Developing Countries: A Cross-Cultural and Institutional Approach*, Cheltenham: Edward Elgar, 156–72.

Wennekers, S. and Thurik, R. (1999) Linking entrepreneurship and economic growth, *Small Business Economics*, 13(1), 27–56.

Wennekers, S., van Stel, A., Thurik, R. and Reynolds, P. (2005) Nascent entrepreneurship and the level of economic development, *Small Business Economics*, 24(3), 293–309.

Werker, C. and Athreye, S. (2004) Marshall's disciples: knowledge and innovation driving regional economic development and growth, *Journal of Evolutionary Economics*, 14(5), 505–23.

Winder, B. P. (2010) Sovereign wealth funds: challenges and opportunities, *Middle East Policy*, 17(2), 31–7.

Wink, R. (2007) Transregional institutional learning in Europe: prerequisites, actors and limitations, Unpublished manuscript, Leipzig: Hochschule für Technik, Wirtschaft und Kultur (HTWK).

Wójcik, D. and Burger, C. (2010) Listing BRICs: stock issuers from Brazil, Russia, India, and China in New York, London, and Luxembourg, *Economic Geography*, 86(3), 275–96.

Wolfe, D. A. (2010) The strategic management of core cities: path dependence and economic adjustment in resilient regions, *Cambridge Journal of Regions, Economy and Society*, 3(1), 139–52.

Wolfe, D. A. and Gertler, M. S. (2006) Local antecedents and trigger events: policy implications of path dependence for cluster formation, in Braunerhjelm, P. and Feldman, M. (eds), *Cluster Genesis: Technology-Based Industrial Development*, Oxford: Oxford University Press, 243–63.

Wong, C. (2002) Developing indicators to inform local economic development in England, *Urban Studies*, 39, 1833–63.

Wong, P.-K., Ho, Y.-P. and Singh, A. (2007) Towards an 'entrepreneurial university' model to support knowledge-based economic development: the case of the National University of Singapore, *World Development*, 35(6), 941–58.

Wonglimpiyarat, J. (2006) The Boston Route 128 model of high-tech industry development, *International Journal of Innovation Management*, 10(1), 47–63.

Wood, P. (2006) The regional significance of the knowledge-intensive services in Europe, *Innovation: The European Journal of Social Sciences*, 19(1), 51–66.

Woolcock, M., Isham, J. and Pritchett, L. (2001) The social foundations of poor economic growth in resource-rich countries, in Auty, R. M. (ed.), *Resource Abundance and Economic Development*, Oxford: Oxford University Press, 76–92.

World Bank (1993) *The East Asian Miracle*, New York: Oxford University Press.

World Bank (2005) *World Development Indicators 2005*, Washington, DC: World Bank.

World Bank (2007) *The Road not Traveled: Education Reform in the Middle East and North Africa*, Washington, DC: World Bank.

World Economic Forum (2012) *Global Competitiveness Report, 2012–2013*, Geneva, Switzerland: World Economic Forum.

Wu, W. (2007) State policies, enterprise dynamism, and innovation system in Shanghai, China, *Growth and Change*, 38(4), 544–66.

Wu, W. (2010) Managing and incentivizing research commercialization in in Chinese universities, *Journal of Technology Transfer*, 35(2), 203–24.

Wydra, S. and Nusser, M. (2011) Diffusion and economic impacts of biotechnology: a case study for Germany, *International Journal of Biotechnology*, 12(1/2), 87–103.

Wymbs, C. (2004) Telecommunications, an instrument of radical change for both the 20th and 21st centuries, *Technological Forecasting and Social Change*, 71(7), 685–703.

Yang, C. (2009) Strategic coupling of regional development in global production networks: redistribution of Taiwanese personal computer investment from the Pearl River Delta to the Tangtze River Delta, China, *Regional Studies*, 43(3), 385–407.

Yang, D. T., Chen, V. W. and Monarch, R. (2010) Rising wages: has China lost its global labor advantage?, *Pacific Economic Review*, 15(4), 482–504.

Yildirim, J., Öcal, N. and Özyildirim, S. (2009) Income inequality and economic convergence in Turkey: a spatial effect analysis, *International Regional Science Review*, 32(2), 221–54.

Yuan, S.-J. (2011) Educational policies and economic growth in BRICs: comparative perspectives, *Journal of US-China Public Administration*, 8(2), 188–97.

Yukon Economic Development (2006) *Pathways to Prosperity: An Economic Growth Perspective 2005 to 2025*, Whitehorse: Yukon Government.

Yurtsever, Ş (2011) Investigating the recovery strategies of European Union from the global financial crisis, *Procedia Social and Behavioral Sciences*, 24, 687–95.

Yusuf, S. and Nabeshima, K. (2005) Creative industries in East Asia, *Cities*, 22(2), 109–22.

Zabala-Iturriagagoitia, J. M., Jimenez-Saez, F., Castro-Martinez, E. and Gutierrez-Gracia, A. (2007) What indicators do (or do not) tell us about regional innovation systems, *Scientometrics*, 70, 85–106.

Zhang, A., Huang, G. Q. and Liu, X. (2012) Impacts of business environment changes on global manufacturing in the Chinese Greater Pearl River Delta: a supply chain perspective, *Applied Economics*, 44(34), 4505–14.

Zhao, X. B. and Tong, S. P. (2001) Unequal economic development in China: spatial disparity and regional policy, 1985–95, *Regional Studies*, 34(6), 549–61.

Zhao, Y. (2002) Earnings differentials between state and non-state enterprises in urban China, *Pacific Economic Review*, 7(1), 181–97.

Zheng, C., Sossay, C. and Hyland, P. (2008) Manufacturing to Asia: who will win the emerging battle for talent between Dragons and Tigers?, *Journal of Manufacturing Technology Management*, 19(1), 52–72.

Zhou, Y., Sun, Y., Wei, Y. H. D. and Lin, G. C. S. (2011) De-centering 'spatial fix': patterns of territorialization and regional technological dynamism of ICT hubs in China, *Journal of Economic Geography*, 11(1), 119–50.

Zucker, L. G., Darby, M. R., Furner, J., Liu, R. C. and Hongyan, M. (2007) Minerva unbound: knowledge stocks, knowledge flows and new knowledge production, *Research Policy*, 36, 850–63.

Index